THE PRACTICE OF WAR

PRODUCTION, REPRODUCTION AND COMMUNICATION OF ARMED VIOLENCE

Edited by
Aparna Rao, Michael Bollig
and Monika Böck

Berghahn Books
New York • Oxford

FOUNDATION®
BOOKS

Delhi • Bengaluru • Mumbai • Kolkata • Chennai • Hyderabad
Pune • Thiruvananthapuram

Published by
Cambridge University Press India Pvt. Ltd.
under the imprint of Foundation Books
Cambridge House, 4381/4 Ansari Road, Daryaganj, **New Delhi** 110 002

Cambridge University Press India Pvt. Ltd.
C-22, C-Block, Brigade M.M., K.R. Road, Jayanagar, **Bengaluru** 560 070
Plot No. 80, Service Industries, Shirvane, Sector-1, Nerul, **Navi Mumbai** 400 706
10 Raja Subodh Mullick Square, 2nd Floor, **Kolkata** 700 013
21/1 (New No. 49), 1st Floor, Model School Road, Thousand Lights, **Chennai** 600 006
House No. 3-5-874/6/4, (Near Apollo Hospital), Hyderguda, **Hyderabad** 500 029
Agarwal Pride, 'A' Wing, 1308 Kasba Peth, Near Surya Hospital, **Pune** 411 011
T.C. 25/ 2731 Lukes Lane, Ambujavilasam Road, **Thiruvananthapuram** 695 001

This edition is published by Cambridge University Press India Pvt. Ltd. by arrangement with Berghahn Books Ltd.

First South Asia Edition 2014

ISBN 978-93-82993-17-9

Published by Manas Saikia for Cambridge University Press India Pvt. Ltd. and printed at Bhavish Graphics, Chennai

CONTENTS

Part III: Organizing, Encouraging and Dissuading: The Uses of Kinship, Gender and Religion

Part IV: The Inscription of War in Mediated Worlds

Part V: Peace Building at the Crossroads: Appropriations of War, Ambivalences of Interest

List of Figures and Tables

Figures

Tables

List of Contributors

Jon Abbink
The African Studies Centre, University of Leiden

Mariam Abou Zahab
Centre d'Etudes et de Recherches Internationales, Paris

Heike Behrend
Institute of African Studies, University of Cologne

Eyal Ben-Ari
Department of Anthropology, Hebrew University of Jerusalem

Monika Böck
Department of Social and Cultural Anthropology, University of Cologne

Michael Bollig
Department of Social and Cultural Anthropology, University of Cologne

Elisabeth Colson
Department of Anthropology, University of California, Berkeley

John Darby
The Joan B. Kroc Institute for International Peace Studies, University of Notre Dame

Jan-Bart Gewald
Institute of African Studies, Leiden University

Iris Jean-Klein
Department of Anthropology, University of Edinburgh

Henner Kirchner
Institute of Oriental Studies, University of Giessen

Edna Lomsky-Feder
Department of Anthropology, Hebrew University of Jerusalem

Elaine Martin
Department of Modern Languages and Classics, University of Alabama

Matthias Österle
Department of Social and Cultural Anthropology, University of Cologne

Julia Pauli
Department of Social and Cultural Anthropology, University of Cologne

Aparna Rao
Department of Social and Cultural Anthropology, University of Cologne

Michael Schnegg
Department of Social and Cultural Anthropology, University of Cologne

Katharina Schneider
Department of Social and Cultural Anthropology, University of Cologne

Yoginder S. Sikand
International Institute of the Study of Islam in the Modern World, Leiden

Marilyn B. Young
Department of History, New York University

PREFACE

For years issues such as ethnicity, xenophobia and cultural difference, scarcity of resources, relative deprivation and various modes of colonial domination etc. have dominated the anthropological discourse on conflict and war. Many studies have offered in-depth ethnographic accounts of war: how it is organised, its ritual ramifications and socio-economic consequences, and the ultimate and proximate causes of organized violence. War and society/culture were rendered as two independent variables: war was seen as the phenomenon to explain and society/culture the entity to explain it with. In the current debates, however, growing attention is paid to the question of how war produces 'culture' and 'society'. In a rhizomatic way war pervades all aspects of everyday life and transforms major structural variables. Only an understanding of these mechanisms of war in everyday practice can lead to meaningful efforts to institute peaceful conflict resolution.

The purpose of this book is to discuss and analyse social, economic and cultural practices connected to and generated by violent combat through a cross-cultural perspective. The chapters focus on processes that occur during or immediately after periods of prolonged and extreme violence. Two highly interrelated themes will be addressed: the reinforcement or disintegration of existing social networks; and the manner in which those involved in war are represented, or represent themselves and their cause. The first theme covers concepts of solidarity, altered definitions of social status and identity, the construction of new social links produced by war and the subsequent extension of existing networks across local, regional, or national borders. The second theme deals with a range of actors: the state, the military, liberation groups, militias, individual combatants, so-called civilians (non-combatants, women and youth), members of the diasporas and also human rights groups and refugee communities and looks at how images produced, reproduced and often globally circulated have a direct impact on violence-prone or violence-averse strategies of local actors.

The introductory chapter of the book by Elisabeth Colson reviews recent anthropological studies of war, and outlines several contemporary situations of armed conflict and warfare. Many wars in recent decades are not constituted by armed conflicts between states and organized armies, but between states and their 'own' people, who may be claiming a right to membership in other, sometimes still non-existent states. Occasionally the state will not be a significant actor in violent conflicts at all, but rather appears unable to control the violent activities of various non-state actors. In the course of such conflicts international intervention usually takes place. Contemporary warfare appears in many forms and – depending on the perspective of the interlocutor – may be presented as rebellion, civil war, liberation struggle, crusade etc. Strategies range from guerrilla warfare, gang violence, witch-hunts, cyber war, to 'terrorism', violent state repression, etc. It can take the shape of high intensity battles or of prolonged low intensity warfare, which periodically goes through processes of peace only to be followed by spurts of violence. Contemporary warfare also surfaces as simmering, armed conflict at the level of banditry, in which armed gangs terrorize local communities or indulge in raiding and looting.

The introduction is followed by three contributions addressing dimensions of low intensity warfare and drawing on case studies from Africa. The first two case studies from Kenya (Michael Bollig and Matthias Österle) and Ethiopia (Jon Abbink) illustrate how the international trade in small arms leads to local arms races fuelling violence beyond the control of the state. Rapid militarization and continued violence in both cases leads to profound changes of social interaction. As the gun becomes a means of production in the hands of juniors the power of seniors wanes. Violence is progressively commoditized and instrumentalized by outsiders. The spoils from violent interaction are often not redistributed and ideas of reciprocity that underlie exchanges between kinship groups and age-based groups are eroded. In parallel to these two cases the third case study on violence in western Uganda (Heike Behrend) shows the effects of social fragmentation after the experience of violence and trauma. The violent strategies of a rebel faction (ADF) and high mortality rates due to HIV/Aids are connected to spurts of internal terror. A war is waged within a war as local inhabitants conduct 'crusades' against witches and cannibals in their communities who are thought to have brought violence and misery. External threats are conceptualized in the idiom of witchcraft. In all three cases renegotiations of moral orders are of importance and local actors desperately try to make sense of a reality which slips further and further out of the control of established authorities – it is not so much a question of how and why to engage in violence, but rather how to bring an end to it. These first three chapters demonstrate that violence is produced and reproduced in every day life, and becomes an integral part of social interaction causing social tension and personal dramas.

The contributions of Part II 'Memory, Trauma, and Redemption' show how the experience of higher intensity war scenarios is embodied in collective memories (Jan-Bart Gewald) and epistemic structures which inform discourses on mental health (Edna Lomsky-Feder and Eyal Ben-Ari). Gewald describes the way in which Namibia's Herero community has dealt with the trauma of genocide inflicted upon them by German colonial forces at the beginning of the twentieth century. He shows, in some detail, how Herero society was recreated by consciously hybridizing images of the pre-colonial past and the present. The rekindling of ancestral fires is described as an intentional act to re-link the post-genocide fragments of Herero society with their pre-genocide ancestors. At the same time new elements are introduced: the *otruppe*, a guild of mock-soldiers, dressed in colonial uniforms and bearing the names of authorities of the German army, not only mimicked the former colonial power but also linked local actors to the United Negro Improvement Association spreading from the U.S. and the Caribbean to Africa at the beginning of the twentieth century and served as a means of re-establishing networks of solidarity. Gewald's contribution parallels the other two chapters from this part of the book in that it interprets the powerful images of violence and suffering as a lens through which identity is constructed. Lomsky-Feder and Ben-Ari show how the episteme 'trauma' and concomitant traumatic-therapeutic discourses provide a set of cultural models through which war and its effects are interpreted in contemporary Israel. The authors show how 'trauma' has become a hegemonic figure of thinking into which academia, public policy, media and local actors feed. The concept is stretched in that not only individuals but also sub-groups and even the entire society is thought of as traumatized. He shows how the discourse on trauma on the one hand helps to maintain social solidarity, produces and reproduces social hierarchies and undermines the critique of war and on the other hand routinizes war into social life. Mariam Abou Zahab's analysis of the militant Pakistani Islamic movement of Lashkar-e Taiba also shows the emergence of epistemic structures directly connected to violence. The *martyr* and *jihad* are salient concepts in the discourse on violence in Kashmir. They are more than mere rhetorical concepts but are rather to be thought of as schemata setting culturally appropriate goals and thereby guiding cultural practice. They offer young men who feel estranged by corrupt politicians and frustrated by their own powerlessness and economic vulnerability a feeling of moral superiority.

Part III 'Organizing, Encouraging and Dissuading: The Uses of Kinship, Gender and Religion' begins with a contribution by Elaine Martin which draws attention to a perspective which has been frequently muted in anthropological discourses on war. Violent conflict is always gendered and war offers itself as an arena to play out sexual hierarchies and power relations. Not only does violence mirror gender relations within a society but is in itself a gendering activity. Martin concentrates on perspectives of German women on gender during the Second World War. More specifically she analyses the emic views of women who have jotted down their experiences in autobiographies and other genres of literature. Drawing on both written documents and interviews, Martin explores the close relation between fascism and a patriarchal value system. The production of a warrior/soldier mentality is related to the denigration of women and a general oppression of the Other. These insights link Martin's chapter along with those of Bollig and Österle, and Abbink who also explore the cultural ramifications of militarism and authoritarianism in two African societies and show how violent interaction shapes gender and age relations. Iris Jean-Klein's contribution deals with continuities and discontinuities of patterns of social organization and moral identity during the First Palestinian Intifada (1987–1991/92). She uses the theme 'management of collaborators' as a window to view social and cultural change in Palestinian society. Traditionally constituted by patronymic associations, in which 'people of the same blood' are kept conceptionally different from clients and affinal relations, Palestinian society adopts less exclusive and less fragmentary forms of social organization during the conflict. Intifada intellectuals strongly criticized the patriarchal value system and tended to emphasize other kinship concepts which were more focussed on bilateral recruitment and emotional closeness. Committee movements were becoming constitutive for Palestinian society in the 1980s. Although their organization recalls patronymic patterns, concepts of closeness and solidarity beyond narrow kinship confines shape social practice and morality within committees. The discourse on collaboration with the enemy (Israel) and the daily experience of violence emphasizes traditional values of (blood) retribution, honour, duty, steadfastness, firmness and Islamic justice, and mould these epistemic structures into one Intifada related value system. Yoginder Sikand's analysis of the historical roots and social history of the Lashkar-e Taiba is the second chapter to deal with this extremist Islamic movement (see also Abou Zahab, this volume). He explores the emergence and evolution of the extremist group both in Northern India, Kashmir and Pakistan and traces Lashkar's origins to the Ahl-i Hadith movement of northern India during the nineteenth century. This religious reformatory movement wanted to purge Islam from syncretist elements and confronted the Hanafi Islamic tradition as well as local Sufism. The Ahl-i Hadith movement developed a separate religious and elitist minority identity in which followers identified themselves as the true bearers of the *jihad* ideology. Strong feelings of moral superiority and avant-garde thinking constituted a binding element amongst followers. The movement grew rapidly in Pakistan during the 1980s, established its own parastatal structures with schools and even a university specialising in the training of *mujahidin*. It was especially the *jihad* in Afghanistan which brought ever more followers to the Ahl-i Hadith movement of which the Lashkar developed as a militarist splinter again emphasizing avantgardeness and militaristic strategies. Many of the elements Jean-Klein traces in her analysis of Palestinian committees resound in the chapters of Sikand and Abou Zahab: radical moral values, visions of an Islamic modernity and fraternity beyond patriarchal authoritarianism are key concepts in those movements.

Part IV 'The Inscription of War in Mediated Worlds' adds the dimension of communicating violence in a global arena. While the Internet is a key source in Sikand's chapter already, contributions to this part focus on the manifold ways in which media, and especially new media, shape networks of actors impacting on a conflict and become constitutive means framing ideologies of violence and peaceful cooperation within a globalized world. But as a start this part discusses the 'old media' in their crucial role as battlegrounds or surfaces upon which war is imagined. Marilyn Young's contribution analyses filmic presentations of the first Gulf War and their use in the formation of collective memories on violence. She emphasizes that many of those films (treating *Courage under Fire* [1996] and *Three Kings* [1999] in more detail) are directly linked to earlier filmic discourses on war and national identity. Films on the Gulf War ostensibly distance themselves from filmic representations of the Vietnam war, a 'war that went wrong' in U.S. American public opinion. However, they try to draw links to films on the Second World War. Images of 'the good soldier', of bravery and male camaraderie are evoked. In an interesting manner Young gives an insight into the close relations Hollywood producers and politicians are engaged in, in order to generate a common understanding of a national collective memory on war and identity. The chapter by Aparna Rao, Monika Böck, Katharina Schneider and Michael Schnegg concentrates on a specific form of Internet communication, taking place in mailing lists or e-groups, and its relation to the Kashmir conflict. While Abou Zahab and Sikand focussed on the analysis of one extremist group within this conflict, here the emergence and development of an online community directly relating to the conflict is analysed. The online community mainly constituted by expatriates from Kashmir, as well as other parts of India and Pakistan, living all over the world emerges from a drawn out virtual conflict on the righteousness, of their discourse and of them being a separate web community. They constitute themselves as a moderated online community thereby acknowledging modes of moderation and control in order to promote communication flow and condone fissioning. Concepts like cyberwar and online exodus as well as insults and accusations presented online show that Internet constituted groups heavily borrow epistemic elements from real-world discourses on conflict. Visions of togetherness, often formulated in relation to the embracing concept of *kashmiriyat* (referring to a peaceful coexistence of Kashmiris of different denominations and different class), bring about cohesiveness and constitute the basis for a more enduring dialogue. Henner Kirchner traces the use of the Internet by Palestinian Islamists. Acknowledging that the Internet is the fastest growing communication medium in Palestine, Kirchner analyses the structure of diverse Internet presentations of organizations such as Hamas and the Jihad Movement. It is of some interest that there seems to be an inverse relationship between the growth of Internet communication and state control: where state control is low (such as in Palestine but also for example in Somalia) the Internet opens channels for quick and efficient dissemination of information, for the promulgation of images and texts and for the formation of discourses. Kirchner details the structure of virtual presentation and discusses the issues of authorship and the public addressed by virtual messages. The successful use of communication technology and its organisational structures as well as the capacity to network in the virtual space are constitutive for the domination of public opinion. The chapter by Michael Schnegg and Julia Pauli focuses on the virtual ramifications of the Mexican Chiapas conflict. They analyse why the Zapatistas have been highly successful and have outdone the Mexican government on the cyberspace battlefield. Zapatistas and their sympathizers have succeeded in gaining international attention and acknowledgement for the justness of their cause through skilfully networking and efficiently using text and images. This success seems to be even more astonishing as actors within the cyber network participating in the discourse on the conflict were highly heterogeneous, international, multi-lingual and multi-organizational. Notably, the Zapatistas themselves did not directly participate in disseminating virtual information but left space for a multitude of different actors, which ranged from Mexican NGOs hoping to foster the democratization of their country to international activists participating in other forms of struggle. Hence the local agenda of the Zapatista movement became entwined with anti-globalization and pro-democratization agendas. These actors are interconnected in a cohesive network of closely linked websites. Schnegg and Pauli argue that the cohesiveness of this network and the resemblance of images and texts shown create a form of collective memory underlying the moral justness of the Zapatistas' texts and feats.

In the final Part V 'Peace Building at the Crossroads: Appropriations of War, Ambivalences of Interest' John Darby analyses peace processes. He concentrates his comparative study on the time period between ceasefire and longer lasting peace agreements. Drawing on several case studies Darby looks for factors constraining and promoting processes of peace. The chapter begins with the observation that out of thirty-eight formal peace accords signed between 1988 and 1998 most failed to last longer than three years. Making peace is a difficult process and gets more difficult the longer the duration of violence. Taking off from the main tenet of previous chapters, that violence pervades diverse subfields of society and eventually gives rise to a culture of violence, Darby asks how such structures can be changed successfully. He identifies three sources of post-ceasefire violence: the state, militants and the community. Drawing on examples from Sri Lanka, Spain and South Africa Darby shows that it is difficult to disband formerly well established governmental counter-insurgency networks. Experienced and well-armed forces feel threatened by demobilization and may be eager to destabilize the peace process to ensure their organizational survival. Militants have frequently been active in a war-economy which at once fuelled violence and also brought personal profits to them. A rescheduling of a war-economy threatens economic options and precludes further accumulation by militants. On the other hand zealots break away from major militant factions to follow the 'true course'. Such zealots Darby identifies in Palestine, taking up ideas from Jean-Klein's and Kirchner's study on the same context. Violence by militants can also be used within the peace process to press for specific aims and enforce a greater willingness for compromise with the (former) enemy. The fragmentation of paramilitary organizations and the militarization and criminalization of entire communities during prolonged violent conflicts brings about a plethora of problems to the peace building process: economic alternatives to criminal activities, processes of grass-roots mediation and control have to be installed all at the same time. Darby's chapter opens a wide perspective on further detailed studies on specific cases of peace building. It becomes clear that the anthropology of war and violence has to expand its agenda to include post-ceasefire processes and peace building into their agenda.

The idea for this book grew out of an international workshop organized at the University of Cologne in November 2001. Little did we know while planning the workshop, that the debate on war, armed aggression, terror and cultural imperialism would involve us all after September 11. As editors of the volume we feel, and so do our authors, that there is a pressing need to discuss and analyse the issues addressed by these various chapters. The contributions forward new empirical material and open theoretical dimensions on the intricate relation between war, society and culture. It took a long time to finalize the volume as contributions attempted to include new empirical material and reviewers thoroughly assessed and commented on the manuscript. Aparna's untimely death in June 2005 prevented her from seeing the volume in its final form.

INTRODUCTION
THE PRACTICE OF WAR

Elizabeth Colson

The Meaning of War

When this workshop was proposed, none of us knew that war would so intimately involve us all by the time we met or that our attention would be so firmly focused on just what it means to frame events in terms of war. Terrible as what happened on 11 September was, I have pondered what might have happened if the American government had not immediately tried to frame the attack on the World Trade Center and the Pentagon as acts of war, and whether those who planned and implemented the attack could have done so if they had not framed their actions as legitimate acts of war. A comment that came through the Internet, written by a Zambian who has lived in the United States for some years, gave me a clue to what it means to provide such a frame, when he said, 'war-time morals are not judged by the same standard as in civilian life. This is the very reason why it is called "war". The rules of engagement are different, and the whole world understands that in war, there will be a reasonable expectation of collateral damage.' The historian Richard Overy (2001: 6) said much the same thing when he wrote, 'The purpose of war [waged by stages] is to impose the will of one state on that of another. Killing is one of the many means to achieve this purpose, not an end in itself.' He continues, 'Economic pressure, psychological warfare, the intelligence war, political initiatives, strategic planning are all ingredients in the waging of war alongside military conflict.'

Overy is right in emphasizing that war uses many means but he is led astray by the general readiness to think of the world as divided up into nation states which hold a monopoly on warfare. The vast majority of wars during recent decades have not been between states. Some have been between states and rebels against that state, who may be claiming the right to membership in another, sometimes still non-existent state. Others have pitted elements of a population against each other. Sometimes conflict is at the level of brigandage when armed gangs terrorize a countryside not yet mobilized to resist them.

With mobilization may come a new political community born of warfare and resistance. A large number of conflicts now being fought for one cause or another may have the end result of transforming a vague feeling of ethnic differences into national identities.

The belief that war involves conflict between states dies hard, but such belief implies that labelling a conflict as war legitimates claims to statehood. Indonesia recognizes this when it claims to be fighting separatist Indonesian terrorists rather than a war with a Papuan or East Timorese state (Gedicks 2001: 182). The United States finds itself in a dilemma when it proclaims a war against terrorists who have no territory and form no state and is therefore reduced to attacking Afghanistan which meets the definition of a suitable opponent.

The fact is that war comes in many guises and its effects continue to be felt long after peace is proclaimed. This challenges the anthropologists who write of war as participant observers. Participant observation inevitably deals with the here and now, with the highly specific. It is only over the long view that one can begin to see the commonalities that emerge from the different forms of conflict and can begin to generalize. But we already know that the effects of violence are long-lasting, pervasive and unexpectedly complex.

Anthropologists and the Study of War

In 1974, Klaus-Friedrich Koch wrote that ethnographic literature so far said little about warfare that was based on observation and that instead it relied on old men's reminiscences which were reported in the ethnographic present. Oral traditions about wars were mistakenly treated as factual reports of what had happened, but there was little reason to think that they provided the real reasons why people fought or the way in which they fought or even the outcome of any war (Koch 1974: 52–53). The style of writing reflected a continued anthropological preoccupation with small-scale societies, despite the fact that some of the anthropologists, in the United States at least, who were writing of war in the 1960s and 1970s were veterans of the Second World War or the Korean War or had undergone military training (Otterbein 1970; Givens and Nettleship 1976; Ember and Ember 1997). They were spurred to write about war because of what was then happening in Vietnam. But they did not deal with their own hands-on experience. They drew lessons from archaeology and the ethnographic record to ask when warfare emerged in human history and if our genetic heritage entails an aggression that makes warfare inevitable or if warfare is primarily economically motivated and whether it was born with the state or fostered the emergence of the state. Sociobiology, Freudianism and various forms of Marxism provided them with theoretical guidelines.

Archaeologists (Ferguson 1984, 1997; Haas 1990; Keeley 1996) are still intrigued with such questions, for they deal with the past rather than with the effects of warfare stark before their eyes. Social and cultural anthropologists, however, were writing of contemporary warfare by the 1980s although rarely from personal experience (Foster and Rubinstein 1986; Rubinstein and Foster 1988). They also recognized that anthropological thought and practice had been affected by the recruitment of the United States academy in the service of the Cold War (Nader 1989, 1997). Simons (1999) has summarized much of this literature. More recently it has become difficult to disregard war and its consequences. Ethnographic work in the latter half of the twentieth century exposed a large number of anthropologists to the immediate apprehension of violence. Sometimes they themselves have been on the scene. More often they have heard of the devastation of communities where they once worked. Frequently they encounter those whose lives have been distorted by war. Even those who thought to escape the rigours of the post-colonial world by doing ethnography at home have had to take cognizance of the arrival on their doorsteps of refugees from here, there and everywhere. Civil war in the Sudan means Nuer trying to make a living in Minneapolis; wars in Vietnam, Afghanistan and Eritrea have transformed the population of California; Tamil Tigers in Canada solicit funds to continue the civil war in Sri Lanka. And Germany faces questions of identity as it absorbs refugees from Palestine, Turkey, former Yugoslavia and the Soviet Union, while France has been profoundly altered by the arrival of those who fled independence and post-independence wars in Algeria. Today threatened civil war in Zimbabwe is sending a stream of people south to South Africa, where increasing local violence sends another stream of people out to Australia, New Zealand, Europe and North America. Everywhere we look we see what this means as people occupy common space without sharing common language, religious symbols, political values or common memories. This could make for an explosion of creativity, as relationships are negotiated and renegotiated, or it could make for further violence.

Robben and Nordstrom are of the generation of anthropologists who began ethnographic research in the 1980s, who have watched wars engulf and sometimes destroy those among whom they work. They ask why the 'chaos of warfare and the incomprehensibility of violence for its victims' is 'so seldom addressed in scholarly writings'. 'Why do we find so many intricate studies about war and so few about human suffering?'(1995: 1) In fact, intricate studies of warfare written by anthropologists are few and far between, and if they existed they would have to deal with far more than human suffering. We now have many studies of those who suffer, but few of contemporary actors and institutions who benefit or expect to benefit from warfare or other forms of violence. Admittedly it is difficult to study military establishments, guerrilla bands, mercenary companies, the intermeshing of the armament industry or smuggling networks through which arms today so often travel, or the black-market networks which spring up with every interruption in normal trade, although Ben-Ari (1998) has examined an Israeli military unit and Zulaika

(1995) has studied Basque political violence. Others have looked less directly at the motivations and structuring of war. Richard Werbner (1998), for one, has shown how national monuments and state rituals speak to memories of war and are continually reappraised as people evaluate the present against the past and plan for the future. Jennifer Cole (1998) too has probed conflicting memories to examine the aftermath of civil war in Madagascar and their continuing influence within the political arena. This suggests that our subject matter lies around us.

The chapters in this book explore possibilities for further work as they examine how warfare lingers on in memory, in organizations war brings into being, and in verbal and visual symbols affecting action. That is, they write of what happens when peace is declared. In the spirit of the workshop on which the book is based, then, let me look more closely at some of the implications that war has for people, their lived-in communities and their larger political orders.

War as Mentality

Bourdieu has written of habitus or 'socialized subjectivity', Foucault of the colonization of the mind through the imposition of thought patterns that confine the subject and produce governmentality. The habitus or socialised subjectivity of anthropologists emerges from a world that dedicates a very high proportion of its assets to the provisioning of war. Its social order is predicated on the existence of military establishments, which expect to be supported, both financially and morally, and whose existence is justified in terms of some perceived threat. To be a state it must have not only a territory, a flag and an anthem. It must also have an army, and perhaps a navy, and these must have arms. The existence of the United Nations seems to have done little to reduce such thinking.

Public thought in the United States, during the last fifty years, has been increasingly dominated by metaphors and images drawn from military usage as the military establishment inherited from the Second World War has come to have a significant role in determining economic and social policy (Johnson 2000). Despite the fact that the rituals of Memorial Day, which valorized death in battle, have largely vanished from the ritual calendar, popular culture in the United States is dominated by metaphors of war, and the playing with war through video games, television, films and print teaches children that war is glorious and something to be desired (Grossman and DeGaetano 1999; Reyna 1999: 15). Almost any purposive activity is framed as a kind of war and, whether we like it or not, we think war, however much we may call for peace. Indeed, Mary LeCron Foster has asked if, given the militarization of national patriotic symbols, patriotism could continue to exist without reference to past and future enemies (1986: 72).

Organization for any purpose in the United States is likely to invoke the imagery of war. Political parties have campaigns and war chests. Charitable organizations wage campaigns. We have wars on drugs, poverty, pornography, crime, welfare mothers. Sometimes these wars are not purely metaphorical, for the metaphor permits those who wage war to exercise wartime violence within the civil sphere. This happened in Los Angeles in 1992 when the city government bulldozed houses suspected of housing drug-dealers in a manner reminiscent of Israeli moves against Palestinians who may or may not be associated with violent resistance (Swedenburg 1995: 37). Evoking the necessities of war is very much a factor in current attempts to reduce the legal rights of those suspect of dealing in drugs, engaging in physical violence or in any way abetting possible terrorists. These are defined as warring on the social fabric in a way that those profiting from white-collar crime do not.. Once action is labelled as war, who can legitimately oppose the rightness of mobilization and battle?

Civil society in the United States is thus permeated by a culture or habitus of war. I do not know how true this is elsewhere, though it may be more common than I think, for Western Christian discourse seems rich in military motifs. We speak of the Church Militant, urge onward Christian soldiers, and address God as 'Lord of hosts' or even as 'God of battle'. Greenhouse found Christian fundamentalists in the southern United States justifying the morality of wartime killing by reference to the higher good. For them, war created an opportunity for service that was both right and sacred, and those of the community who fought in Vietnam did so as 'artists of war' (1986: 56). Elsewhere, too, where Christian values should have high valence, violence is justified as a righteous cause. Jeffrey Sluka reports that his informants in Northern Ireland, largely adherents of the Irish Republican Army, were convinced of the rightness of violent actions, and he comments, 'Conflict and violence may be the result of rational and pragmatic appraisals of moral obligations, and they may represent an affirmation of the legitimacy of moral systems rather than a sign of their breakdown' (1988: 108).

Others do not appeal to abstract morality to justify the violence they perpetrate on others, but base themselves on pragmatic expedience. An Argentinian general interviewed by Robben, called war 'a social phenomenon' and replied to questions about the morality of the treatment of political opponents during the 'dirty war' by asking 'What is licit and what is illicit, when war presupposes that I am going to kill my enemy?' Other officers were content to cite precedent such as the bombing of Hiroshima and Dresden, or the violence perpetrated during the Algerian struggle for independence (1995: 90). Atrocities thus become a precedent rather than a barrier to further atrocities.

Membership within a profession has its own consequences for mentalities. I have been told by former students that no matter what they do they continue to think as anthropologists. So it is to be expected that members of military professions should think in military terms. Donna Brasset (1989), in one of the few ethnographic studies along with that of Ben-Ari that deal with military communities, found that officers belonging to the United States military elite were trained not only to think as soldiers but to think in terms that became part of military thinking in the Second World War. They continued to think of war as an enterprise focused on defending or attacking a bounded territory, despite the fact that nuclear weapons had made such thinking obsolete, and were unable to adjust strategic thinking to match revolutionary changes in technology. Because experience of war in Vietnam went against the grain of their training, they learned little from it beyond the belief that they must rein in the press to avoid repercussions from the American public which they tended to view as the ultimate enemy. Experience in the Gulf War seems only to have reinforced this way of thinking.

It is no major discovery, this knowledge that we live with mentalities that link back to the Second World War since such mentalities are encoded in military organizations and training. Even without such means of perpetuating the past, memories live on. Meanwhile, new wars are creating new mentalities. Guerrilla warfare is now endemic in much of the world. It is frightening to think how many people have been directly exposed to violence and how their experience may condition the future. The twentieth century has been called the century of refugees, given the enormous number of people who have been displaced by warfare or other violence. Thereafter they see the world through different eyes. By flight, they cut loose from many of the bonds of belonging and identity that provide the givens of social existence. Even those who flee as families find familial roles transformed (Colson 1987; Muecke 1995: 38). Many have written of the sense of loss and disassociation expressed by refugees whether they are living in camps or have found permanent asylum in a new country (Hitchcox 1990; Abdulrahim 1993; Eastmond 1993; Malkki 1995; Voutira and Harrell-Bond 1995; Sommers 2001). Peteet (1995: 168) found Palestinian refugees in the 1990s still speaking of the bewilderment and trauma they felt in the 1940s and 1950s, immediately after being driven into exile, and of the continued longing to return home:

> For many, the first years of exile were like a period of mourning. The loss of land and the rupture of identities and social relations grounded in it was akin to the loss of a loved one. Unable to defend their communities, landless and penniless and now recipients of relief and charity, they felt an intense loss of trust in themselves.

Similarly, sixty years after their 1920s' displacement from Asia Minor, Greek-speakers resettled in Greece identify themselves in some contexts by reference to their former homes, while Greek neighbours of other origins still see them as different (Karakasidou 1997; Hirschon 1998). Former refugees, long settled in Britain or the United States, have spoken to me of their sense of continuing to live in transit, as one said 'with suitcases always packed', or as another said 'with antennae always out for possible trouble'. When home, which was considered a refuge, a safe place, is invaded and neighbours once considered friends or at least reasonable associates turn on one, the ability to trust people or accept the surface tranquillity of a new home is profoundly affected (Daniel and Knudsen 1995).

Yet refugees and those displaced within their own country, including those who survive torture, do make new lives for themselves. Barnett, indeed, has argued that being uprooted gives space for experimentation and new growth (1953). Research on refugees from the Second World War suggests that, in the immediate aftermath of war, life pressed in again and memories were repressed as people put their energies into jobs and child rearing. It was when these pressures lessened as they approached their late fifties that they began to relive experiences and suffer bitterly the loss of home and childhood associates. We see something of the same phenomenon among veterans of the Vietnam War, who today suffer from what some call post-traumatic stress disorder. We probably need to rethink the trajectory of wartime experience to cover at least the lifetime of those who fought and suffered through it.

Communities in Construction and Reconstruction

Part of the creativity of those uprooted has gone into inventing new institutions that help to transform world organization. One striking consequence of twentieth century wars has been the emergence of new diaspora communities. Diasporas are an old story, but the contemporary world fosters their emergence and persistence. With jet travel, telephones and the Web, we are released from the need to mobilize territorially and are able to live, so to speak, between worlds. Despite the role diaspora communities have played in fomenting wars of resistance in their countries of origin and underwriting emergent ethnic communities as in Poland in the early twentieth century and in Ukraine and East Timor at the century's end – ethnographic studies of such diasporas are rare and recent. Fuglerud's study, whose subtitle is *The Tamil Diaspora and Long Distance Nationalism* (1999), is evidence that they are possible and important. A principal ethnographic site of the future may well be the Internet and the chat room, reflecting the globalization of meaningful networks through which histories are being created and values debated and reaffirmed.

This does not mean that we can ignore the implications of territory. After all the primary purpose of a diaspora organization may be tied to obtaining a territorial state that will embody its nation. Moreover, some ethnic communities bestride international boundaries and are demanding the redrawing of maps. The flow of refugees, smugglers, freedom fighters and aid organizations across such boundaries fosters the emergence of new political entities intent on recognition as states or calling for the redrawing of political boundaries to permit the reunification of those now subject to different states. Though

Zambia, where my research is centred, so far has been unscarred by civil war, old ethnic associations are being revived through linkages established by those who come to Zambia as refugees or as freedom fighters. There have been calls for the revival of a Lozi state to include portions of Angola, Namibia and Botswana along with Zambia's Western Province. There are also calls for the joining together of people who live astride the boundaries of Zambia, Angola and the Democratic Republic of the Congo in a new Lunda empire.

A large number of conflicts now being fought for one cause or another usually involve some relationship to territory and the end result may be the transformation of a vague feeling of ethnic differences into national identities. Turton (1999: 146) sees the Mursi on the Ethiopian border waging war with their neighbours as a means of defining themselves as political entities and describes such warfare as a reciprocal activity by means of which groups assert their independence of each other and enter into orderly relationships. For him, warfare is not a breaking down of normal political relations, but their underpinning. This sounds perilously like a distortion of old functionalist arguments, and Turton agrees that recent Mursi wars followed territorial encroachments. Danforth (1995: 18) rather similarly describes Macedonia as emerging through processes that focused attention on precise territorial boundaries and then to a call for the creation of a homogeneous national community in opposition to so-called enemies, who became the epitome of otherness. It may be that the Mursi, unlike the Macedonians, will be content with being a nation and not go on to claim recognition as a state, but the United Nations has member states with populations no greater than the Mursi. Are the processes underlying the Mursi definition of the self much different from those that underpin the drive to statehood elsewhere?

Contested boundaries and nations will be ethnographic commonplaces of the twenty-first century. Gledhill (2001: 151–52) speaks of the possible emergence of a larger Maya political community thought into existence when Maya took refuge from the civil war in Guatemala in Maya communities in Mexico and elsewhere in Central America, and he cites Montejo (1999) as saying that survival and resistance in exile have overridden old cultural/linguistic divisions to create new symbols associated with a common unity and this in turn may foreshadow future Maya collective action. It may be no accident that the Zapatista movement in Mexico arose in Maya territory, where those who fled Guatemala found asylum.

International policy, however, emphasizes the reinforcement of old communities rather than support for new ones. While international rhetoric insists that the best and sometimes the only appropriate solution to what is called the world's 'refugee problem' is repatriation or return home of those who fled, this passes the burden to areas still smarting from the violence of war and to people whose whole existence has been transformed because of it. The ethnographies of the return have begun to emerge and they indicate that, while one may be able to go back to an old area, one cannot go home again

(Black and Koser 1999). Everyone has changed. If people do learn to live together again, they do so as a new community (Jansen 1998). Guatemalans who spent years of exile developed new forms of organization, a new ethos and a history that justified resistance. They returned to Guatemala with an agenda and organizational resources including links with international allies and a sense of a wider community. Even if they had returned without memories of betrayal and violence and without claims to land and property usurped by others in their absence, they would have been a threat to the existing political structure and those who had lived under it who had spent the same years developing different histories and different justifications of the past (de Rivero 2001: 9–10). Hostility to those who return after civil war appears to be common. In Sudan, the peace, negotiated in the 1980s floundered back into civil war as those who had fought each other continued to contest jobs and other economic assets. The divisiveness of religion is only part of the Sudanese story (Karadawi 1999). In South Africa, I have been told, those who left to become freedom fighters or in simple protest against a regime they found oppressive or indecent on return often found scant welcome from those who saw themselves as having borne the brunt of the struggle against apartheid. In Bosnia–Herzegovina, as in Kosovo and for that matter in East Timor, restoration of community is an international myth. Bosnians who have tried to return to former homes are said to be disillusioned about the possibility of living in peace with former neighbours or obtaining protection from local authorities (Hovey 2001: 21). Indeed, it has been said of Bosnia, as elsewhere, that the most positive agents linking members of different ethnic communities are black-market smugglers who serve the market rather than ideological communities (Englbrecht 2001: 18).

The divisiveness fostered by war lingers on. Nordstrom (1997: 141) sees hope for reconciliation within Mozambique in the emergence of rituals used to remove violence from people and return them to peaceful coexistence, playing a role that elsewhere may be delegated to peace and reconciliation tribunals. The rituals she describes are ancient devices that have been used to purge alien influences and return warriors, murderers and labour migrants to normal social life. But do they work beyond the moment? Do they put the past to rest, or are they temporary expedients comparable to attempts to reduce community anxieties through rituals employed to identify and cleanse witches of their powers for evil? Do they persuade those long socialized to warfare who identify with the power to inflict violence? We know that communities that have been racked with warfare are giving thought to such matters, as have Nuer, who fear the pollution of homicide but now must kill (Hutchinson 1998). The attempt to transcend a violent past by membership in new communities may also lie behind the rapid spread of Pentecostal churches in war-torn Congo (de Boeck 1998) or in Zimbabwe (Schmidt 1996), but Pentecostalism is also spreading rapidly elsewhere. So far youngsters who were caught up in the civil wars of Sierra Leone have proved resistant to rituals of demobilization when demobilization promises them only a drab existence. They have lost the years in which they might have been in school or learned a trade. Many have lost or been alienated from their families. They have little to look forward to that would disenchant memories of a past in which they found security among fellow guerrillas and in the guns that gave them power over others (Richards 1996; Fanthorpe 2001). I do not know if any effective means have so far been discovered to break the ongoing influence of violence on children.

We do know that men who are veterans of warfare try to retain something of the comradeship they felt with other men through the formation of associations that give them meeting space, rituals and symbols to memorialize the past and networks of mutual assistance. We also know that such veteran organizations seek to exert political influence.

War seems to give less legitimacy to the association of women veterans. The demands of war legitimate the recruitment of women as soldiers, industrial workers and political activists. But, once war ends, women in such positions are seen as out of place and therefore as polluted and polluting (Douglas 1966). In Eritrea, Zimbabwe and Guinea Bissau where women were recruited as freedom fighters and battled alongside men, peace brought rapid demotion. Eritrean women comprised about one third of the Eritrean People's Liberation Front, but the very qualities that brought them regard as good soldiers and comrades have stigmatized them as wives and potential wives. They are seen as having experienced independence, sexual freedom and equality with men, including the freedom to kill men. As a result, according to Bernal (2000: 61), 'Their morality is suspect, their femininity is doubtful, and their ability to behave as obedient wives questionable.' Eritrean women, who found refuge in countries such as Canada, struggle with host expectations and the continued demands of an Eritrean community where freedom to move and work is defined as unfeminine and a reflection upon husbands and families (Matsuoka and Sorenson 1999). On return from exile Guatemalan women, who took part in resistance and used their exile in Mexico to build organizations to continue the struggle, find themselves under communal authorities who regard women's organizations as an infringement on male authority and want to suppress them (de Rivero 2001: 10). I suspect this is a common aftermath of war, for much the same thing happened in the United States following the Second World War when it became popular dogma that a woman's place was in the home or working as an unpaid volunteer.

The immediate aftermath of war can be bitter for women who have to live with knowledge of their vulnerability. They may be repudiated because they are seen as defiled by rape or exposure to wartime experiences (Muecke 1995; Olujic 1995). They may be badly disadvantaged in a struggle for livelihood because kin who should represent them before the law have been killed or fled. In Mozambique and Ruanda, women have found it difficult to regain or maintain control over land because they are seen as vulnerable by kin, neighbours and government officials (Rose 2000). In Cambodia, where conflicts over land are frequent and bitter, female-headed households have been particularly vulnerable to dispossession (Bennett 2001: 23).

Reconstructing of social life is made no easier by the way male roles are challenged during conflict, in refugee camps and in countries of asylum. Some have attributed the violence against women, so characteristic of refugee camps, to the loss of male status when jobs and political power are swept away and family status is no longer reinforced by control over economic resources or an ability to mediate with others. Men accustomed to authority find it bitter when they must rely upon children as interpreters and mediators, and sometimes on wives, who will take the menial jobs that men find one more assault on their dignity. Yet it does not follow that support for male pride and status alleviates the lot of women. When Afghan men were given unusual autonomy in the organization and running of refugee camps in Pakistan, including control of international assistance, they closed schools for women and girls, restricted freedom of movement, tried to bar them from employment and banned any activities that might lead to their empowerment (Carmack 1999). It made no difference that the men were in control or could pride themselves on their status as *muhajirin*, who from the safety of the camps continued to fight to fulfil Islamic religious and political objectives (Shahrani 1995: 2000). The Taliban have only implemented policies already enforced in the camps in Pakistan and some have justified this as protecting women from male violence in an Afghanistan torn by war.

The Fomenting of War

Rebuilding communities is problematic because those who must build are moulded by experience informed by conflict. It is made no less problematic because war continues to be profitable to many actors and these continue to foment conditions that fuel new sources of unrest, distrust and eventually conflict.

One does not have to be a Marxist to recognize that economic factors are intimately involved with war and with fomenting the instability that leads to war. For one thing, wars and preparation for war are expensive and a drain on economic resources. In contemporary states, preparation for war is often the largest single economic activity, as it has been in the United States in the years since the Second World War. In the 1980s, for instance, the military budget was the largest single finance capital fund in the United States and exceeded the net profits of all corporations (Melman 1984: 391–92; 1986). One consequence, largely ignored by those who argue for larger military budgets, is that overall gains in productivity are minimized because military procurement largely disregards rules of industrial efficiency. In the United States the priority given to military spending has destroyed an earlier productive advantage, and military decisions have contributed to the radical change from a manufacturing to a service economy (Johnson 2000). Factory closures and job losses are reflected in the blighting of industrial cities and the displacement of families dependent on workers. Furthermore, those who work within the military/industrial complex, and they are many, are said to 'acquire a trained incapacity for functioning in a civilian economy with ordinary technical and economic competence' (Melman 1984: 392). The downsizing of military budgets and establishments is thus not easily accepted by those who will be displaced.

The economic consequences of military budgets have global repercussions. Guns require more metal than ploughshares. Combat uses more petrol than peaceful transport: a B-52 Stratofortress, for instance, consumes 3,612 gallons of fuel per hour (Gedicks 2001: 185). Access to strategic metals and oil has obvious international implication and much military strategy is aimed at ensuring access. This we all recognize. We also recognize that the continuation of civil wars in Sierra Leone, Angola and the Democratic Republic of Congo rests upon control over such things as diamonds and oil.

What is less discussed is the arms trade itself (but see Boutwell et al. 1995). In 2000, military spending by the world's governments rose to $798 billion dollars, of which $36 billion was spent by so-called developing countries (Lederer 2001). Almost half of their purchases were made from the United States, followed by Russia, France, Germany, Britain and China. Arms sales to other countries is a major activity of the military establishment of the United States, an activity that implicates it in fomenting warfare elsewhere. Chalmers Johnson reports that the United States government 'employs some 6,500 people just to coordinate and administer its arm sales program in conjunction with senior officials at American embassies around the world, who spend most of their "diplomatic" careers working as arms salesmen' (2000: 87). Attempts to ban the use of depleted uranium in ammunition ran up against a Pentagon blockage, for the Pentagon finds this ammunition both extremely effective against tanks and also a profitable trade item (Tashiro 2001: 39). Much foreign aid involves military equipment. It should also be noted that arms sales are made to both recognized governments and those rebelling against such governments. When African governments recently called for a UN ban on selling arms to rebel groups, the United States, China, Russia and other arms-producing countries opposed it. African governments then drafted an OAU resolution calling upon their governments to draw up uniform laws that would make it more difficult for arms smugglers to operate (Walt 2001: 6–7).

While anthropologists have argued about whether warfare could exist prior to the formation of the state, there is complete agreement that wars have intensified with the growth of states and over the last two centuries with the spread of guns (Cohen 1986: 260; Reyna 1999). The history of Chad over the last several centuries gives good evidence of this (Azavedo 1998). So does that of Uganda. When Idi Amin armed the Pokot on the Uganda/Kenya border, they developed a booming trade in guns, which in turn fomented inter-group hostilities in Kenya (Walt 2001: 5). When Amin and later Obote were driven out, their disbanded soldiers took their guns with them to be used in continuing hostilities throughout northern Uganda and neighbouring countries (Vincent 1999). Warfare escalated among the Mursi and their neighbours on the borders of Ethiopia as guns dispersed from armies fighting in Ethiopia and Sudan (Turton 1999).

Peace entered into by states does not mean disarmament: it releases stocks of arms for sale elsewhere and forces arms manufacturers to search for new markets. In Cambodia, the aftermath of two decades of civil war is a large stock of weapons and a culture of violence: it is estimated that two thirds of the households in Phnom Penh have weapons and these are used to settle even petty disputes (Charle 2001: 9). Here, as elsewhere, supplies are being replenished as armaments continue to circulate through covert international trade routes. Gun smuggling may be the most lucrative employment available locally, as a Somali refugee in Kenya maintained. He estimated that he could make between $1,500 and $2,000 per month, enough to support himself and ten members of his family still living in UN refugee camps after more than a decade of exile (Walt 2001: 7).

Arms sales imply organized networks composed of manufacturers, salesmen, traffickers and buyers (Nordstrom 2000). The latter include governments of Third World countries. Governments that invest in arms acquire debts as well as armaments and have diminishing resources to use for other purposes. In Africa, this makes governments vulnerable to the demands of international powers, including the International Monetary Fund and the World Bank. It also encourages the burgeoning of an international flotilla of NGOs, which take over governmental functions such as the provision of health, education and extension services and the running of refugee camps and much else, while government agencies wither from lack of support. In the end, the only effective state agency may be the army. With little in the treasury to reward its supporters, governments further lose control as the ambitious mobilize ethnic clienteles to contend for what is left. In various regions, and not only in Africa, we have had a de facto demise of the state as contenders for power set up their own fiefdoms (Stavenhagen 1996: 6), much as fiefdoms emerged in tenth- and eleventh-century Europe with the demise of the Carolingian empire (Bloch 1961; Barraclough 1976). That ambitious men fish in ethnic waters to find supporters is not surprising, nor is the emergence of ethnic hostilities in the place of national citizenship.

I would also direct attention to the powerful influence exercised by new communities formed of those who become roving mercenaries. The end of any prolonged war, such as the Hundred Year War between France and England, has probably always provoked the emergence of roving bands of ex-soldiers who move from country to country, wherever they can find employment (Perroy 1965: 154). The phenomenon of mercenary soldiers who live by what Nordstrom (1997: 53) calls 'an economy of predation' is not peculiar to the twentieth century nor to Africa. Some companies operating in Africa are locally formed. Others are international in scope. They are a source of an evolving repertory of terror, for they hone their skills as they move from Congo to Sierra Leone to Mozambique to Angola and onwards. What is new is the emergence of international mercenary forces under the United Nations, engaged as peacekeepers but sometimes preying upon the civilian populations they are sent to guard (Nordstrom 1997: 71).

Conclusion

This book examines the ways of war and the effects of war. War may have been seen as most needing our attention because it is regarded as problematic, as a break in the pattern that needs repair, as something out of control. Of even more moment, however, may be the problematic of peace as individuals, communities and nations try to find ways of overcoming the inevitable conflicts of interest that put us at odds with one another. Hobbes saw the answer to that conflict in the creation of the state, which he thought must be preserved at all costs, but major conflicts are often between states or are caused by state oppression. Obviously something other than the state is needed. The expansion of the role of international law may be one answer, but as anthropologists we know that law is enforceable only when there are mechanisms for enforcement and when it responds to what people accept as legitimate. How does one change minds and ensure that people think peace rather than war?

War is a great many things, some of which may seem quite unrelated to each other (Rappoport 1976: 206). But, as the Zambian speaking through the Internet insisted, it always claims the right to escape the legalities with which we try to discipline and safeguard civilian life. It is for this very reason that attempts have been made throughout known history to bring war back under the control of law, through defining what is to be considered justifiable provocation and so constitute action as 'a just war', through the creation of such pacts as the Geneva Convention to define what cannot be regarded as legitimate actions no matter how 'just' the war, through the creation of international tribunals to judge those who are indicted as war criminals because they have claimed the right to do what they would under the rubric of war. What we have not done is create conditions throughout the world that would nourish the mentalities that would see war itself as an illegality that cannot be tolerated in a globalized world with its interdependencies.

Acknowledgements

My thanks to Laura Nader, who made very pertinent comments on earlier drafts of this chapter and alerted me to some neglected sources of information. Also to Judith Justice for her reading of the typescript. And to participants in the Cologne workshop, 'The Practice of War', who listened and commented, and especially to Aparna Rao, Monika Böck and Michael Bollig, who invited me to join the workshop, and to Nicole Körkel for help with logistics.

References

Abdulrahim, D. 1993. 'Defining Gender in a Second Exile: Palestinian Women in East Berlin', in G. Buijs (ed), *Migrant Women: Changing Boundaries and Changing Identities*. Oxford: Berg, pp. 55–82.

Azavedo, M.J. 1998. *Roots of Violence: A History of War in Chad*. Amsterdam: Gordon and Breach.

Barnett, H. 1953. *Innovation: The Basis of Culture Change*. New York: McGraw-Hill.

Barraclough, G. 1976. *The Crucible of Europe: The Ninth and Tenth Centuries in European History*. Berkeley: University of California Press.

Ben-Ari, E. 1998. *Mastering Soldiers: Conflict, Emotions, and the Enemy in an Israeli Military Unit*. Oxford: Berghahn.

Bennett, J. 2001. 'Participatory Planning in Cambodia: Reconciling Communities', *Forced Migration Review* 11: 22–24.

Bernal, V. 2000. 'Equality to Die For? Women Guerilla Fighters and Eritrea's Cultural Revolution', *Political and Legal Anthropology Review* 23(2): 61–76.

Black, R. and K. Koser (eds). 1999. *The End of the Refugee Cycle? Refugee Repatriation and Reconstruction*. Oxford: Berghahn.

Bloch, M. 1961. *Feudal Society*. London: Routledge and Kegan Paul.

Boutwell, J., M. Klare and L. Reed (eds). 1995. *Lethal Commerce: The Global Trade in Small Arms and Light Weapons*. Cambridge: Committee on International Security Studies.

Brasset, D. 1989. 'U.S. Military Elites: Perceptions and Values', in P.R. Turner, D. Pitt and Contributors (eds), *The Anthropology of War and Peace: Perspectives on the Nuclear Age*. Gramby, Mass. Bergin & Garvey, pp. 32–48.

Carmack, D. 1999. 'Gender Relief and Politics during the Afghan War', in D. Indra (ed.) *Engendering Forced Migration*. Oxford: Berghahn, pp. 95–123.

Charle, S. 2001. 'Confronting Cambodia's Culture of Violence', *Ford Foundation Report, Fall*: 9.

Cohen, R. 1986. 'War and War Proneness in Pre- and Postindustrial States', in M.L. Foster and R.A. Rubinstein (eds), *Peace and War: Cross-Cultural Perspectives*, New Brunswick: Transaction Books, pp. 253–67.

Cole, J. 1998. 'The Uses of Defeat: Memory and Political Morality in East Madagascar', in R. Werbner (ed), *Memory and the Post Colony: African Anthropology and the Critique of Power*. London: Zed Books, pp. 105–25.

Colson, E. 1987. 'Introduction: Migrants and their Hosts', in S. Morgan and E. Colson (eds), *People in Upheaval*. New York: Center for Migration Studies, pp. 1–16.

Danforth, L.M. 1995. *The Macedonian Conflict: Ethnic Nationalism in a Transnational World*. Princeton: Princeton University Press.

Daniel, E.V. and J.C. Knudsen (eds). 1995. *Mistrusting Refugees*. Berkeley: University of California Press.

de Boeck, F. 1998. 'Beyond the Grave: History, Memory and Death in Postcolonial Congo/Zaire', in R. Werbner (ed), *Memory and the Postcolony: African Anthropology and the Critique of Power*. London: Zed Books, pp. 21–57.

de Rivero, J. 2001. 'Reinventing Communities: The Resettlement of Guatemalan Refugees', *Forced Migration Review* 11: 8–10.

Douglas, M. 1966. *Purity and Danger*. London: Routledge and Kegan Paul.

Eastmond, M. 1993. 'Reconstructing Life: Chilean Refugee Women and the Dilemmas of Exile', in G. Buijs (ed), *Migrant Women: Crossing Boundaries and Changing Identities*. Oxford: Berg, pp. 21–34.

Ember, C.R. and M. Ember. 1997. 'Violence in the Ethnographic Record: Results of Cross-Cultural Research on War and Aggression', in D.L. Martin and D.W. Frayer (eds), *Troubled Times: Violence and Warfare in the Past*. Amsterdam: Gordon and Breach, pp. 1–20.

Englbrecht, W. 2001. 'Bosnia and Herzegovina: No Future without Reconciliation', *Forced Migration Review* 11: 18–20.

Fanthorpe, R. 2001. 'Neither Citizen nor Subject? "Lumpen" Agency and the Legacy of Native Administration in Sierra Leone', *African Affairs* 100 (400): 363–86.

Ferguson, R.B. 1984. 'Introduction: Studying War', in R.B. Ferguson (ed), *Warfare, Culture and Environment*. New York: Academic Press, pp. 1–81.

———. 1997. 'Violence and War in Prehistory', in D.L. Martin and D.W. Frayer (eds), *Troubled Times: Violence and Warfare in the Past*. Amsterdam: Gordon and Breach Publishers, pp. 321–55.

Foster, M.L. 1986. Is War Necessary? in M.L. Foster and R. Rubinstein (eds), *Peace and War: Cross-Cultural Perspectives*. New Brunswick: Transaction Books, pp. 71–78.

Foster, M.L. and R. Rubinstein. 1986. 'Introduction', in M.L. Foster and R. Rubinstein (eds), *Peace and War*. New Brunswick: Transaction Books, pp. xi–xviii.

Fuglerud, O. 1999. *Life on the Outside: The Tamil Diaspora and Long Distance Nationalism*. London: Pluto Press.

Gedicks, A. 2001. *Resource Rebels: Native Challenges to Mining and Oil Corporations*. Cambridge, Mass South End Press.

Givens, R.D. and M. Nettleship (eds). 1976. *Discussions on War and Human Aggression*. The Hague: Mouton.

Gledhill, J. 2001. 'Deromantizising Subalterns or Recolonizing Anthropology? Denial of Indigenous Agency: Reproduction of Northern Hegemony in the Work of David Stoll', *Identities – Global Studies in Culture and Power* 8(1): 135–61.

Greenhouse, C.J. 1986. 'Fighting for Peace', in M.L. Foster and R. Rubinstein (eds), *Peace and War: Cross-Cultural Perspectives*. New Brunswick: Transaction Books, pp. 49–60.

Grossman, D. and G. DeGaetano. 1999. *Stop Teaching Our Kids to Kill: A Call to Action against TV, Movie and Video Game Violence*. New York: Crown Publishers.

Haas, J. 1990. *The Anthropology of War*. Cambridge: Cambridge University Press.

Hirschon, R. 1998. *Heirs of the Greek Catastrophe: The Social Life of Asia Minor Refugees in Piraeus*. New York: Berghahn Books.

Hitchcox, L. 1990. *Vietnamese Refugees in Southeast Asian Camps*. Oxford: Macmillan in association with St Anthony's College.

Hovey, G. 2001. 'Discontent with Assistance to the Bosnian Return Process', *Forced Migration Review* 11: 21.

Hutchinson, S. 1998. 'Death, Memory and the Politics of Legitimation: Nuer Experiences of the Continuing Second Sudanese Civil War', in R. Werbner (ed) *Memory and the Postcolony: African Anthropology and the Critique of Power*. London: Zed Books, pp. 21–57.

Jansen, S. 1998. 'Homeless at Home: Narrations of Post-Yugoslav Identities', in N. Rapport and A. Dawson (eds), *Migrants of Identity: Perceptions of Home in a World of Movement*. Oxford: Berg, pp. 85–110.

Johnson, C. 2000. *Blowback: The Costs and Consequences of American Empire*. New York: Henry Holt.

Karadawi, A. 1999. *Refugee Policy in Sudan 1967–1984*. Oxford: Berghahn.

Karakasidou, A.N. 1997. *Fields of Wheat, Hills of Blood: Passages to Nationhood in Greek Macedonia 1870–1990*. Chicago: University of Chicago Press.

Keeley, L.H. 1996. *War before Civilization*. Oxford: Oxford University Press.

Koch, K.-F. 1974. *The Anthropology of Warfare*. Reading, Mass. Addison-Wesley.

Lederer, E. 2001. 'Poor Nations Step Up Spending on Armaments', *San Francisco Chronicle*, 31 August, A-13.

Malkki, L. 1995. *Purity and Exile: Violence, Memory, and National Cosmology among Hutu Refugees in Tanzania*. Chicago: University of Chicago Press.

Matsuoka, A. and J. Sorenson. 1999. 'Eritrean Canadian Refugee Households as Sites of Gender Renegotiation', in D. Indra (ed), *Engendering Forced Migration*, Oxford: Berghahn, pp. 218–41.

Melman, S. 1984. 'The End of War', in R.B. Ferguson (ed), *Warfare, Culture and Environment*, New York: Academic Press, pp. 387–96.

———. 1986. 'The War-Making Institutions', in M.L. Foster and R. Rubinstein (eds), *Peace and War: Cross-Cultural Perspectives*. New Brunswick: Transaction Books, pp. 193–208.

Montejo, V. 1999. *Voices from Exile: Violence and Survival in Modern Maya History*. Norman: University of Oklahoma Press.

Muecke, M. 1995. 'Trust, Abuse of Trust, and Mistrust among the Cambodian Refugee Women: A Cultural Interpretation', in E.V. Daniel and J.C. Knudsen (eds), *Mistrusting Refugees*. Berkeley: University of California Press, pp. 36–55.

Nader, L. 1989. 'The Drift to War?' in P. Turner, D. Pitt and Contributors (eds), *The Anthopology of War and Peace*. Gramby, Mass: Bergin and Garvey, pp. 79–86.

———. 1997. 'The Phantom Factor: Impact of the Cold War on Anthropology', in N. Chomsky et al. (eds), *The Cold War and the University: Toward an Intellectual History of the Postwar Years*. New York: The New Press, pp. 107–48.

Nordstrom, C. 1997. *A Different Kind of War Story*. Philadelphia: University of Pennsylvania Press.

———. 2000. 'Shadows and Sovereigns', *Theory, Culture and Society* 17(4): 35–54.

Olujic, M. 1995. 'The Croatian War Experience', in C. Nordstrom and A.C.G.M. Robben (eds), *Fieldwork under Fire: Contemporary Studies of Violence and Survival*. Berkeley: University of California Press, pp. 186–204.

Otterbein, K.F. 1970. *The Evolution of War: A Cross-Cultural Study*. New Haven: HRAF Press.

Overy, R. 2001. 'Beyond the Battlefield', *The Times Literary Supplement* 5143: 6–7.

Perroy, E. 1965. *The Hundred Years War*, transl. W.B. Wells. New York: Capricorn Books.

Peteet, J.M. 1995. 'Transforming Trust: Dispossession and Empowerment among Palestinian Refugees', in E.V. Daniel and J.C. Knudsen (eds), *Mistrusting Refugees*. Berkeley: University of California Press, pp. 168–86.

Rappoport, A. 1976. 'Comment', in R.D. Givens and M.A. Nettleship (eds), *Discussions on War and Human Aggression*. The Hague: Mouton, pp. 206–08.

Reyna, S.P. 1999. 'Introduction: Deadly Developments and Phantasmagoric Representations', in S.P. Reyna and R.E. Downs (eds), *Deadly Developments: Capitalism, States and War.* Amsterdam: Gordon and Breach Publishers, pp. 1–21.

Richards, P. 1996. *Fighting for the Rain Forest: War, Youths and Resources in Sierra Leone*. Oxford: James Currey.

Robben, A.C.G. and C. Nordstrom. 1995. 'Introduction: The Anthropology and Ethnography of Violence and Sociopolitical Conflict', in C. Nordstrom and A.C.G. Robben (eds), *Fieldwork under Fire: Contemporary Studies of Violence and Survival*. Berkeley: University of California Press, pp. 1–23.

Robben, A.C.G. 1995. 'The Politics of Truth and Emotion among Victims and Perpetrators of Violence', in C. Nordstrom and A.C.G. Robben (eds), *Fieldwork under Fire: Contemporary Studies of Violence and Survival*. Berkeley: University of California Press, pp. 81–104.

Rose, L.L. 2000. 'African Women in Post-conflict Societies: Rethinking Legal Research and Program Implementation Methodologies', *Political and Legal Anthropology Review* 23(2): 107–26.

Rubinstein, R. and M.L. Foster. 1988. 'Introduction: Revitalizing International Security Analysis: Contributions from Cultural and Symbolic Process', in R. Rubinstein and M.L. Foster (eds), *The Social Dynamics of Peace and Conflict: Culture in International Security*. Boulder: Westview Press, pp. 1–14.

Schmidt, H. 1996. 'Love and Healing in Forced Communities: Borderlands in Zimbabwe's War of Liberation', in P. Nugent and A.I. Asiwaju (eds), *African Boundaries: Barriers, Constraints and Opportunities*. London: Pinter, pp. 183–204.

Shahrani, M.N. 1995. 'Afghanistan's Muhajirin (Muslim "Refugee Warriors"): Politics of Mistrust and Distrust of Politics', in E.V. Daniel and J.C. Knudsen (eds), *Mistrusting Refugees*. Berkeley: University of California Press, pp. 187–206.

Simons, A. 1999. 'War: Back to the Future', *Annual Review of Anthropology* 28, 73–108.

Sluka, J.A. 1988. 'Loyal Citizens of the Republic: Morality, Violence and Popular Support for the IRA and INLA in a Northern Irish Ghetto', in R. Rubinstein and M.L. Foster (eds), *The Social Dynamics of Peace and Conflict: Culture in International Security*. Boulder: Westview Press, pp. 107–25.

Sommers, M. 2001. *Fear in Bongoland: Burundu Refugees in Urban Tanzania*. Oxford: Berghahn.

Stavenhagen, R. 1996. *Ethnic Conflicts and the Nation-state*. New York: St Martin's Press.

Swedenburg, T. 1995. 'With Genet in the Palestinian Field', in C. Nordstrom and A.C.G. Robben (eds), *Fieldwork under Fire: Contemporary Studies of Violence and Survival*. Berkeley: University of California Press, pp. 25–40.

Tashiro, A. 2001. *Discounted Casualties: The Human Cost of Depleted Uranium*. Japan: Chugoku Shimbun.

Turton, D. 1999. 'Warfare in the Lower Omo Valley, Southwestern Ethiopia: Reconciling Materialist and Political Explanations', in S.P. Reyna and R.E. Downs (eds), *Deadly Developments: Capitalism, States and War*. Amsterdam: Gordon and Breach Publishers, pp. 133–52.

Vincent, J. 1999. 'War in Uganda: North and South', in S.P. Reyna and R.E. Downs (eds), *Deadly Developments: Capitalism, States and War*. Amsterdam: Gordon and Breach Publishers, pp. 107–32.

Voutira, E. and B. Harrell-Bond. 1995. 'In Search of the Locus of Trust: The Social World of the Refugee Camp', in V.D. and J.C. Knudsen (eds), *Mistrusting Refugees*. Berkeley: University of California Press, pp. 207–24.

Walt, V. 2001. 'Small Arms, Big Trouble', *Ford Foundation Report*, Fall: 4–7.

Werbner, R. 1998.'Smoke from the Barrel of a Gun: Postwar of the Dead, Memories and Reinscription in Zimbabwe', in R. Werbener (ed), *Memory and the Post Colony: African Anthropology and a Critique of Power*, London: Zed Books, pp. 71–102.

Zulaika, J. 1995. 'The Anthropologist as Terrorist', in C. Nordstrom and A.C.G. Robben (eds), *Fieldwork under Fire: Contemporary Studies of Violence and Survival*. Berkeley: University of California Press. 206–22.

PART I

CHANGING QUALITIES OF VIOLENCE: CASE STUDIES FROM AFRICA

CHAPTER 1

'WE TURNED OUR ENEMIES INTO BABOONS': WARFARE, RITUAL AND PASTORAL IDENTITY AMONG THE POKOT OF NORTHERN KENYA

Michael Bollig and Matthias Österle

Introduction

Northern Kenya has become an arena of excessively violent interactions between various local groups and external power groups such as army units and police patrols. The character of these conflicts is fairly uniform: usually violent interaction begins with livestock raids by one side, followed by counter-raids by the other side. Due to the escalation of raiding the government is frequently forced to step in with police and/or army units. In the past, violent interactions rarely resulted in drawn-out battles, but rather constituted skirmishes and sudden attacks. But during the 1990s the performance of violent conflicts changed completely: extremely violent clashes with many casualties and acts of ethnic cleansing added to the 'traditional' patterns of cattle rustling and raiding. In a recent contribution Gray et al. (2003: 3) argue that the escalation of warfare 'represents the single greatest threat to [the pastoralists'] biobehavioral resilience and ultimately may have profound evolutionary costs in terms of pastoralists' survival'.

Inter-group violence in northern Kenya is deeply embedded in local cultures and is thoroughly modern at the same time. Since the 1960s guns have been of crucial importance in the region. While during the 1960s and 1970s most battles were still fought with simple rifles, in the 1980s and 1990s automatic guns like the AK-47 and the G-3 replaced earlier rifles. The AK-47 has recently been referred to as a 'change agent' because of its crucial role in changing the household economy, the gerontocratic order and the belief system of pastoralists (Österle and Bollig 2003). Linkages to international arms markets are as important for the understanding of conflicts as local concepts of honour and ideas of violence are. Various recent publications (Hutchinson 1996; Gray, Sundal, Wiebusch, Little, Leslie and Pike 2003; Abbink, this volume) show how local concepts and beliefs are affected and transformed by the current abundance of modern arms and the escalation of violence in many pastoral settings in East Africa.

In this chapter we shall try to show how external links and local factors together generate a dilemma situation: while warfare offers opportunities for militant youths, the majority of the population suffers from violence. Endemic low-intensity warfare and a steadily deteriorating ratio of livestock to people today endanger pastoralism – the resource base of the major part of the population – not only in northern Kenya, but in many parts of East and North-East Africa (Österle and Bollig 2003). We shall focus first on the pastoral Pokot of Baringo District and offer a dense description of the economic, social and cultural ramifications of violence in their society. We shall attempt to show how the recent dynamics of violence have impacted Pokot society. Drawing upon a growing body of literature on violence and social organization in pastoral communities, we shall draw connections from the Pokot study to other well-documented cases.

First, some introductory notes on the pastoral Pokot of Baringo District. According to the latest census carried out in 1999 they are estimated to number about 63,000 people (Republic of Kenya 2001) and inhabit the semi-arid plains north of Lake Baringo, subsisting mainly on mixed herds of cattle, camels and small stock. Pokot herders protect themselves against the various risks of a drought-prone environment by means of mobility, herd diversification, dispersal of livestock property and widespread exchange networks. Due to pressures on the local economy (demographic growth, herd decline, degradation) the traditional economy has changed since the late 1980s: young men have taken up trading, women and men have gone for ten-cent jobs (e.g., brewing, collecting firewood, charcoal burning) and many households have started small-scale agriculture. The social organization is based on patrilineal descent groups, age- and generation-sets and extended personal networks (Peristiany 1951; Schneider 1953; Bollig 1998). Neighbourhood councils and ritual specialists solve internal conflicts. Chiefs were installed by the colonial authorities and later by the Kenyan Ministry of Home Affairs. In the 1990s a young educated elite started to establish itself in the growing centres of Pokotland. Businessmen, politicians and local development workers wield a certain influence. Whereas the power of elders waned, parallel authority structures emerged. Surrounding pastoral groups, like Turkana and Samburu, are organized in similar ways. Sedentary agricultural economies in the region (Marakwet, Tugen, Il Chamus) show a much higher degree of market integration and stratification.

The Conflict: Character, Course and Causes

Intra-ethnic conflict management amongst the Pokot has been characterized mainly by peaceful strategies. Physical violence is only permitted in certain highly ritualized contexts. The use of 'sharp weapons' (spears, knives, arrows and guns) is prohibited altogether. Internal conflicts are resolved through negotiations, mediated by neighbourhood councils and ritual specialists, and finally prevented by opponents leaving a neighbourhood. In the case of murder or manslaughter within the group a harsh compensation system (*lapai*) prevents the escalation of violence. In a *lapai* case the entire lineage of the culprit is affected and has to compensate the victim's paternal and maternal lineages. Frequently such cases end in the impoverishment of the culprit's household and close kin. Whereas the government first rejected this kind of compensational system and worked towards its abolishment in the 1990s it nowadays condones this way of internal conflict management.[1]

In sharp contrast to this, inter-group conflicts are exceedingly violent. While the colonial regime had succeeded in keeping inter-group violence at low levels for some decades, inter-group raiding flared up once again in the late 1950s. Due to the easy access to guns the conflicts escalated into a state of permanent low-intensity warfare by the middle of the 1970s, with organized large-scale raids comprising several hundred men. Armament in one group led to the acquisition of guns in neighbouring groups. In the late 1960s and 1970s Pokot started to acquire guns in large quantities by bartering cattle with itinerant arms traders and raiding was frequent all through the 1970s.

Raids were social and military events at the same time: before a raid, ritual specialists had to be consulted and warriors were cleansed and blessed by elders. Local police forces quickly lost out to these well-armed petty armies. In the late 1970s and early 1980s large-scale raiding and subsequent army reprisals became the order of the day. The appendix gives the administration's records for just one year. Over a period of roughly eight years (1976–1984) inter-group conflicts remained at a high level. In addition to traditional bands of warriors, well connected gangs of bandits mainly of Turkana origin (the so-called *ngoroko*) roamed the area and they supplied urban livestock markets with their loot (Best 1991; Hendrickson, Mearns and Armon 1996). Then, in 1984, the army used a serious drought to disarm both Pokot and Turkana. After a peaceful interlude of some five years, raiding resurfaced in 1990. The demise of armies in Ethiopia, Somalia and the Sudan led to a massive redistribution of modern weaponry in rural populations. Rebel factions in all countries bordering north-western Kenya used guns to barter for food and consumer goods. Arms traders transported AK-47s, so to say, 'on donkeys' backs' from the battlefields and arsenals in Somalia to northern Kenya, where they exchanged guns and ammunition for livestock, which they later sold in central Kenyan markets. Although the prices of arms declined massively from some twenty-five head of oxen in the 1970s to just three oxen in the 1990s to be paid for an AK-47, the arms trade still seems to have been attractive enough to lure men into this illegal and risky business. During the 1990s Uganda became the main source for guns. Pokot men went on their own to their kinsfolk in Uganda to stock themselves with weaponry.

After 1992 violence reached a new climax. Violent clashes took place not only between pastoralists, but between herders and agriculturalists, raiders and army units, militias and police patrols, etc. In addition to the 'normal' cattle rustling other forms of violence emerged. An outstanding example is the Pokot attack on a school in Marakwet District, which left about fifty pupils dead. Many Pokot claimed this to be an act of revenge: Marakwet had killed Pokot women on their way to the market and had stolen livestock; but they had not sold or killed this livestock for food; they had now simply mutilated the cattle, hacking away their feet. During the second half of the 1990s Pokot attacks became so intense that Marakwet retreated into the Cherangani hills, leaving behind good agricultural land in the Kerio Valley. In 1996 an alliance of Samburu and Pokot warriors attacked a Turkana community near Baragoi where Turkana had been living for decades. Informants summarily reported that many Turkana, irrespective of age and sex, were killed and that the remaining vicitims left the place in horror. In fact, large tracts of land that had been held by Turkana in the past now became accessible for Pokot and Samburu. The 'Lopurkoyan case' constituted an attempt to conquer large tracts of land. In 1995 Turkana invaded Pokot territory in great numbers and attempted to occupy a vast portion of it. These Turkana were under the leadership of a younger war-leader called Lopurkoyan.[2] This man wore plaited hair – in strange and astounding contrast to Turkana traditions – and he behaved like a military leader, being flanked by 'his men' in later negotiations. The Turkana under Lopurkoyan were not organized as raiders but were in the company of young women and children and they brought a lot of livestock along with them. In the end they were defeated by Pokot (Pokot say 'devastatingly') and moved back into Turkana District after losing a huge number of people and livestock. By that time the region had entered into a state of permanent low-intensity warfare. Some newspapers clippings and reports give some idea of the intensity of warfare:

> On March 12, several hundred young Pokot, many carrying AK-47s mounted a raid on the Marakwet, their neighbours to the south and west. By the time the raiders retreated back to their side of the Kerio river, the valley had been dubbed The Valley of Death. Schools, houses and shops had been torched, and most of the 47 dead were women and children. (Washington Post, 8. July, 2001)

> At least 40 persons were killed in a March 4 cattle raid by Pokots on Turkana in the Turkwell Gorge area. At least 15 persons were killed in an October 24 cattle raid by Pokots on the Marakwet village of Tot; raiders killed 10 women and children waiting for polio vaccinations at a health clinic. (Kenya Report on Human Rights Practices for 1999, Bureau of Democracy, Human Rights and Labor, U.S. State Department, February 2000)

The regional arms race led to an enormous accumulation of automatic weapons in the hands of the civilians. Kamenju et al. (2003) claim that, among the pastoralists of West Pokot, Turkana, Samburu and East Baringo, most, if not all, adult males possess guns. Mirzeler and Young (2000: 408) estimate the number of AK-47s in neighbouring Karamoja to be between 30,000 and 40,000. After the end of the Pokot-Marakwet conflict in late 2002, East Pokot experienced a phase of relative tranquillity before the latest escalations of conflict with the Turkana in the border town of Kapedo in 2004 and with the Il Chamus in 2005. The current balance of power that has developed between well-armed neighbouring groups like Turkana and Pokot makes it very risky for any group to raid livestock from the other, so that current violent conflicts between those groups are mainly restricted to the border zones. On the other hand, neighbours of such highly militarized groups who are less well equipped with modern firearms, have become more vulnerable and rely on assistance by the Kenyan government, as was drastically demonstrated in early 2005 when raiders from East Pokot attacked the Il Chamus community in the Lake Baringo Region. After several weeks of almost daily raiding by the Pokot, the vast majority of Il Chamus had fled to Marigat (a small town about 30 kilometres from Lake Baringo with a considerable contingent of police forces) after not being able to defend themselves and their property against the Pokot invaders in any effective way. If the Kenyan government had not decided to send the Kenyan Army to confiscate livestock from households in East Pokot to compensate the Il Chamus (a measure which triggered of further problems because it was carried out as 'communal punishment'), to launch a disarmament campaign and to threaten the Pokot at the same time with even more severe consequences, the Il Chamus would have permanently lost a big portion of their territory and several thousand animals without being able to resist the Pokot in any considerable manner. Emic views reflect this state of affairs. The Pokot themselves consider the Il Chamus as very weak and they describe it as a very easy task to raid them. It does not even require proper planning and – most importantly – no spiritual backup by a prophet is needed. In stark contrast, the Turkana are considered as very brave and powerful opponents. Raiding them requires proper planning and the backup by a prophet is a necessity for being successful. The Il Chamus were in a state of shock after experiencing the superior strength of the Pokot and one old man in Marigat summarized the situation when he said: 'We only have some few weapons to defend ourselves whereas the Pokot are a full-fledged army!'

Inside the Raid: A Dense Description of Violence

During fieldwork in the late 1980s detailed accounts were collected on how inter-ethnic violence was practised. The information pertains to the 1970s and 1980s, although informants dubbed ways of planning and preparing for a raid or the ritual cleansing of people who had killed during raids as 'traditional'. However, it seems problematic to draw unbroken lines from the pre-colonial past to the practice of violent conflict in the 1970s and 1980s. The dire need to obtain bullets before a raid or the blessing of guns is clearly something specific for conflicts in Kenya's post-colonial society. It is obvious that the changing character of conflicts in the 1990s also changed the performance of violence. But not only did the character of conflicts change, so also did the entire socio-economic set-up. Impoverishment, social differentiation and the demise of gerontocratic power with the concomitant rise of new elites (young educated job holders, traders, etc.) led to comprehensive social and cultural changes. Data on the social and cultural ramifications of these new forms of violence are still somewhat scanty and will be mentioned here only where trends are clearly visible.

Psyching Up for Battle and Raid

The capacity to organize a raid adequately (*ketech luk* or *ketech setat*) is seen as a major cultural achievement through which Pokot males distinguish themselves from their agricultural neighbours. Oral traditions deal at some length with the transformation of conflict patterns in the pre-colonial past. Whereas the non-pastoral, agricultural predecessors of the pastoral Pokot only knew how to 'steal' livestock, the ability to plan and carry out large-scale raids involving hundreds of men and ritual preparation is depicted as a major step of cultural development signifying the transition to pastoralism. The archaeologist John Sutton supports oral history with his interpretation of findings that Sirikwa settlements, which had dominated much of highland western Kenya for centuries, were terminated in the late eighteenth century. The palisaded Sirikwa settlements did not offer any security against large gangs of marauders (Bollig 1992: 54) and the very beginning of the Pokot as a distinctive ethnic unit is connected to the adoption of large scale raiding, probably in the late eighteenth century (Bollig 1992: 54–59). At the same time Pokot men point out that women are not able to carry out raids. According to a small story, women once went for a raid; during the night, however, in their preparatory meeting, none of the women wanted to sleep at the fringe of the meeting place because they were afraid of enemy attacks. Women placed at the fringe took refuge in the middle and thus the planned raid soon ended in complete disorder. It is exactly this orderliness – the ability to plan over long sequences of time and to involve many people in collective action – that is thought of as a predominantly male characteristic. Also agriculturalists are said to be unable to organize a raid: they may steal livestock but are not capable of organizing a large group of men for a raid.

A raid (*setat* or *luk*) is emphatically distinguished from armed theft (*chorisyö*). While theft is 'uncultured' and non-prestigious, raids are thoroughly planned and highly ritualized affairs. It takes several weeks, sometimes months, to organize a raid; hence Pokot speak of *ketech luk* – literally 'to build a raid'. Frequently the original idea for a raid is born in a meat feast (*asiwa*). Eating meat in a group of men renders an appropriate scene to discuss the prospects of future raids, which are initiated by young men eager to foster their esteem within the male community. They display determinedness and ferocity. During the *asiwa* they stage their own courageousness by adopting an agitated style of speech – short sentences and a clipped manner of speaking – and a specific gait – spear held high over the head with the sheath (*malyan*) removed. To initiate such talks is seen as essential for *nyakan* – courageous men. Once the plan for a raid is in the air, a group of men sets off to consult a ritual specialist (*kapolokyon*) who equips them with blessings and magic for their spying expedition (*ghot*). He blesses their guns with white colour and casts a spell on their sandals, intending to make their tracks invisible. For a week or two the men scrutinize the enemy's territory during nightly walks. They try to identify neighbourhoods where large numbers of livestock congregate. Coming back they spread the news that a raid is pending. As Pokot men own many different guns the acquisition of ammunition usually takes another few weeks.

Before the men congregate in a huge final ritual (*kokwö luk*) the 'owners of the raid' – those who have participated in the spying expedition – consult a prophet (*werkoyon*), a ritual specialist who forecasts future events on the basis of his dreams. Only if his visions for the attack are promising will the raid go ahead. In the entire Pokot area only two or three prophets were active in the 1980s. Their identity is usally not disclosed to outsiders. Prophets who foretell the success of raids and warn of enemy attacks are important nodal points in the network of information flows. In times of escalating raids they are frequently consulted in order to find out about raids and army patrols or to learn about the prospects of own future raids. In the 1990s prophets were targeted by the administration and some were put in prison. This, however, did not result in the reduction of violent activities but led to the prophets going underground and/or young men going for raids without consulting experts or elders.

After the raid has been sanctioned by the prophet, men gather in a preparatory meeting, the *kokwö luk*, which can last for one to two weeks and is used to 'psych up' warriors. Practically and emotionally warriors prepare themselves for the raid and war dances, martial songs, speeches and blessings feature importantly. Livestock is slaughtered and eaten communally in the sacred half-circle of men (*kirket*), which in a nutshell is a visualized presentation of Pokot social order. Renowned courageous men (*nyakan*) recount the exploits of previous successful raids. They point out how shameful anxiety (*nyokoryö*) and how manly ferociousness (*sirumoi*) is (see Figure 1.1 for a schematic presentation of feelings of aggression). The ability to deliver such fiery speeches which draw hesitant men into the mood, is regarded highly. Successful raids of the recent past are condensed in songs.[3]

Singer: *Ekirepe loyangatome*
ekirepe nyikwa Yelele
This is the raid of the yellow guns
This is the raid of Yelele's son
Group: *aliwori ngichomi kanyi kwiapa, ooh*
We turned the inhabitants of that country into baboons
Singer: *ooh yalelo*
ooh yalelo
Singer: *ekirepe nyikwa Asiriyara,*
ekirepe nyikwa Kilikili
This is the raid of Asiriyara's son,
This is the raid of Kilikili's son
Group: *remerupe nyeriongo aliwori ngichominia kanyakwapa, ooh*
we attacked in spring and brought back cattle,
those with horns pointing downwards
we turned the inhabitants of that country into baboons
Singer: ooh yalelo
Singer: *ekirepe nyimeritome, ekirepe ngingatome kireme Marti*
the raid of the speckled guns, the raid of the yellow guns
which attacked Merti forcefully
Group: *aliwori ngichominia kanyakwapa, ooh*
we turned the inhabitants of that country into baboons

This song was composed in 1978 after a successful raid on Merti. Yellow guns (AK-47s) and speckled guns were of particular importance in this raid. The raid was very successful, depriving the attacked community of livestock and rendering it dependent on food gathered from the bush.

During the preparatory meeting the men attending it have to obey several rules to maintain the purity (*tililyö*) of the raid. Sexual intercourse and quarrelling are prohibited during the preparatory meeting and the subsequent raid. Men who have seriously violated these norms or those who are caught up in cases of adultery and theft or who think of themselves as being cursed should not attend the meeting. They would inevitably draw misfortune onto the entire group. The final day of the meeting is a day of dancing and ferocious speeches. Finally the men and their arms are blessed by prominent elders with specific earth colours, which prevent misfortune. In a final act all men crawl through the spread legs of a standing elder. In this way a group of raiders is 'tied together' (*kerat luk*) and magically prevented from getting dispersed by enemy crossfire or helicopter attacks by army units.

The raid is now on its way. Without showing much concern for secrecy the warriors run and march. The attack usually takes place during the early morning hours. In small groups the raiders 'comb' the area, attacking single homesteads, randomly shooting at inhabitants and driving off livestock. After a few hours the group starts to retreat. By then the attacked community has managed to congregate and frequently police and/or army units are on the heels of the raiders. Because of the looted livestock the retreat is slow and usually the raiders have to fight their way back. Mortalities among the raiders are highest in this phase, especially when army units pursue them with helicopters and open fire from the air. Frequently parts of the looted herd are lost again. Reaching safer grounds, the herd is immediately divided but there are no clear-cut rules as to how to divide the loot. Those who have participated in the spying expedition, the so-called 'owners of the raid', may take their animals first, and some animals are also given to the ritual experts consulted before the raid and during the preparatory meeting. Then those who participated in the raid with automatic guns take their share. Informants described the distribution of the loot as a very uneasy event that frequently results in quarrels. For fear of reprisals the group disperses rapidly, no communal feasting and no celebrations of the spoils of war taking place. Those who have killed, however, may not go back to their homesteads. For them a period of ritual purification starts immediately after the raid.

There is some evidence that the ritual aspect of preparation for a raid became less prominent in the 1990s. While preparatory meetings did take place, they were obviously smaller in size and – perhaps more importantly – drew less on the legitimizing power of elders. The number of violent acts not sanctioned by elders clearly rose: an attack on neighbouring Samburu and the armed attack on an Indian trader were rejected by many elders. There are accounts that some elders condoned and blessed raids secretly, hoping to participate in the loot but thereby undermining the consensus within their age group. The decrease of elders' power to control and contain violence corresponded to their waning power in local politics and a dwindling resource base. Elders' control of livestock competes with the control of firearms through young men. Elders' power is further curtailed by the growing importance of politicians, agents of various development organizations and rich local traders. To what extent the new elites have any impact on the proliferation of violence is unclear in the Pokot case. A first impression is that the young and educated town dwellers and job holders have only very limited impact, if any. Especially livestock traders may have benefited from looted livestock; however, after a raid local livestock markets frequently collapse as police units control trading points or prohibit marketing activities altogether. There is one account of a late parliamentarian from neighbouring West Pokot coming to the region for an electoral campaign and asking Somali traders openly to bring more guns to the region. However, if politicians and office holders are asked directly about their opinion, they emphasize the defensive qualities of armament – thereby justifying the large number of guns in their constituencies.

The Ideal Emotive and Moral Orientation of a Warrior

The *nyakan* is the ideal warrior: he is distinguished from others by his determination, his emotional state and his fulfilment of goals. Young men usually have little chance to attain prestige as rich herd-owners – too great a herd would make them fall prey to witching and cursing by elders. Throughout the 1990s drought and livestock diseases as well as a dramatic increase in population have led to pastoral impoverishment. Many young men not only felt that they were poorer than their forefathers, but they actually were much less well off than their fathers and grandfathers. At the same time they could not achieve the status of ritual specialists during their youth. Ascent is rigidly controlled and defined within a gerontocratic system: people never increase their status as individuals but only go up the ladder as a well-defined group. While alternative sources of income like trading and paid labour were eagerly sought after, these did not convey any prestige. Only the ideal of the courageous warrior (*nyakan*) is attainable for them: this includes the preparedness to act violently during external conflicts and to control aggressive feelings in internal conflicts. Somebody who can claim to have raided plenty of livestock and boast of having killed enemies accumulates personal prestige. The symbolic capital a successful raider has accumulated is made visible: he wears scarifications on his shoulders, includes a red feather in his headdress and cuts the ears of his name-oxen in a special way. He also reorganizes the praise songs for his favourite oxen in such a way that his prowess is adequately emphasized.

The foundation of this ideal character is an emotional predisposition: the control of aggressive emotions. Under no circumstances should aggressive feelings result in immediate action. While they are articulated in non-violent ways in internal disputes (verbal aggressions, cursing, witching), they are transformed into intentional, controlled violent behaviour in external conflicts. Pokot language offers a variety of terms denoting aggressive feelings (see Figure 1.1). Aggressive emotions are categorized into different fields of emotion terms: the Pokot differentiate between *ghöityö* (a general and intense bad feeling towards a fellow Pokot), *sinyoryö* (an irritation) and *kilemasat* (anger). These feelings are connected to envy (*ngatkong*) and pain (*ngwönin*). In disputes within the community these aggressive feelings are regarded as the most disruptive feelings; these emotions frequently materialize in acts of verbal and magical aggression. Even a general 'bad will' (*ghöityö*) towards an opponent may already have disastrous consequences. These feelings are regarded as socially disruptive and everybody fears them. These emotions are regarded as 'violent acts', not as mere feelings awaiting materialization. A number of ritual specialists are at hand to control the effects of such negative aggressive feelings (Bollig 1992: 176–83).

Aggressive feelings directed against an opponent outside one's own ethnic group are not conceptualized in the same way. Labelled *sirumoi*, the aggressive feeling in inter-ethnic conflict is best understood as a mixture of determinedness, ferocity and rage. As mentioned above, when warriors are preparing for a raid they undergo a 'psyching up for battle'. War dances and speeches are aimed at inflaming the *sirumoi* of all participants. This highly emotionalized state

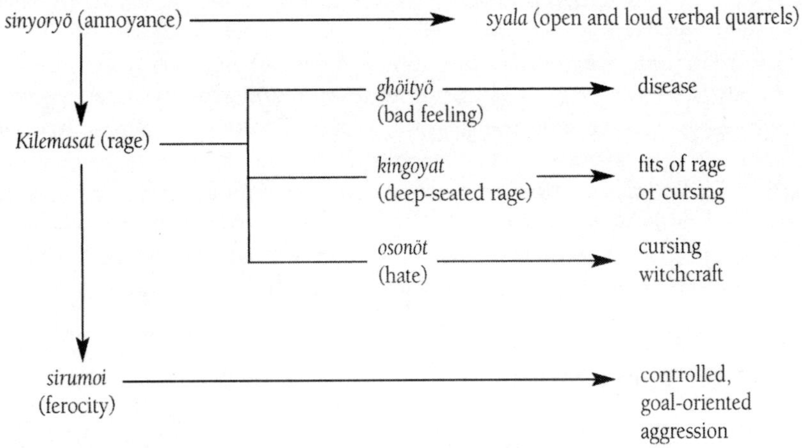

Figure 1.1: *Schematic representation of relations between emotions and actions as perceived by Pokot informants*

expresses itself in shivering (*potenö*) and, in extreme cases, in short fits of unconsciousness (*longunogh*). The capacity of being perceptive to *sirumoi* and this emotion's physical reverberations add to the prestige of a warrior.

Clearly there has been a differentiation in the role of male youths over the past two decades. Numerous young men have finished secondary school education, some went to universities and several hold high-salaried jobs in Kenya's cities or in Kenya's national administration. Some have joined the Kenyan army and taken part in UN missions as far afield as Eritrea and Sierra Leone. Some of these soldiers came back as rich men, documenting their wealth with prestigious stone-built houses in the small centres of Pokotland. There can be no doubt that there are well-accepted, alternative life careers for males nowadays. However, many of these new perspectives are not open to young men who lack education[4] and only successful trading may be a viable alternative to violent activities. While in the past the warrior ideal was clearly dominant, other highly valued alternatives are available nowadays. Not only are violent activities no longer embedded in the structures of the gerontocratic system, but women also look for spouses with different orientations. To adhere to the moral code of conduct of a *nyakan* seems to be much less desirable nowadays. There is a clear tendency for young men no longer to invest the same amount of capital and time in their personal decoration: beaded personal ornament is rarely worn outside major rituals; the finely coloured mud-cap of which most men were still proud in the 1980s is hardly seen any more. The dressing code seems to be much more relaxed than before and most young men resort to cheap second-hand clothing. More and more, violence committed by young men is negatively commented upon by other members of the society and thereby becomes the activity of a societal subgroup, blocked in its aspirations and convinced of its relative poverty. Most of them are not likely to establish wealthy pastoral households, nor will they be able to make alternative careers outside the pastoral sector. Transitions to banditry and criminal activities are a possible outcome of this process. Events in the 1990s point towards this direction: on several occasions young men went in small groups for raids without the consent and blessing of elders; several times traders on their way to the small market centre Nginyang, the major livestock market in the region, were attacked and some of them even killed.

Killing and Ritual Healing

While killing a fellow Pokot results in a complex mechanism of compensation and is perceived as a collective catastrophe, killing a non-Pokot sets off a process of ritual purification. The post-conflict careers of warriors who have killed in battle are determined by communal efforts to resocialize them. Seen as endangering physical and social reproduction within the homestead, initially they themselves have inhibitions about re-entering their homestead, thereby being barred from the realm of culture. The presence of such a warrior is thought of not only as polluting, but also as outright dangerous. When killing an enemy (*pung*) a shadow (*rurwö*) falls onto the person who has killed. This shadow condenses an array of supernatural dangers that may befall the slayer. If this shadow is not treated adequately, a disease called *anges* will slowly waste away the warrior. His untreated shadow inevitably destroys all fertility in his surroundings, that of women as well as of livestock.

First rituals of purification begin immediately after the deed and are meant to ban the dangers of 'spilled blood', which may result in infertility and disease. Still standing near the corpse of the slain victim, the slayer should call upon some friends and together with them sing a song called *kiorontö*. This song emphasizes the necessity of the deed, underlines the radical discipline of the warriors and mocks the slain victim. This first part of the purification ritual, however, rarely happens today, as most mortalities are caused by heavy gunfire and nobody risks approaching the victim's body for fear of being shot. Killing by gun is ostensibly more anonymous than killing by spear.

Kiorontö

Aya lope yo, oh lope yo, oh lope yo oh
Aya, spirit of the dead, oh spirit of the dead, oh spirit of the dead
Onyoru koko kawaghe, a ya yo oh, lope yo
I killed the wife of hyena

Onyochö koko kawaghe
I have beaten you, wife of a hyena
Aya lope yo, oh lope yo, oh lope yo oh
Aya, spirit of the dead, oh spirit of the dead, oh spirit of the dead

Ahh, lapuröröro, ah lahooh, aah, lapröröro, aah lahooh,
Indeed this being is stone-dead
Onyoru koko kawaghe, ah lahooh, aah lapurörö, aah lahooh
I killed the wife of hyena, she is stone-dead
Onyochö koko kawagh, ah lahooh, aah lapurörö, aah lahooh
I have beaten you, wife of a hyena, yes she is stone-dead

Ore ye, ore ye, ore ye
[meaning not clear]
onyochö koko kawaghe, ore ye, oh, ore ye oh
I have beaten you, wife of a hyena
Ore ye oh, ore oh. Apar kichongone, ore ye oh,
I have pierced her …

ato kilenchin nchile, inchil,
if you are told 'jump', then jump
kilowowisa iwis, iwi le sipirir
if you are told 'jump on your tiptoes', then jump on your tiptoes
inam nyu kiyona
you take this thing [death] [instead of me]

On the way back from the raid a further minor purificatory ritual takes place, without which the slayer would not be allowed to eat or drink anything. Some initiated *kolïn*, those who have already gone through the entire process of purification, have taken pieces of the magical *moikut* root (*Cyperus rotundus*) with them on the raid. This root is frequently used to cure states that seem to go out of human control: long-festering wounds are anointed with the sap of the root, and a homestead head may spit the sap of *moikut* towards a bull going on the rampage. In this small ritual an initiated *kolïn* squats together with the person who has just killed. He chews parts of the magic root and spits bits of it on the initiate's heart, then under his armpits, on his chest and finally on his forehead, in order to dispel the ill-effects of the shadow.

Despite these purificatory rituals a man who has killed is confronted with a number of other taboos. He may not enter his or any other homestead, may not drink milk and may not himself cut the meat he eats. Usually he stays near the homestead in the bush and his food is brought to his hideout by young girls or elderly women beyond menopause. Fertile women would be endangered as the shadow of the slain person could easily fall upon them. It would be easy to translate the image of the shadow of the slain as a conceptualization of 'sin'. However, this kind of thinking would lead in the wrong direction: women who have had a miscarriage or whose baby child died are also affected by the shadow, and so too are people who carried a dead person to his/her grave. It is rather the pollution brought about by the direct contact with death that has to be treated in order to prevent disease and infertility.

Shortly after the return from the raid a black goat is slaughtered – black in this context symbolizing death, and an initiated *kolïn* then anoints the man with the stomach contents of this goat. The killing of the black goat signals the beginning of the *kimokat* ritual. The slayer has to stay on in the bush until the new moon rises. The final part of this ritual takes place in the meeting place of men (*kokwö*), taking the man from his hideout in the bush back to a public space. There a white goat is slaughtered – white symbolizing harmony and peace. Again the initiate is smeared with the stomach contents of the slaughtered goat, whose skin is cut into many long strips (*maasa*). For the final stage of the ritual a set of calabashes is prepared containing various medicines (a concoction of *siyoyowö* [*Ficus dekdekana*] and *lakatetwö* [*Barleria eranthemoides*]), honey-beer and a mixture of honey and the milk of a cow that has never been sick (*chepö roriyon*). The *kolïn* 'washes' the initiate with these medicines and finally anoints him with honey. Then he binds the strips of the goat's skin on all the joints of the slayer. Symbolically, these strips 'prevent the body from falling apart'. In the following years the initiate wears these strips, or some of them, on festive occasions.

While from now on the slayer may participate in everyday life, he is still restricted in ritual contexts: he may not undertake the final marriage ceremony (*koyogh*), spear an ox in a ritual of the age-set or generation-set or cut the sacred *amurö* meat from oxen slaughtered in ritual settings. Only some years later will the final purification ritual, the *dia* ceremony, be celebrated. Early in the morning, before the sun rises, two *kolïn* bring the initiate into the middle of the livestock enclosure. They are festively adorned with red-painted ostrich feathers. Once again they tie the *maasa* strips onto the joints of the initiate and anoint him with red ochre. Then his cattle herd is driven onto the ceremonial ground and he spears an ox from within the herd. In contrast to other rituals of initiation, nobody is blessed with the stomach contents of this animal: the occasion for which this animal was slaughtered is regarded as impure – as '*mötilinye lasiny eghintö*' ('this ox is not completely pure'), it is still polluted by bloodshed.

The core of the initation starts only late in the afternoon. Both *kolïn* and the initiate squat in the middle of the sacred half-circle of men just in front of the stomach contents of the oxen, which have been heaped right in the centre of the ceremonial ground. Just as during the *kimokat* ritual, calabashes with various medicines have been prepared. The only difference is that the honey has been mixed with millet. Then the ritual experts undress the initiate. Ceremoniously they take off the *maasa* strips and his clothing. He is then washed with these medicines and finally anointed with the mixture of honey and millet. After the cleansing he is walked around the ritual centre of the ceremonial ground and given a mixture of blood and milk to drink. A reddened ostrich feather is put into his hair and he squats down again with the *kolïn*. The initiate will now be given an honorary name. The ritual expert explains briefly to the public that the initiate needs to be given a new name and he asks the men in the half-circle, 'what name shall he be given?' He calls out a specific *nom de guerre*: these names are easily distinguishable from ordinary Pokot names: the suffix *-moi* indicates that a woman was killed, the suffix *-le* indicates a man was killed. Habitually the men do not respond at the first suggestion. The ritual expert calls out further names and with each name the crowd murmurs more loudly. The last name is shouted three or four times to the crowd and their consent is heard louder and louder. The community of men has now given a new honorary identity to the slayer. Finally the ritual expert greets the initiate with his new name. He is now a fully initiated *kolïn* and may treat pregnant women for various diseases. Pregnant women are thought of as most susceptible to shadows, but the *kolïn* has successfully domesticated 'his' shadow and this has therefore enabled him to cure all diseases connected with shadows. During Bollig's fieldwork in the late 1980s he found that there was hardly a pregnancy that was not treated by *kolïn* (Bollig 1992: 297). Soon after his ritual of initiation (the *dia*) the slayer will ask a specialist to cut the scarifications on his shoulder – on the left if he has killed a woman, on the right if he has killed a man. In many rituals the new *kolïn* will be given prominence and he will also occasionally conduct healing rituals.

The changing character of warfare and the impact of modern weaponry on local belief systems and/or ideologies have been documented in recent studies (see, for example Abbink 1994, 1999, 2001 on the Surma; Hutchinson 1996 and 2001 on the Nuer; Gray 1999 on the Karimojong; Mirzeler and Young 2000 on the Karimojong and the Jie). The fact that guns have widely replaced spears in fighting and killing has led to the transformation of religious concepts concerning killing and homicide among the Nuer; take, for example, the concept of *nueer*, which Evans-Pritchard described as 'the most important of Nuer sin concepts' (1956: 183). According to *nueer* the blood of a man who has killed someone is polluted in a very dangerous and contagious way and to avoid severe and deadly consequences the killer has to undergo specific purificatory rites. The increasing number of killings by guns and bullets and the specific nature of these killings required the transformation and extension of *nueer* by integrating new ideas of sin and pollution to make it compatible with this peculiar and particularly devastating form of violence. A Nuer warlord prominent all through the 1980s and 1990s succeeded in introducing a conceptual division between so-called 'internal wars' and 'government wars'. Whereas deaths resulting from internal wars were to be compensated and the slayer ritually cleansed from the blood of his victim, deaths resulting from government wars were considered completely secular, requiring neither compensation nor cleansing. This warlord established that all wars fought under his command against rival rebel factions, Nuer and Dinka alike, were government wars, thereby releasing the militias under his command from all fear of spiritual pollution (Hutchinson 2001). Karimojong and Jie also differentiate between the power of spears and the power of modern firearms and automatic weaponry (Mirzeler and Young 2000). Their elders consider 'modern wars' to be mere profane events, lacking the spiritual sanctions that were characteristic of 'traditional' armed conflicts. In contemporary Karimojong belief, death caused by automatic guns such as the widespread AK-47s has far-reaching consequences for the spirits of the victims: they are not sent to the bush – the place where the ancestral spirits live – but have to move to unknown locations instead.

What, then, are the changes in Pokot beliefs and rituals connected with warfare and killing? Apparently no new ideology of killing and purification has arisen as it has among the Karimojong and Nuer. However, rituals of purification (especially the final *dia* ceremony) are obviously delayed a lot. We spoke to young men who had delayed the key purification ceremonies for about ten years, but insisted that they still thought that they should proceed with it. Many men of the younger generation do not want to be addressed any longer with their honorary *nom de guerre* as they do not wish to publicly disclose that they have been involved in raiding. Many young men will have killed more than one person during the 1990s when violence escalated, but they will undergo the ritual only once. While the exact ramifications of these changes are yet to be seen, a de-ritualization of killing does seem to have taken place over the course of the last decade.

The Embeddedness of Local Conflicts and Socio-economic Change in Pastoral Systems

The final section of this chapter identifies some of the economic and social consequences of low-intensity warfare in the region and compares processes observed among the Pokot with the dynamics reported upon in neighbouring communities. An attempt is made to show the degree to which low-intensity warfare contributes to the transformation of pastoral systems in the broader region.

The Economics of the Weapons Trade and Cattle Rustling in Northern Kenya

A survey of guns used by the Pokot during the conflicts of the 1970s and 1980s pointed to the close relationship between local conflict, regional wars and the international arms trade. Weapons that the Pokot owned in the 1980s were (besides spears and bows) old-fashioned rifles, guns from the Second

World War and some modern automatic guns. All these had been used earlier somewhere in East Africa – in other words, the Pokot were second- and third-hand users. Only after the previous owner had acquired a better weapon, or was killed, did the gun enter the illicit trade network. The oldest gun Bollig found had an Austro-Hungarian designation and had been produced in Budapest, probably before 1914. It was rusty in the extreme and probably as much a danger to the person shooting as to the person being targeted. Table 1.1 sets out the manner in which Pokot differentiated guns in 1988–89. During the late 1980s and the 1990s most older guns were replaced by AK-47s and G-3s. Kamenju et al. (2003) estimate the number of automatic guns in East Pokot to be around 7,500 – an enormous number that suggests that by far most adult Pokot men own automatic guns.

How do Pokot obtain these guns? Until the middle of the 1990s they bought them mainly from itinerant Somali traders, who in their turn bought them in Somalia, or more frequently in north-east Kenya from other Somali traders. From the 1920s to the 1960s camels were traded along the same route as guns in the 1980s and Pokot were accustomed to Somali traders, who exchanged precious goods for oxen. Once a load of guns arrived, men potentially interested in the deal would contact the trader and invite him home. There the trader would wait until the customer had gathered the necessary number of oxen and cash. For some time the trader continued to gather oxen in this manner. Once he had sold his goods he embarked on tracking the cattle to one of the nearby livestock markets. This system of

Table 1.1: *Pokot differentation of guns in 1988–89*

Type	Local Term	Origin
SLR		Origin not clear, used during the Ogaden war
F/N	Epen	The Fabrique Nationale, Belgium; probably from licensed production in Congo; traded through Uganda on to northern Kenya
Freign Gun	Fram	Great Britain; guns in northern Kenya of this type probably originate from magazines of former Somalian police
Pintup	Pintap	Lee-Enfield, used during Ogaden conflict and during the shifta rebellion of Kenyan Somali
4 KL	Pokela	Not identified
2/5	Topay	AK-47 of Russian origin, from magazines of the former Somalian or Ethiopian armies
G3	–	German gun, produced by Heckler and Koch; used by the Kenyan police and the Somalian army
?	Anawuchir Namechir Atakore	Different guns named after their sound by Pokot; I did not succeed in identifying the precise type of guns and their origin

weapon supply changed thoroughly during the middle 1990s. Since then almost no guns have been obtained from the Somali side; instead Pokot have taken up the weapons trade themselves. They venture into Uganda, where they obtain guns from Ugandan Pokot. The source of these guns is not entirely clear and there are allegations that some Pokot have connections with Joseph Kony's Lord's Resistance Army (see Behrend this volume) and obtain guns via this channel. Pokot gun traders obviously feel more at ease trading guns with distant relatives, clan and/or age mates and are of the opinion that by doing it this way the risk of being cheated is much lower.

Losses Due to the Acquisition of Guns

When asked who gained the most from raids – Pokot, Turkana or gun dealers – young Pokot men unanimously admitted that the highest gains were probably made by the gun dealers. Throughout the 1970s and the 1980s Pokot had to pay very high prices for guns. The better weapons cost thirty head of cattle and above, and even an old-fashioned gun was still sold at ten head of oxen and more. Table 1.2 gives an overview of cattle spent on guns in five households (household no. 3 had to acquire a second gun after a first one was lost during a raid). The figures clearly indicate that the Pokot were forced to pay heavily for guns and these expenses, it is suggested, forced men to raid in order to compensate for the extraordinarily high losses of livestock involved in the acquisition of guns.

Some young men recounted how they had to postpone marriages because they lacked enough cattle to pay bridewealth after buying a gun. As yet guns are not offered as bridewealth payment, as Hutchinson (1996) reports for the Sudanese Nuer. Obviously, young men were interested in recouping some of their losses, but did they succeed in doing so? Apparently they were faced with

Table 1.2: *Livestock paid for guns in the 1970s and early 1980s*

	Price paid				
Household	**Oxen**	**Cows/heifers**	**Small stock**	**Camels**	**TLU**
1	15	36	0	1	52.2
2	20	5	0	0	25.0
3a	24	1	0	0	25.0
3b	2	10	30	0	17.0
4	25	12	0	1	38.2
5	18	22	0	2	42.4
6	9	11	0	0	20.0

a dilemma: when the loot was distributed mainly those men who participated in the raid with a gun got the lion's share, while those who took part without a gun got only a few animals. It is said that men owning a gun contributed disproportionately to the success of the raid. However, these guns cost tremendous numbers of livestock throughout the 1970s and the 1980s. This shows that raiding begins with profound and rather definite losses due to the expenses on guns and ammunition. Table 1.3 links these expenditures to gains made in raids and shows that all men but one who bought guns made net losses. They had not been able to raid sufficient numbers of cattle to compensate for the purchase of the gun over a span of five years and more. Only the three actors who did not invest in a gun made a marginal profit. Nevertheless, many herders felt forced to buy guns when they saw their enemies arming themselves.

Recent declines in prices for AK-47s have lowered the capital input: Kamenju et al. (2003) report prices of 20,000 to 30,000 KSh, Gray (1999) the price of three to four oxen (see also Mkutu 2001). This not withstanding, data on losses and gains derived from raiding clearly demonstrate that violent inter-ethnic conflict confronts the Pokot – especially young Pokot men – with a dilemma. On the one hand, young men may win numerous head of livestock in a very short period of time if luck is on their side and they may also gain prestige as fierce and brave warriors. This may enable them to establish independent households early on and guarantee them prominent treatment by age mates and seniors. They are favoured spouses, and many men who have accumulated prestige as warriors have in fact married a second and third wife early on. On the other hand, losses are more definite: grazing is lost as each

Table 1.3: *Gains and losses due to raiding and purchases of guns between c. 1975 and 1989*

		Received in TLU		
Household	**Spent in TLU**	**Total gains from raiding**	**gains per raid**	**Total gain/loss**
1	52.2	13.0	1.9	–39.2
2	25.0	30.0	5.0	+5.0
3	42.0	28.3	3.5	–13.7
4	38.2	27.0	4.5	–11.2
5	42.4	24.2	3.5	–18.2
6	20.0	15.4	2.2	–4.6
7	0	1.8	0.6	+1.8
8	0	2.2	1.1	+2.2
9	0	0.4	0.2	+0.4

* Figures vary slightly from those in a table published in Bollig (1990). Small-stock units were counted differently and raided donkeys are included here too.

raid inevitably provokes a counter-raid, livestock has to be paid to weapon dealers to obtain guns and more continuously to obtain ammunition, and, last but not least, livestock are lost to raiders and to army operations. However, those few people who gain from raiding are not necessarily those who lose most during counter-raids. Losses of grazing land are borne by the entire community, losses of livestock due to raids are frequently borne by seniors because their populous households are less mobile, and raids often hit households in an unpredictable manner simply because they happen to be in the way of raiders. There is little doubt that with the recent decline in arms prices raiding became more profitable in the 1990s, but one wonders how much more substantial the gains of raiders are.

The arming of one population leads to that of neighbouring populations and the competition between young males within an egalitarian society is motivation enough to take to high-risk investments. Clearly, guns do not function only as a 'means of production' but contribute to the prestige of young males as well. Inequalities in arms frequently lead to an immediate upsurge in violence. When the Karimojong raided the Moroto army barracks left behind by fleeing Idi Amin soldiers, the comparative advantage was immediately realized in raids on the Dodos. Turton and Tornay report on similar cases in south-western Ethiopia. The balance of power between the various pastoral groups of Ethiopia's 'Southern Peoples' Region' was disturbed dramatically when the Nyangatom managed to arm themselves with automatic weapons on a large scale at the beginning of the 1980s. The Nyangatom obtained these guns through an alliance with the Sudanese Toposa, who were first in line with the Sudan People's Liberation Army but later changed sides and supported the Sudanese government. From both relationships the Toposa-Nyangatom alliance gained a lot of weaponry which enabled them to put heavy pressure on their enemies, the Mursi and the Surma, with partly devastating consequences (Tornay 1993; Turton 1993, 1994, 1996; Abbink 2001). The Mursi and Surma lost many lives and large parts of their territories and their only chance to regain pastures and successfully defend the remainder was to acquire automatic weapons on a large scale too. While rapid arming of one party usually had disastrous consequences for less armed neighbours, disarmament campaigns frequently had the same effect. Especially across international boundaries there has hardly been any coordination of army-based disarmament campaigns. So, once massive campaigns in Karamoja had brought down the number of guns in this region, Kenyan Turkana took their chance and raided the Karimojong.

Local arms races have led to an immense accumulation of automatic guns in the hands of civilians. Mirzeler and Young (2000) estimate the number of AK-47s in Karamoja at between 30,000 and 40,000, and Kamenju et al. (2003) claim that, among the pastoralists of West Pokot, Turkana, Samburu and East Baringo, most, if not all, adult males possess guns. Of course, human mortalities count higher than losses in pastures and livestock. There is an uncontroversial reporting of an increased number of deaths connected to the introduction of automatic guns. Gray reports that in 1999 alone over 4,000 Karimojong were killed in large-scale attacks and helicopter-borne repressive operations by the army. Tornay (1993) and Turton (1994) mention several hundred casualties in isolated raids in south-western Ethiopia. The loss of human lives has been tremendous and Turton (1979) considers that the rapid armament of adversaries could lead to the annihilation of entire communities, in both physical and cultural terms. This argument has been extended by Gray et al. (2003), who show that adult mortality has increased tremendously and as a further consequence of displacement and impoverishment, child mortality has increased as well.

Socio-economic Change Brought About by Low-intensity Warfare

Guns have been discussed as a new 'means of production', highlighting the potential gains from raiding and other illicit actions backed by the threat of lethal weapons. However, there has been little proof that guns are in effect consistently used in an economic way so as to accumulate scarce resources. The case study from Pokot presented above points in another direction. In contrast, damage from violent conflicts has been widely reported by anthropologists and by the staff of development organizations working in pastoral conflict settings. However, a detailed quantification of losses and damage is rarely presented.

Diminished Access to Grazing

In order to evade violent conflicts Pokot herders moved away from border areas. A no-man's-land at least some 100 kilometres long and some 50 kilometres wide was not used. If a modest stocking rate of one head of cattle per 20 hectares of land is taken, 5,000 km^2 would offer space for roughly 25,000 head of cattle. These are the high opportunity costs of inter-ethnic raiding! And these costs are still higher if (a) increased degradation in overstocked areas is taken into account, (b) the negative impact of under-grazing on the development of the vegetation is rated and (c) the detrimental effect of violence on communal resource management is weighed:

(a) Environmental degradation is extreme in the southernmost locations of Pokotland and around the few centres where Pokot concentrated, hoping for better protection through police and army. However, this imbalance led to a situation in which probably more than two-thirds of all livestock were kept on a fraction of the land.

(b) One may be tempted to hypothesize, then, that pastures that are not used for some time will recover and perennial grasses re-establish themselves after the stress of grazing by large herds of herbivores is diminished. However, the opposite seems to happen: bush encroachment is rampant in the areas that are not grazed any more. Conant (1982: 117ff.) shows, on the basis of satellite imagery, aerial photography and ground-truthing, that grassland communities were replaced by acacia thorn bush on a large scale in areas that were not grazed any more in the north-western Baringo plains. In the absence of herding, *Acacia* spp. doubled their distribution and grass retreated from 38 per cent in 1973 to 13 per cent in 1978.[5]

(c) Pokot found it more and more difficult to manage key resources such as pastures and watering-places communally. Widespread violence led to a constant move of people from one grazing community to another. In a situation in which there was no guarantee that resources could be used the next season there is little incentive to manage them in a sustainable way. Furthermore, due to the presence of internally displaced herders, i.e., actors who are present in the community for one or two seasons only, the community responsible for the management of collective goods becomes blurred. The increase of inter-ethnic violence contributed a great deal to the fact that Pokot communal resource management turned into open-access management.

The loss of grazing land has been widely reported in accounts of violence in pastoral areas. Almagor (1979) on the Dassanetch, Turton (1979, 1994) on the Mursi, McCabe et al. (1999) on the Turkana and Gray (1999) on the Karimojong all report the widening of no-go zones where people fear to bring their cattle because of the high risk of being raided. This dilemma frequently results in the existence of highly overused pastures near settlements and close to police stations. Furthermore, low-intensity warfare precludes the emergence of situations that allow for a clear definition of people using a resource, hinders local authorities from policing and sanctions, and precludes any forms of reasonable co-management.

Losses due to Livestock Theft

Each raid by one party provokes a counter-attack by the raided party. Hence, the raiding economy offers simultaneous gains and losses. Furthermore, army units are in the game as a third party. They confiscate livestock of the offending party – defining all inhabitants of a region as offenders – and give livestock back to the damaged party. However, actors from both parties claim that some confiscated animals stay with the army units.

The overview on stock losses and recovered stock (i.e., livestock confiscated by the army and given back) in northern Baringo for the years 1976 and 1977 proves that net losses were high. In 1976 the Pokot lost some 700 cattle and in 1977 almost 5,000 (about 10 per cent of the total herd at that time). Goats that were stolen in both years were hardly compensated for: more than 7,000 goats were lost within one year, about 5 per cent of the total herd. A closer look at the literature published in recent years on the southern Turkana suggests that at least some Pokot managed to gain in livestock numbers during this period of heavy losses. Johnson (1990: 182f.) reports that about half of the twenty-two Turkana households he worked with were raided by the Pokot during the early 1980s and lost substantial numbers of livestock. Significant shifts in wealth in livestock took place. During raids it is especially young men who gain livestock and it is the older, well-established households who lose most.

A massive decline of herds is also reported from other pastoralists as well as from neighbouring agro-pastoralists. The fact that livestock numbers dwindle due to systematic bombing, gunfire and raiding crops up in many accounts. Exact numbers, however, are usually missing. The Karamoja case is an exception. Mirzeler and Young (2000: 417) report that Acholi lost massively to Karimojong herders: within a period of twelve years (1985–1997) cattle numbers in Acholi country declined from 300,000 to a mere 5,000, mainly due to Karimojong raids. Gray (1999) asserts that the herds of the Bokora Karimojong were reduced so heavily in recent years that many people dropped out of pastoralism. Mkutu (2000) estimates that in 1996 alone livestock worth over 320 million Kenyan shillings was lost to raiders in Samburu, and that Baringo District (mainly referring to Pokot and Njemps) lost 420 million between 1995 and 2000 (Mkutu and Marani 2003). McCabe (1985) lists losses for individual Turkana households: his figures show that losses hit households at random and devastatingly. Clearly cattle rustling has levelling effects and its lottery character exacerbates the uncertainty herders have to bear with anyhow.

Changes in Socio-political Organization and Inter-community Relations

Intra-group relations changed profoundly due to the escalation of violence. In eastern Uganda the power of elders was destabilized. Young men, usually the owners of the automatic weapons or at least the people having the skill to deal with them, acted independently and out of control of elders. The decline of the gerontocratic system, so typical for East African pastoral nomadism, has been reported for southern Ethiopia (the Surma case) and some areas of northern Kenya and Somalia as well. The Pokot case too shows that the escalation of violence in the 1990s was linked to a demise of gerontocratic power. Mirzeler and Young (2000) as well as Fleisher (1999) describe for eastern Uganda and south-western Kenya how young men spend their gains from raids by entertaining themselves on beer and consumer goods, continuously reinforcing their soldierly camaraderie. Elders as well as women and children are excluded from these forms of exchange. Abbink (2001: 132, see also Abbink this volume) describes the decline of the age-grade system for the south-west Ethiopian Surma (Suri), detailing the loss of authority of elders. Generally the trend seems to be clear: with the gun becoming an ever more important means of production, a means of production firmly in the hands of young men, gerontocratic power wanes, and with it a realm of norms and standards of social conduct. To the extent that elders decline as policing and sanctioning institutions, almost anarchic conditions arise in many pastoral communities. In fact, the rise of 'lawlessness' and the non-existence of any internal policing and sanctioning agency has been noted in several articles (Gray 1999, Mirzeler and Young 2000, Hutchinson 2001).

Several authors have also stressed that the escalation of warfare has led to the emergence of or to the increase of internal violence. While the feud had been a traditional means of conflict management amongst the Nuer, all-out wars as practised recently between competing Nuer warlords are a new phenomenon (Hutchinson 2001). Gray (1999) and Mirzeler and Young (2000) report that the unity of the Karimojong is called into question by the increase of fighting between the three Karimojong factions, Matheniko, Bokora and Pian. In fact 'guns were used for resolving disputes at every level of Karimojong society from the homestead to the territorial section' (Gray et al. 2003). Abbink (2001) also observed the rise of intra-Suri violence in the Sudan/Ethiopia borderlands which works to the detriment of the entire group. In Turkana internal raids have become prominent since the 1970s. While raids between Turkana sections have been reported in older ethnographic reports, the violence reported on in recent commentaries is unprecedented. Among the Kenyan Pokot internal warfare is thought of as a severe breakdown of moral standards and is considered a 'sin': nevertheless internal raids took place as early as in the 1970s, with West Pokot sections preying on East Pokot cattle. However, such large-scale internal violence within Pokot society is still rare.

Conclusion

Pastoral societies have changed drastically over the last century – this is a commonplace in the ethnography of East and North-East African herder societies. However, changes brought about by the escalation of warfare seem to be particularly rapid and detrimental. Automatic guns as change agents have perhaps sparked off a deeper transformation of these pastoral societies than any repressive colonial measures in the past. Gray et al. (2003: 21) conclude their study on violence in East Uganda thus: 'It might be reasonably argued that AK-47 raids currently present the single greatest risk to the persistence of the pastoralist systems considered here and to the continued survival of pastoralists themselves.'

Our contribution has shown that, while guns can be well interpreted as a means of production, unlike other pastoral means of production it is ambiguous and gains are as a rule accompanied by losses. Moreover, gains are short-term advantages for perpetrators: they can gain resources and prestige among peers in a situation of relative impunity, because the age-grade system does not work properly and there is no restraining of authority (Abbink 2001: 135). There is little doubt that the long-term effects of enormous accumulations of firearms are detrimental: loss of human lives, dissolution of households and erosion of networks of exchange are some of many consequences. Taking the south-west Ethiopian Suri as an example, Abbink (2001) has argued that 'all in all the inclusive fitness of families and lineages is reduced. In such circumstances it appears that aggression "does not pay".' In extension we may argue that an entire mode of existence seems to be endangered because of the failure to cope socially and politically with the introduction of automatic guns. Vayda (1976: 87ff.) shows that the introduction of firearms in New Zealand led to the disintegration of Maori political systems and society in the nineteenth century. Will African pastoralists go the same way? As yet, these pastoral societies have not found an answer to the large-scale influx of guns and fail to manage extreme firepower coupled with an exaggeration of youth power. Fratkin (1997: 252) observes that: 'Pastoralists … are moving into the twenty-first century with less ability to maintain their subsistence livestock economies than at any time in their past.' The militarization of East and North-East Africa has contributed a great deal to this pessimistic view.

Are there viable ways out of this dilemma? Various governments have tried at several points in time to disarm pastoralists. We have reported on disarmament campaigns among the Karimojong of Uganda and the Pokot of Kenya, but these campaigns seem to be successful only in the short run. Since it is nearly impossible to disarm an entire region at once, disarmament frequently leads to disarmed people immediately becoming prey to armed neighbours. While the effects of enforced disarmament are doubtful, such campaigns lead to strained relations between state agencies and the local population. It may be necessary to focus more seriously on peacemaking initiatives that come from within. Strecker (1998) understandably maintains that not all people in a society (he takes the Ethiopian Hamar as an example) are bound to resort to violence. Some individuals may opt for peaceful strategies simply because they perceive the personal losses that will result from violent conflict. The stereotype of the violent East African herder has clouded the fact that there are always hawks as well as doves in such violent social contexts. Strecker (1998) reports on how leading figures amongst the Hamar make use of rituals to condone the tendency of youths to engage in violence. But peace initiatives are not confined to traditional contexts and Gray (1999) reports on Karimojong politicians who are active in setting up peace talks at the local level. Another outstanding attempt of cross-border peace talks between Karimojong and Turkana was a peace meeting in Moroto in 1996. The meeting resulted in the following joint communiqué:

> We, the people of Karamoja in Uganda and the Turkana in Kenya, have come together to make peace for the sake of our own security, accelerated sustainable development and that of posterity, hereby come together ... to declare our commitment and resolve to end hostilities between the various communities in the presence of our two governments. We also wish to propose a set of principles to galvanise actions that will ensure the said peace pact is holding. (Anon. 1996: 1)

This contract-like document clearly spells out rules for the mediation of conflict, institutes policing and sanctioning institutions and is signed by traditional as well as modern political leaders of the two parties. It is interesting that this initiative took place as a kind of co-management effort between regional elites and the concerned governments. Another experiment in the application of local-level peacemaking intiatives in a pastoral context is the institution of elders' councils in Somaliland (Höhne 2002). There are also a number of development projects which currently use an approach of supporting local level peace making institutions.

Despite the recent spate of contributions on the effects of violence in pastoral settings, as yet there has been little in-depth anthropological research on the problem. A comparative perspective seems to be lacking completely. If there is only limited research on the escalation of violence, there is nearly no research on local-level or co-managed peace initiatives (for a notable exception see Heinrich 1998). Future anthropological research on pastoralists should focus on the effects of low-intensity warfare, its socio-political origins and efforts to cope with the crises.

Appendix: *Baringo District Annual Report 1977, Ngoroko Incidents*

The following are some of the Ngoroko incidents (as they are usually known) of the year:

(1) On 6th February 1977 Turkana Ngorokos attacked Pokot Manyattas, killed one woman and took off with a large number of cattle.
(2) On 11th March another Pokot was killed by Turkana Ngorokos who staged a raid and killed many heads of cattle.
(3) On 29th March 1977 Turkana Ngorokos attacked Maron area in Kolloa Location killed 3 Pokot and took with them some cattle. However, the Police intervened and after an exchange of fire, all the stolen animals were recovered.
(4) On the 7th of April 1977 Pokot took retaliatory measures by staging an attack on villages around Kapeddo in Turkana District. Dring this raid 45

Turkana were injured. Only 3 Pokot were killed and a number of cattle were stolen from the Turkana during this raid.

(5) On the 25th April 1977 Turkana raided Nginyang area and stole 2,000 heads of cattle leaving 3 Pokot dead. Then the raiders encountered Police and in the exchange of fire which ensued eight Turkana were killed and all the stolen animals recovered.

(6) On the 24th May Turkana attacked Komolion area and stole 1,500 heads of cattle. Police followed and killed 3 Turkana and one GSU constable was injured.

(7) On the 22nd September Turkana attacked Churo area and killed 7 Pokot leaving 3 others wounded. All stolen cattle were recovered.

(8) On the 25th October Pokot attacked Tugen of Ngoroa Location and stole over 300 heads of cattle.

(9) On the 29th October 1977 the Pokot again attacked Ngoroa Location and stole over 300 heads of cattle.

(10) On the 31st October 1977 the Pokot again attacked Ngoroa Location and stole 40 heads of cattle. Two people were injured.

Notes

1. In early 2004 some informants stressed that recently there had been considerable misuse of the *lapai* system, as people try to enrich themselves using the compensation system.
2. The odd side-story of Lopurkoyan's plaited hair is told by all Pokot informants. The man seems either to have adopted a style of urban rappers or – more likely – to have been in contact with the LRA leader Joseph Kony who also appears on some photographs with plaited hair.
3. This song, like many other Pokot songs on cattle and warfare, are in the Turkana language. Pokot assert that the Turkana language simply sounds better than their own in these contexts.
4. Until the late 1980s the proportion of school-going children was small. Many families did not send any children to school others sent one boy. Seemingly school-goers stemmed either from rich or from very poor families.
5. We would like to add that Pokot informants contested this finding: they said that to go back to no-go zones after some years is highly profitable from a herding perspective.

References

Abbink, J. 1994. 'Changing Patterns of "Ethnic" Violence: Peasant–Pastoralist Confrontation in Southern Ethiopia and its Implications for a Theory of Violence', *Sociologus* 44(1): 66–78.

———. 1999. 'Violence, Ritual, and Reproduction: Culture and Context in Surma Dueling', *Ethnology* 38(3): 227–42.

———. 2001. 'Violence and Culture: Anthropological and Evolutionary-Psychological Reflections on Inter-group Conflict in Southern Ethiopia', in B. Schmidt and I.W. Schröder (eds), *Anthropology of Violence and Conflict*. London, New York: Routledge, pp. 123–42.

Almagor, U. 1979. 'Raiders and Elders: A Confrontation of Generations among the Dassanetch', *Senri Ethnological Studies* 3: 119–46.

Anonymous. 1996. 'A Joint Communique on the Resolutions of the Turkana–Karamoja Peace Meeting at Moroto, Uganda held on 3–5.6.1996' (document available to the authors).

Best, G. 1991. 'Bemerkungen zum modernen Viehraub in Kenia', in F. Scholz (ed), *Nomaden, mobile Tierhaltung: Zur gegenwärtigen Lage und zu den Problemen und Chancen mobiler Tierhaltung*. Berlin: Das Arabische Buch, pp. 157–64.

Bollig, M. 1990. 'Ethnic Conflicts in North-West Kenya: Pokot, Turkana raiding 1969–1984', *Zeitschrift für Ethnologie* 115: 73–90.

———. 1992. *Die Krieger der gelben Gewehre: Intra- und interethnische Konfliktaustragung bei den Pokot Nordwestkenias*. Kölner Ethnologische Studien 20, Cologne: Lit.

———. 1998. 'Moral Economy and Self-Interest: Kinship, Friendship, and Exchange among the Pokot (N.W. Kenya)', in T. Schweizer and D.R. White (eds), *Kinship, Networks, and Exchange*. Cambridge: Cambridge University Press, pp. 137–57.

Conant, F. 1982. 'Thorns Paired, Sharply Recurved: Cultural Controls and Rangeland Quality in East Africa', in B. Spooner (ed), *Desertification and Development*. New York: Academic Press, pp. 111–22.

Evans-Pritchard, E. 1956. *Nuer Religion*. Oxford: Clarendon Press.

Fleisher, M.L. 1999. 'Cattle Raiding and Household Demography among the Kuria of Tanzania', *Africa* 69: 238–55.

Fratkin, E. 1997. 'Pastoralism: Governance and Development Issues', *Annual Review of Anthropology* 26: 235–61.

Gray, S.J. 1999. 'A Memory of Loss: Ecological Politics, Local History, and the Evolution of Karimojong Violence', *Human Organization* 59(4): 401–18.

Gray, S., M. Sundal, B. Wiebusch, M.A. Little, P.W. Leslie, and I.L. Pike. 2003. 'Cattle Raiding, Cultural Survival, and Adaptability of East African Pastoralists', *Current Anthropology* 44 (suppl.): 3–30.

Heinrich, W. 1998. 'Konfliktforschung, Entwicklungszusammenarbeit und Konfliktbearbeitung – und die Rolle der Ethnologie', *Entwicklungsethnologie* 7(2): 49–63.

Hendrickson, D., R. Mearns and J. Armon. 1996. 'Livestock Raiding among the Pastoral Turkana of Kenya: Redistribution, Predation and the Links to Famine', *IDS Bulletin* 27(3): 17–30.

Höhne, M. 2002. *Somalia zwischen Krieg und Frieden: Strategien der friedlichen Konfliktaustragung auf internationaler und nationaler Ebene*. Hamburg: Institut für Afrikakunde.

Hutchinson, S.E. 1996. *Nuer Dilemmas: Coping with Money, War, and the State*. Berkeley, Los Angeles, London: University of California Press.

———. 2001. 'A Curse from God? Religious and Political Dimensions of the Post-1991 Rise of Ethnic Violence in South Sudan', *Journal of Modern African Studies* 39(2): 307–31.

Johnson, B.R. 1990. *Nomadic Networks and Pastoral Strategies: Surviving and Exploiting Local Instability in South Turkana*. Ann Arbor: University Microfilms International.

Kamenju, J., M. Singo and F. Wairagu. 2003. *Terrorized Citizens: Profiling Small Arms and Insecurity in the North Rift Region of Kenya*. Nairobi: Security Research and Information Council.

McCabe, J.T. 1985. *Livestock Management among the Turkana: A Social and Ecological Analysis of Herding in an East African Pastoral Population*. Ann Arbor: University Microfilms International.

McCabe, J.T., R. Dyson-Husdon and J. Wienpahl. 1999. 'Nomadic Movements', in: M.A. Little and P.W. Leslie (eds), *Turkana Herders of the Dry Savanna: Ecology and Biobehavioural Response of Nomads to an Uncertain Environment*. New York: Oxford University Press, pp.109–22.

Mirzeler, M. and C. Young. 2000. 'Pastoral Politics in the Northeast Periphery in Uganda: AK-47 as Change Agent', *Journal of Modern African Studies* 38(3): 407–29.

Mkutu, K. 2000. *Cattle Rustling and the Proliferation of Small Arms: the Case of Baragoi, Samburu District*. Paper presented at the Conference 'Improving Human Security through the Control and Management of Small Arms'. Arusha, March 23–25. (Typescript).

———. 2001. *Pastoralism and Conflict in the Horn of Africa*. Nairobi and London: Africa Peace Forum Report.

Mkutu, K. and M. Marani. 2003. *Human and Economic Costs of Small Arms: A Comparative Study of Two Districts on Kenya*. (Typescript).

Österle, M. and M. Bollig. 2003. 'Continuities and Discontinuities of Warfare in Pastoral Societies: Militarization and The Escalation of Violence', *Zeitschrift für Entwicklungsethnologie* 12: 109–43.

Peristiany, J.G. 1951. 'The Age-Set System of the Pastoral Pokot', *Africa* 21: 188–206.

Republic of Kenya. 2001. *The 1999 Population and Housing Census: Counting our People for Development*. Nairobi: Government Printer.

Schneider, H. 1953. *The Pākot (Suk) of Kenya with Special Reference to the Role of Livestock in their Subsistence Economy*. Ann Arbor: University Microfilms International

Strecker, I. 1998. 'The Temptations of War and the Struggle for Peace among the Hamar of Southern Ethiopia', in G. Elwert, S. Feuchtwang and D. Neubert (eds), *Dynamics of Violence: Processes of Escalation and De-escalation in Violent Group Conflicts*. Supplement to *Sociologus* 1. Berlin: Duncker and Humbolt, pp. 227–59.

Tornay, S.A. 1993. 'More Changes on the Fringe of State? The Growing Power of the Nyangatom, a Border People of the Lower Omo Valley, Ethiopia (1970–1992)', in T. Tvedt (ed), *Conflicts in the Horn of Africa: Human and Ecological Consequences of Warfare*. Uppsala: Uppsala University, pp. 143–63.

Turton, D. 1979. 'War, Peace and Mursi Identity', *Senri Ethnological Studies* 3: 179–210.

———. 1993. '"We must teach them to be Peaceful": Mursi Views on Being Human and Being Mursi', in Terje Tvedt (ed), *Conflicts in the Horn of Africa: Human and Ecological Consequences of Warfare*, Uppsala: Uppsala University, pp. 164–80.

———. 1994. 'Mursi Political Identity and Warfare: the Survival of an Idea', in K. Fukui and J. Markakis (eds), *Ethnicity and Conflict in the Horn of Africa*. London: James Currey; Athens: Ohio University Press, pp. 15–33.

———. 1996. 'Migrants and Refugees: a Mursi Case Study', in T. Allen (ed), *In Search of Cool Ground: War, Fight and Homecoming in Northeast Africa*. London: UNRISD in association with James Currey, Trenton: Africa World Press, pp. 96–110.

Vayda, A. 1976. *War in Ecological Perspective: Persistence, Change, and Adaptive Processes in Three Oceanian Societies*. New York: Plenum Press.

Chapter 2

Culture Slipping Away: Violence, Social Tension and Personal Drama in Suri Society, Southern Ethiopia

Jon Abbink

Introduction

In 1992 during fieldwork among the Chai-Suri people in Ethiopia, I witnessed a collective ritual held for raiders: armed Suri young men who were preparing to go to raid back cattle stolen from them by their southern neighbours, the Nyangatom, some months earlier. The ritual chief of the Chai led a protective blessing ceremony, lasting several hours. In the closing stages, one young man accidentally shot and killed one of his age mates with his automatic weapon. The perpetrator quickly fled to the bush, as is the custom. The ceremony was not concluded and the raid was called off.

The ritual leader or *komoru*[1] said to me, with an uncharacteristic air of resignation and despair:

> Look, look now what happened … This is the fate of the Chai in this time of guns. We were preparing to hit back the Bume and now this comes along, a boy of our own killed for nothing, lying dead on the ground, his family in trouble. Our people have guns and can defend themselves but instead they shoot each other … The guns have not brought anything good … They take possession of us, we don't control them. How can we ever recover like this?

The death of this boy, in a freak killing, made a deep impression in the Suri community where I was living. The customary mourning and compensation ceremonies were eventually completed, but the father of the victim, his eldest son, took it hard. He suffered silently and seemed not to have a way to express his grief – Suri rarely, if at all, talk about the dead once they are buried. In subsequent months, his health deteriorated. He became taciturn and sombre, and died a year later.

At the time, this case provided me with the first glimpse of the social effects of violence among the Suri, a society of agro-pastoralists in southwestern Ethiopia. Since then, the number of lethal confrontations, both with non-Suri neighbours and within their own society, has only increased. In fact, there is no family that is untouched by the loss of a close relative through violence. The crisis of interpersonal relations and social order resulting from intensified violence seems fairly general in most pastoralist societies in East Africa: the Karimojong in Uganda are a prime example (Mirzeler and Young 2000; Simonse 2003), but also the Toposa, the Nuer (Hutchinson 2001) and, of course, the Somali (Adam 1999; Abbink 2003).

Small-scale societies not only are relevant as comparative case studies demonstrating the decline of regional security in parts of Africa, thus having a political dimension – witness southern Sudan or Uganda – but can also be seen as 'social laboratories' where more general, pan-human ways of dealing with violence and its aftermath can be studied closely. The insights emerging from such case studies are, in my opinion, useful for a wider understanding of violence in other contexts. The increase of interpersonal violence is not only an African problem but a global one, and a comparative understanding of the wider societal causes, effects and escalation patterns, as well as of the reasons why mediation and culturally rooted methods of control and conciliation seem to lose force, is as relevant as ever. On the other hand, in the East African region of which I am talking there are also some agro-pastoral societies that do not seem so negatively affected, like the Turkana, Hamar, Nyangatom or Borana, although they face similar conditions, and the reasons for the divergence might be found in the social organization and values of these groups.

In this chapter I trace some of the effects of warfare and violence on Suri family life, social cohesion and personal relations.[2] The Suri number about 28,000 people, have their own administrative district (*woreda*) in the Southern Regional State of federal Ethiopia and live in a marginal and volatile border area. They have three subgroups: the Chai (largest), the Tirmaga and the Baale, each with diverging origin histories and group identity. The Baale speak a language only partly intelligible to the Chai and Tirmaga. The Mursi are a group closely related to the Chai, speaking virtually the same (South-East Surmic) language. The Suri have armed themselves relatively fast since 1988, following developments among neighbouring groups, and now have tense relations with most of their neighbours. Since 1996 there has been an Ethiopian state army contingent (in Amharic: *fet'no derash*, or 'rapid reaction force') of some 100–130 people quartered in one of their villages, but its record is not impressive.

Much of the literature on violence and suffering (e.g., Kleinman et al. 2001; Das et al. 1997) deals with the effects of external, political violence imposed by a war situation or by state oppression. In the case of the Suri there is also growing interference of the state (including targeted violent repression), but more notable is an interactive setting of armed confrontation between them and their neighbours, e.g., Toposa, Nyangatom, Anywaa and Me'en, as well as the growing internal friction, leading to more fatal casualties. Much of the suffering is therefore generated by the multiple exercise of violence by Suri themselves, in- and outside their own group.[3]

The theoretical perspective taken here is based on a political ecology model (see Dentan 1992) but one that integrates the relatively autonomous role of cultural and cognitive factors as semiotic elements that both structure, and are the cumulative result of meaning creation and socially adaptive behaviour in human society. While attention to ecological factors in anthropology has a long tradition (see Vayda 1979, 1989), there have been problems with its explanatory procedures, often neglecting the role of human agency and the dynamics of 'culture' interacting with ecological factors. I follow a general critical realist epistemology (Bhaskar 1986; Archer et al. 1998) in trying to integrate structure and agency in the understanding of human behaviour and society in such a way as to look at the generative social mechanisms that produce their dialectic.

The familiar problem in writing about violence is how to locate its 'normalcy'. Violence, while rejected and avoided by most people in any society, is more frequent in some groups, and is conceptualized differently. In academic writing and in the Western tradition in general violence has been seen as an aberration, as a failure of the social order, and in need of explanation with reference to special conditions giving rise to it. While this view is not necessarily wrong – in the sense that violence usually is infamy and constitutes the unacceptable imposition of hurt and humiliation on others – it presupposes that violent behaviour is rare in ordered, functional societies. As we know, this is not correct. In certain historical phases there is indeed a marked decline but some conditions promote a sudden upsurge in violent performance. Virtually all societies have to confront the issue of killing, maiming, humiliating and arbitrary lethal force to which innocents fall victim. The practices should be recognized as a part of social life, although they are always contested and never normative. The long dominant Western discourse about the 'barbaric violence' and 'savagery' of non-Western societies not only rings false in light of European history of colonialism and mass destruction, e.g., in the Second World War, but also when viewing the high rates of everyday crime, intimidation and arbitrary 'leisure violence' that have become pronounced in recent decades in many Western societies (see Duclos 1996; Baumeister 1997). Paradoxically, as John Keane has said, civil democratic societies usually 'are plagued by endogenous sources of incivility' (1996: 63): the freedoms of the modern democratic state tend to create their own challenges and crises, and the states may go down into fragmentation and chaos if the fragile achievement of freedom and the rule of law is not cultivated in politics, public policy and education.[4]

In many pastoral and other smaller, technologically simple societies like Bellona (Kuschel 1988), Gebusi (Knauft 1987), Gisu (Heald 1999) or the !Kung (Lee 1979), violence in the form of assault or homicide seems disproportionately high. It does not necessarily mean that cruelty, humiliation, torture or rape is prevalent as well. All of these latter forms seem to be higher in centralized state societies, dictatorships or highly fragmented and 'anomic', postmodern industrial cultures. Violence in segmentary societies is in the nature of maintaining a balance of deterrence and of asserting and defending rights both individually and collectively, e.g., on the basis of clan solidarity (such as, notably, among the Somali; see Prunier 1997; Abbink 2003).

The thesis of this chapter is that social rules and cultural values within Suri society enhance individualism and independent behaviour, which, when articulated with the wide availability and instrumental use of firearms, has led to escalation and to fragmentation of kinship and other integrative networks. The Suri political order, as well as the low level of state interference, has not contained the centrifugal force of violent performance by Suri males. Increased violence has led to more social tensions within Suri society, which have yielded frequent personal drama, further undermining people's recovery chances and confidence in the future.

The political ecology of conflict in the Ethio-Sudanese border areas is therefore marked by self-reproducing instability, conflicting value systems and a lack of institutional capacity to mediate or adjudicate. Persistent conditions of resource pressure (competition for gold-panning places, pastures, cultivation sites), migration, cattle raiding and judicial impunity have affected patterns of violence in recent years. The trade in and availability of modern rifles and ammunition since the mid-1980s are a contributory cause, but function as the trigger or means through with conflicts are played out and intensified. As mentioned above, cultural values relating to warrior status, male independence and manhood are also at play. On the ground, local people, victims of the violence, usually refer to the idiom of different cultural values and representations of the value of life of the perpetrating group to explain what happens.

The Issue of Violence: New and More Intensive Forms of Armed Conflict

A 'non-complex' society like the agro-pastoral Suri people, who live in a small-scale, egalitarian social order, shows patterns of violence and conflict resolution different from those of peasant or industrial societies. The radical militarization of Suri society – one that should be seen as part of a wider political and cultural system of ethnic group relations in the Ethio-Sudanese border area – parallels developments among other agro-pastoralist societies in East Africa (see Österle and Bollig 2003). In the Suri case, the underlying problems relate to territorial expansion of their southern agro-pastoral neighbours, the Nyangatom, assisted by their Sudanese brethren, the Toposa, a people heavily armed by the Sudanese government as a 'tribal militia' in the civil war. They have been preying on Suri since about 1990 and are expanding into what is Ethiopian territory (Suri pasture and cultivation areas) from the west. This problem is basically one of international relations, but the Ethiopian government does not address it. Suri are thus hemmed in and cannot expand towards the highlands without coming into conflict with Dizi and Me'en people, neighbouring highland cultivators. This leads to resource pressure. I divide the last sixty years of Suri history into three periods, following the type of regime in Ethiopia, and take the issue of intra-Suri violence as a core measure, because it is the main factor of social decline of Suri society. Table 2.1 summarizes this, based on data from interviews in 1991–99.

There is no need to resurrect a myth of an integrated, harmonious Suri society in the past, because there always was rivalry, conflict and raiding, but what can be said is that Suri social institutions were able to canalize, or mediate, the effects of violence if it occurred. It was of lower intensity due to the nature of armaments (spears, knives, clubs) and there was an option of migration or fission. Violent incidents with the neighbouring groups were also 'accepted' as facts of human social life, tied in with their mobile and independent lifestyle as cattle herders. They were 'processed' via social mechanisms of compensation, reconciliation, and sometimes fission or ostracism. There was, until a few years ago, little Ethiopian state influence (via administration, police, prisons or courts), only a self-regulating system of checks and balances in Suri society. However, the state context – it has always been there since 1898 but in quite different shapes – is now slowly but inevitably changing local expressions of violent performance, to be discussed later.

Among the Suri, assertive, aggressive behaviour is frequent. Youths are encouraged by their parents to be self-conscious and active, and to talk – and hit – back at others wanting to take advantage of them. Being loud and assertive is a virtue, seen as important in a tough society. Present-day violence not only takes the form of raiding, gun battles, ambushes in the context of

Table 2.1: *Levels of violence among Suri in three recent historical periods*

	Political regime		
Type of conflict	**Imperial regime (1941–74)**	**Derg (1974–91)**	**EPRDF (1991–)**
Inter-ethnic conflict *	Medium	High	Very high
Chai–Tirmaga–Baale conflict	Low	Medium	Medium
Internal conflict within Chai orTirmaga†	Very low	Medium	Very high

* With Dizi, Me'en, highland villagers, Anywaa, Nyangatom or Toposa.

† I have only superficial information on internal conflict within Baale.

fights with rival pastoral groups and other neighbours, but also that of frequent personal fights, drunken brawls, beatings and homicide within their society. However, Suri do not know rape[5] or torture, and while open insults are frequent, there is no vicious verbal intimidation or humiliation and constant talk about competition and 'war', as we know it in Western consumer culture (see Tannen 1998).[6] In the more formal setting of Suri public debates people also insult each other, but in indirect and metaphorical ways.

Since the 1990s, in conjunction with the growth in the number of automatic weapons possessed, Suri society shows signs of intensifying violence (i.e., more dead and wounded), breakdown of conflict resolution mechanisms and anomie. The question is whether this is a present-centred view, ignoring the fact that in the past things were the same, or if there is indeed deterioration. I argue the last: there is a gradual loss of meaning and a fallout of growing violence outside the 'cultural bounds' of the past, felt by the protagonists. Some illustrations to be given below are the increased tension between the generations, the lack of restraint on the expression of emotions, and the crisis in gender roles. I have treated aspects of the crisis repeatedly in other publications (Abbink 1993, 1998, 2000a, 2000b, 2004), and would like to focus here only on the social and cultural dimensions of the problem, not the political.

My central question is therefore about the relationship between violence, social tension and personal drama in Chai-Suri society, and in what way this process can be said to signify a 'slipping away of culture'. This expression was used by some young Suri and also Dizi, to indicate that the Suri were 'going bad and did not follow the norms and precepts of their own culture any more'. (They hereby always assumed that these were fixed and good in themselves.)

The main types of violent engagements of Suri in the current period (i.e., late 1990s and early 2000s) are the following:

(1) Raiding for cattle and other property. This continues an old pattern of 'exchange' with their agro-pastoral neighbours, notably Nyangatom, Toposa and Me'en.
(2) Ambushing travellers and traders, and raiding the outskirts of highland villages, populated by Dizi and other non-Suri people.
(3) Attacking peasants working in the fields, male and female. Especially Dizi[7] and Me'en people are the victims.
(4) Random killing of members of another group, even elders, local leaders or visitors. Often these are Dizi again.
(5) Internal violence arising in disputes around girls and women, the distribution of raided cattle, unsolved feuds and drunkenness at collective gatherings. The number of occasions of violent dispute has shown a remarkable rise in the past decade. The situation is now such that any disagreement can lead to a Suri man grabbing his rifle and threatening or shooting. My count of the past eight years reveals dozens of such incidents.

The increase in type 4 and 5 violence suggests that the control of aggression, more marked in the past (see also the Pokot case: Bollig 1993: 180) is on the decline: when the gun is always present, people grab it and shoot. Violent behaviour is not – or cannot be – 'punished', thus generating feelings of impunity, certainly vis-à-vis members of neighbouring groups. Killing within the group carries the threat of feuding (see below).

Effects of Intensified Violence on Suri Social Life

The Suri have had access to automatic rifles (mainly M-16s and AK-47s) and ammunition since the late 1980s, illicitly trading them for cattle and alluvial gold with Sudanese groups across the border, and with traders, ex-soldiers and neighbouring groups in the Maji area. There has been no official check or limit on the distribution of arms or ammunition, and today every Suri adult has now at least one (semi-)automatic rifle (see Table 2 for an example). They see it also as investment and, as Bollig (1993: 182) noted for the Pokot, 'gun-owners are awarded disproportionately large amounts from the booty' (of raided cattle). But as important is that the arrival of this weapon fed into an existing pattern of Suri values and ideals of male behaviour[8] that emphasized personal valour and achievement in fighting: within Suri society in ceremonial stick duelling, and in relations with certain non-Suri groups the occasional killing of an enemy, in which case the killer when returning home was greeted with a praise song and could make a prestigious marking on his arm.

Guns are now highly visible, and lend their owners power and 'status' among peers. Like the wooden headrest of a male Suri, they are carried around everywhere. (The older types are usually left at home, except when Suri go to a government meeting or to Maji town: then they leave the new ones behind for fear of arrest or confiscation.)

Initially, in the 'armament phase' (*c.* 1988–92), Suri women encouraged their husbands and/or sons and brothers to acquire the new rifles and use them. Today, however, the awareness of the social damage wrought by them predominates. In brief, the results of multiple gun use are many: sudden loss of male partners, fragmented families, shrinking of resource access and more poverty, a weakening

Table 2.2: *Estimate of number of guns in Makara village, 1992–93 (43 households,* c. *300 people)*

	Type of rifle					
	AK-47	**M-16**	**GM-3**	**Warahólí, a non-automatic rifle with bayonet**	**Meskobitch, a Russian Second World War rifle**	**Other old-type rifles (3 or 5 bullet)**
Number	28	8	4	6	9	7

Source: field data. The numbers have probably increased since then, because the price of guns has gone down markedly.

of females within the wider lineage and extended family, traumatized children who do not understand what is happening and sink into mute sadness and insecurity, a growing number of unresolved feuds, and more disputes about compensation rituals and other culturally appropriate mechanisms.

It may be surprising – at least, it was initially to me – that this social downturn is happening in a society that was known for social cohesion and solidarity, especially vis-à-vis outsider groups. This view, however, underestimated the nature of the individualism and independent agency that Suri people always valued, despite their kinship and ethnic identification, as well as the weak structure of political authority (of elders and ritual leaders). Below, I look at a few crucial social domains where the effects of violence can be noted.

Exchange Relations

Exchange is the foundation of Suri society through which relationships are forged: clan groups, families, bond friends and neighbouring groups exchange persons (marriage partners), livestock (as bridewealth, compensation payments), products (pottery for grain, cabbage and iron tools), beer (for labour service) and ritual acts and items in life-cycle rituals. Suri individuals build ego-centred networks that yield them support in times of need. Although brothers and sisters of a deceased person take in his orphaned children and inherit part of his cattle, the corporate identity of kin groups is weak, and people do not expect much support from kinsmen in cases of stock loss, fire, destruction of property, etc.

Bond-friend exchange relations were concluded mainly within the Suri population, but also a few with neighboring groups (Dizi, Nyangatom, Me'en). For about the last fifteen years, however, no more inter-ethnic bond friendships have been established, nor are existing ones honoured, due to the state of enmity between groups. But also with Suri bond partners there is more argument over the 'balance of payments', and as a result the institution is in decline. While obviously exchange remains important, the new activities of gold panning and theft from neighbours have led to a more short-term, individualist accumulation of cash and property, de-emphasizing long-term exchange relations. Faced with the growing diversion of resources of their husbands and/or male relatives, women are more forced to develop their own activities, and apart from cultivating their own fields with the help of collective (beer-paid) labour they try to raise small stock and do petty trade. Few, if any, Suri do paid jobs outside their own home area to gain income. Some policemen, members of the Surma Mikir Bet (the government-installed local council in Kibish village) and some workers and language helpers on the missionary Surma Project in Tulgi village have salaried jobs, all in the Suri area.

To summarize, the idea of reciprocity underlying exchange is being eroded: people try to avoid their obligations. In Suri the notion of reciprocity was in any case one imbued with rivalry, people jealously guarding the balance. In many instances one might speak of an ethos of negative or 'revenge reciprocity'.

Descent-group Relations

Suri live in a society structured by ideas of patrilineal descent. Clan groups (*kèno*) and lineage membership define marriage partners, ritual obligations and reconciliation procedures in times of dispute. These groups were never characterized by a strong corporate feeling. More important in daily life were the *b'uran*, the territorial herding units, bringing together people from a variety of clans or lineages for herding purposes.

In several domains we see that kin relations and their ritual mediation are declining. On the subject of feuding, the following case is a telling one. In January 2002, the MP for Suri in the Ethiopian parliament, Mr Guldu Tsedeke, was killed by a Suri man (when he was trying to mediate his surrender for homicide). The custom in such a case is to open complex negotiations for compensation, but this was refused by the family of the victim. Time went by and the two lineages lived in great tension. About a year later, a brother of Guldu shot and killed the murderer. After that, the cycle was considered closed: arrangements were made for a 'reconciliation meal', for which cattle would be killed and the peritoneum cut and worn by males of both parties as a sign of peace. So, instead of paying the traditional compensation in the form of six to ten head of cattle and a young girl from the lineage of the killer to that of the victim, the 'debt' was now only cancelled out by another killing. This case illustrates a trend, and indicates: (a) the growing reluctance of patrilineal kin to provide 'blood cattle' for compensation of a misdeed of a lineage member. This leads to many unresolved feuds; and (b) the growing 'déritualization' of Suri life, as individual action backed by force is replacing the ritual coding of social encounters.

A final aspect to be mentioned is the sheer magnitude of some killings: in one fight in a Suri village in 1996, a man shot dead seven people with a Kalashnikov. What to do about the cattle compensation payment for homicide? The number of victims would necessitate about seventy cattle to be paid to the families of the slain: the family of the killer simply cannot pay this. This in itself encourages revenge killing instead of compensation.

Gender Relations

Male–female relations among the Suri were based on equality and complementary division of labour. Suri women were independent and assertive and central decision-makers. They had their own fields, prepared and sold beer and had rights in cattle. Mothers were highly respected. Suri girls chose their lovers and marriage partners themselves (e.g., during duelling contests), and did not wait for men to come. Arranged marriages were not common. Suri wife beating was hardly known (she would hit back). This equality and independence, however, have declined with the rise of young male power based on guns. An image of the Suri male as an economically independent, aggressive, gun-toting person afraid of no one and with the capacity to use force to realize his aims has settled in Suri society. This new 'masculine' identity builds on traditional notions of male gender, but reinforces aggression and arbitrary behaviour also vis-à-vis the female sex, and is a far cry from the former Suri 'warrior' persona of the old days, some one who defended the herds, had a code on the proper use of violence, and did not kill women and children on raids: in today's inter ethnic raids women and children are purposely sought out and killed by Suri raiders (also by their adversaries, the Nyangatom and Toposa).

Sex and Marriage

Changing gender conceptions are related to changes in the choice and treatment of (female) partners by men and in marriage patterns. Not only are adulterous relations more frequent – to judge from the conflicts about women – but also forced sex and the abandonment of married women. Suri men live under the illusion that they can always marry another wife or more wives with the cattle (for bridewealth) they will accumulate force, but they forget that the spoils of raiding are quite short-lived, as the enemy group often raids them back. The net profit of the raiding is virtually zero, while the risk it carries to be killed is much greater.

The pressure on the bridewealth system has increased: not only have guns entered the system as part of the deal (the 'wife-giver' group wants an automatic), but also arguments about the exact size and division of the animals to be handed over are more acute. There is a growing demand by 'wife-giver' clans to receive more, and faster as well. Husband-wife relations have become more strained and this change in the bridewealth system may be a cause for males to increasingly neglect spouses and their children. While marriages are not easily dissolved because of the bridewealth agreement between families, especially not if there are children born, abandonment without formal divorce is on the increase. The levirate, a widow going to a brother of the deceased husband, is also less accepted.

When a child was born out of wedlock, the young mother could not perforate her lower lip and insert the lip disc (a distinctive custom of the Suri). Now they do it anyway. The number of children born out of wedlock is much higher than in the past, and the father cannot be forced to either marry the girl or pay the customary compensation (in head of cattle). The children will then be socially recognized as children of the girl's future husband.

Family Life

A random survey of twelve households in three Suri villages[9] revealed that all were affected by violent death. Violence as an almost daily occurrence has imprinted itself on the minds of the young generation. Children see their parents or relatives die or being wounded, and their household deprived of labour power, affection and social support. Such life-history experiences generate feelings of insecurity and grief, the frequency of which inhibits people's – especially children's – long-term well-being. There were even a few cases of suicide (two girls, one man) during my fieldwork in the mid 1990s, previously very rare among Suri.[10]

Three households of the twelve were female-headed, with two women having lost their husband in violence, while another was abandoned for another wife. In general I noted that the stability of marriages had declined. Men did not really divorce their (older) wives, but just abandoned them, and let them take care of their own. Male children usually move to the new household of the husband, girls stay with the mother. In more households malnourishment is seen, and female-headed households have a less stable and lower labour input than an average household.

Chiefly Families

Ritual leaders or *komorus* have lost authority and are not heeded. Among the Tirmaga, there are two *komorus*. Some fifteen years ago one of them (the incumbent *komoru* called Wolezoghi) was killed. The feud that emerged after his death was still not over by 2004. The second *komoru* is still a caretaker, provisionally taking over the role of the previous one, deceased in 1994. His authority is slight. The Chai *komoru* Dollote Londósa was a well-respected person (see Abbink 2004) and had some restraining influence. But he died in July 2000, and a successor is not yet installed (by late 2004). His eldest son cannot be installed as *komoru* because he killed someone. Thus, the *komoru* function is still there and is respected in principle, but the incumbents have lost authority and ritual function. Their families have become enmeshed in disputes and fighting.

Age-grade Relations

As I showed in other publications (Abbink 1993, 1998), the crisis in the age-grade system, specifically the loss of authority of the reigning age grade of elders over the youngsters, is evidence of notable internal disarray, especially among the Tirmaga section. The relationship between the grade of the unmarried young men, the so-called 'warriors' (or *tègay*, i.e., uninitiated) and that of the junior elders (*rórà*) was seriously upset because of the younger grade getting weapons and having earlier an independent economic base by gold panning and building up their cattle herd (partly by raiding). The youngsters could ward off ritual and other claims of the elders, and even stall their own initiation into 'adulthood' – a responsibility they did not yet want.

Other Social Institutions

The decline in observing 'Suri custom' is evident in other institutions. In ceremonial duelling, which used to be a strictly regulated male combat sport between different herding units, the display of aggressive and dangerous behaviour has increased, as duelling grounds become arenas for settling scores that have nothing to do with the duelling itself (see Abbink 2000a). A 'cleansing' after homicide (ritual isolation and washing in the blood of a sheep, supervised by an elder) is often dispensed with. Mourning customs, e.g., a ban on games and dancing in the months after a death, are neglected. Peace or truce agreements with neighbouring groups, which have an elaborate ritual and take days to accomplish, have hardly been held over the past few decades, and if so they have not been honoured by Suri, because some young men don't know of it or don't care. A big government-sponsored effort in 1991 (see Abbink 2000b) did not bring peace either; it was broken a few months later. A similar fate met three other efforts in 1992, 1993 and 1995.

Beliefs and Values

Dizi people, in their search for explanation of Suri violence, often say: 'the Surma don't care about human life, it is nothing for them to kill or even to lose some one'. Some Suri confirm this. The Suri worldview, if one may generalize, is quite secular and not informed by religious inhibitions to killing. Suri are also reluctant to speak about death and killing, and also avoid any talk about 'guilt'. But, as evident from often-heard private complaints, many Suri survivors and bereaved have trouble in dealing with the effects of death and loss. However, they do not know how to stop the violent behaviour and see no alternatives. For the young generation, practical examples of how conflict can be solved are now few in number, and children thus do not learn the appropriate cultural procedures of mediation.

One might also say that the Suri world view does not allow one to invoke God (the sky god Tumu) in times of trouble. In a way, God is 'unreachable'. Ancestors are appealed to, but the messages that people claim to have received from them (in dreams) confirm the social disarray and the need to overcome violence and infighting.

What has emerged among male youngsters is a kind of secular 'cult of the gun': seen as their most cherished possession, a means of self-protection and a 'means of production' which no one can take away from them. This ties in with the reinforced ideal of assertive masculinity.

One other remarkable development is the emergence of the '*kay*', female diviners/magicians among widowed, older Suri females. They are consulted by people to get information about the future, to cast a spell or curse on some one, and to cure afflictions. This function was known among the Dizi and Me'en, but not among Suri before *c.*1990. Perhaps one might interpret it as a compensation gesture of impoverished, abandoned females to deal with misfortune and powerlessness, or, on the side of the customers, as a coping mechanism to face the risks and insecurities of life.

Finally, since the late 1990s there has been a small Christian community among the Suri in and around the village of Tulgi (where a primary school and a development project have been established), and church services are held regularly. But this community has no noticeable effect yet on the levels of violence among the rest of the Suri.

The Non-acknowledged Problem: Personal Drama and Social Suffering Resulting from Violence

As we have seen in the above account, Suri know that their brothers, fathers and husbands occasionally kill outsiders, but now also see their own people being killed, within their own society, including women and youths. This is a relatively new problem, certainly in scale. While the violence initially was directed against those non-Suri 'others', that is, the neighbouring peoples and enemies, they now see that it now rebounds, destroying families, marriages, and even kinship bonds.

Recent studies (e.g., Kleinman et al. 1997; Das, et al. 2001) have highlighted the nature of social suffering caused by violence and theorized on its causes and effects. In these studies less attention is paid to the internal socio-psychological processes resulting from violence perpetrated from within a social group or society than from the violence of outside forces. No doubt, the effects of state suppression and violent attacks by neighbouring groups are visible in the Suri case, but they are not as pervasive as in most other cases, as Suri were able to maintain a good deal of autonomy. My interest in this chapter has been to focus on the processes resulting from frequent violence within Suri society, i.e., to study the unintended consequences of conscious, intended (violent) action, which the perpetrators could not, or did not care to, anticipate. These consequences are far-reaching in the personal life histories of people.

Remarkably, there is no pronounced public discourse among the Suri on the suffering caused by violence or at least the victims are powerless to effectively contest and prevent it. There is also a Suri cultural rule prohibiting people from memorizing and talking about the dead and departed: one rarely hears this. People complain in private or suffer mutely and with incomprehension. Personal drama is all around but people do not vent their grief. When asked, children fall silent about the fate of their father or brother or playmate. I personally found it distressing to hear from these youngsters, bit by bit, that their loved one or close relative was killed and then to see their numb and repressed tearfulness, having no option, no way out, to express their silent anger or sadness.

Suri Culture Slipping Away? The Declining Repertoire of Options

The foregoing should not suggest that Suri society in the past – before the current period of turmoil – was a completely harmonious and peaceful one and that crisis has come only now. This would be subscribing to the myth of 'primitive harmony', rightfully criticized by, for example, Edgerton (1992). This idea is in itself historically the result of a failure in the anthropological discipline to fully consider the role of human conflict and violence, present in virtually every society. The phenomenon of violence is often not integrated in the analysis or is badly conceptualized. A sober view of the data in 'tribal' or traditional societies shows a fair amount of violence, but also higher levels of its 'tolerance' as well as ritual mediation. Edgerton's view is extreme in that he sees all traditional or 'tribal' societies as dismal complexes of repression and internal tension without modes of redress, which is not true. The function of *komoru* within Suri society, as a living symbol of social order, indicates that values of peace and mediation were present.

In Suri society today there is an awareness of crisis – and an inability to set things right. A Dizi chief in Maji once said to me, in 1993:

> It's not that they [Suri] have turned bad only in these days: in the past they were already unreliable and full of tricks. They killed also in the past. In Italian times [1936–41] they killed a mail runner, and were punished for it. Nevertheless, what we see now beats everything we have known. And these problems will not go away.

He has been proved right in subsequent years. Especially, the Tirmaga section (which still has not completed its age-grade initiation ceremony) is in dire straits, showing more disintegration tendencies than the Chai section. Many people say they even don't know the requirements of the various rituals any more.

Whatever the wider political, ecological and demographic reasons that condition the limitation of options for a pastoral society like Suri, situated in a volatile border area awash with arms and ammunition and persistent threats of drought, famine and cattle disease, a radical reconfiguration of 'Suri culture', as a more or less coherent set of values and notions that create meaning and orient behaviour, is going on. Both the habitus of Suri social behaviour and the ritual idiom of action are fragmenting. Also the transmission of Suri culture as a defining, identity-creating process is questioned by the people themselves. While their cognitive focus on 'cattle culture', independence and personal achievement is maintained, integrative social values and principles of reciprocity are de-emphasized. This puts the cohesion, social reproduction and long-term survival potential of Suri society in danger, and makes them vulnerable to outside pressures from stronger groups and the state. These wider connections will become more important, and will include the threat of HIV/AIDS and state resettlement schemes, which will import Ethiopians from elsewhere to live in the Maji area.[11]

Conclusions

One might almost speak of a traditional society passing through the 'postmodern' phase: Suri no longer have an overarching cultural narrative giving meaning to society as a cohesive whole, and they evince a loss of ideological elements founding the social order. In the absence of the *komorus* and the elders of the 'reigning' *rórà* generation being able to exercise restraint and leadership, it is only the peer group, kinship bonds and the inescapable duties resulting from lineage or clan membership that bind Suri. Young men tend to bond more strongly in peer groups of 'warrior-raiders', and also go together to the gold-panning places. The age grade of *tègay* has definitely gained in power at the expense of the *rórà*, basically because the young could become economically independent by wielding their guns. The kin and clan obligations relate to ritual duties and to, for example, the need to contribute cattle for bridewealth for a patrilineal relative who marries. There is some countervailing force of women, who largely reject the excessive use of violence displayed,[12] but so far with little result. Women turn towards their own economic and household activities, try to claim their existing rights in cattle, raise small stock, work their fields, brew *gèso* beer for sale and try to take care of their children.

There is also a contagious effect of violence. While my account has focused on the Suri, it is not only they who exercise violence: also Dizi highlanders and Me'en are known to be involved in acts of theft, killing and cruelty, although there is a less unified picture of social and cultural change as a result of all this. Groups are seemingly caught in a mimetic cycle of violence that spreads as victims experience loss and grief and retaliate.

Suri, like other East African pastoralists, are thus in an irreversible process of change, endangering their social order and survival options. The human toll of violence – death, impoverishment, fragmentation and psychological damage – has been high. Authority relations, gender relations, parent-child relations and economic exchange relations show decline and change into a habitus of force and intimidation. This story of 'decline' is not particularly new, but the above account has shown the accelerating and transformative role of persistent violent action in the process. We see a society that is losing its resilience, and capitalizes on violent but unsustainable male self-assertion. We might now indeed speak of a Suri 'culture of violence', and by definition this cannot last very long. Either core notions of traditional culture will reassert themselves due to pressures from within (women, the elders, the ritual leaders, new religious orientations), or the state military and administrative machinery will assert itself and append the Suri to a new state order where they will be disempowered and lose their autonomy of action.

Acknowledgements

I am very grateful for the support and patience of many Suri and Dizi people in the Maji area over the past years (1995–2000), a debt difficult to repay. Special gratitude I owe to *Ato* Dishiburji in Adikyaz village, and to the late Guldu Tsedeke. I also thank the authorities in Tum and Maji, including EPRDF forces in 1991–92, for their cooperation and tolerance. Finally, I would like to express my deep appreciation for the help and cooperation of Mike and Andrea Bryant and Ulrike Beyer, SIL language workers and teachers among the Suri since 1994, as well as to John and Gwennyth Haspels of the Surma Project in Tulgi.

Notes

1. I described the role model and functions of this priest-like mediator elsewhere (Abbink 1997; 2004). See also Turton 1975 on the Mursi *komoru*. The *komoru* is a religious figure only and is not supposed to exhibit aggression or encourage violent action. Compare the case of the Pokot *kapolok* (Bollig 1993: 180).
2. A more general assessment of the crisis affecting the Suri was given in Abbink 2000a.
3. The subject of this paper is closely related to my fieldwork experiences (1990s). The fact that several personal Suri, Me'en and Dizi friends and acquaintances whom I came to know closely over a decade were killed or seriously wounded in the violence of the past years compels me to raise the issue. In general, anthropologists during their fieldwork increasingly note that the societies or groups they study are marked by an intensification of violence. My account is based on data from several periods of fieldwork among the Suri in the 1990s and on information from correspondence kept up during the past four years with people in the area. Final editing of this chapter was done in mid-2005.
4. This even apart from the coming challenges to equity and democracy to be posed by genetic engineering (cf. Baudrillard 2001) and new technologies in, e.g., artificial reproduction.
5. However, the definition of the word 'rape' is contested. There are cases of forced sexual contact among the Suri, and it seems increasingly so. I think this is a direct reflection of their growing contacts with non-Suri, the negative impact of government security

forces in the area, and with being gradually exposed to stories about the wider Ethiopian society and to global audiovisual media images. It can thus be predicted that rape cases will increase. Still, forced sex among the Suri today is quite different from the violent rape known, e.g., from Western-industrial societies. Inter-group rape, for example during raids or ambushes on non-Suri groups, is not practiced. However, in one incident in 1998 the body of a young Dizi girl, killed by Suri, was found with a stick in her vagina (Abejje 1999: 45). This kind of thing was never reported before and deeply shocked the Dizi.

6. Witness the average films and videos screened, also in the public media.
7. The case of the Dizi people, whom the Suri call *Su* and despise, is tragic, because they are the almost weekly target of a Suri attack. The government does not adequately protect them, nor allows them to carry arms for proper self-defence. The frequent attacks have not only resulted in hundreds of deaths in the past decade, but also reduced many Dizi farmers to dismal poverty, because Suri also take their cattle, grain, clothes, etc. In 1993 I called attention to the tragedy of the Dizi (Abbink 1993), and several times I appealed to the authorities in the Southern Region to better assist them, but not much has changed. See also Abejje's report (1999).
8. See Michael Bollig's interesting study (1993: 180, 183) on similar ideals among the Pokot.
9. In Makara, B'eelya, and near Tulgi (1993, 1999).
10. Informants could even recall the few cases over a thirty-year period.
11. See the daily *Ethiopian Herald* of 19 December 2003, "SNNPRS to resettle over 50,000 households this fiscal year". SNNPRS is the Southern Ethiopian Regional State.
12. It has to be said that when an inter-ethnic dispute or homicide case is at issue, the women still encourage the men to take revenge. In several cases known to me, an unwilling brother or husband was 'forced' by the widow of a victim to retaliate.

References

Abbink, J. 1993. 'Ethnic Conflict in the "Tribal" Zone: The Dizi and Suri in Southern Ethiopia', *Journal of Modern African Studies* 31(4): 675–83.

———. 1997. 'Authority and Leadership in Surma Society (Ethiopia)', *Africa* (Rome) 52(3): 317–42.

———. 1998. 'Violence and Political Discourse among the Chai Suri', in G.J. Dimmendaal and M. Last (eds), *Surmic Languages and Cultures*. Cologne: R. Köppe, pp. 321–44.

———. 2000a. 'Restoring the Balance: Violence and Culture among the Suri of Southern Ethiopia.' in Göran Aijmer and Jon Abbink (eds), *Meanings of Violence: A Cross-Cultural Perspective*. Oxford/New York: Berg, pp. 77–100.

———. 2000b. 'Violence and the Crisis of Conciliation: Suri, Dizi and the State in Southwest Ethiopia', *Africa* 70(4): 527–50.

———. 2003. 'Dervishes, *Moryaan* and Freedom Fighters: Cycles of Rebellion and the Fragmentation of Somali Society, 1900–2000', in J. Abbink, K. van Walraven and M. de Bruijn (eds) *Rethinking Resistance: Revolt and Violence in African History*. Leiden: E.J. Brill, pp. 328–65.

———. 2004. 'Remembering Londósa: Mediator and Counterpoint in a 'Violent' Society', in Verena Böll, Denis Nosnitzin, Thomas Rave, Wolbert Smidt and Evgenia

Sokolinskaia (eds), *Studia Aethiopica. In Honor of Siegbert Uhlig.*Wiesbaden: Otto Harrassowitz, pp. 371–82.

Abejje, B. 1999. *The Dizi People and their Neighbours: Report to the House of the Federation, Project on the 'Least Known Peoples of Ethiopia'.* Addis Ababa: Department of Sociology and Social Administration, Addis Ababa University.

Adam, H.M. 1999. 'Somali Civil Wars', in T.M. Ali and R.O. Matthews (eds), *Civil Wars in Africa: Roots and Resolution.* Montreal/Kingston/London/Ithaca: McGill-Queen's University Press, pp. 169–92.

Archer, M., R. Bhaskar, A. Collier, T. Lawson and A. Norrie (eds). 1998. *Critical Realism: Essential Readings.* London, New York: Routledge.

Baudrillard, J. 2001. *The Vital Illusion.* New York: Columbia University Press.

Baumeister, R.F. 1997. *Evil: Inside Human Cruelty and Violence.* New York: W.H. Freeman.

Bhaskar, R. 1986. *Scientific Realism and Human Emancipation.* London: Verso.

Bollig, M. 1993. 'Intra- and Interethnic Conflict in Northwest Kenya: A Multicausal Analysis of Conflict Behaviour', *Anthropos* 88: 176–84.

Das, V., A. Kleinman, M. Lock, M. Ramphele, and P. Reynolds (eds). 2001. *Remaking a World: Violence, Social Suffering and Recovery.* Berkeley, Los Angeles, London: University of California Press.

Dentan, R.K. 1992. 'The Rise, Maintenance, and Destruction of Peaceable Polity: A Preliminary Essay in Political Ecology', in J. Silverberg and P. Gray (eds), *Aggression and Peacefulness in Humans and Other Primates.* New York: Oxford University Press, pp. 214–70.

Duclos, D. 1996. *The Werewolf Complex: America's Fascination with Violence.* Oxford, New York: Berg.

Edgerton, R.B. 1992. *Sick Societies: Challenging the Myth of Primitive Harmony.* New York: Free Press.

Heald, S. 1999. *Manhood and Morality: Sex, Violence and Ritual in Gisu Society.* London, New York: Routledge.

Hutchinson, S.E. 2001. 'A Curse from God? Religious and Political Dimensions of the Post-1991 Rise of Ethnic Violence in South Sudan', *Journal of Modern African Studies* 39: 307–31.

Keane, J. 1996. *Reflections on Violence.* London: Verso.

Kleinman, A., V. Das and M. Lock (eds). 1997. *Social Suffering.* Berkeley, Los Angeles, London: University of California Press.

Knauft, B.M. 1987. 'Reconsidering Violence in Simple Human Societies: Homicide among the Gebusi of New Guinea', *Current Anthropology* 28: 457–500; 29: 629–33.

Kuschel, R. 1988. *Vengeance is their Reply: Blood Feuds and Homicides on Bellona Island.* Volume 1: *Conditions Underlying Generations of Bloodshed.* Volume 2: *Oral Traditions.* Copenhagen: Dansk Psychologisk Forlag.

Lee, R.B. 1979. *The !Kung San: Men, Women and Work in a Foraging Society.* Cambridge: Cambridge University Press.

Mirzeler, M. and C. Young 2000. 'Pastoral Politics in the Northeast Periphery in Uganda: AK-47 as Change Agent', *Journal of Modern African Studies* 38(3): 407–30.

Österle, M. and M. Bollig. 2003. 'Continuities and Discontinuities of Warfare in Pastoral Societies: Militarization and the Escalation of Violence in East and North-East Africa', *Entwicklungsethnologie* 12(1/2): 109–42.

Prunier, G. 1997. 'Segmentarité et violence dans l'espace somali, 1840–1992', *Cahiers d'Etudes Africaines* 146(XXXVII-2): 379–401.

Simonse, S. 2005. 'Warriors, Hooligans and Mercenaries: Failed Statehood and the Violence of Young Male Pastoralists in the Horn of Africa', in J. Abbink and I. van Kessel (eds), *Vanguard or Vandals: Youth, Politics and Conflict in Africa*. Leiden/Boston: Brill, pp. 243–66.

Tannen, D. 1998. *The Argument Culture: Moving from Debate to Dialogue*. New York: Random House.

Turton, D. 1975. 'The Relationship between Oratory and the Exercise of Influence among the Mursi', in Maurice Bloch (ed), *Political Language and Oratory in Traditional Society*. London: Academic Press, pp. 163–83.

Vayda, A.P. 1979. 'War and Coping', *Reviews in Anthropology* 9(2): 191–98.

———. 1989. 'Explaining why Marings Fought', *Journal of Anthropological Research* 45: 159–77.

Chapter 3
Catholics and Cannibals: Terror and Healing in Tooro, Western Uganda

Heike Behrend

Introduction

When in 1998 I came to Tooro in western Uganda, originally to do a study[1] on the re-establishment of the kingship, I was more than surprised to find people talk about *abali babantu*, man-eaters or cannibals. Women and men from all social classes, in towns as well as in rural areas, complained that cannibals were killing and eating their relatives, friends and neighbours. Cannibals had disappeared from Africanist anthropological discourse since the end of the 1970s; they had finally been discovered to be the stereotype of the Other. Europeans had accused Africans of being cannibals and, likewise, Africans thought Europeans were man-eaters. Both had done so to construct their radical Other (Arens 1979). In Tooro, however, the cannibal had been resurrected. Cannibals and to a certain extent also vampires had become very real, not so much at the margins of or outside Tooro, but in the midst of the kingdom. While in the 1970s, man-eaters were still assumed to live contained in a certain place named Kijura in Mwenge district, since the 1980s they had greatly multiplied and spread into other regions. In 1998, people told me that cannibals were everywhere;[2] in some regions where they had become epidemic a sort of moral panic, or internal terror (Lonsdale 1992), reigned.

I had not planned to do an ethnographic study on cannibals in Tooro. On the contrary, after having done a study on war and religion in northern Uganda, I had seen too many people suffering and had looked for a peaceful spot in Uganda to continue doing research. In 1995, I was invited to attend the coronation of King Oyo Olimi of Tooro; at this time, there was peace in Tooro and I did not hear of cannibals. Thus, I decided to do some research on the invention of traditions in the context of the re-establishment of kingship in

Tooro. By the time funding was granted by the Volkswagen Foundation in 1997, the situation in Tooro had changed dramatically. In 1996, the Allied Democratic Force had started to wage war against the government and Tooro had been turned into a war zone.

Yet, as an anthropologist, I had been trained to take up and respect the subjects the people I was living with were concerned about. When more and more cannibal stories came up and even my research assistant told me that her little brother had been eaten up by a cannibal, I decided to find out more about the production of cannibals and their local history. I soon learned that a lay movement of the Catholic Church, the Uganda Martyrs Guild (UMG) was trying to deal with this situation of internal terror. While in pre-colonial Tooro it had been the duty of the king in times of internal terror to cleanse the country from witches and cannibals, since 1996 members of the UMG had begun to hunt witches and cannibals. By identifying and healing witches and cannibals they attempted to put an end to the internal terror. While the local government and especially the police, themselves an agent of terror, failed completely to deal with the situation, the Catholic Church started using witch and cannibal hunts as instruments of political action, and as a dramatic discourse of discovery in the public sphere, in which moral order could be negotiated and reconstructed (Comaroff and Comaroff 1999: 293, 309). Hence, while, on the one hand, they succeeded in finding scapegoats and thus contributed to the cleansing and healing of the country, on the other hand, they affirmed and even spread the reality of witches and cannibals, thus reproducing the enemy they were fighting against. By trying to deal with, explain and terminate the crisis, they themselves ended up participating in the very process of producing the crisis – a self-referring chain (Mbembe and Roitman 1995: 325).

In the following, I wish to show how in some regions of Tooro a situation of external and internal terror emerged that was characterized by a dramatic rise of occult forces, an epidemic of cannibals. Against the tendency to find the origin of the rise of occult forces in the invisible hand of the capital or millennial capitalism (Comaroff and Comaroff 1998), I would like to argue that it is, above all, the strong increase of the death rates through the Aids epidemic and the local war that, interpreted in the idiom of witchcraft and cannibalism respectively, should be seen as responsible for the dramatic activation and expansion of occult forces, and especially the rise of cannibals.

First of all, I shall analyse the social and cultural conditions that contributed to the emergence of a situation of external and internal terror and, likewise, the rise of the UMG as a movement hunting witches and cannibals. Thus I shall deal with the war of the Allied Democratic Forces (ADF), the 'invasion of immigrants', economic depression, corruption and Aids. Then I shall analyse the attempts of the UMG to counter the dramatic rise of witches and cannibals, to heal the country and to re-establish a new Christian moral order.

External and Internal Terror

In early 1990s, various scholars showed that wars generate violence not only against an outside enemy, but also against people who belong to the 'inside'. In her book on the war of liberation in Zimbabwe Norma Kriger (1992) wrote about a 'war within a war'; John Lonsdale when writing about Mau Mau coined the term 'internal terror' (Lonsdale 1992: 355) and called Mau Mau an imploded debate on Kikuyuness, while Colin Leys and John Saul (1995) entitled their book about Namibias liberation war 'The Two-edged Sword' thus referring not only to SWAPOs fight against the South African army but also to the internal power struggles and killings within SWAPO, in the course of which thousands of so-called dissidents were imprisoned and killed in 1976 and during the 1980s. In my work on the Holy Spirit Movement and its war against the government in northern Uganda (Behrend 1999), I also followed this trajectory and attempted to give some insights into the complicated dialectics of external and internal violence. I argued that, for an understanding of a 'war within a war', local discourses on witchcraft and sorcery have to be included in the analysis. With increasing death rates, not only are social tensions, fears and anxieties expressed in the witchcraft and sorcery discourses, but they also put in operation a mechanism creating a vicious circle that intensifies violence and killings, sometimes to such an extent that Hobbes' nightmare of a [secret] war of all against all may be realized. This happens because often the responsibility for death is not so much attributed to the alien enemy soldier or the epidemic (as a 'natural' cause, as the ancestors' or God's punishment) but instead is turned inside: relatives and neighbours at home with whom the deceased lived together are made the culprits by being identified as witches, and so instead of creating solidarity an aporia is produced that radicalizes and escalates the unbearable situation even more.

The War of the ADF

Since 1996, Tooro (Kabarole District) and Kasese have become the operation areas of the Allied Democratic Forces (ADF), a fundamentalist Islamic guerrilla movement, operating from the Congo, fighting the Ugandan government of Yoweri Museveni and getting support – for some time – from the Congo and the Sudanese Government.[3] The ADF consisted of various remnant groups from Uganda, Congo and Rwanda, soldiers from different guerrilla movements that were mushrooming over the last few years: old Rwenzururu fighters who did not come down from the mountains in 1982 but decided to continue the fight under the leadership of Amon Bazira in a movement then called NALU (National Army for the Liberation of Uganda) (Amon Bazira was killed in Kenya in 1993), remnants of the West Nile Bank Front I, Tabliqs of the Salaf sect organized under a group called the Uganda Freedom Fighters Movement

(UFFM) led by Jamil Mikulu, soldiers of the Uganda Army who had been in Congo under the command of the late Brigadier Tizihwayo, groups of the former Rwandan Army of the Habyarimana regime, the Interahamwe (militias strongly involved in the genocide in Rwanda), and parts of Mobutu's defeated army. In addition, the ADF recruited from various parts in Uganda, from Jinja, Iganga, Mbarara, Kampala and Masaka as well as among the youth from Kasese and Bundibugyo, activating old Rwenzururu sentiments to recreate the Bakonjo kingdom.

In their manifesto, made public through the Internet, the ADF declared that they went to the bush in May 1996 to challenge the presidential elections and overthrow Museveni in order to return to democracy and a multiparty system. They accused the present government of being led by 'kaffirs' and one of their goals was to enforce shariah law in Uganda. Obviously, the ADFs political agenda is rather simple. In addition, the manifesto is based on xenophobia ('Museveni is a foreigner, a Tutsi from Rwanda, intending to install his Tutsi Empire of the Great Lakes Region') and a complementary discourse celebrating pure Ugandaness and radical nationalism ('we emphasise that we are Pure Ugandans, BAANA NZAALWA, from various parts of our beloved country'). The ADF declared their war a liberation war, 'a war of nationalism and for a genuine independence from foreigners' ruling the 'motherland'. Denied in the manifesto is the fact that they are 'a mixture of defeated Zairian soldiers and Nalu rebels, a mixture of Interahamwe and former Rwandan soldiers, Muslim fundamentalists and former Amin soldiers' (http://www.admadf.ccom.co.uk).

In the last years (up to 2002), the ADF movement has increasingly resorted to isolated massacres, often targeting not so much the soldiers of the Ugandan Army, but instead the local population. They increasingly – as a conscious and systematic policy of recruitment – kidnapped children under the age of fourteen ('if they are older they are useless'), not only to use them as porters for looted and plundered goods, but also to train and use them as soldiers. In the camps in the Ruwenzori Mountains and the Congo, children were trained to kill at random. Parents of kidnapped children told me that they feared their own children because they were used by the rebels to lead the way to their homes. Indeed, often the children were forced to turn against their relatives, to loot and kill their own people. By killing their own kin, their return home became impossible; they were made asocial, cut off from their own community, while at the same time their bond with the ADF was strengthened – a strategy used also by other guerrilla movements, for example the RENAMO in Mozambique and the Lords Resistance Army in northern Uganda (Behrend 1999: 195). This brutal practice of kidnapping children likewise enabled the ADF to establish a negative network with the local population, the inverse of what the king and the chiefs did in pre-colonial times. In the old days, parents deliberately gave some of their children to the king and his chiefs to be trained in the etiquette of the court, and thereby to ensure their future political career. Yet, at the same time, the children also formed a sort of pawn to prevent their parents from rebelling against the king. Soldiers of the ADF, however, took the children by force and, as in pre-colonial times, used them as pawns and hostages to prevent the parents from taking action against them. Thus, parents of kidnapped children were desparate, fearing not only that their own children would kill them, but also fearing that their own action against the ADF might have deadly consequences for their children.

Although the ADF, in contrast to the Holy Spirit Movement (HSM) of Alice Lakwena in northern Uganda, did not succeed in gaining substantial local support in Tooro, its existence created deep local divisions. As in northern Uganda, certain men and women used the ADF for denunciating their neighbours or other people they hated by telling government soldiers or the police that this or that person was collaborating with the ADF. I was told that some people in Tooro used the ADF to kill immigrants, very often Baciga, who, so they claimed, were stealing their lands. And there were rumours that even a few very high-ranking politicians who were against Museveni secretly gave support to the ADF. Whenever there was an attack, certain local people were suspected to have collaborated with the rebels. Thus, a clear boundary between friend and foe, between inside and outside, could not be drawn. Instead, every threat from the external enemy was likewise suspected to be also an internal one. Furthermore, as in northern Uganda, the deaths inflicted by ADF guerrillas were often attributed to occult forces, evil spirits, witches or cannibals. The enemy's bullet that killed a man was not seen as the real cause of his death, but instead relatives or neighbours of the deceased with whom he had been in conflict were suspected to have bewitched (*kuroga*) him and so ensured that the enemy's bullet hit him rather than someone else. Thus, through the idioms of witchcraft – what Peter Geschiere (1994) referred to as the dark side of kinship – the external terror practised by the ADF was turned inside, against people who should have lived in peace and solidarity with one another.

'Invasion' of Strangers

In addition, an increasing scarcity of land and the intrusion of immigrants created bitter feelings among local people. Especially in some areas, such as Kijura or Kyarusozi, Batooro accused the strangers of stealing their land and their women. The settlement of immigrants not only altered the composition of communities – in some areas Baciga turned locals into a minority in their own parishes – they also changed the conditions of leadership. Some Batooro told me that they felt dominated by the immigrants and like strangers in their own kingship. Furthermore, at the height of the war against the ADF around 2000, camps for internally displaced people were established as parts of already existing villages in some regions of Tooro, near the Ruwenzori Mountains. Their existence also contributed to the threat felt by many Batooro of being invaded by strangers.

Economic Depression, Corruption and Aids

Since the beginning of the 1990s, western Uganda has experienced an acute economic depression – certain people nonetheless accumulating great amounts of wealth – and various instabilities and ruptures of all kinds. In addition, the growth of economic inequality increased witchcraft and sorcery fears and accusations. Furthermore, the growing retreat of the state and the corruption in the local government also led to a strong feeling of insecurity. It is not by chance that Tooro is said to have the highest rate of 'mob justice' in Uganda.[4] People resorted to violence and lynching of notorious thieves and suspected witches, I was told, because the police were so corrupt that no justice could be expected and, worse, the criminals' revenge after their release had to be anticipated.

Also, since the beginning of the 1990s, in Tooro, the Aids epidemic has spread to a terrifying degree. People of all social classes were and are affected. 'There are not enough tears left to mourn all the dead,' people say in Tooro (as well as in Congo) (de Boeck 1998: 50). Nearly every day funerals take place, sometimes more than one. Besides the xenophobic discourse that blamed the West for producing Aids, there existed other competing discourses, for example, the one led by the Christian churches where Aids is seen as a punishment by God, or the one led by 'traditionalists', for whom the general neglect of traditions is a reason for the epidemic. However, the dominant discourse attempting to explain the epidemic was the witchcraft[5] discourse, and, as its radicalization, the cannibal discourse.[6]

Local Cannibal Discourses

Cannibalism (like incest) in its various forms, in the West as well as in Africa, violates one of the most fundamental human interdictions. It is such an abominable act that there exists no law (in Uganda or Germany) against it. It is part of the standardized nightmares in which societies portray their evil Other.

The cannibal discourse in Tooro seems to be rather old. It already appeared in the context of the slave trade, slave catchers and traders being suspected of enslaving local people for the purpose of killing and eating them, as Mr. Yosoni Kyemulesire told me (see also Pierson 1993; Turner 1993). In addition, cannibals formed part of a local ethnographic map, in which some of Tooro's neighbours, especially those in the west, in the Congo, were said to be cannibals. As Mr Yosoni Kyemulesire explained to me, in the Congo people practised cannibalism openly; they would eat humans during the daytime. The Abahuku, Ababire, Abangwetu and Ababulebule were all people from the forest and cannibals. They would not bury a person, but eat him or her; they would eat their own people, even relatives, and they called other people *manyama*, meat. In this ethnography, other foreigners, such as Europeans, were also suspected to be cannibals. Thus, the figure of the cannibal formed part of the local xenophobic repertoire of othering.[7]

However, cannibals were not only the radical Other outside of Tooro, but, as already mentioned, they were also found inside of Tooro, confined to a certain place called Kijura in Mwenge district. Two texts from the 1970s about Kijura (Mulindwa 1972; Ruyonga 1977/78) and my own research open up a rather complicated perspective. On the one hand, it seems that at the beginning of the twentieth century some groups of people from the Congo settled in Kijura and brought with them the tradition of mortuary cannibalism, the eating of dead relatives as an act of piety and respect. Yet this positive practice of incorporation as part of ancestor worship became integrated into the witchcraft discourse as an epitome of evil. Witches turned into cannibals and *mahembe*, horns filled with various substances or medicines, were said to be used by witches and cannibals to get human flesh (Ruyonga 1977/78: 4).

While the positive aspects of (endo)cannibalism had disappeared completely when I did my research at the end of the 1990s, the negative ones continued to determine the present cannibal image. In Tooro, cannibals were said to form some sort of 'secret society'. In contrast to witches, they ate in groups. They were bound together in an exo-cannibalistic system of reciprocity; if a cannibal of a certain village killed a relative he invited the cannibals of another village to share the ensuing feast. Later the cannibals of the second village would reciprocate by inviting their previous host to a feast at which they would serve a victim from their own village. Cannibals searched for their victims among people they hated or envied. But they also killed because of greed, of lust for human flesh; and they killed their own kin as well as strangers. In addition, cannibals were said to bring the dead back to life, not so much to work for them, but instead to be eaten, to be killed a second time. After the victim's funeral, the cannibal is said to blow a whistle, then a strong wind blows and the corpse is – like Jesus – resurrected from the grave to be killed and eaten a second time during the cannibals' sinister banquet.

The cannibal discourse is, as already mentioned, part of the witchcraft discourse. 'All cannibals are witches, but not all witches are cannibals,' I was told. However, it is a radicalized witchcraft discourse: while witches kill only once, cannibals kill twice, their banquet appearing as a blasphemous inversion of the Eucharist, a diabolic caricature of the Christian theophagy.[8]

Furthermore, in this discourse not only the living, especially those close to oneself, but also the dead have become a terrible threat. Because so many people were dying of Aids and through war, the expensive and long-lasting funeral rites had to be drastically reduced. This is why some people fear that the dead might feel neglected and to punish their living relatives send sickness and misfortune to them. Thus, the boundary between the living and the dead has become ever more permeable and insecure, resulting in a sort of 'zombification' of post-colonial life in Tooro – as in other regions of east and central Africa (de Boeck 1998: 49).

Catholics and Cannibals: the Uganda Martyrs Guild

While before 1980 cannibals were more or less confined to Kijura, by the end of the 1980s it was believed that the number of cannibals had greatly multiplied and that they now ranged over the entire area of northern Tooro bordering Bunyoro. Around this time, a new Christian movement founded by a Catholic named Bisaka split off from the Catholic Church and started hunting witches and cannibals and healing them. Many people also in other parts of Tooro joined this movement, and especially the Catholic Church lost a substantial number of followers (Kassimir 1999: 262ff. Ndyabahika 1999:143ff.). When around 1996 a lay movement of the Catholic Church, the Uganda Martyrs Guild (UMG), began to do the same in other regions, they succeeded in regaining some of its former members. Thus, the witch- and cannibal hunts became political instruments in a power struggle between various Christian movements and churches and the cannibals became increasingly associated with the 'pagan' and the 'satanic', the Other of Christianity.

The Uganda Martyrs Guild has its origin in the persecution and killings of Protestant, Catholic and Muslim pages at the court of King Mwanga in Buganda in 1885 and 1886. In 1920, the Catholic martyrs were beatified and in October 1964 declared to be saints by the Catholic Church. In 1897 Archbischop Henry Streicher who trained people to help in the evangelization process, founded the UMG as a lay organization. While for a long time, in spite of the attempts of the Catholic Church, the Uganda martyrs did not gain much local importance, at the beginning of the 1990s, the UMG changed into a charismatic movement. This transformation has to be seen in the context of a more global development, the development of Christian fundamentalism, which started as early as the 1960s[9] with a Pentecostalist turn in the Protestant and later a charismatic renewal in the Catholic Church. From the U.S.A., the charismatic movement spread to Uganda and to Tooro where it became localized and connected to already existing religious practices.

Thus, in Tooro, to the surprise of the more conservative clergy, members of the UMG, mostly poor people with little education, began trembling, falling to the ground, speaking in tongues, being filled and possessed by the Holy Spirit. Evil or satanic spirits were exorcized; and healing became one of the most important ministries in the church. A few years later, around 1995–96, when the war with the ADF started, the UMG, with the strong support of an American priest, organized so-called crusades in regions where meanwhile cannibals were said to have become epidemic. Thus, the UMG turned into a Christian witchcraft-eradication movement, countering the epidemic of cannibals by mass possessions by the Holy Spirit.

'Crusades' and the Production of Cannibals

Before some members of the UMG went for an 'operation' or 'crusade', they announced their plans in monthly papers and on the radio. They sent letters to the local council and to the police, and sometimes, when they feared fierce resistance they asked for some policemen to protect them. The day before the operation they fasted; the night was spent in church singing and praying rosaries until their bodies were filled or 'loaded' with the Holy Spirit. In the early morning they took off in lorries. As Mr Kasaija, the president of the UMG, explained to me, they had to be very careful because witches would put up traps to fight the UMG. After arrival in the villages, they walked from house to house, an 'operation' that was called 'carpet bombing'. Thus, in their terminology, they used the vocabulary of modern warfare.

They moved in groups of twelve to twenty people, every group having a secretary, who recorded what was said and done. UMG members were not allowed to eat anything in these houses because people might try to poison them. When they reached a house the Holy Spirit used their bodies as an indicator for the presence of something satanic. If there was a 'satanic' object, then some especially gifted members of the UMG, often children, fell violently to the earth, rolling and scratching the ground; they cried, became wild, their eyeballs disappeared and they fell on their knees and begged the hesitant sinners to bring forth all the things of evil. Other UMG members ran on their knees and found the 'fetishes' hidden in the roof and in the bush. When all the satanic things had been collected – such as pots used by cannibals, a dried human hand, a woman's breasts, pieces of cloth belonging to people who had died and been eaten, horns (*mahembe*) and all sorts of medicine – they were displayed outside to be seen by everybody and photographed, the photographs supplying the proof of the veracity of the event. The pictures were circulated and put into albums, which were shown to visitors as a sort of trophy or memory of the UMG's power and success. In addition, politicians were called to witness the event.

To heal cannibals and witches, besides praying and laying hands on their heads, they were also made to vomit – to reverse the process of incorporation that had produced their greediness for human flesh. To end a crusade, members of the UMG offered night-session preaching and praying, and they gave answers to questions from the local population; and the Catholic parish priest served Holy Communion.

I was told that the first crusades of the UMG were extremely violent. In a village called Kabende the Christian witch and cannibal hunters identified an old lady to be a notorious cannibal. When she turned into a black cat, members of the UMG caught her and started to burn her. Yet, already in flames, the cat transformed again into the old lady, who – with bad burns – had to be taken to hospital. She sued some members, who went to prison. After this incident, the Catholic Church decided to first train the UMG. For two years, they were not allowed to go for any crusade. They participated in workshops and learned to hunt witches and cannibals without using violence. While before this the identified witches and cannibals were beaten up and then forced to confess in public, the UMG now only prayed for them. However, part of the healing process is the cannibal's confession in which the accused has to narrate in detail when, how and whom he/she has eaten. Thus, the confessions produce more detailed knowledge about witches and cannibals, leading to a further proliferation and differentiation of the cannibal discourse: cannibals now are organized in grades and classes; some cannibals of the upper classes can turn into cockroaches; they have agents to help them; they use cars and modern media, especially photography; victims are identified through photographs, etc.

In addition, as already mentioned, if a cannibal was identified he/she had to give the names of the cannibals he or she had been working with. As during the times of the Inquisition in Europe, in Tooro whole networks of people were established and then put under pressure to confess their satanic deeds. Thus, the fight of the UMG against evil produced and spread even more the reality of the evil agents. When I visited the areas that had been the targets of the UMG's first crusades, people told me that they had not realized how many cannibals were living in their villages before the UMG came. In addition, when I asked some policemen for evidence that certain people were cannibals, they explained that they never succeeded in getting trustworthy evidence and that only members of the UMG had produced such proofs. Thus, it is obvious that the UMG participated in the production of the enemy they were fighting to provide evidence of their own power and the power of their (Catholic) god. In their war against witches and cannibals, the Catholic Church, as an alternative institution to the state and the kingship, regained members and political legitimacy; the churches, which in some parts of Tooro had been empty for a long time, were now filled with people. As an American Catholic priest told me, before the war against cannibals people came to him only to get money, nowadays they come to get healed.

Re-establishing the Moral Order

Most of the people I talked to welcomed the UMG's work of cleansing their villages from cannibals and witches. More critical and outspoken were some traditional healers, who felt intensly persecuted by the UMG. Some of them accused the UMG of being an accomplice in the production of cannibals and witches. To demonstrate their power, the UMG would bring false evidence against people they hated.

Yet, like the Holy Spirit Movement in northern Uganda, the UMG not only tried to eradicate witchcraft and cannibalism, but also attempted to re-establish the moral order. Members had to follow the Ten Commandments; in addition, they were not allowed to commit adultery, drink alcohol, smoke, go to discos, 'eat bribes', visit witch-doctors or 'practise satanic traditions'. Members who were not living a life according to these standards were counselled, preached, prayed over and helped so that they became 'holy'. Members would collect money so that couples who lived together without being married could finally wed in church. If a person had to be hospitalized, members would collect money, visit and care for him or her. They would help one another in building houses and tending gardens. Thus, the UMG was also a sort of self-help group – not so much on the basis of neighbourhood and kinship, but instead on a religious basis. By doing so they tried to re-establish some sort of Christian solidarity among people who feared their relatives and neighbours were witches and cannibals.

When I visited Tooro the last time in August and September 2002, the ADF had disappeared and there was peace. Nobody knew where the rebels had gone. Some suspected that they had dissolved themselves after having been defeated, while others guessed that large parts had joined the Lords Resistance Army (LRA) in northern Uganda, which launched a serious military campaign against the government army.

Although the war in Tooro had ended, the UMG kept on organizing 'crusades' in various regions healing cannibals and witches by delivering them from evil. Yet the epidemic of Aids continued to kill people. And cannibals continued to be held responsible. From January to September 2002 in Kijura alone, five people suspected of being cannibals were killed by enraged villagers. As long as the UMG continues to fight cannibals and thereby to strengthen and confirm their existence, the situation of internal terror will not end. Only when witches and cannibals cease to be taken as a primary explanation for death and when instead Aids becomes 'medicalized' as a natural disease or is interpreted as a punishment by God or the ancestors might the vicious circle of terror and healing be dissolved.

Conclusion

The holy war (or the crusades) of the UMG is the attempt to cleanse society from evil and to establish an 'instant millennium'. It has to be seen as an answer to the failure of the local government and the kingship to deal with the situation of internal terror. In the crusades, women and men – themselves to a large extent excluded from economic and political power – took the chance to 'become holy' and to empower themselves by identifying others as cannibals and witches and thereby excluding them. Yet, because of the UMG's invention of practices of healing, the identified cannibals and witches – if they repented – were reintegrated into the villages. Thus, although some people were victimized, the healing practices of the UMG succeeded in containing violence.

Also in Tooro – as in Rwanda – the situation of internal terror could have escalated into a genocide (against the Baciga, for example). In a contribution to the aesthetics and politics of violence in Central Africa, Wyatt MacGaffey confronts the imaginary violence of witchcraft with Western warfare. He shows that, in contrast to the First World War, the wars of the Bakongo were divinatory ordeals or trials that ended after the first casualties. Maybe also in Tooro the excessive imagination of violence that found its expression in the figure of the cannibal has contained real violence. Thus, it may be that imagined violence – at least sometimes – substitutes for the real thing (MacGaffey 2000: 74).

Notes

1. This study was generously funded by the Volkswagen Foundation and I am grateful for this assistance. This chapter is part of a more substantial study in progress on the cannibal discourse in Tooro and its relation to Christian missionary teachings.
2. The existence of cannibals was not restricted to Tooro or Africa, as a fervent Catholic told me; instead, he said, cannibals were also to be found in Europe, especially in the Black Forest of Germany.
3. The war of the ADF from Congo was one of a variety of reasons why the Ugandan army started fighting in the Congo. The Ugandan army had built up an alliance with Rwanda (which later was interrupted) to fight Kabila, who had given protection to Hutu Interahamwe. There were also, of course, economic interests in gold, other minerals, timber and diamonds and, in addition, an interest to keep the army busy because, at least at that time, northern Uganda was relatively peaceful.
4. See the special report in *The New Vision*, 8 October, 1999, p. 4
5. Various forms of witchcraft, sorcery, poisoning and cannibalism are distinguished in Tooro. However, as all are subsumed by English-speaking Batooro under the more general term 'witchcraft', in what follows I shall use 'witchcraft' in this general sense.
6. The connection between the rise of occult forces and Aids (or other epidemics) is also made in Yamba (1997), Schoffeleers (1999) and Stewart and Strathern (1999).
7. It is interesting to note that not all neigbouring peoples were seen as cannibals. For example, the Baganda or the Bakonjo were excluded from the local cannibal ethnography. Thus, this more detailed and differentiated ethnography, attributing cannibalistic practices to some people but not to others, criticizes the rather simple thesis of Arens (1979) that the cannibal is a stereotype of the Other. As new research has shown, it cannot be excluded that cannibalism as a practice did and does exist in certain contexts. Even Evans-Pritchard could not deny that among some groups of the Azande cannibalism had been practised (Evans-Pritchard 1965; Gebauer 2000: 51ff.).
8. This aspect will be elaborated in a forthcoming publication that attempts to interpret the resurrected cannibal in Tooro as a variation of the Eucharist. There I will show in more detail how the Christian discourse and practices that the missionaries brought to Tooro around the 1890s became localized and 'othered' and thus inverted and integrated into the witchcraft discourse.

9. It is possible, of course, to trace various waves of renewal and so go back at least to the nineteenth century.

References

Arens, W. 1979. *The Man-Eating Myth: Anthropology and Anthropopaghy*. New York, Oxford: Oxford University Press.

Behrend, H. 1999. *Alice Lakwena and the Holy Spirits: War in Northern Uganda 1985–97*. Oxford: James Currey. (First published in 1993).

Comaroff, J. and J. Comaroff. 1999. 'Occult Economies and the Violence of Abstraction: Notes from the South African Postcolony', *American Ethnologist* 26(2): 279–303.

De Boeck, F. 1998. 'Beyond the Grave: History, Memory and Death in Postcolonial Congo/Zaire', in R. Werbner (ed), *Memory and the Postcolony*. London: Zed Books, pp. 21–57.

Evans-Pritchard, E.E. 1965. 'Zande Cannibalism', in E.E. Evans-Pritchard (ed), *The Position of Women and Other Essays in Social Anthropology*. London: Faber and Faber, pp. 133–64.

Gebauer, N. 2000. ‚Menschenfresser in Zentralafrika', MA thesis. Cologne: Institute of African Studies, University of Cologne.

Geschiere, P. 1994. 'The Dark Side of Modern Kinship: Domesticating Personal Violence: Witchcraft, Courts and Confessions in Cameroon', *Africa* 64(3): 323–41.

Kassimir, R. 1999. 'The Politics of Popular Catholicism in Uganda', in T. Spear and I. Kimambo (eds), *East African Christianity*. Oxford: James Currey, pp. 248–74.

Kriger, N. 1992. *Zimbabwes Guerilla War*. Cambridge: Cambridge University Press.

Leys, C. and J.S. Saul (eds). 1995. *Namibia's Liberation Struggle: The Two-edged Sword*. Athens: Ohio University Press.

Lonsdale, J. 1992. 'The Moral Economy of Mau Mau', in Bruce Berman and John Lonsdale (eds), *Unhappy Valley*. London: James Currey, pp. 265–468.

MacGaffey, W. 2000. 'Aesthetics and Politics of Violence in Central Africa', *Journal Of African Cultural Studies*, 13: 63–75.

Mbembe, A. and J. Roitman. 1995. 'Figures of the Subject in Times of Crisis', *Public Culture* 7: 323–52.

Mulindwa, P. 1972. 'The Abacwezi and Embandwa in Tooro', MA thesis. Kampala: Department of Religion and Philosophy, Makerere University.

Ndyabahika, J. 1999. *New Religious Movements in Uganda*. Kampala: Fountain Press.

Pierson, W. 1993. *Black Legacy. America's Hidden Heritage*. Amherst: University of Massachusetts Press.

Ruyonga, A.E. 1977/78. Cannibalism as an African Culture: In the Kijura People of Toro District, BA thesis. Kampala: Makerere University.

Schoffeleers, M. 1999. 'The AIDS Pandemic, the Prophet Billy Chisupe, and the Democratization Process in Malawi', *Journal of Religion in Africa* 29(4): 406–441.

Stewart, P. and A. Strathern. 1999. 'Feasting on My Enemy: Images of Violence and Change in New Guinea Highlands', *Ethnohistory* 46(4): 645–669.

Turner, P. 1993. *I Heard it through the Grapevine: Rumour in African American Culture*. Berkeley: University of California Press.

Yamba, B.C. 1997. 'Cosmologies in Turmoil: Witchfinding and AIDS in Chiawa, Zambia', *Africa* 67(2): 200–223.

Newspapers and Websites

http.//www.admadf.ccom.co.uk
The New Vision, 8 October 1999

Part II

Memory, Trauma and Redemption

Chapter 4

Coming Through Slaughter: The Herero of Namibia, 1904–1940

Jan-Bart Gewald

Introduction

The Herero were a pastoral people living in south-western Africa. In 1904, under the leadership of Samuel Maharero, they became involved in a genocidal war against the armies of Imperial Germany. In the following four years an estimated 80 per cent of the Herero were killed. Of late a number of authors have sought to deny or at least downplay the genocide, and allow historical discussion to spiral into a demeaning and frankly meaningless debate about numbers. The debate was given new input by the publication, shortly before the independence of Namibia, of Brigitte Lau's 'Uncertain Certainties: The Herero–German War of 1904' (Lau 1989; for critique see Dedering 1993; Gewald 1994). Lau's article was followed by a series of articles and books that have sought to deny the genocide, or at the very least, called for a revision of histories dealing with the war (see Sudholt 1975; Kühne 1979; Poewe 1985; Spraul 1988; Nuhn 1989). Within Namibia, Herero survivors, the majority of whom were women and children, were incarcerated in prison camps and put to work as forced labourers for the German military and settlers. The prison camps, with their categorization of 'fit for labour and unfit for labour' (*arbeitsfähig und arbeitsunfähig*) prisoners and preprinted death certificates with 'death by exhaustion following deprivation', were finally abolished in 1908. But this did not mean that Herero were free to go and do as they chose. The colonial administration passed laws that stipulated that each and every African above the age of seven had to permanently carry a numbered metal tag around his or her neck. Furthermore, Herero were prohibited from owning land or cattle – the two basic necessities of any pastoral society (Gewald 1999).

This chapter seeks to discover and describe the manner in which, through time, Herero society sought to deal with the trauma of genocide and war. The essay builds upon the work of other historians and indicates how, during the remaining years of German occupation and thereafter, Herero society came to be re-established. It came to be re-established in keeping with deep-seated ideas with regard to what it was that constituted Hereroness, ideas that at all times were subject to the lingering social, cultural and historical effects of the war.

The contribution is divided into nine sections, which chart aspects of Herero society through the course of the twentieth century. The first section seeks to indicate that it is necessary to bear in mind, that even in the most adverse of conditions, people within societies always have some, however limited, room to manoeuvre. It provides an overview of the Herero–German war and links this to historical traces, both hidden and blatant, which are gaped at by tourists in present-day Namibia. The second and third sections detail the relationship between Herero war survivors, the mission and the ethnically exclusive reserves established by the South African administration in the 1920s. This section argues that the reserves provided a place in which Herero ideas regarding society, identity and history could come to fruition. In this process various widely divergent strands of thought and ways in which people and societies constitute themselves were drawn upon. Thus, as is discussed in sections four to nine, strands of pan-Africanism, German militarism and colonial ethnography were drawn together and used to inform and determine Herero society as it is presented at Herero annual commemorations of the war. The chapter argues that, in coming to terms with the Herero–German war, Herero war survivors and their descendants drew upon a wide variety of historical experiences and ways of being to determine their society in the present. In effect, as is sketched very briefly in the last section of the text, this has led to the effective effacement of separate and distinct historical Herero identities prior to the outbreak of the Herero–German war. In the end, contemporary Herero society is what it is on account of the Herero–German war of 1904–1908, and not, as it could very well have been, a society that traces its history and identity beyond 1904.

The Peace of the Graveyard

> 'German imperialism had largely broken the Herero's and Nama's power to resist, so that in the remaining years of German colonial rule the peace of the graveyard reigned in the territory' (Drechsler 1980: 231).

Writing in the 1960s, the East German Horst Drechsler was the first historian to seriously question the role of German imperialism in Namibia, thereby initiating a debate that was taken up by the West German historian Helmut Bley relating to the nature of German imperialism and the development of totalitarian society. Though both provided insights into the nature of Imperial Germany and Herero society, both failed to expand upon the history of the

Herero prior to, during and after the bloody conflict. In fact, discussion as to the history of the Herero, their resistance and their reaction to colonization was subsumed in a discussion relating to the society and colonial policy of Imperial Germany. Working through the mass of detailed archival material stored in Potsdam, Drechsler stumbled from one shocking event to the next. Having personally experienced and been traumatized by the experiences of what Nazism had wrought in Europe, Drechsler was shocked to discover echoes of the same inhumanity in Germany's colony of German South West Africa. Couched in the rhetoric of historical materialism, Drechsler sought to give vent to his feelings and came to describe the remaining years of German occupation in Namibia as being 'the peace of the graveyard'. Apart from the string of revisionists (Nordbruch 2002, 2004) who sought and still seek to deny the validity of Drechsler's findings, there are those who recognized the enormity of what had happened in Namibia and yet sought to flesh out and nuance 'the peace of the graveyard': historians who sought to restore agency to the African actors caught up in the terror of what constituted German colonial rule in Namibia. Foremost amongst these historians was the young German Philip Prein, who in 1994 published an article that clearly indicated that there was room for manoeuvre, however limited, within the confines of totalitarian German colonial rule. Prein's work proved to be an impetus and inspiration for further work, most notably that conducted by German and Namibian historians Gesine Krüger and Dag Henrichsen (Krüger 1995, 1999; Krüger and Henrichsen 1998). The present contribution falls within this paradigm and builds on the themes raised by these historians (most notably, see Gewald 2000), focusing particularly on aspects of agency. In doing so, it in no way seeks to diminish or play down the horrors of colonial occupation and colonial warfare; yet at the same time it seeks to explore and highlight the agency of people seeking to overcome and deal with war.

War, Genocide and Remembrance

To the many thousands of tourists who annually visit Namibia, the long dresses and spectacular headdresses of Herero women have come to form one of the most significant markers of Namibia. That this should be so is an intriguing aspect of history, for between 1904 and 1908 the Herero were defeated in a genocidal war against Imperial Germany. In the aftermath of the Herero–German war, the Herero had to all intents and purposes been destroyed. General von Trotha and his commanders had put into action that which he had extolled in brave words:

> 'I know enough of African tribes to understand that they give way only to violence. To exercise this violence with crass terrorism and even with gruesomeness was and is my policy. I destroy the rebellious tribes with streams of blood and streams of

money. Only from this seed something new will emerge, which will remain' (Drechsler 1966: 180; JBG's translation)[1]

Herero were killed, driven into the desert, incarcerated in concentration camps. Apart from being systematically abused, the majority of the survivors, women and children, were put to work as forced labourers for the colonial army, businesses and individual colonial settlers. All forms of Herero society appeared to have been destroyed and all Herero made to conform to the regimentation of camp life. Herero leadership, with the exception of a few Christian evangelists, had been killed or driven from the country. Herero boys, in so far as they had not been incarcerated in the camps, became the mascots and servants of the victorious army (Gewald 1999: 141–230).

Life in the prisoner-of-war-camps established by the German military in the settlements under its control was generally short and brutish. The doyen of Namibian anthropology, Heinrich Vedder, who was a missionary in Swakopmund at the time, described conditions in the camp in which he worked when he first arrived in the territory:

> When [I] arrived in Swakopmund in 1905 there were very few Herero present. Shortly thereafter vast transports of prisoners of war arrived. They were placed behind double rows of barbed wire fencing, which surrounded all the buildings of the harbour department quarters [*Hafenamtswerft*], and housed in pathetic [*jämmerlichen*] structures constructed out of simple sacking and planks, in such a manner that in one structure 30–50 people were forced to stay without distinction as to age and sex. From early morning until late at night, on weekdays as well as on Sundays and holidays, they had to work under the clubs of rough overseers [*Knutteln roher Aufseher*], until they broke down [*zusammenbrachen*]. Added to this, the food was extremely scarce: Rice without any necessary additions was not enough to support their bodies, already weakened by life in the field [as refugees] and used to the hot sun of the interior, from the cold and restless exertion of all their powers in the prison conditions of Swakopmund. Like cattle, hundreds were driven to death and like cattle they were buried. This opinion may appear hard or exaggerated, lots changed and became milder during the course of the imprisonment but the chronicles are not permitted to suppress that such a remorseless brutishness [*rucksichtslose Roheit*], randy sensuality [*geile Sinnlichkeit*], brutal overlordship [*brutales Herrentum*] were to be found amongst the troops and civilians here that a full description is hardly possible. (Translation JBG)[2]

At present, in Windhoek, the capital of the Republic of Namibia, many tourists admire the numerous German monuments scattered throughout the city. Yet, standing in front of these monuments, few of them will have realized that between 1904 and 1908 to the right of the *Alte Feste* (Old Fort), where a secondary school is now situated, a Herero POW camp was situated. It was with labour from this camp that the building of the *Tintenpalast*, which currently houses the Namibian parliament, was started. Even fewer of them will have realized that immediately behind the *Alte Feste*, where the sports fields of the secondary school are now to be found, the German military had established a separate camp in which Herero women were kept specifically for the sexual gratification of the German troops.[3] The situation was no different in any of the other Namibian towns and villages where German forces were stationed. Suffice to say the impact of the wholesale rape of Herero women by German soldiers continued long after the formal ending of the war in 1908. Between 1906 and 1909 more Herero children were born of German than of Herero fathers (see also Krüger 1999: 152). As Herero informants told Steenkamp in 1922:

> In these villages and on these farms they [our wives and daughters] came in contact with immoral whites and soldiers, contacted gonorrhoea, and when after years they were again met by their husbands and fathers they were sterile. At Windhoek a house of prostitution was opened for the German military. Our daughters were placed in it and when they returned from there and got married to Herero men, they were sterile. … So keen were they to convince me that the Herero were not acquainted with that disease before white occupation that they quoted the example of those Hereros who had fled with Samuel Maharero to Bechuanaland and Northern Transvaal. These were not sterile but on the contrary had large families. (Steenkamp 1922: 19)

In the aftermath of the war the camps were abolished. Henceforth, the Herero were enmeshed in a series of laws that sought to transform the survivors of Germany's colonial wars in Namibia into a single amorphous black working class.[4] Herero were deported from their former areas of residence and allocated to those settlers and businesses requiring labour. Ancestor worship and the maintenance of *Okuruuo* (holy fire)[5] was prohibited. All forms of leadership, with the exception of the Christian evangelists, was also prohibited. The ownership of cattle, essential to the maintenance of a pastoralist society, such as the Herero were, was prohibited. Herero boys continued serving in the German army. In short, it appeared as if the settlers' dreams of creating a pliable leaderless working class was coming to fruition. In 1911 a colonial official in German South West Africa initiated a bureaucratic file on the Herero. He captioned the file with the following words, '*die aufgelösten Eingeborenenstämme*', or 'dissolved Native Tribes'.[6] Ninety years later the 'dissolved Native Tribe' of the Herero, which forms a mere 7 per cent of Namibia's total population, has come to dominate the western image of Namibia and its history. No tourist folder, TV programme or public political discussion on Namibia is complete without inclusion or mention of the Herero; their women in brightly coloured 'traditional' dress, or their *Otruppe* at the annual commemorations of the dead. Indeed, one could argue that today the Herero form one of the most distinctive and well-known cultures of southern Africa.

As noted above, recent research has brought to the fore that, though Herero were subject to all manner of constraints in the immediate aftermath of the war, it is a mistake to view Herero society at the time as being solely acted upon or Herero as mere objects. Herero were actively engaged in manipulating the pass and labour laws that had been imposed upon them. Evidence also exists indicating that Herero were engaged in re-routing labour allocations, i.e., changing to whom and when they were allocated for wage purposes and attempted to exercise to the best of their abilities their independence, within very sharply defined parameters to their own advantage (Krüger 1999). Herero evangelists, the only Herero who were permitted some form of mobility and literacy,[7] informed other Herero, as they travelled from farm to farm, about the news of the world and the conditions of their families and friends. Indeed, Herero evangelists were so successful in their function as purveyors of the latest news that German settler farmers referred to them as weekly tabloids. Added to this, Herero living beyond the confines of the colonial administration successfully established communities, which were regularly in contact with Herero confined to the settler farms. All in all, in the aftermath of the war, though Herero society appeared to have been destroyed in the war, Herero were actively engaged in attempting to regulate their lives though not necessarily as Herero (Krüger and Henrichsen 1998).

Herero, Mission and Reserves

In the aftermath of the Herero–German war, the majority of the Herero in Namibia became Christians, attached to the Rhenish Missionary Society, which had been operating in Namibia since the 1840s (see Oermann 1999).[8] The Herero formally became Christians for a number of reasons. The first, which should not be discounted, is simply that of true belief; i.e., Herero actually believed that the gospel being taught by the missionaries was correct. Secondly, Christianity gave the Herero an identity beyond the confines of German control.[9] Thirdly, being a Christian provided a certain amount of protection from abuse by the colonial administration and/or settlers. Given that the Herero religious, military, political and economic leaders had been systematically liquidated in the war,[10] the survivors were faced with a fundamental problem: how does one run a society when all those with expert knowledge are dead? Or, to put it another way, how does one conduct marriages, circumcision ceremonies and the like when all the ritual specialists have been killed? This, essentially, was the problem that faced Herero society. The re-establishment of what it is that makes a person and a society uniquely Herero has been a process that started in the immediate aftermath of the Herero–German war and has continued into the present.

The South African invasion of Namibia in 1915 brought about a dramatic change and improvement in the living conditions of the African inhabitants of the territory. As the South African forces rolled through Namibia, Herero who had been confined to specific areas assigned to them on account of German labour demands, were able to leave their former employers and return to the lands of their birth. Often they absconded with the cattle of their employers, many of whom abandoned their farms in the face of the advancing South African forces. Within a year of the South African invasion, extensive stock-owning Herero communities had come into being in central Namibia on farms abandoned by their former German occupants. In due course, as the new South African administration sought to enforce its own form of government in the territory, it came into conflict with the Herero, who for their part had sought to re-establish their rights to the land. Due to the larger numbers of Herero the new administration, anxious to avoid any costly conflicts for the duration of the Great War, agreed to the establishment of territories reserved solely for the Herero and their stock. In effect, the administration was forced to accept the reoccupation of parts of Hereroland, and to formalize this acceptance through the establishment of a number of reserves. In a process that developed from tacit acceptance of Herero occupation of grazing lands, through the establishment of grazing reserves and the collection of grazing taxes, to the declaration of administered reserves set aside solely for Herero occupation, the new administration sought to gain control over the Herero.

With the establishment of reserves, Herero could withdraw beyond the sight and influence of the mission. Though, in the immediate aftermath of the Herero–German war the mission churches, both Catholic and Lutheran, had provided structural support for the survivors, this support had only been provided on the condition that Herero repudiated their former faith. As the South African administration strengthened its control over the Herero, the Rhenish Missionary Society increasingly lost control over its Herero converts. Already during the days of the South African campaign, Herero had deserted their former German bosses in droves. Associated with this move out of enforced employment and the re-establishment of themselves as Herero pastoralists was the decreasing need for certain aspects of mission Christianity. For example, Herero men and women no longer needed to prove that they were married in missionary-sanctioned Christian wedlock to prevent their families from being split up in the interests of settler labour allocation. Safe on parts of their reoccupied lands, Herero no longer needed missionaries to intercede on their behalf with cruel masters. Added to this, as the Herero re-established themselves with newly acquired cattle on the lands of their ancestors, so too they were increasingly able to begin attempting to re-establish what they believed were the forms of governance and belief of their ancestors. Needless to say, the missionaries, whom the Herero partly blamed for the destruction of their ancestral faith and governance, thus now had but a small role to play in Herero social life, a role that grew increasingly smaller.

In the early 1920s influences of the Ethiopianist movement elsewhere in Africa did not leave the Herero untouched. As early as 1921 Herero evangelists were being expelled from the Lutheran mission for conduct considered unbecoming for Christians, but becoming among Herero. As they reacquired and redefined their identity, Herero became increasingly more critical of the established mission churches. No longer did they live in the vicinity of the mission stations that had been established in the urban settlements of the country. On the reserves the Herero, as they sought to rebuild their society, had very little need for the mission, and did very little to encourage the missionaries and evangelists who visited them. Many a time visiting missionaries were told, "We are not Christians, we are Herero'. Increasingly, Herero on the reserves owned and maintained *Okuruuo*, even if they did not all immediately know the ritual practice associated with this. Missionaries and missionary evangelists reported on the holy fires being kindled and reported that the ritual practices associated with the *Okuruuo* were lost (Gewald 2000: 196–201). Added to this, some Herero in the reserves established their own syncretic churches, and preached to their own followers. Thus, after a few initial attempts, the mission refrained from attempting to minister in the reserves and steered clear of them.[11]

Concepts of Hereroness

In keeping with what the Herero believed their ancestors did and would have liked, Herero men and women would come to submit themselves to self-mutilations, rites of passage, abstentions and forms of gender-specific relations which for the greater part of Herero society had ceased to exist a generation earlier. Indeed, the striving of the greater mass of the Herero, between their first contact with the 'modernism' of the Cape Colony in the 1840s and the funeral of their paramount chief, Samuel Maharero, in 1923, had been for their wholehearted inclusion in the 'modern' world. Much as Herero royals could boast of rectangular as opposed to round houses and wore the latest in Cape fashion in the 1880s, so too, before his death in 1923, Samuel Maharero and his followers had anxiously sought to acquire and appropriate the goods, ways and means of the 'modern' world. All this changed with the death of Samuel Maharero.

Samuel Maharero was a chief who had been installed when the Herero were still paramount over their own lands and destiny. He died in a phase in which the Herero had lost control over their own lands and destiny. In his life Samuel Maharero carried the extremes of Herero existence, independence and colonial subjugation. His death forced the Herero to rethink and discuss the life and times of Samuel Maharero and thus provided the Herero with a link back into their own past. It took a full nine months to bring Samuel's body from Botswana to Okahandja (lead coffins, permits and the like had to be arranged), where he was to be buried. This provided the Herero with ample time to discuss his funeral and to analyse the causes of their downfall. In due course Herero argued and reasoned that the cause and reason for their downfall was to be found in their having turned their backs on the ways of their forefathers.

It was this that had caused their downfall. To heal and restore Herero society they had to return to the ways of their ancestors.

In order to become what was deemed to be a true Herero, men and women took to knocking out their lower incisors and filing an inverted V in their upper incisors. Though Herero women had to abdicate political control over Herero society to men, this did not prevent them from effectively ensuring that henceforth Herero men were to be circumcised. From the 1840s onwards circumcision had been discouraged and finally prohibited by the mission. However, following 1923, Herero men and women, confronted with the low birth rates that characterized Herero society in the first two decades of the century, believed and argued that it was the uncircumcised nature of Herero men that had prevented Herero women from bearing children in the manner in which they had done in the past.[12] Women argued that they did not want to have intercourse with 'children' (*ovanatje*), and thereby pressurized men to get circumcised. As a consequence, adult men allowed themselves to be circumcised by professional circumcisers who travelled across the land peddling their trade. The impact of this event cannot be overestimated and bespeaks the tremendous changes that were taking place within Herero society at the time (see Gewald 1998).

In all societies women are surrounded by a series of strictures and taboos that seek to control and possess the specific powers they are supposed to have. If these powers remain unchecked they can turn upon, pollute and injure society itself. On account of the war, Herero women were demographically dominant, and as long as they were not confined within the constraints of marriage they posed a danger to Herero society. Herero men argued that another prime reason for their downfall was the fact that, at the urging of the missionaries, they had agreed to monogamous marriages. Added to this, Herero men reasoned, another cause for the low birth rate and singular lack of children was simply that they were monogamous, something their ancestors had not been.

In 1903, when Andreas Kukuri became the last major Herero chief to convert to Christianity, he extinguished his *Okuruuo* or holy fire, which Herero believed was the embodiment of their forefathers. By submitting his ancestral fire sticks to the missionaries, Kukuri did not merely put out a fire, he extinguished the continued existence of his ancestors in favour of the gospel of Jesus Christ. In contrast, twenty years later, the burial of Samuel Maharero's body next to the graves of his father and grandfather once again underscored and emphasized Herero belief in the importance of being close to one's ancestors. Members of the funeral cortège that escorted Samuel's body from Botswana came from a colonial territory where the maintenance and possession of the *Okuruuo* had never been prohibited. Indeed, in the Bechuanaland Protectorate the *Okuruuo* of a number of powerful ancestors had been maintained since the 1890s. It was thus to members of Samuel's funeral cortège that Herero turned for the rekindlement of their *Okuruuo*. In the event, many Herero must have been disappointed, as Frederick Maharero, the leader of the delegation, was a practising Christian and thus at pains to avoid dealing with the *Okuruuo*. This was not the case with Samuel Shepherd, a descendant of Saul Shepherd, who in the 1870s had been granted fire from the *Okuruuo* of Maharero Tjamuhua with which to kindle his fire. In the early 1920s Samuel Shepherd travelled through much of Namibia, Botswana and northern South Africa, where he visited Herero communities (see also below, 'The Universal Negro Improvement Association').

In the months immediately following the funeral of Samuel Maharero, Herero ritual specialists travelled throughout Hereroland, lighting *Okuruuo*. Though many Herero heads of households (*Omuhona*) kindled *Okuruuo* in their homesteads (*Onganda*), this did not mean that they knew the ritual procedure associated with the *Okuruuo*. This was knowledge that in the past had been acquired during initiation and circumcision ceremonies. Thus, following the rekindling of the *Okuruuo*, a number of Herero ritual specialists travelled from homestead to homestead, giving instructions to men who did not know how to deal with the *Okuruuo* (Gewald 2000: 145–207).

Needless to say, the rekindling of the *Okuruuo*, the resumption of male circumcision, the re-establishment of polygyny and the reintroduction of the practice of knocking out and filing teeth led to a storm of protest and condemnation on the part of the mission. For their part, the Herero reasoned that it was precisely because they had decided to follow the ways and listened to the advice of the mission in the past that disaster had befallen them. They argued that, had they remained faithful to their forefather ways, they would have remained in control of their own destiny. Missionary Meier reported the critical statement of a Herero:

> Priest, don't think that the Herero will ever return; they are through with God, everywhere! The fulfilment of the Word is there: 'the break will be great'. You missionaries are guilty of our present defeat. You have not only made us propertyless, you have also taken away our rights. For us God's word has been a calamity. In the past we were the owners, and today it is the whites. To whom does the land now belong, and where are the huge herds that our fathers once owned? It has been like this everywhere where God's word has arrived; from South Africa all the way to Togo. If only our fathers had not become Christians, then matters would have been very different with us. (Translation JBG)[13]

Missionary opposition to Herero expression of their new-found identity did very little to deter the Herero from increasing their self-confidence and, if anything, served to alienate them further from the mission. The Rhenish mission's policy of paying its evangelists, missions and missionaries with money collected from its congregants exacerbated the situation.

Interestingly, though, the move away from the church was to a large extent gender-specific. Though nearly all Herero men turned away from the mission, large numbers of women and children in urban areas remained members. In the towns, where women remained employed and in charge of their own 'purse', they continued to attend the mission church, whereas in the reserves, where women were effectively cut off from forms of cash employment, women stayed clear of the mission. For payment was expected from Herero for their membership of the church. With the move to the reserves, women were no longer in direct employment and thus no longer in a position to pay. A further reason for the gender-specific and urban church attendance bias was the simple fact that women who could prove that they were church members and had regularly attended services were exempted from the regular degrading experience of forced internal vaginal examinations. In the alleged interest of combating sexually transmitted diseases, black women in urban areas were forced to undergo regular gynaecological examinations (Wallace 2002). Though the Herero turned away from the mission and church, they often justified their actions on the basis of theological arguments taken from the Old Testament. In discussions with the missionaries, Herero would refer to the laws of Leviticus, the polygamy of the prophets and the circumcision of the people of Israel. At times, the missionaries were hard put to counter the arguments of their former congregants and devoted a substantial amount of time at their annual conferences to the search for arguments with which to refute those of the Herero.

Following the funeral of Samuel Maharero, the majority of Herero sought to create a society in their image of the past; however, other possible paths into the future were also tried out. There were, as mentioned above, Herero women and children, as well as a few men, who sought to continue as Christian Herero associated with the mission and all that this entailed. More spectacularly, there were those Herero who were inspired by the wave of *bekennende* apostolic evangelism that swept southern Africa in the decades following the establishment of the Union of South Africa. Here many Afrikaner farmers, who found themselves on the downside of life, took to apostolic evangelism (see also Hexham 1980).[14] Afrikaner soldiers and farmers brought this form of religion with them to Namibia, where they preached to and clearly inspired members of Namibia's Herero population. There was a spectacular syncretization of apostolic evangelism and elements taken from Dama and other societies. Certain Herero men refrained from cutting their hair, carried sticks mounted with cow tails, and allowed themselves to become possessed by spirits, as they sought out and dispelled the evil that was so clearly manifest in their societies.

The Universal Negro Improvement Association

As the Herero established themselves on the lands of their ancestors and increasingly turned their backs on the missionaries, they did not only turn to the past for inspiration. They also found what they were looking for in the Africanist message being propagated by the Universal Negro Improvement Association

(UNIA) of Marcus Garvey. Marcus Garvey was a Jamaican man of African descent who founded the first pan-Africanist movement (UNIA) in 1914. The movement spread rapidly through the activities of West Indian stevedores, dock workers and sailors, and in 1920 the movement held its first convention in New York. Branches came to be established in the United States of America, Africa and Europe – even in Hamburg, Germany. The movement called for the unification of all people of colour, a return to Africa and the equality of all people. In the aftermath and partly on account of the First World War, UNIA spread through much of the African continent and around the world. Partly on account of the devastation that the Herero had experienced at the hands of the Germans, UNIA found a great deal of support among the Herero of central Namibia.[15] Within two years of its introduction into the territory by West Indian dock workers and sailors, the majority of the movement's positions of office in all the branches in central Namibia had been taken over by Herero, particularly by those descended from the former ruling families.

In part, UNIA was organized as a paramilitary organization, with its own ranks, uniforms and titles, and it was this aspect that found a certain resonance amongst a substantial section of the Herero – notably those who had associated with or served as soldiers and police of low rank in the German colonial military. Immediately after the collapse of the German military in Namibia, these men had established their own social support network, based on the organizational structure of the German army. Within this Herero paramilitary organization, which became known as the Otruppe,[16] Herero men carried rank, held exercises, wore uniforms and sought to form support for members of their organization. As with UNIA, for certain regions of Hereroland there was an effective twinning between those in leadership positions in the *Otruppe* and those descended from the former leading families. Thus, for example, in the Okahandja region, Alfred Maharero, one of the sons of the last Herero chief of Okahandja, held the office of *Kaiser* in the *Otruppe*.

Otruppe

As noted earlier, a number of Herero survived the war as child servants in the German army, where they assisted in all manner of tasks, from taking horses out to graze to washing clothes or serving at table. As they grew older, they, along with their associates, found within the confines of the German army the structures and institutions around and within which they could re-establish their lives as social beings. Needless to say, with the defeat of the German army in Namibia in 1915, these people could have been expected to lose the structures that had given their lives meaning. This, however, was not the case; Herero had appropriated and inculcated the structures and institutions of the German army for their own ends. Within a few months of the German defeat, Herero soldiers had established their own nationwide social support system, which was modelled and based on the organization of the recently defeated German military. These young Herero men appropriated the names and titles of their former commanders. They sent telegrams in German to one another. Not possessing rifles, the *Otruppe* drilled with sticks and dressed in German uniforms, which, at times, were adorned with medals and ostrich feathers. Specific areas were cleared for purposes of military drill and throughout the year regular training exercises were held. These exercises ensured regular contact between participants from widely dispersed settlements, who issued one another military passes, pay books and commands. The regiments collected cash dues, which were used for welfare purposes and operated as burial and benefit societies.

Particularly striking is the fact that the Herero chose the structure of precisely that institution – the German army – which had destroyed their former society to establish a new social order. The *Otruppe* were organized into regiments that corresponded with magisterial districts. Regiments were characterized by specific uniforms, designations and names. Thus, the *Otruppe* of Windhoek wore a khaki uniform, those of Keetmanshoop wore whites and those of Lüderitz khaki tunics and white trousers (Werner 1990). The regiments also had different designations. Thus, *Otruppe* of Okahandja were known as an infantry regiment, and those of Windhoek as a machine-gun regiment. The areas under the control of the various *Otruppe* regiments were given new names. Significantly Okahandja was named *Paradies* (paradise) and was headed by the *Kaiser*, otherwise known as Eduard Maharero, the brother of Traugott Maharero, one of the relatives of Samuel Maharero, who for a while led the Herero of Okahandja.[17]

An initial glance at the documents captured from the *Otruppe* by the South African colonial administration in 1917 gives the impression of a surreal world: A world in which His Excellency, Gouverneur von Deimling (Governor), Staatssekretär Heighler (State Secretary); 'Treasurer von Ministermann', 'Oberst Leutenants (First Lieutenants) Leutwein, Franke and von Estorff', 'Major Muller' and 'Hauptmann und Adjudant Schmetterling von Preusen' correspond with one another in a mixture of German and Herero. The archives are full of patrol reports, military passes, payslips and notices of promotion and regimental transfer, written on music paper and the discarded stationery of the German colonial administration. On closer inspection, it becomes clear that the messages refer to collected contribution dues, letters of attestation to other regiments and the payment of fines and assistance out of regimental funds on behalf of regimental members. Information that was of importance to regimental members, such as a magisterial ban on marching, were passed on by circular telegrams.[18] A member of a regiment, travelling through the district of another regiment and who was able to produce a letter of attestation, a *Reisepaß*, from his regiment commander, was guaranteed the support of the regiment he was visiting. Thus in May 1917 a telegram was sent to Lt. Col. Franke (aka Erastus) requesting him to pay Ober Leutenant von Mausbach, who had travelled from

Omaruru, the sum of 3 shilling so that he could continue on his journey to Windhoek. The telegram was sent by Schmetterling von Preussen, Hauptmann und Adjudant des Ettapenkommando (aka Fritz).[19] Effectively, by copying the structures and images of the German military, young Herero men had set up a countrywide support and information network for themselves: a network that extended from Lüderitz and Keetmanshoop in the south, to Gobabis in the East, Tsumeb, Grootfontein and Otjiwarongo in the north, Swakopmund and Omaruru in the West and Okahandja and Windhoek in the centre of the territory (Henrichsen and Krüger 1998). The regiments formed an organization that looked after the welfare of its members, a social structure to replace the society they did not have or were only marginally part of.

Herero Ethnography

Prior to their defeat in the Herero–German war, Herero had been extensively involved in the fashioning of Herero ethnography, if only as informants for the Rhenish Missionary Society missionaries who were active in their midst.[20] At their annual conferences a number of Rhenish missionaries presented ethnographic studies of aspects of Herero society and life. In order to be able to convert the Herero to Lutheran Christianity, the missionaries had to come to an understanding of what it was that the Herero believed in, and what it was that would have to be transformed before a Herero convert became an acceptable Christian in their eyes. More often than not the studies presented at the annual conferences were based on the extensive and intensive questioning of Herero converts as to their lives. Information divulged by the Herero was used as a gauge of commitment to the mission and conversion. Thus, for instance, the conversion of Chief Kukuri in 1903 was seen as being genuine on the basis of the fact that Kukuri surrendered his *Otjiha*, fire sticks used to kindle the *Okuruuo*, to the missionaries. In some instances Herero converts introduced Rhenish missionaries into areas that were ritually off-limits to all but Herero ritual practitioners. Interestingly, the products of this cooperation have come to form the basis for much of what is now known as Herero society and culture in the present. Herero presently engaged in attempting to determine what Herero tradition is meant to be are dependent on the earlier works of the Hahns and Irle (e.g., J. Hahn 1868; T. Hahn 1869; Irle 1917; C.H. Hahn 1985), and thus at one remove from the information of their ancestors.

The greatest ethnographic source on the Herero is the voluminous work of the Rhenish missionary Heinrich Vedder. Vedder, who, as we have seen had as his first active posting the Herero prisoner-of-war camp in Swakopmund, became Namibia's self-trained and self-appointed ethnographer-historian, whose work has come to form the flawed basis upon which most of all Namibian ethnography and history is based (Lau 1981; Kinahan 1989). Following the

First World War Namibia was placed in the care of South Africa as a mandated territory of the League of Nations. In the early 1920s as the South African government sought to impress upon the League of Nations its rights to the territory, the new administration sought to make ethnographic sense of the mass of people that had become its new subjects. To this end, experts were appointed by the administration to assist in the definition and determination of Namibias population. Part of this work is to be found in a book entitled *The Native Tribes of South West Africa* (Hahn, Vedder and Fourie 1928), which was commissioned and written with the express purpose of convincing the League of Nations of South Africa's good conduct in the territory.

Needless to say these experts, and in this case specifically Vedder, were dependent on indigenous informants for their information. Exactly who Vedder's informants were is still not clear, and an analysis of how Vedder conducted his research still remains to be done. Suffice it to say that Herero informants will have had their own agenda when assisting Vedder in his ethnographic study of the Herero. However, Herero definitions of the ethnographic self have not been limited to the definition of the self to others, as was the case of informants with Vedder, missionaries and administrations, but Herero themselves have also been continuously anxious to define exactly what it was that constituted Herero ethnicity. Thus, aside from reacting in response to state investigations into the ethnic condition of Namibia, Herero, too, have initiated projects to define their own ethnicity.

Herero Annual Commemorations

The aspects – history, religion, ethnicity and the *Otruppe* – which Herero use to determine, define and display their own identity as Herero come together in their annual commemorations of the dead. During the course of two days the Herero attempt to see the way in which others see them and to redefine themselves as a grouping distinct from the rest of the world in terms of their religion, history, dress and norms. Effectively they seek to reach an agreement as to what Herero identity should be and consists of.

Annually, at various sites in Namibia and Botswana, the followers of three flags (*omarapi* – derived from the Dutch word *lapje*, piece of cloth) gather for two-day ceremonies to commemorate the dead. At present there are three main flags. These flags have different colours and different sites of commemoration. The red flag, *erapi rotjiserandu*, has the largest following in Namibia and is the best known of the flags. Essentially the red flag represents the Herero of central Namibia and commemorates the royal house of Tjamuaha centred on Okahandja. The green flag, *erapi rotjigreeni*, is centred on ceremonial sites in Okahandja, Okaseta and Botswana and is generally equated with the followers of the royal house of Kahimemua. A number of the followers of the green flag refuse to define themselves as being Herero, choosing instead to define themselves as Ovambanderu. The black and white flag, *erapi rotjizemba*, is centred in western Namibia on Omaruru and represents the followers of the royal house of Zeraua. Following independence, the followers of lesser chiefs have also sought to institute their own annual commemorations and flags.

Participants arrive on Saturday and are introduced to the ancestors at the *Okuruuo*. During the course of the day participants greet and meet friends and relatives, and practise for the events of the following day. In the evening cooked cattle meat is distributed amongst all the participants and formal men and womens dances evoking the past are held. On the following day, Sunday, the actual ceremony takes place. Long before dawn participants are dressed and start assembling into marching troops on the central parade ground. In this melee women sing songs and troops indulge in some last-minute practice and start forming up into the order in which they will march to the graves. Eventually, shortly after the sun has risen and the *ovandangere* (ritual experts dealing with the holy fire) have deemed it fit, the participants head off towards the graves, led by horsemen and followed by the marching men and women. Arriving at the graves, permission is asked of the ancestors, whereafter the participants are led past the various graves, and if they are newcomers they are introduced to the ancestors. Following the visit to the graves, the participants return to the parade ground. Here speeches detailing historical events and current affairs are given. Topics can range from the presence of researchers in their midst to what a speaker believes the correct approach to sales tax should be, as long as the topic is considered to have a bearing on the community as a whole. Hereafter the various troop contingents display their marching skills and seek to be appointed as winners of the occasion. Once the winners have been chosen by public acclaim the ceremony is over and participants begin to pack up and go home.[21]

Herero History and Historians

> A man who catches History's eye is thereafter bound to a mistress from whom he will never escape. History is natural selection. Mutant versions of the past struggle for dominance; new species of fact arise, and old, saurian truths go to the wall, blindfolded and smoking last cigarettes. (Rushdie 1984: 123)

Many years ago, when I started my work on Herero history and society, my ideas regarding this topic were determined by my own observations as a child and the works of Bley (1971), Pool (1979), Drechsler (1980) and Bridgman (1981). All these authors, and my own schoolboy observations of Herero day celebrations, in which Herero marched in uniforms and to commands based on Wilhelmine German militarism, centred on and were essentially about the Herero–German war of 1904–8. The main purpose of my work, when I started my project, was that I wanted to get beyond the war. I wanted to get beyond the Herero–German war as the be-all and end-all of Herero history and society: the year zero upon which all that is defined as being Herero is based and in terms of which all that is Herero is to be understood. Thankfully, in the first years of my research I was able to go beyond the war. I could and did venture into a world as yet uncharted and as yet totally unrelated to the war. A quote from my research report written at the end of my first year in the uncharted history will serve to illustrate the point that I am trying to make:

> With regard to the collected information the following very preliminary results can be given. At present certain points stand out which will entail a considerable revision of the accepted views on central Namibian history. Most notably, it has become clear that Herero society was much less monolithic than originally thought. Ethnic divisions were far from clear cut, and very porous. Herero society, if such can be defined, was riven by tensions and splits which extended beyond the Herero as conventionally defined, so that the incoming Germans were able to play off one leader against another, thereby facilitating their conquest.

What I had come across was far from monolithic, and this, I must admit, was a surprise to me. Instead, what I saw developing throughout the nineteenth century were the evolution and disintegration of polities and ethnicities, be they Herero, Ovatjimba, Ovahimba, Damara, Ovambanderu or Nama. At times, polities and ethnicities were concurrent; at other times polities evolved that were clearly, and consciously, multi-ethnic. I saw, under the influence of guns, powder, horses, bibles, pens and ink, what I believe was the emergence of such a thing as Herero identity. I watched groups of people, now referred to as Herero, coalesce, centralize, split and move northwards into lands previously occupied by others; I saw five Herero chiefs emerge and contest the spoils of the land with one another. I watched as one chief, Samuel Maharero, successfully rode the tiger of German imperialism and eliminated his many opponents through the use of German arms. And eventually I saw how Samuel Maharero, now as paramount chief of all the Herero, was unseated from his mount and consumed along with his people in the hellfire of war. In other words I travelled beyond the war: I successfully charted Herero history before the war, I reconstructed the past.

Herero had also reconstructed the past, but in distinction to my approach their history is centred on the Herero–German war. All that has occurred, or is believed to have occurred in Herero history, is centred on the war. The Herero–German war is seen and presented as the be-all and end-all of Herero identity and history. Everything that relates to Herero society, history and identity is made understandable and explainable in terms of the war. In much the same way that the Nazi genocide has come to determine much of Jewish identity and being in the present, so too Herero have been and continue to be affected by the war. The events of the war have come to dominate Herero historical thought and its lessons are used to appreciate and inform action in the present, to situate and authenticate Herero identity in the present.

Conclusion

In dealing with Herero society in the aftermath of the Herero–German war, one sees that the war has come to act as the catalyst that has fused separate histories and identities into one. The war is seen and referred to as the touchstone through which all of Herero society can be defined and determined. The war has effectively come to form a lens through which all that is considered to be Herero can be brought into focus and examined. It is a lens that is not only used by Herero themselves, but also by the majority of those who occupy themselves professionally with the social, cultural and historical aspects of Herero society. In effect, through being the single most dominant event in Herero history, the war has rubbed out and obscured all other ways of viewing and dealing with Herero society. In this, all attempts at analysing the social, cultural, historical and some might say economic aspects of Herero society are subject to the war. Unfortunately, this has also come to mean that Herero society is only definable in terms of the Herero–German war.

Notes

1. 'Ich kenne genug Stämme in Afrika. Sie gleichen sich alle in dem Gedankengang, dass sie nur der Gewalt weichen. Diese Gewalt mit krassem Terrorismus und selbst mit Grausamkeit auszuüben, war und ist meine Politik. Ich vernichte die aufständischen Stämme mit Strömen von Blut und Strömen von Geld. Nur auf diesser Aussaat kann etwas Neues entstehen, was Bestand hat' (after Drechsler 1966: 180, referring to RKA Nr. 2089, Bl. 100–102, Trotha an Leutwein, 5.11.1904).
2. Als [ich] 1905 nach Swakopmund kam, waren dort nur sehr wenige Herero anwesend. Bald kamen aber grosse Transporte von Kriegsgefangenen an. Dieselben wurden hinter einem doppelten Stacheldrahtzaun, der das umfassende Gebäude der Hafenamtswerft einschloss, in jämmerlichen, aus einfachen Sackleinen und Latten hergestellten Raumen untergebracht, und zwar so, das in einem einzigen Raum 30–50 Personen ohne Unterschied des Alters und Geschlechtes zu bleiben gezwungen waren. Vom frühen morgen bis zum späten Abend mussten sie am Werktag sowohl als am Sonn und Feiertagen unter den Knütteln roher Aufseher arbeiten, bis sie zusammenbrachen. Dabei war die Ernährung mehr als dürftig: Reis ohne jegliche Zutaten war nicht genügend, den durch das Feldleben geschwächten und an die heisse Sonne des Innern gewohnten Korper die Kälte und ruhelose Auspannung aller Kräfte in der Swakopmunder Gefangenschaft ertragen zu lassen. Wie Vieh wurden Hunderte zu Tode getrieben und wie Vieh begraben. Dies Urteil mag hart erscheinen ... aber die Chronik darf es nicht verschweigen, dass eine solche rücksichtslose Roheit, geile Sinnlichkeit, brutales Herrentum sich hier unter der Truppe und Civil breitmachte, dass ein Übertreiben in der Beschreibung kaum möglich ist. (Archiv ELCRN V.31 Chroniken Swakopmund; Archives of the Evangelical Lutheran Church in the Republic of Namibia (ELCRN) V. Ortschroniken Swakopmund).
3. Vereinte Evangelische Missionsarchiv Wuppertal (VEMA) 1623, Wandres in Windhuk, 9/9/08, to inspector: 'Of the free Natives no girl went there, therefore people resorted

to the prisoner of war Herero girls, who of their free-will accepted this dirty business. I personally doubt this free-will … the kraal existed about 100 metres behind the fort.' (Von den freien Eingebornen ging kein Mädchen dort hin, man griff deshalb auf Kriegsgefangenen Herero Mädchen zurück, die sich freiwillig dem schmutzigen Geschäft apserten [sic]. Ich persönlich, bezweifle diese Freiwilligkeit … etwa 100 meter hinter der Feste bestand jener Kraal.)

4. For the war, see Bley (1971). For copies of the legislation regarding the control of Herero see NNAW, ZBU, 2023 *Verwaltung der Eingeborenen angelegenheiten*, WII a 4–a 10. For published texts see *Verordnung des Gouverneurs von Deutsch-Südwestafrika, betr. Dienst- und Arbeitsverträge mit Eingeborenen des südwestafrikanischen Schutzgebiets, Verordnung des Gouverneurs von Deutsch-Südwestafrika, betr. Maßregeln zur Kontrolle der Eingeborenen*, and *Verordnung des Gouverneurs von Deutsch-Südwestafrika, betr. die Paßflicht der Eingeborenen*, all of 18/8/07 and also NNAW DKB, 15/12/07, pp. 1179–1184. For a detailed discussion of this legislation, see Bley (1971) and Zimmerer (2001).
5. The term *Okuruuo* is generally translated as 'holy fire'. In essence the *Okuruuo* is held to embody the patrilineal ancestors of a household head. It is through and with the *Okuruuo* that a household head ministers to his ancestors and seeks their advice and guidance in daily life.
6. Namibian National Archives (NNA), Zentrales Büro (ZBU) 2027.
7. On the prohibition of literacy see Hillebrecht (1992); on the role of evangelists, see Prein (1994: 99–121) and Gewald (1996: 253–55).
8. See Gewald (1996: 55) for a more detailed discussion on Herero conversion to Christianity.
9. For a detailed discussion on the relationship between the Herero and the Mission between 1915 and 1940, see Chapter 6, '"When the Lord Jesus Milks my Cows, then I Will Come to Church Service": The Herero and the Church, 1920–1940', in Gewald (2000).
10. Andreas Kukuri the last major Herero chieftain to convert to Christianity, converted in 1903, only to be hanged in 1906.
11. There are a number of detailed descriptions dealing with developments within Herero society in the run-up to Samuel Maharero's funeral in 1923. Central to these are Krüger (1994, 1999).
12. Herero birth rates are something that has fascinated not only the Herero. In the 1920s Steenkamp wrote a pamphlet entitled *Are the Herero Committing Race Suicide?* (Steenkamp 1922). Not to be outdone, H. Vedder wrote a number of documents dealing with the same issue and Herero forms of abortion (Steenkamp 1922: VEMA 2635b Vorträge und Aufsätze zu SWA Band 2 Der künstliche Abortus bei den Herero und Ovambo).
13. 'Muhonge, denk nicht daran, dass die Herero je wieder zurückkehren werden; sie sind fertig mit Gott, und zwar überall. Die Erfüllung des Wortes ist da: der Abfall wird gross werden.' Another one said:

    Ihr Lehrer seid schuld daran, dass wir heute erledigt sind; nicht nur besitzlos habt ihr uns gemacht, sondern auch rechtlos. Für uns ist Gottes Wort ein Unglück gewesen. Früher waren wir die Besitzenden, und heute sind's die Weissen. Wem gehört jetzt das land, und wo sind die grossen Herden, die unsere Väter einst besaßen? So ist es überall gewesen, wo Gottes Wort hingekommen, von Südafrika bis hin nach Togo. Wären doch unsere Väter nie Christen geworden, es stände heute anders um uns. (VEMA 2533 b. Meier, Windhoek, 28 January 1924, Jahresbericht der Herero Gemeinde)

14. In the early years after the First World War, unskilled Afrikaners were increasingly marginalized in South African society, creating what became known as the 'poor white' problem. The discontent felt by these people came to the fore in the Rand Revolt of 1922, as well as the election of Herzog as prime minister of South Africa in 1924. Those seeking an introudction to the South African 'poor white' problem are advised to see Vincent (2000).
15. The effective 'proletarianization' of the Herero by the German military meant that the Herero had more in common, in terms of experience, with the urban blacks of continental America than with most Africans elsewhere in Africa. As a result the message of the UNIA found a ready reception amongst them.
16. The *Otruppe* was a movement that came to be established predominantly among Herero-speakers in central Namibia in 1915. A substantial literature has been written on this topic, of which the most imporant is Werner (1990).
17. NAN, SWAA 432, Truppenspieler 1917–1918, Vol. 1.
18. NAN, SWAA 432, enclosure 11, circular telegram 1/7/16.
19. NAN, SWAA 432, enclosure 4, telegram 5/5/17.
20. For a critical overview of these informants, see Irle (1917) and Lau (1995).
21. This description, written in the much maligned ethnographic present, is based on the author's personal observation and participation in these commemorations on and off between 1977 and 2001. Those seeking additional material are advised to refer to Hendrickson (1992).

References

Bley, H. 1971. *South West Africa under German Rule, 1894–1914*. London: Heinemann V.

Bridgman, J.M. 1981. *The Revolt of the Hereros*. Berkley: University of California Press.

Dedering, T. 1993. 'The German-Herero War of 1904: Revisionism of Genocide or Imaginary Historiography?' *Journal of Southern African Studies*, 19(1): 80–8.

Drechsler, H. 1966. *Südwestafrika unter deutscher Kolonialherrschaft : Der Kampf der Herero und Nama gegen den deutschen Imperialismus (1884–1915)*. Berlin: Akademie-Verlag.

———. 1980. *'Let Us Die Fighting': The Struggle of the Herero and Nama against German Imperialism (1884–1915)*. London: Zed Press. (Translation from German Original Published 1966)

Gewald, J.-B. 1994. 'The Great General of the Kaiser', *Botswana Notes and Records* 26: 67–76.

———. 1996. *Towards Redemption: A Socio-political History of the Herero of Namibia between 1890 and 1923*. Leiden: Research School CNWS.

———. 1998. '"*We will Go to the Jews": The Reintroduction of Circumcision, Polygamy and Ritual Mutilation, and the Redefinition of Gender Relations in Central Namibian Herero Society, 1920 – 1940*', Paper presented at the 41st Annual Meeting of the African Studies Association, Chicago, 29 October–1 November.

———. 1999. *Herero Heroes: A Socio-political History of the Herero of Namibia, 1890–1923*. Oxford: James Currey.

———. 2000. *'Thought we would be Free ...': Socio-Cultural Aspects of Herero History in Namibia, 1915–1940*. Cologne: Rüdiger Köppe Verlag.

Hahn, C.H. 1985. *Tagebücher 1837–1860: a Missionary in Nama- and Damaraland (in 5 Vols.)*. Ed. by B. Lau. Windhoek: Archives Services Division of the Department of National Education, SWA/Namibia.

Hahn, J. 1868. 'Das Land der Ovaherero', *Zeitschrift der Gesellschaft für Erdkunde zu Berlin*, 3: 194–243.

Hahn, T. 1969. 'Ein Rassenkampf im nordwestlichen Theile der Cap-Region', *Globus* 14: 270–71.

Hahn, C.H.L., H. Vedder and L. Fourie. 1928. *The Native Tribes of South West Africa*. Cape Town: Cape Times for the Administration of South West Africa.

Hendrickson, H. 1992. 'Historical Idioms of Identity: Representation among the Ovaherero in Southern Africa', Ph.D. thesis. New York: New York University.

Hexham, I. 1980. 'Dutch Calvinism and the Development of Afrikaner Nationalism', *African Affairs* 79(315): 195–208.

Hillebrecht, W. 1992. 'Habe keinerlei Papiere in Deiner Kiste ...', *WerkstattGeschichte* 1: 57–8.

Irle, J. 1917. 'Die Religion der Herero', *Sonderabdruck aus dem Archiv für Anthropologie Neue Folge* 15: 337–67.

Kinahan, J. 1989. 'Heinrich Vedder's Sources for his Account of the Exploration of the Namib Coast, *Cimbebasia* 11: 33–39.

Krüger, G. 1994. *'"He Has Come. He Is Going. The Sun": Aspekte von Kriegsbewältigung, Identität und Rekonstruktion in der Hererogesellschaft'*. Paper presented at the University of Hanover, 14 November.

———. 1995. *'"(...) so schicke uns jemanden mit einem Brief von Dir." Alltagsgeschichtliche Quellen zur Nachkriegszeit des Deutsch-Hererokriegs 1904–1907'*. Working paper no. 1, presented in Basel 27 September, 'Basler Afrika Bibliographien'.

———. 1999. *Kriegsbewältigung und Geschichtsbewusstsein: Realität, Deutung und Verarbeitung des deutschen Kolonialkriegs in Namibia, 1904 bis 1907*. Kritische Studien zur Geschichtswissenschaft 133. Göttingen: Vandehoeck and Ruprecht.

Krüger, G. and D. Henrichsen. 1998. '"We have been Captives Long Enough, We Want to be Free": Land, Uniforms and Politics in the History of Herero during the Interwar Period', in P. Hayes, J. Silvester, M. Wallace and W. Hartmann (eds), *Namibia under South African Rule: Mobility and Containment 1915–1946*. Oxford: James Currey, pp. 149–74.

Kühne, H. 1979. 'Die Ausrottungsfeldzüge der "Kaiserlichen Schutztruppen in Afrika" und die sozialdemokratische Reichstagsfraktion', *Militärgeschichte* 18: 206–16.

Lau, B. 1981. '"Thank God the Germans Came": Vedder and Namibian Historiography', in *Africa Seminar Collected Papers*. Cape Town: Centre for African Studies, University of Cape Town, Vol. 2, pp. 24–53.

———. 1989. Uncertain Certainties: The Herero–German War of 1904, *Mibagus* 2: 4–8.

———. 1995. 'Johanna Gertze and Emma Hahn: Some Thoughts on the Silence of Historical Records, with Reference to Carl Hugo Hahn', in A. Heywood (ed), *History and Historiography*. Windhoek: Discourse/MSORP Publications.

Nordbruch, C. 2002. *Der Hereroaufstand 1904*. Stegen am Ammersee: Vowinckel.

———. *Völkermord an den Herero in Deutsch-Südwestafrika?: Widerlegung einer Lüge*. Tübingen: Grabert.

Nuhn, W. 1989. *Sturm über Südwest: Der Hereroaufstand von 1904; ein düsteres Kapitel der deutschen kolonialen Vergangenheit Namibias*. Koblenz: Bernard & Graefe Verlag.

Oermann, N.O. 1999. *Mission, Church and State Relations in South-West Africa under German Rule, (1884–1915)*. Stuttgart: Steiner.

Poewe, C.O. 1985. *The Namibian Herero: A History of their Psychosocial Disintegration and Survival*. Lewiston: Edwin Mellen Press.

Pool, G. 1979. *Die Herero-Opstand 1904–1907*. Cape Town: Haum.

Prein, P. 1994. 'Guns and Top Hats: African Resistance in German South West Africa, 1907–1915', *Journal of Southern African Studies* 20(1): 99–121.

Rushdie, S. 1984. *Shame*. London: Picador.

Spraul, G. 1988. 'Der "Völkermord" an den Herero', *Geschichte in Wissenschaft und Unterricht* 39: 713–39.

Steenkamp, W.P. 1922. *Are the Herero Committing Race Suicide?* [Cape Town]: [Unievolkspers].

Sudholt, G. 1975. *Die deutschen Eingeborenenpolitik in Südwestafrika: Von den Anfängen bis 1904*. Hildesheim: Olms.

Vincent, L.D. 2000. 'Bread and Honour: White Working Class Women and Afrikaner Nationalism in the 1930s', *Journal of Southern African Studies* 26(1): 61–78.

Wallace, M. 2002. *Health, Power and Politics in Windhoek, Namibia, 1915–1945*. Basel: Schlettwein Publishing.

Werner, W. 1990. '"Playing Soldiers": The Truppenspieler Movement among the Herero of Namibia, 1915 to ca. 1945', *Journal of Southern African Studies*, 16(3): 485–502.

Zimmerer, J. 2001. *Deutsche Herrschaft über Afrikaner: Staatlicher Machtsanspruch und Wirklichkeit im kolonialen Namibia*. Hamburg: Lit Verlag.

CHAPTER 5

TRAUMA, THERAPY AND RESPONSIBILITY: PSYCHOLOGY AND WAR IN CONTEMPORARY ISRAEL

Edna Lomsky-Feder and Eyal Ben-Ari

At the base of most scholarly studies of the impact of war lies a rather strong assumption about the nature of such an event. In these works, war is assumed to be a traumatic occurrence that has a host of negative and destructive implications. Given that the traumatic meaning of war is socially constructed, we seek to examine the central discourse by which this kind of meaning is created in present-day Israel. Our contention is that this traumatic–therapeutic discourse – one centring on trauma, suffering and therapy – provides a ready set of cultural models through which war and its effects are interpreted and acted upon. More specifically, we argue that this discourse 'normalizes' violent conflict in this society by sustaining and routinizing war in social life. It does so by establishing and maintaining social solidarity around war, producing and reproducing social hierarchies, and by diluting and undermining critical appraisals of war and the military.

War, Trauma and Social Construction

Violence has been the object of rather intense anthropological scrutiny in the past decade or so. The stress in much of this literature has been on its constructed nature, the symbolism within which it is embedded, and especially its destructive and traumatic effects (Nordstrom and Robben 1996; Abbink 2000: xv; Sluka 2000). In these studies violence has been linked to issues related to cultural representations and images, to the 'body' and personal experiences. Typical examples are works on the representations of suffering (Kleiman and Kleiman 1997), the experience of torture survivors in particular cases such as Sri Lanka (Daniel 1996), Indian riot victims (Das

1990) or ethnic and national identity as they are implicated in war-making (Gilsenan 1996). This academic interest is part of a global shift towards the recognition of 'trauma' as the outcome of large-scale collective violence and the introduction of a variety of proposals to deal with it. One example has been the opening of 'trauma' projects alongside those for food or health provided for civilian victims of war (Bracken and Petty 1998: 1). Arising out of an intricate relation between academia, public policy and the media, over the past two decades or so the language of trauma has become part of the vernacular and in many Western cultures has provided a model for interpreting war: '[W]hilst a mass audience may find modern warfare, waged against ordinary civilians, almost unimaginable in its scale and brutality, when the experience is translated into the everyday language of stress, anxiety and trauma, its character changes and it becomes less challenging' (Bracken and Petty 1998: 1).

It is precisely these understandings of war in psychological terms that interest us.[1] Over the past decades, the discipline of psychology has developed a host of concepts, theories and models that are used to categorize, explain and treat various victims of armed conflict. It is this kind of disciplinary discourse that has led to the establishment of a culture of trauma, as Shephard (2000: 385) explains: 'The concept of Post-Traumatic Stress Disorder created a standardized model of how victims respond to trauma… [which] made [it] possible to build bridges between the "trauma of war" and other kinds of trauma such as rape, child abuse, and civilian disasters, which were then attracting attention' (Shephard 2000: 385). In the same way, Suarez-Orozco and Robben (2000: 4) depict a historical development from 'shell shock' to 'post-traumatic stress disorder' and then to 'massive trauma' arising out of collective violence. These kinds of interpretations, again, form part of a wider set of cultural understandings. Blok (2000) has suggested that in Western societies as the means of violence have been monopolized by the state, and as society has been pacified, people have developed strong feelings about using and witnessing violence. These understandings have travelled into the academy and most of the scholarly literature sees violence as something that is problematic and that has to be either constantly controlled or bears intense implications for personal and collective crises and distress. Thus violence has come to be seen as anomalous, irrational, senseless and disruptive – as the reverse of social order, as the antithesis of 'civilization' (Blok 2000: 23). Along the same lines, the overwhelming stress in much scholarly understanding of war has been on its negative or destructive implications. Thus, for instance, in the past two decades, it has come to be generally assumed that the term PTSD captures 'the fundamental psychological disturbance after any particular type of trauma/extreme event' (Bracken and Petty 1998: 4).

However, a number of studies have also recently appeared examining and critiquing the social and cultural processes by which 'trauma' has taken up such a central place in the understanding of collective violence and armed conflict. The primary focus has been on how trauma is basically a Western concept, which is based on strong, culturally embedded, psychological assumptions. Thus Bracken (1998), following scholars such as Gaines (1992), points out that because psychiatry is a Western discipline, such notions as PTSD derive from a particular cultural understanding of suffering. Consequently, he suggests, relevance to non-Western communities is very limited. Similarly Peters and Richards (1998) point out that assuming that every child who goes through war is traumatized is too simplistic. Another set of critiques have been spearheaded by such scholars as Allen Young (1997) who talks about how PTSD is a political concept that is historically situated. He shows how, from being understood in bodily terms, the concept of trauma was widened to cover the psychological outcomes of highly distressing experiences. In the context of the treatment of Vietnam veterans in the United States, he shows how the spread of understandings of PTSD was caught up with the veterans' interest in getting specialized help free of charge (in Chester 1999).

It is within this broad series of studies that explore the cultural associations between trauma, suffering and violence that our analysis should be seen. At its beginnings, the discourse on war as trauma or traumatic contained critical elements that focused on the moral foundations of acts in war (Eisenhart 1975; Shatan 1977). In Israel too, this discourse has often dealt with the traumatic aspects of war and has emphasized private suffering and pain, rather than collective mourning (Bilu and Witztum 2000). Indeed, the very existence of voices expressing pain and anguish is evidence of a critical element that subverts the idea that war is necessary and therefore 'natural'. We do not deny these elements, and without doubt they offer a base from which much protest in Israel has drawn its power, especially during the Israel Defence Force's (IDF) debacle in Lebanon (1982–85) and the first Intifada (1987–92).

We, however, take the discussion in a different direction to show another side of this discourse – one that we think is growing stronger – its normalizing variants. In another essay (Lomsky-Feder and Ben-Ari n.d.) we have attempted to provide a broad overview of the variety of psychological discourses found in contemporary Israel, and the way in which they relate to war and compulsory military service. In this chapter we focus on one such discourse: the traumatic-therapeutic one.[2]

Our Sources

The Palestinian–Israeli conflict has a long history and is part of the wider Arab–Israeli conflicts that have been going on in one way or another for over a hundred years (for an excellent overview see Jean-Klein, this volume). Indeed, since its establishment in 1948, Israel has been involved in nine major conflicts[3] and numerous other kinds of attacks and reprisals (see, Gilbert 1993; Pappe 1999; Bregman 2002 for good overviews). The present conflict, sometimes called the Second or Al-Aqsa Intifada began in September 2000. It represents the latest round of conflicts and struggles, and forms the immediate background to our analysis since it represents a change in the scale of terror attacks and civilian victims. Yet our argument is wider both in terms of Israel as a case study and in terms of the more general relations between psychological discourses and armed conflict, especially as they appear in Western countries.

Because we focus on public debates and discussions, we have deliberately chosen to utilize a rather eclectic set of sources as our data: daily, weekly and monthly news reports, articles in magazines, television programmes, academic studies, advertisements and blurbs, professional books and handbooks, popular novels about military service, and some interviews and observations gleaned from scholarly texts. It is only on the basis of this kind of variety that we can get an idea of the popularity and pervasiveness of the psychological discourses we have set out to explore. The rationale for this kind of eclecticism follows from Ehrenhaus's (1993) contention that psychological discourses appear as fragments and rarely as fully formulated and internally consistent texts. Psychology's various shapes as an academic discipline, a healing industry, a class ideology, a form of popular entertainment (movies, books and dramas) and a repository of ideas about and metaphors of the emotions (Schnog 1997: 4; see also Illuz 1997) suggest that we need to be sensitive to the multiplicity of sites where it appears.

Social Hierarchies and Trauma

We argue that, while ostensibly a private, an individual syndrome, trauma figures prominently in the creation of social hierarchies and boundaries around groups. In every war, soldiers return home after having undergone testing experiences. In many cases they continue to suffer painful memories. In more recent times, casualties of various kinds of terror attacks have been added to the ranks of people suffering from such anguish and grief. Sociologically speaking, however, it is social definitions that govern the extent to which the voices of such individuals will be heard and the ways in which they will be construed. Distressing recollections can only be expressed by those people who have received social sanction to do so. This point is especially apparent in situations that are socially perceived as critical for the community. In her book on the life stories of veterans of the war in 1973, Lomsky-Feder (1998, 2001) explores these patterns in Israel. These ex-soldiers' stories reflect how the period after the war was characterized by a lack of social consent to express traumatic memories. The social imperative voiced at the time was to continue their lives after the war as if it had not occurred. The underlying view, at the time, was that there is a clear link between the way one performed in the war and its effect on one's life. According to this ethos, combat soldiers are expected to cope and perform properly during the war and in its aftermath. Moreover, in the Israeli case, and perhaps in others, there is no difference here between individuals who volunteer to fight (that is, professionals) and those people who are conscripted.

Indeed, a breakdown in social and individual functioning, whether during the armed conflict or at its end, implied lack of control over one's very self. It is this same attitude that lay at the base of how 'battle reactions' were understood at the time. Until the 1970s such conditions were stifled both by the Israeli military authorities and by other institutions, such as the Ministry of Defence. Since the Yom Kippur war of 1973 ex-soldiers suffering from such reactions have become much more noticeable in public, and new treatment programmes have been instituted for them within and outside the army (Moses et al. 1976). Indeed, it is only recently that they have been acknowledged as requiring arrangements similar to those awarded to the physically wounded (Barzilai 1998). But at times people suffering from battle reactions are still treated in rather unsympathetic terms by members of parliament and senior military commanders. Because of the cultural assumption about how deficient performance in war is related to lack of functioning in everyday life, these people not only have often become an 'anti-model' for behaviour in war, but symbolize in a negative manner the norm that one should return to life after war as if it did not occur.

Yet there is an added complexity in this situation. It is these war veterans who have the 'right' to voice criticism of war and of military service. In reality, the right to express a sense of personal calamity and criticism is acceptable precisely because these soldiers have met the decisive national plea for personal sacrifice. Moreover, these men may voice their personal pain and social critique precisely because they do not fundamentally challenge the essence of the fighter's ethos – the hegemonic masculinity. In fact, only those who have epitomized the ethos, who have proven control over their body and emotions during the war and, at times, those individuals who have been severely wounded, are entitled to be affected by the war. These men may therefore allow the war to infiltrate their lives without questioning the ethos on a social level and without threatening their self-image as males. This connection between participation in combat and traumatic experiences is also found in a variety of sites of popular culture, such as literature and the cinema, or in the popular press (Meidan 1998; Ronen, 1998; Argeman-Barnea 2000; Tsvi 2000; Blau 2001). What is important to note is that even if such people are disparaging about war, they always derive their licence to voice criticism from their actual mobilization into combat roles.

Indeed, these soldiers do not threaten the ethos of the warrior, but rather reproduce it. In the national discourse, their stories are symbols of the war and can be regarded as a type of 'living monument' in its commemoration (Shamgar-Handelman 1986). Their stories actually allow other ex-soldiers to displace the war from their private lives. Through these stories, other soldiers channel the traumatic and critical elements in the memory of this specific war to the public sphere, and thus can adhere to the normalized meaning of war in Israeli society. In this way, the very soldiers who express the other voice – the voice that presents the war in a critical tone as a crisis – paradoxically reinforce society's demand to normalize the war. Via their deep affinity with the fighting ethos, their memories are linked to the hegemonic ideology and its basic premises about nation, war and citizens.

This point has wider import because the intense cultural fixation on the experience of combat soldiers, who are always a distinct minority of any armed force, underlies the 'naturalization' of war in present-day Israeli society. Moving narratives of battles or hostilities may ironically allow people who have not participated in them to ventilate their emotions and in that manner to erase war from their lives. This situation occurs because emotional expressions seldom lead to any intensive enquiry about the implication of being perpetrators or victims of violence. This cathartic function is best seen around such events as Remembrance Day or anniversaries of various wars. There are many newspaper articles and television and radio programmes stressing the pain and suffering brought about by war. The intense debates with regard to the price of war that take place during such occasions channel the pain, anger and protest to the collective arena and thus allow individuals to undergo a process of catharsis (to feel 'purified') and to thus continue their lives as if war does not have an impact on it. It does not really matter if public discussions stress the awe-inspiring or repulsive aspects of warfare, since the very preoccupation with war in so many arenas and in an everyday manner brings about a situation in which the collective arena appropriates the right to come to grips with war from the private arena.

'Everyone Traumatized': Therapy and the Ordinariness of Violence

As in many armed forces around the world, so within the IDF one finds research and therapeutic techniques centred on 'combat reactions' and its closely related synonyms, such as 'shell shock', 'battle fatigue' 'or functional debilitation' (Gabriel 1987: 48, 74; Shalit 1988: 103). The basic stance in these studies and therapies is recuperative and restorative, that is, of returning soldiers to active duty as quickly as possible after they have been harmed (Moses et al. 1976; Greenbaum et al. 1977). Along with wider developments in the helping professions around the world, in Israel the same kind of reasoning is now applied to anyone who has been affected by armed conflict. One instance is a special issue of *Psychologia* (1994), the journal published by the Israeli Psychologists Association and the departments of psychology at Israeli universities. This special issue is devoted to the first Gulf War[4] and includes studies that deal with the effect of this war on different parts of the population and the kinds of treatments offered them. The common base of the different studies involves the traumatic–therapeutic perspective, which in principle, is applied everywhere in the world. What is important, however, is that the universalistic assumptions about war as a crisis are so strong that they conceal the fact that war and its meanings are contextual phenomena that are socially constructed (Young 1996). Thus, paradoxically, through the pathologization of war, the traumatic discourse establishes its hold on daily life. In other words, this period signalled the transition from an understanding of war as somehow necessary and 'natural' to an understanding of it as bringing about serious psychological illnesses and costs. While no doubt related to the fear of chemical warfare that characterized this period, this transition is related to wider developments encompassing the psychologization and pathologization of war around the world. What is significant, however, is that since the first Gulf War this discourse has been gradually generalized and 'civilianized' to apply to all Israelis (mainly Jewish but including, at times, Palestinian citizens of Israel). In one such instance which is an excerpt from a volume about children in emergency and stressful conditions, the editors (Klingman et al. 2000: 375) describe the reality of Israel: 'We live in difficult and confusing times, under the constant threat of crisis and tragedy – and this theme takes on many forms … everyone is perforce a victim.'

The process of gradual traumatization of the whole society has become much stronger since the beginning of the recent Al-Aqsa Intifada. Convinced that this latest conflict is influencing the mental health of the city's residents, the new director of Jerusalem's psychiatric hospitals suggests setting up communal emergency rooms, a psychiatric ambulance and new mental health centres in the city's suburbs (Even 2001). Another case is that of 'Natal' – the Centre for Mental Support in Situations of Pressure and Trauma Deriving from a National Setting – whose aim is furnishing support, not only to soldiers suffering from battle shock but to anyone who has been harmed by a trauma resulting from a national conflict (Natal 2001). The centre caters for anyone suffering the consequences of 'the trauma of the Arab–Israeli conflict: terror attacks, bereavement, battle shock, returning POWs [from Israel's various wars], second generation to the trauma, residents of settlements on the line of conflict, parents of combat soldiers and others' (Argeman-Barnea 2000). Set up in 1998, the centre has taken on national prominence since the beginning of the Al-Aqsa Intifada. On Memorial Day it published a bulletin in which the chairperson observed that the centre:

> [g]rew out of a real need of many in the Israeli public to grapple with the moral crisis that we are now part of. The process of deterioration of the binding frame that unites Israeli society weakens the emotional strength of the society and its ability to grapple with situations of pressure and trauma … A preoccupation with themes such as people suffering from battle reaction, their families, and a second generation of such people, and the general subject of trauma following from national conflict, are slowly entering public awareness. (Natal 2001)

The centre also holds various seminars for people who suffer from battle shock and terror attacks, and carries out fund-raising activities such as a concert with the Israeli Philharmonic Orchestra (Argeman-Barnea 2000).

Similarly, new 'mental health hotlines' for the general population have been established around the country. One example is provided by the lines established and operated by the main medical institutions under the direction of the Ministry of Health and operated whenever there is a disaster (Rosenblum 2002). Another case is a telephone centre for parents of male and female soldiers who are in distress (*Ha'aretz*, 17 January 1997). Staffed by volunteer mental health professionals (many of whom were mental health officers in the IDF), the centre received thousands of calls during its first year of operation. A clinical psychologist working at the centre explains: 'We direct [people] about how to act and who to turn to. We work primarily as a support group for the soldier and his parents.' The emphasis, as the founders of the hotline insist, is not to go against the military but rather to help it: by treating the soldiers in distress they are helping the IDF. Their language is suffused with terms such as 'abuse' of soldiers, 'distress', 'suicide', 'sexual harassment', and then again 'treatment' (*tipul*), 'support' (*tmicha*) and 'facilitate' (*ezra*). Another example is a website (http://construct.haifa.ac.il/~azy/counseling.htm) established by the Israeli Institute for the Treatment and Study of Stress, which specializes in 'stress and trauma' (Maytal 2002). Not surprisingly, this institution is modelled on the American National Center for PTSD (http://www.ncptsd.org/facts). In addition to these endeavours, the IDF ombudsman also deals with psychological issues (Chen 1999).

In a related manner, traumatic discourse has entered the everyday lives of Israelis. As a Jewish settler from the U.S. living in Hebron told the journalist Robert Friedman (2001): 'Most of the people [settlers] in the West Bank are suffering from what we in America knew or learned was called post-traumatic stress syndrome … It happens when a population is under constant threat or constant pressure.' Notice how this man applies a term for a syndrome developed with regard to individuals to whole populations. Similarly, Halevi (2002) contends that, in the wake of terror attacks on Israel, 'a whole society [is] in the early stages of shell shock'. These developments are related, at one level, to the changing nature of violent conflicts, in which terror attacks have blurred the conventional distinction between the 'front' and the 'rear'. From the perspective of our analysis, the general point, as Nolan (1998: 9; see also Bracken 1998: 38) suggests, is that as 'the therapeutic perspective has spilled into the culture more broadly, so has the belief that a growing number of human actions represent diseases or illnesses that need to be healed'. What is important here is that war and armed conflict are seen to breed ailments that must and can be treated through psychological methods.

In like manner, psychologists have turned into central experts who are invited to discuss the 'national social situation'. The process began during the first Gulf War (Bilu 1995) and has clearly been continuing since the beginning of the second Intifada. For example, during a workshop held by the Israel Teachers Association on 'The Military Conflict and the National Resiliency', apart from two politicians, two psychologists were invited to present their professional views on the situation (*Ha'aretz*, 16 June 2001). More widely, as Allen Young observes in an interview (Chester 1999), this kind of understanding of trauma as developed in America was later adopted by many organizations, states and movements out of a wish to emulate the Americans and their 'advanced' medical establishment.

This routinization of the psychological perspective into cultural discourse is also articulated in academic studies that adopt psychological models that have been developed with regard to individuals to describe the national situation and social developments. One case is the work of Malkinson and Witztum (1996), which explores processes of national mourning with theories developed with regard to individual mourning. Another instance is a book published by the psychologist Dan Bar-On, which is described by a journalist thus: 'the profile of Israeliness is sketched through the prism of the traumas that Israelis have undergone – from the shadow of the Holocaust, through the wars, and to the peace process' (Rotem 2000). Yet another case is that of the head of Tel Aviv University's psychiatry department, who is asked by a journalist to comment about the national situation and provides an answer centring on collective grappling with mourning and the price paid for the conflict with the Palestinians (Ringel-Hoffman 2002).

In this manner, the very fact that so many people and groups are held to be 'traumatized' trivializes both the word and the experience. From being a phenomenon that is somehow unique to certain individuals or groups, trauma has now come to be a general concept that characterizes a whole, a public. In this context, even the physicians working in hospital admissions rooms have begun to seek psychological support. The words of a middle-aged man interviewed by Lomsky-Feder epitomise the trivialisation of the concept of trauma (1998: 122): 'I am sorry, but we are all shell-shocked. There is no one that it has not affected in one way or another. But it doesn't matter, just as anyone who becomes a father is birth-shocked.' This man turns everyone into shell-shocked persons and the very use of a term borrowed from a 'natural' process indicates how banal war has become.

Distress and the Emotional Strength of the Population

Another central site into which psychological-traumatic terms have entered is that of collective mourning. Whereas in the past the culture of bereavement focused on soldiers as heroes and stories of bravery were prominently narrated, in the past twenty or so years, the bereaved, grieving family has become the centre of attention. Pictures of victims, weeping soldiers and stunned or screaming family members accompany military-related events and are displayed in the media. Individual family members – say, relatives of a soldier who has been killed – are often depicted struggling, undergoing pain and being critical. Here again, through accounts of suffering and anguish, war and armed conflict continue to be at the centre of public attention (Rosenthal 2001). While there may be differences between groups of Israeli Jews in terms of who is allowed to weep and how, to the best of our knowledge, no systematic studies of this point have been carried out. What does seem to be important, however, is that the media regularly depict a very large variety of soldiers and family members who are openly emotional at the gravesides of kin, friends and comrades.

Indeed, this relatively new pattern in which the vulnerability of (Jewish) Israelis has become a central concern for social commentators began with the infantilization of soldiers in many discussions about the IDF. If in the past the image of the soldier was of an adult, a grown-up person who has taken on social responsibility, now the governing imagery is that of the soldier as a child, a youngster who is dependent and vulnerable. 'Honey, The Soldiers Have Shrunk' warns Doron Rosenblum (1994), a publicist with a biting sense of humour, in the title of a newspaper item dealing with this issue. Two recent autobiographical volumes (Neumann 2001; Spivak 2001) that portray military service as characterized by suffering, crisis and depression were described in a television programme as a 'documentation of trauma' (Bar-El 2001). While, at one level, such depictions suggest a critique of the masculine portraits of Israeli soldiers, they also help to express and define the growing importance of psychological and therapeutic models in dealing with situations of pressure and crisis and of the greater involvement of parents in the army (itself an outgrowth of the fact that that majority of parents of soldiers in contemporary Israel have served in the military). During a helicopter accident in which tens of troops died on their way to deployment in southern Lebanon, fathers and mothers complained that commanders did not allow psychologists into the units where soldiers were killed so as to aid their sons in grappling with the tragedy (Zohar 1997). The moral strength of the soldiers is no longer the main question but rather their emotional health. Kalman Binyamini, one of the founding fathers of educational psychology in Israel, reacted to this situation in which soldiers weep at times of bereavement and loss of their comrades:

> During the Yom Kippur War [1973] we sat, a few psychologists, with the units in Egypt. There were guys there who were paralyzed; couldn't function; and we helped them to cry but that was after the action. There is a difference between that and the attempt to see the soldiers as children, as kindergarten children. Today soldiers are allowed to complain, they are spoilt enough, with the constant accompaniment of their parents ... When soldiers are allowed to cry, then I have a problem. (Katzman 1991)

Indeed, the issue of whether soldiers should be allowed to cry in public has become a subject of intense public debate (*Ma'ariv*, 15 September 1997;

Becker 2000). A recent article in the official journal of the IDF – *Bamahane* – solicited opinions from military commanders, social commentators and members of the helping professions in this regard. In this debate different interpretations of soldiering and manhood compete, as one military correspondent in rather cynical terms describes: 'The stress on "hitting at them" and "we'll break their bones" is now replaced by weeping … Spartan emotionality is transformed into exaggerated [emotional] expressions' (Becker 2000). Binyamini, who is wary of the weeping of soldiers, is very much the exception among his psychologist colleagues and among them the mental health officers within the military. In his article, a former head of the military's mental health department 'explains how the IDF has turned from a body that automatically spits out weak people into an organization that extends its hand and gives legitimacy to tears' (Eilon 2001). More generally, psychologists encourage soldiers to unburden themselves of negative emotions, caution against the dangers of obstructing them, and warn about the severe problems of functioning faced by people who do not cry as soldiers and as civilians (Lieblich 1979: 17; Zohar 1997). To be sure, the distinction between soldiers and civilians is not always clear-cut for many Israeli Jewish men (who often serve in the reserves for long periods of their lives), but there is a strong cultural assumption at the base of such arguments that there is a carry-over effect between the two realms.

Indeed, every once in a while when a crime is committed, there is reference to the trauma that the perpetrators underwent in the military. One case involved a man who was prosecuted for the murder of a tourist from England and the wounding of his girlfriend. In his defence he argued that he was suffering from post-trauma that he incurred during his military service (involving the killing of a terrorist) and that on the basis of this argument he was recognized by the army as handicapped (Harel 2000). In ways similar to the reasoning with regard to some Vietnam veterans, traumatic aspects of war are invoked as excuses in order to turn criminal acts into various kinds of (individual) psychological problems.[5] Along these lines, a clinical psychologist (Ofir-Shacham 1999), providing a general overview of traumatized veterans, states that 'people who have been mentally injured in war often experience intense anger and they may not control their urge to express it'. The problem with this kind of reasoning is that, along with the focus on suffering, the perpetrators of violence are absolved of moral responsibility.[6]

Suffering, Liability and the Critique of War

The reaction of the IDF to Tsipora Melet, a mother who criticized the army when her son was killed in a game of Russian roulette, is indicative of another dimension of the psychologization of debates about the armed forces (Rosenthal 2001: 98). In this case, her son, who was a conscript at the time, played the game with his friends without any apparent control or intervention on the part of his commanders. The IDF attempted to silence her criticism by turning her into a 'crazy person' (*meshuga'at*), attributed to the intensity of her bereavement. Indeed, the fact that she committed suicide on her son's grave only strengthened the allegation that it was mental instability that lay at bottom of her harsh criticism of the IDF. Such psychological reasoning, and especially terms that turn people into passive victims of circumstances, and thus negating their agency, are often mobilized by defenders of the IDF in order to defuse critical stances towards the military and its various actions. Weiss (1997) provides an account of two artists who mounted exhibitions highly critical of the IDF. Unlike combat soldiers, these two artists based their 'right' to be critical on the fact that they were members of bereaved families. What is more noteworthy, however, is the reaction to an exhibition that one bereaved father published in the Bulletin of the Association of Bereaved Families. His conclusion was that more attention should be paid to the orphans of wars (which the artist was) and that they should be monitored psychologically (Weiss 1997: 97). By using a psychological discourse this man attempted to 'neuter' the core of the criticism. He did this by interpreting the artistic appraisal as an expression of trauma, as a non-normative, non-normal reaction of an orphan, and thus as an expression of mental damage. More generally, a number of the IDF's military commanders have labelled bereaved parents critical of the Israeli military 'crazies' (*metoraphim*) (Rosenthal 2001: 108).

These processes are similar to the manner in which the 'therapeutic motif' has contained and co-opted Vietnam veterans in America as a voice of political opposition. This motif:

> renders veterans harmless by casting them in terms of metaphors of psychological dysfunction, emotional fragility, healing and personal redemption; it effectively silences the voice of the veteran as a source of legitimate knowledge about the nature of contemporary warfare, thus subverting a potentially effective challenge to discourses advocating the use of 'legitimate' state-sanctioned violence as a tool of national policy. (Ehrenhaus 1993: 78)

By drawing attention to the suffering and sacrifice of individuals, the therapeutic motif distracts us from wider concerns about the nature of war, its use as an instrument of states and the mythic obligations that link individuals to the collective.

Because of the ongoing conflict, simultaneously with the individualization and victimization of the soldiers, there is also a move – especially during the last two Intifadas – towards the traumatization and (then) treatment of the whole of the (Jewish) population. Sentiments of victimhood and the memory of trauma are basic elements of the national identity and the creation of solidarity in Israel (Handelman and Katz, 1991; Ram, 2000). As a commentator rather scathingly describes it: 'We are the unfortunate to whom everything is owed. In the morning we were King David and in the evening

Anna Frank. This is a feature of every nationalism, the national variation of manic-depression' (Kaspi 2001). Since the 1980s, at the same time as there is an erosion of the moral standing of Israeli society in the western world, the traumatic discourse and sentiments of victimhood are growing.

One expression of this pattern at the individual level is the growing tendency – cutting across social cleavages and groups – of (Jewish) Israelis to read popular psychology books that deal with spiritual matters, anxieties and depression. According to publishers 'the Israeli reader who is stuck in a war without a solution, looks for explanations that are outside of the political arena' (Manheim 2002). The wider moral implications of these developments are echoed in the words of Binyamini, the educational psychologist quoted previously:

> For me the therapeutic culture and its scarecrows are empty. Mental health and health in general, in my eyes, are not the goal but rather means … Christopher Lasch, also a sociologist of culture, talks about 'cultural narcissism' – an immersion in yourself that lowers political and social desires and ambitions. I allow myself to say that, for Israeli society in its present geopolitical situation, and with a constant danger to its existence, I find in this attitude a lowering of its ability to stand and a weakening of its power. (Katzman 1991)

Binyamini's words confer a renewed emphasis on the demand to grapple with war, to control emotions and not to let that kind of experience hinder life. But his words also caution against Israelis receding into themselves, while disregarding their responsibility for their and other people's suffering, distress and misfortune. Moreover, the placement of the self-as-victim at the centre of attention blinds many Israeli Jews from seeing the 'other', from perceiving themselves as powerful and as occupying another people, and from grappling with the moral implications of this situation. While in the Six Day War (1967) the morality of the soldiers was up for debate, since the Lebanon war (1982–85) and especially since the 1990s the emotional strength of the Israeli soldier is the central theme in public discussions. Take the following example. After the Six Day War of 1967, the book *The Seventh Day: a Conversation with Soldiers* (Hakkibutz Hameuchad 1968) was published. The book was a best-seller and translated into a number of other languages. At the same time, however, it was criticized by both right- and left-wing commentators for taking a pseudo-moral stance towards the war and what it had done to the civilian populations of the occupied territories. In a retrospective article, attempting to explain why such a book would not appear now, one journalist wrote: 'Today they also cry. But if you listen to them closely, they cry especially for themselves. In all of the conversations with the combat soldiers… the soldiers complain about their fate, about what "this" has done to them. Few pay attention to the other' (Galili 2001). Again and again, Jewish Israelis perceive themselves to be victims whose morality is taken for granted. In an ironic manner, then, the therapeutic-traumatic discourse not only has equalized the Israeli and Palestinian cases in the eyes of many Jewish Israelis, but in fact inverts them by turning them into victims. As Nolan (1998: 15) observes more generally, because the language of victimhood is much more visible and available today, the self is not seen as the perpetrator but as the victim of a disorder.

Finally, the institutional expression of the neutering of criticism is apparent in the next case. In Israel, conscientious objectors are very rarely recognized by state authorities and released from military service (*Ha'aretz*, 22 May 1998). It was only in the late 1990s that special committees were set up granting such referrals. The most common pattern, however, is for such individuals to receive their exemption from service via a psychiatric discharge: a psychological reason is substituted for an ideological or moral one. Apparently, because the IDF is not interested in awarding discharges on moral grounds (and makes it virtually impossible to do so), it informally encourages youths to declare that they have certain psychological problems so that they can be released on the basis of lack of suitability for service (Harel 1998, 2000).

On the 'Effectiveness' of Psychological Discourses

Young (1996) suggests that psychology as a discipline has been of central importance in developing the understanding of war as a traumatic event. We go further, to contend that the therapeutic discourse on war and armed conflict is 'effective' in normalizing war because of three of its characteristics. The first is the 'scientific' nature of psychology as a field of knowledge. The 'scientific', 'objective' validity of its contentions are based on the fact that psychology is rooted in research and associated with academia. Science – often perceived as a progressive, rational, 'objective' enterprise – is used not only as a description and analysis of how certain phenomena have developed; it is also used as a legitimizing device. In this manner, it also blurs the ideological bases of its models and of the very phenomena it seeks to explain (Griffin 1993; Wexler 1996).

The second feature is the professional ethos that pervades the discipline and which implies that it has a practical side that is institutionalized in the 'helping' or 'caring' professions. Psychology is defined as a 'healing' profession, marked by recipes for action that are based on 'objective' knowledge. This profession is carried by what Nolan (1998: 7) calls the 'new priestly class' of psychiatrists, psychologists, social workers, counsellors and therapists who understand and can decipher the emotional language emanating from people. In Israel, as around the western world, members of this class have been granted a high level of prestige and social recognition for their ability to help individuals make sense of life in the modern world. As Quinn and Holland point out (1987: 9–10), in many contemporary societies, explanations of human behaviour that are devised by groups of socially designated experts – in this case psychologists – come to provide models for making choices in, and for making sense of, the everyday world.

The third element is the popularization of psychological models. Psychological models have been 'translated' into widespread folk knowledge, which is accepted as legitimate and even preferred among wide segments of society, and especially among dominant groups (Illuz 1997). This situation implies that psychological interpretations and explanations can readily be mobilized to clarify complex situations. The fact that everyday interpretations are rooted in, and often formulated with, concepts borrowed from psychology does not make them any less 'folk' interpretations. Indeed, with the popularization of science and with the spread of mass higher education, it is not surprising that scientific models are incorporated into the models people use in their everyday lives.

Conclusion

Anthropology has long dealt with various issues related to violence and its place in diverse cultures and societies. Yet, in most of these studies, violence has been analysed from one of three major perspectives. The first has been a functional one and has stressed the idea that certain activities, such as rites and ceremonies, allow the controlled displacement of aggressive impulses so as to allow the continuation of social structures and groups. Thus Girard (1977) has argued that ritual controls, channels and represses human violence so as to allow ordered social life (see also Watson 1996; Bouroncle 2000: 55). The second strand of research includes studies focused on the causes of warfare (Rubinstein 1994; Harrison 1996) and sees war as providing opportunities for mating and reproduction or competition between individuals (Chagnon 1988), or as the outcome of inter-group competition for scarce resources such as land, food or trade opportunities (Ferguson 1984). The stress in the newer literature has been on a third aspect of violence: on its constructed nature, the symbolism within which it is embedded and its destructive and traumatic effects (Nordstrom and Robben 1996; Abbink 2000: xv). Here the primary links have been made to issues related to cultural representations and images, or to the body and personal experience (Kleiman and Kleiman 1997). In all three respects, however, anthropology has contributed to relevant discussion in the documentation of how violence is pre-eminently collective rather than individual and social rather than asocial or antisocial, and how it is culturally interpreted (Riches 1986; Spencer 1996).

In our chapter, we have taken many of the insights provided by these previous studies in another direction. Most importantly, as we showed, violence does not only belong to the realm of the pathological but is woven into the very fabric of normal everyday life. Along these lines, the focus of this essay was on how the therapeutic discourse normalizes war and armed conflict in societies such as Israel. Historically speaking, we contend that the past few decades in Israel have witnessed a change in how violent conflict is understood, interpreted and acted upon. What we have called the therapeutic discourse has emerged during this period as a result of global changes such as the stress on suffering and victimhood, and more Israeli-based patterns entailing the spread of popular psychological models among the population at large. The major point from which this transformation took place was the Yom Kippur War of 1973. It was during this conflict, and especially after it, that silencing of war trauma among soldiers was ended and subsequently pathologized (in the sense of turning it into a medical and psychiatric problem). Later, during Israel's war in Lebanon (1982–85) and the first Intifada (1987–92), the traumatic discourse was considerably widened to cover soldiers who participate in combat. Here the change was expressed in debates about the emotional strength of troops rather than about the moral implications of their actions. But it was only the cumulative effect of the first Gulf War (1991) and the second Intifada (2000 to the present) that saw the 'trivialization' of trauma. This effect was the outcome of the bombing of civilian areas by Iraq during the Gulf conflict and the long series of terror attacks targeting civilians during the latter struggle. The labels of 'traumatized' or 'traumatic' were broadened to such an extent as to make them lack specific meanings. It is within this process that the turning of Israelis into victims and the consequent 'equalization' with Palestinians should be seen. This trend has been the direct result, we suggest, of the terror attacks waged against Israelis and the violence perpetrated against Palestinians. When linked to global trends stressing suffering and victimhood, this process has resulted in a sort of 'competition' over which group is more distressed and has suffered the more serious casualties.

The emergence of the therapeutic discourse, we showed, has led to three implications. First, it creates a basis for social cohesion. In a highly conflictual society such as contemporary Israel, the stress on suffering – everyone is a traumatized individual – allows the creation of social solidarity because it offers a very basic common denominator with which many people can identify. Secondly, the traumatic discourse produces and reproduces social hierarchies by allocating different groups the right and justification for voicing pain and distress. In this manner, what is created is a ranking of groups according to how they have suffered and been traumatized. While it is usually men who have been labelled as suffering from the trauma of war, it is women, children and the elderly who have entered these social hierarchies through being victims of terror attacks. The third is that through the stress on pain, bereavement and suffering, criticisms of war and armed conflict are diluted. They are diluted because the focus of discussions and debates has become one of emotional strength (especially during the last two decades or so), rather than moral justification or the effects of perpetrating violence that were prevalent up until the 1980s.

Notes

1. We follow previous scholars (Schnog 1997: 3–4; Nolan 1998) in defining the 'psychological' as encompassing the public life of the psychological disciplines (in research institutions, intellectual traditions, social policy and popular culture), as changing cultural visions of the psychological interior (as the soul, the 'real' part of selfhood) and as a set of 'common-sense' or 'folk' models for interpreting social phenomena.
2. We clearly distinguish between the traumatic discourse found in public sites and concrete cases of individuals who have been defined as suffering from trauma or post-trauma. The very existence of a discourse on people suffering from war trauma is an indicator of the traumatic effects of war, but in everyday usage the term trauma (the very same word is used in Hebrew) is most often used without reference to the specific medical syndrome. In other words, we clearly recognize that specific individuals have paid a heavy price for participating in armed conflict, but suggest that alongside this recognition there is a need to understand how psychological language and models affect the ways in which war is understood in societies such as ours.
3. These conflicts include the 1948 war, the war in 1956, the Six Day War of 1967, the war of attrition between 1970 and 1972, the Yom Kippur War of 1973, the Lebanon war between 1982 and 1985, the first Gulf War in 1991, the first Intifada between 1987 and 1992 and the ongoing second or Al-Aqsa Intifada, which began in 2000.
4. Israel's involvement in the first Gulf War was passive. During the war, over thirty Iraqi rocket-propelled bombs fell in the urban centres of Tel Aviv and Haifa and near Israel's nuclear installations in the south.
5. Within the American military, the:

   > [e]xpansion of mental health and self-help programs in military hospitals, increased treatment efforts to stem the reported growth of domestic violence among military children and their parents by army psychiatrists, and the growing presence of military psychologists to help soldiers work through stress and other war-related psychological difficulties are other indicators of the influence of the therapeutic impulse in the U.S. military. (Nolan 1998: 280)

6. As Allen Young in an interview (Chester 1999) observes, it is ironic that in 1980 the American Congress initially rejected the notion of PTSD, fearing that it would open up a can of worms in terms of possible demands for compensation. But now the American authorities welcome it in the wake of the first Gulf War since it is easier to investigate it as a medical problem rather than examine the political implications of the war or ask what in the first place caused soldiers to be traumatized.

References

Abbink, J. 2000. 'Preface: Violation and Violence as Cultural Phenomena', in G. Aijmer and J. Abbink (eds), *Meanings of Violence: A Cross Cultural Perspective*. Oxford: Berg, pp. xi–xvii.

Argeman-Barnea, A. 2000. 'The Paintings After the War', *Yediot Aharonot,* 26 March. (Hebrew)

Bar-El, T. 2001. 'Everything is Memory', *Ha'aretz*, July, 27. (Hebrew)

Barzilai, A. 1998. 'Ministry of Defense Has Formulated a New Process of Detecting Post-Traumatic Disorders among Battle-Shocked Veterans', *Ha'aretz*, 23 February. (Hebrew)

Becker, A. 2000. 'The Flag of Fear', *Ha'aretz*, 18 February. (Hebrew)

Bilu, Y. 1995. 'From Anxiety to Methodology', *Ha'aretz*, 7 November. (Hebrew)

Bilu, Y. and E. Witztum. 2000. 'Transformations in the Construction of War-Related Loss and Suffering in Israeli Society', *Israel Studies* 5 (2): 1–31.

Blau, U. 2001. 'Ministry of Defense Recognizes Mental Injuries that were Caused to Sharon's Assassination Units', *Kol Ha'ir*, 25 May. (Hebrew)

Blok, A. 2000. 'The Enigma of Sensless Violence', in G. Aijmer and J. Abbink (eds), *Meanings of Violence: A Cross Cultural Perspective*. Oxford: Berg pp. 23–38.

Bouroncle, A. 2000. 'Ritual, Violence and Social Order: an Approach to Spanish Bullfighting', in G. Aijmer and J. Abbink (eds), *Meanings of Violence: A Cross Cultural Perspective*. Oxford: Berg, pp. 55–76.

Bracken, P.J. 1998. 'Hidden Agendas: Deconstructing Post Traumatic Stress Disorder', in P.J. Bracken and C. Petty (eds), *Rethinking the Trauma of War*. London: Free Association Books, pp. 38–59.

Bracken, P.J. and C. Petty. 1998. 'Introduction', in P.J. Bracken and C. Petty (eds), *Rethinking the Trauma of War*. London: Free Association Books, pp. 1–8.

Bregman, A. 2002. *Israel's Wars: A History Since 1947*. London: Routledge.

Chagnon, N. 1988. 'Life Histories, Blood Revenge and Warfare in a Tribal Population', *Science* 239: 985–92.

Chen, Y. 1999. 'In the Name of the Son', *At*, January, 45–51. (Hebrew)

Chester, B. 1999. 'A Most Stressful Disorder', *McGill Reporter*, 4 November, 1–5.

Daniel, E.V. 1996. *Charred Lullabies: Chapters in the Anthropography of Violence*. Princeton: Princeton University Press.

Das, V. (ed). 1990. *Mirrors of Violence: Communities, Riots and Survivors in South Asia*. Delhi: Oxford University Press.

Ehrenhaus, P. 1993. 'Cultural Narratives and the Therapeutic Motif: The Political Containment of Vietnam Veterans', in K.D. Mumby (ed), *Narrative and Social Control: Critical Perspectives*. Newbury Park: Sage, pp. 77–96.

Eisenhart, R.W. 1975. You Can't Hack it Little Girl: A Discussion of the Covert Psychological Agenda of Modern Combat Training', *Journal of Social Issues* 31(4): 13–23.

Even, D. 2001. 'A Rise in Demand for Psychological Help', *Kol Hazman*, 6 July. (Hebrew)

Ferguson, R.B. (ed). 1984. *Warfare, Culture and Environment*. Orlando: Academic Press.

Friedman, R.I. 2001. 'And Darkness Covered the Land', *The Nation*, 24 December.

Gabriel, R.A. 1987. *No More Heroes: Madness and Psychiatry in War*. New York: Hill and Wang.

Gaines, A. (ed). 1992. *Ethnopsychiatry: The Cultural Construction of Professional and Folk Psychiatries*. Albany: State University of New York Press.

Galili, L. 2001. 'Today There Are Those Who Shoot and Those Who Cry', *Ha'aretz*, 27 May. (Hebrew)

Gilbert, M. 1993. *The Routledge Atlas of the Arab–Israeli Conflict*. London: Routledge.

Gilsenan, M. 1996. *Lords of the Lebanese Marches: Violence and Narrative in an Arab Society*. Berkeley: University of California Press.

Girard, R. 1977. *Violence and the Sacred*. Baltimore: Johns Hopkins Press.

Greenbaum, C.W., I. Rogovsky and B. Shalit. 1977. 'The Military Psychologist During Wartime: A Model Based on Action Research and Crisis Intervention', *Journal of Applied Behavioral Science* 13(1): 7–22.

Griffin, C. 1993. *Representation of Youth*. Cambridge: Polity Press.

Hakkibutz Hameuchad. 1968. *The Seventh Day: A Conversation with Soldiers*. Tel Aviv: Hakkibutz Hameuchad.

Halevi, Y.K. 2002. *A Society in Shell Shock – Israelis Cope with the Routinization of Terrorism*. http://207.168.91.4/vjholidays/independence/53/jta.htm.

Handelman, D. and E. Katz. 1991. 'State Ceremonies of Israel: Rememberance Day and Independence Day', in D. Handelman (ed), *Models and Mirrors: Towards an Anthropology of Public Events*. Cambridge: Cambridge University Press, pp. 191–233.

Harel, A. 1998. 'The IDF and the Pacifists – Conscience is Not Enough', *Ha'aretz*, 27 May. (Hebrew)

———. 2000. 'A New Psychological Profile will Allow Service in the Rear', *Ha'aretz*, 6 June. (Hebrew)

Harrison, S. 1996. 'War, Warfare', in A. Barnard and J. Spencer (eds), *Encyclopedia of Social and Cultural Anthropology*. London: Routledge, pp. 561–62.

Illuz, E. 1997. Who will Care for the Caretaker's Daughter? Toward a Sociology of Happiness in the Era of Reflexive Modernity. *Theory, Culture and Society* 14(4): 31–66.

Kaspi, A. 2001. 'The Time has Run Out', *Ha'aretz*, 6 August. (Hebrew)

Katzman, A. 1991. 'Let's Talk about it Some More', *Ha'aretz*, 8 March. (Hebrew)

Kleiman, A. and J. Kleiman. 1997. 'The Appeal of Experience; The Dismay of Images: Cultural Appropriations of Suffering in Our Times', in V. Das, A. Kleiman, M. Ramphele and P. Reynolds (eds), *Violence and Subjectivity*. Berkeley: University of California Press, pp. 1–23.

Klingman, A., A. Raviv and B. Stein (eds). 2000. 'Preface' to Volume 3, in *Descriptions of Treatment for Stressful Situations*. Jerusalem: Ministry of Education. (Hebrew)

Lieblich, A. 1979. *Tin Soldiers on Jerusalem Beach*. Tel Aviv: Shocken. (Hebrew)

Lomsky-Feder, E. 1998. *As If There Were No War: the Perception of War in the Life Stories of Israeli Men*. Jerusalem: Magnes. (Hebrew)

———. 2001. 'The Meanimg of War through Veterans' Eyes: a Phenomenological Analysis of Life-Stories', in D. Maman, E. Ben-Ari and Z. Rosenhek (eds), *Military, State, and Society in Israel – Essays in Honor of Moshe Lissak*. New Brunswick, London: Transaction Publishers, pp. 269–94.

Lomsky-Feder, E. and E. Ben-Ari. n.d. *The Discourses of 'Psychology' and the 'Normalization' of War in Contemporary Israel*, manuscript. Hebrew University of Jerusalem.

Malkinson, R. and E. Witztum. 1996. 'Psychological Aspects of Mourning in Historical and Literary Studies of Mourning', *Alpaim* 12: 211–36. (Hebrew)

Manheim, N. 2002. 'Enough of Arafat, We Want Psychology', *Y-Net*, 6 June. (Hebrew)

Maytal. 2002. *Israel Institute for Treatment and Study of Stress*. http://www.maytal.co.il. (Hebrew)

Meidan, A. 1998. 'As If There Were No War', *Seven Days*, 25 September. (Hebrew)

Moses, R., D. Bargal, J. Calev, A. Falk, H. HaLevi, Y. Lerner, M. Mass, S. Noy, B. Perla, M. Winokur. 1976. 'A Rear Unit for the Treatment of Combat Reactions in the Wake of the Yom Kippur War', *Psychiatry* 39: 153–62.

Natal. 2001. 'Regarding the Emotions', *Bulletin of Natal* 2 (April): 1–16. (Hebrew)

Neumann, B. 2001. *Good Soldier*. Tel Aviv: Zmora-Bitan. (Hebrew).

Nolan, J. L., Jr. 1998. *The Therapeutic State: Justifying Government at Century's End*. New York: New York University Press.

Nordstrom, C. and A.C.G.M. Robben (eds). 1996. *Fieldwork Under Fire: Contemporary Studies of Violence and Survival*. Berkeley: University of California Press.

Ofir-Shacham, O. 1999. 'Life in the Shadow of Trauma', *Yediot Aharonot*, 18 April. (Hebrew)

Pappe, I. (ed). 1999. *The Israel/Palestine Question: Rewriting Histories*. London: Routledge.

Peters, K. and P. Richards. 1998. 'Fighting with Open Eyes: Youth Combatants Talking about War in Sierra Leone', in P.J. Bracken and C. Petty (eds), *Rethinking the Trauma of War*. London: Free Association Books, pp.76–111.

Quinn, N. and D. Holland. 1987. 'Culture and Cognition', in D. Holland and N. Quinn (eds), *Cultural Models in Language and Thought*. Cambridge: Cambridge University Press, pp. 3–40.

Ram, U. 2000. 'National, Ethnic or Civic? Contesting Paradigms of Memory, Identity and Culture in Israel', *Studies in Philosophy and Education* 19: 405–22.

Riches, D. (ed). 1986. *The Anthropology of Violence*. Oxford: Blackwell.

Ringel-Hoffman, A. 2002. 'We are Still a Strong Society, But the Foundations are Shaking', *Yediot Aharonot*, 22 February. (Hebrew)

Ronen, R. 1998. 'The Time that Stood Still', *Ha'aretz (Health Supplement)*, 23 February. (Hebrew)

Rosenblum, D. 1994. 'Honey, the Soldiers Have Shrunk', *Ha'aretz*, 4 January. (Hebrew)

Rosenblum, S. 2002. 'Distress on the Phone Line', *Yediot Aharonot*, 4 April. (Hebrew)

Rosenthal, R. 2001. *Is Bereavement Dead?* Jerusalem: Keter. (Hebrew)

Rotem, T. 2000. 'The Mental Breakdown is Behind Us', *Ha'aretz*, 23 April. (Hebrew)

———. 2001. 'First the Shock of the Explosion, Then the Fear That They Will Think that I Am a Terrorist', *Ha'aretz, 29* September. (Hebrew)

Rubinstein, R.A. 1994. 'Collective Violence and Common Security', in T. Ingold (ed), *Companion Encyclopaedia of Anthropology*. London: Routledge, pp. 983–1009.

Schnog, N. 1997. 'On Inventing the Psychological', in J. Pfisher and N. Schnog (eds), *Inventing the Psychological*. New Haven: Yale University Press, pp. 3–16.

Shalit, B. 1988. *The Psychology of Conflict and Combat*. New York: Praeger.

Shamgar-Handelman, L. 1986. *Israeli War Widows: Beyond the Glory of Heroism*. London: Bergin and Garvey.

Shatan, C.F. 1977. 'Bogus Manhood, Bogus Honor: Surrender and Transfiguration in the United States Marine Corps', *Psychoanalytic Review* 64: 586–610.

Shephard, B. 2000. *A War of Nerves*. London: Jonathan Cape.

Sluka, J. 2000. 'Introduction: State Terror and Anthropology', in J.A. Sluka (ed), *Death Squad: The Anthropology of State Terror*. Philadelphia: University of Pennsylvania Press, pp. 1–45.

Spencer, J. 1996. 'Violence', in A. Barnard and J. Spencer (eds), *Encyclopedia of Social and Cultural Anthropology*. London: Routledge, pp. 559–60.

Spivak, O. 2001. *Whose Golani?*. Jerusalem: Scena. (Hebrew)

Suarez-Orozco, M.M. and A.C.G.M. Robben. 2000. 'Interdisciplinary Perspectives on Violence and Trauma', in A.C.G.M. Robben and M.M. Suarez-Orozco (eds), *Cultures Under Siege: Collective Violence and Trauma*. Cambridge: Cambridge University Press, pp. 1–41.

Tsvi, A. 2000. Good To Live For Our Country. *Iton Yerushalaim* 28 Jul: 52–3. (Hebrew)

Watson, J.L. 1996. 'Fighting With Operas: Processionals, Politics and the Spectre of Violence in Rural Hong Kong', in D. Parkin, L. Caplan and H. Fisher (eds), *The Politics of Cultural Performance*. Oxford: Berghahn, pp. 145–60.

Weiss, M. 1997. 'Bereavement, Commemoration, and Collective Identity in Contemporary Israeli Society', *Anthropological Quarterly* 70(2): 91–101.

Wexler, P. 1996. *Critical Social Psychology*. New York: Peter Lang.

Young, A. 1996. 'Bodily Memory and Traumatic Memory', in P. Antze and M. Lambek (eds), *Tense Past: Cultural Essays in Trauma and Memory*. New York: Routledge, pp. 89–702.

———.1997. *The Harmony of Illusions: Inventing Post-Traumatic Stress Disorder*. Princeton: Princeton University Press.

Zohar, G. 1997. 'Your Commander is Your Mental Health Officer', *Ha'aretz*, 14 February (Hebrew).

CHAPTER 6

'I SHALL BE WAITING FOR YOU AT THE DOOR OF PARADISE': THE PAKISTANI MARTYRS OF THE LASHKAR-E TAIBA (ARMY OF THE PURE)

Mariam Abou Zahab

> Islamic history is not written, except with the stories of the Shuhada – and with the blood of the Shuhada.
> (Sheikh Abdullah Azzam)

From the 1990s onwards, there has been a transformation in the discourse of the liberation struggle in Kashmir (Sikand 2001a). The early movement, which started in the 1930s and grew after Partition in the aftermath of the first war between India and Pakistan in 1948 over Kashmir, saw itself as a nationalist struggle for an independent state (Racine 2002). The main demand was that India should fulfil its commitment to the United Nations and allow a plebiscite, to enable the Kashmiri people to decide their own political future. These Kashmiri nationalists advocated a secular, democratic Jammu and Kashmir (Zutshi 2004). Their ideology, *Kashmiriyat* (Puri 1995), is an amalgam of both Hindu and Muslim traditions, specific to the Valley of Kashmir, and is characterized by a tolerant Sufi tradition (Sikand 2001b). The main movement was the Jammu and Kashmir Liberation Front (JKLF), established in the mid-1960s in Birmingham, England (see also Rao et al., note 21, this volume). But, from the early 1990s, there was a growing intervention in Kashmir of Islamist groups based in Pakistan, who tend to see the struggle in Kashmir, not only as a jihad between the Muslims of Kashmir and the Indian state, but as a holy war between the Muslims of the world and the Hindus in league with other enemies of Islam, namely the Jews and the Christian West. The nationalist goal of a free Kashmir has thus been marginalized in favour of the Islamist agenda of incorporating Kashmir into

Pakistan and establishing an Islamic state as a prelude to a wider project of reconquering India.[1]

The Islamic revolution in Iran, followed by the largely Western-funded jihad in Afghanistan against communist and Soviet rule, turned Pakistan into a front-line state, which became the staging ground of jihad as an international movement – what Eqbal Ahmed (1998) called Jihad International Incorporated – in whose founding Pakistan, Saudi Arabia and the United States of America played the leading role. Large sums of money and arms poured into Pakistan, mainly from the U.S. and Saudi Arabia. Pakistani Islamic parties were drawn into the jihad and set up or sponsored their own militant wings. There was a mushrooming of religious schools (*madrasahs*), often with sectarian affiliations, patronized by the then President of Pakistan General Zia ul Haq and the Saudis, which trained their students for jihad. The spread of the 'Kalashnikov culture' in Pakistan is one consequence of these factors. Internal conflicts in Pakistan, which had primarily been ethnic (e.g., Baluchistan), now took sectarian forms (e.g., Sunni versus Shia, Deobandi versus Barelvi).[2]

Pakistan's Kashmir policy was also affected in the wake of the armed uprising in Kashmir in 1989. Pakistan first supported the JKLF, but soon realized that the latter's agenda of an independent, democratic and secular Kashmir was a threat to Pakistan's strategic interests and self-image as the state representing all South Asian Muslims. From the early 1990s, therefore, Pakistan, or rather its main agency in charge of external intelligence, the Inter Services Intelligence (ISI), started patronizing radical Islamists who had emerged during the Afghan jihad and began participating in the Kashmiri jihad after the Soviet withdrawal from Afghanistan in 1989 (Sikand 2001b). By 2000, nearly all the militant groups active in Kashmir were Pakistan-based or pro-Pakistan – notably the Hizb ul Mujahidin, linked to the Jama'at-e Islami of Jammu and Kashmir (see Sikand 2002; see also Rao et al., note 22, this volume) – and the JKLF was keeping a low profile. These militant groups act as proxies of the Pakistani government, which uses them to wage a low-intensity conflict against India. Although a kind of privatization of jihad has occurred, the groups who claim to be autonomous of the Pakistani state are still very dependent on it. There is a symbolic Kashmiri presence in their leadership, most of the fighters being Pakistani – and more precisely Punjabi, although the ethnic composition is changing because, since 2003, to spread its message the movement is mainly focusing on Baluchistan and Sind (Jamal 2003) – with a small number of Arabs and Afghans. The unwillingness of Kashmiri militants to target Kashmiri Hindus so as to reduce the Hindu population in Kashmir has also been a factor in the promotion of Pakistani-based groups.

The Markaz Daawat wal Irshad (MDI)

Among the jihadi groups, the most influential is the Lashkar-e Taiba (LeT, the Army of the Pure), which is the military wing of the Markaz Daawat wal Irshad (Centre for Preaching and Guidance).[3] It was set up in 1986 by three Pakistani university professors of the department of Islamic studies of the Lahore Engineering University – Hafiz Mohammad Saeed,[4] Dr Zafar Iqbal (nom de guerre Abu Hamza) and Hafiz Abdul Rehman Makki (Hafiz Mohammad Saeed's nephew), all linked to Saudi ulemas and to Medina Islamic University – and by Sheikh Abdullah Azzam, a Palestinian from the Jenin refugee camp (see Kirchner, this volume), linked to the Muslim Brotherhood (Ikhwan al-Muslimin), who was the ideologue of the Afghan jihad and in those days associated with Maktab ul Khidamat (Bureau of Services for Arab jihadis) in Peshawar and with the International Islamic University in Islamabad.[5] The Markaz's headquarters is located in Muridke, thirty kilometres from Lahore. It is a big, two-hundred-acre complex, allegedly donated by the government of Zia ul Haq, with schools, a farm and factories, and is meant to be a pure city (*Medina al Taiba*) in a purely Islamic environment. The Markaz is affiliated to the *Ahl-e Hadith*[6] or *Salafi* school of Islamic thought, and in the beginning received considerable Arab funds,[7] including some from Osama bin Laden, who also sent them telephonic messages from Sudan and later Afghanistan for several of their general meetings. It is also funded by the large Pakistani diaspora in Europe – mostly in Britain, France and the Netherlands – and in the Middle East, and collects donations in Pakistan (for details see Rana 2002: 243).

The Daawat wal Irshad movement can be described as '*Salafi*-jihadi', in that it has two proclaimed aims to which it accords equal importance: *daawat* (preaching) and jihad, which have a symbiotic relationship and cannot be separated. Hafiz Saeed sees a complementarity between jihad and education. The characteristic of the Markaz is to integrate *daawat* with jihad and to advocate that modern education is not in conflict with religious education. But, without military training, education is meaningless because 'when the Muslims gave up *jihad*, science and technology also went into the hands of others'.[8] For Hafiz Saeed, the main problem facing Muslims as a whole is their subjugation to the West; jihad is thus a means of challenging oppression and establishing the rule of Islam.[9] Contrary to the other *Ahl-e Hadith* movements of Pakistan, who consider jihad as collective duty (*fard kifaya*), the Dawaat wal Irshad considers jihad as individual duty (*fard-e ain*).

Apart from jihad, Daawat wal Irshad wants to purify Pakistani society in particular and Muslim societies in general and purge South Asian Islam of 'Hindu' influences. They also denounce Sufism, which, according to the Markaz, 'has been devised with no other purpose than to dampen the spirit of jihad' and is part of a 'conspiracy hatched by our enemies' (Bin Muhammad n.d.: 78f.). Like most jihadi movements in the area, it sees itself as the inheritor of the legacy of the first jihadi movement in the region (the so-called 'Wahabi movement'), launched in the 1820s by Syed Ahmed Barelvi, who started a jihad in the Pashtun areas against Sikh rule (1825–31) and attempted, in 1827, to set up an Islamic state, the Emirate of Peshawar.

Daawat wal Irshad further believes that jihad is not a means to an end, but an end in itself (i.e., jihad for jihad's sake), and Hafiz Saeed has claimed that, even if the Kashmiri jihad did not succeed, it would not really matter, as his real aim is to make Muslims aware of the importance of jihad. He once remarked, 'People ask what *mujahideen* have achieved from the *jihad* being carried out in [Indian] held Kashmir? It is true that Kashmir could not be liberated so far, but in my opinion awareness of *jihad* among Muslims was much [more] important than other results'.[10] Daawat wal Irshad affirms that many organizations are engaged in *daawat*, but that they have forgotten jihad. For the movement, the current situation, wherein Muslims are perceived as being oppressed throughout the world, demands from them that they engage in jihad against Hindus, who are the worst of polytheists, and against Jews, who are their allies, with the aim of first Islamizing India and then conquering the whole world.[11] Jihad is also presented as essential in preserving the Islamic identity of Pakistan and as the only solution to the evils that plague Pakistani society, notably sectarianism (the Sunni-Shia conflict), which is seen as another conspiracy to divert Muslims from waging jihad against the infidels. This is incidentally one of the reasons why former Pakistani Prime Minister Nawaz Sharif sought their help in 1998 to fight sectarianism in Pakistan.[12] Their success in 'converting' Muslims from different schools of thought to the *Ahl-e Hadith* has, indeed, been phenomenal. They have set up a huge network of over two thousand recruitment centres across Pakistan and from 1994 onwards developed a network of *Al Daawat* model schools,[13] under the leadership of Dr Zafar Iqbal,[14] where children receive Islamic and modern education, with an emphasis on Arabic, English and computer science.[15] The aim is to utilize modern technology to spread the message of jihad and prepare children from a young age to become mujahidin. Textbooks insist on jihad and train young children to focus on the spirit of sacrifice (*qurbani*): Urdu readers for second-year children contain the wills (*wasiatnamah*) of martyrs and exhort children (both boys and girls) to prepare themselves to give their life for the great nuclear power that Pakistan has become.[16] In 2002, Daawat wal Irshad claimed to have two hundred primary schools and 20,000 students, including 5,000 girls.[17] Hafiz Saeed regularly denounces Christian missionary schools, which he describes as 'slaughterhouses where the future of the Muslim youth is being sacrificed' (Jamal 2001).

The Lashkar-e Taiba (LeT)

The LeT was established the late 1980s to train young Pakistanis willing to fight against Soviet occupation in Afghanistan. In 1987, the MDI had set up a training centre known as *Muaskar-e Taiba* in Jaji (Paktia province, Afghanistan, bordering Pakistan), and a second one known as *Muaskar-e Aqsa* in the Kunar province in Afghanistan.[18] It claims that some 1,600 of its trainees participated in the Afghan jihad but only five were martyred.[19] It shifted its focus to Kashmir after the Soviet withdrawal from Afghanistan, as it did not want to involve itself in factional fighting within Afghanistan. The LeT now operates five training centres: four are located in the mountains of Azad Kashmir (i.e., the portion of Kashmir under Pakistani administration – *Muaskar-e Taiba, Muaskar-e Aqsa, Um al Qura* and *Abdullah bin Masood*); the fifth one – *Markaz Muhammad bin Qasim* – is in Sanghar district (Sind), where thousands of mujahidin, among them British Pakistanis and other foreign nationals, have received religious and military training.

The LeT is one of the two largest private armies of jihadis in Pakistan (the other being made up of Deobandi groups – the Sipah-e Sahaba Pakistan and the Jaish-e Mohammad).[20] The LeT entered Kashmir in January 1990, when it ambushed a jeep carrying a group of Indian Air Force personnel. This attack is seen by the LeT as a symbolic start of its operations in Kashmir. In the words of an LeT leader, 'We chose the Indian Air Force because it was instrumental in flying the Indian army into Kashmir between October 27 and November 17 in 1947. This was our way of saying that now it was time for the Indian Air Force to fly their army out of Kashmir' (Abbas 2002).[21]

In early 2002, the organization claimed that, in eleven years, 14,369 Indian soldiers had been 'sent to hell' (*wasl-e jahannam*), while nearly 1,200 militants had 'drunk the cup of martyrdom' (*jam-e shahadat nush karna*) (*Al Daawat*,[22] February 2002). Most of the fighters (over 80 per cent) sent into Kashmir from thirty-two 'launching'[23] points are Pakistanis. From 1996 onwards they concentrated their operations on the border districts of Jammu (Rajauri, Doda and Poonch), to the south of the Kashmir Valley, for two main reasons: first, it is easier here for these militants to merge with the local population, which, whatever its religion, is linguistically allied to Punjabi, and, secondly, non-Muslims (mostly Hindus, but also some Sikhs) are in a majority in these areas. The aim is to cause a mass exodus of Hindus from these areas, thus leading to 'religious cleansing'. LeT fighters are considered by the Indian army to be the best trained among all the jihadi groups active in Kashmir and are characterized by them as practising a high level of brutality. Although they themselves always deny attacking civilians, they were most probably involved in the mass murders of Hindu pilgrims and civilians, including women and young children, with the aim of spreading terror and inciting the few remaining Kashmiri Hindus still in the Valley to leave Kashmir.[24]

In 1999, LeT mujahidin participated in the Kargil operation,[25] together with some two hundred *Ahl-e Hadith* Afghans from Kunar province. After Pakistani Prime Minister Nawaz Sharif's visit to the U.S., they were forced to withdraw against their wishes, the refusal of any truce with the enemy being a basic principle of *Salafi*-jihadism. After the Kargil incident, they announced what they called the second stage of jihad, which consisted of confronting the Indian army in the Kashmir Valley itself with a new tactic of attacks which they called the Ibn Taimiya[26] fedayeen operations. The LeT claims that eleven of its fighters were killed in such operations in 1999,[27] while the number of Indian casualties exceeded two hundred. Ninety-eight operations were carried out in 2000, the attack on the paramilitary Indian Border Security Force (BSF) post in Baramulla in northern Kashmir on 12 July 1999 marking the start of fedayeen missions in Kashmir. The fighting continued for nearly three days, during which a large Indian force failed to overpower a single LeT *fidai*. Thirteen Indian soldiers were killed and the attacker was martyred in the end. In November 1999 they attacked the local Indian army headquarters in Badami Bagh (Srinagar), which boosted their morale after the failure at Kargil. They then claimed that they could strike anywhere in India and proved this in December 2000 when they raided the symbolically crucial Red Fort in the heart of the Indian capital, Delhi. This operation, which officially targeted an interrogation centre of the Indian army and the torture cells where many mujahidin had been martyred, had a highly symbolic value, as the Red Fort was built and lived in by Moghul emperors. Thus the attack symbolized the 'reconquest' of the seat of South Asian Muslim power: as already mentioned, to raise the flag of Islam in Delhi, now the capital of 'Hindu India', is one of the proclaimed aims of the LeT.[28] No *fidai* was killed, injured or captured and all of them went back safely to their base. A second attack was launched on 5 February 2001 on Srinagar airport. In its February 2001 issue, the magazine *Al Daawat* published a long article with detailed charts, explaining the tactics used by the fedayeen for both attacks and, on the occasion of *Eid*, the mujahidin replayed the attack on the Red Fort for a huge audience in the Gaddafi stadium in Lahore. Although the attack on the Indian Parliament on 13 December 2001 was attributed by the Indian government to the LeT, Hafiz Saeed rejects the movement's responsibility: 'One should not expect such an incompetent operation from Lashkar-e Taiba.' He also pointed out that the Parliament was a civilian target, and that the LeT did not attack civilians.[29]

The LeT's modus operandi is extremely efficient: the fighters are well trained and highly motivated and they engage the enemy on its own territory. Small groups of fedayeen (three to five fighters) storm a security force camp and kill as many soldiers as possible before taking defensive positions within the camp and engaging security force personnel till they attain martyrdom. Battles often last twenty hours, if not more. Enemies are invariably described as cowards,[30] and as having no real motivation to fight as the land does not belong to them; many of them are thus 'sent to hell'. These spectacular and well-planned attacks bring the LeT maximum publicity and new recruits. More than the number of casualties inflicted on the enemy, the psychological impact of these attacks has been tremendous because security forces have to resort to heavy fire, destroying their own buildings in the process and causing deaths of their own men in friendly fire. The fedayeen are not like the suicide squads of the Tamil Tigers or the Palestinian and Lebanese suicide bombers. Even if martyrdom is the ultimate aim, they do not go on missions where death is certain; they select missions where they have a chance, however slim it might be, of returning alive. According to Abdul Rehman Makki, when a single mujahid attacks many enemies with the hope of coming back alive or of inflicting maximum damage or if his aim is to terrorize the enemy, then it cannot be called suicide.[31]

Abu Usama, one of their senior leaders, said that 'suicide is to kill oneself in desperation after one fails to achieve the goal that has been set. It is strictly prohibited in Islam, but fedayeen action is very noble. A *fidai* kills himself to achieve a virtuous goal, that is *shahadat*.' According to one mujahid: 'The army says: "You are surrounded, throw down your arms, surrender, we will send you to Pakistan." Then the mujahid is sure that he will attain martyrdom and he decides to fight till the end, in order to inflict maximum casualties on the army before he drinks the cup of martyrdom.'[32]

Who Joins the LeT ?

A study of martyrs was conducted from a randomized sample of about one hundred testaments (*wasiatnamah*) and life stories of martyrs published between 2000 and 2003 in the monthly magazine *Al Daawat* and from taped interviews of relatives of martyrs and would-be mujahidin who were waiting to go to Kashmir.[33] The sociological profile of the martyrs is similar to that of *Ahl-e Hadith* followers (shopkeepers and Saudi Arabia-returned migrants who embraced the *Salafi* form of Islam) and of petty officers of the Pakistani army. Although the LeT claims that the mujahidin are recruited from all social classes, most of them belong to the lower middle class and come from the towns and cities of central and south Punjab and from semi-urban neighbouring villages, whose population grew exponentially in the 1980s through rural-urban migration. Unfortunately, in true *Salafi* tradition, the caste affiliation of the martyrs is hardly ever mentioned, although the caste factor is highly relevant in this context. Indeed, recently, Professor Zafar Iqbal, himself an *Arain*, accused Hafiz Saeed of 'promoting the "*Gujjar baradari*" to which he belonged' (Rana 2004b). Most of the LeT militants do not belong to higher castes, but rather to emergent or lower castes (*kammis*). Although many members of these lower castes have prospered economically in the 1980s and some lower castes have even become locally dominant, their social status remains low in Punjabi society. Moreover, urban, Westernized, middle-class families do not send their sons for jihad in Kashmir. Contrary to what some observers claim, the majority of recruits do not belong to families who migrated from Indian-administered Kashmir after Partition. As most of them come from cities and towns – Faisalabad, Gujranwala, Sheikhupura, Bahawalpur, Sahiwal, Okara, Rahim Yar Khan – where the majority of the population consists of migrants who at the time of Partition came from the eastern part of undivided Punjab, one can infer that most belong to families who migrated. They are thus considered by the 'local population' to be migrants who came from India during Partition (*muhajirs*), but they themselves reject this classification, which they consider pejorative,[34] and describe themselves simply as Pakistanis. These families experienced the trauma of Partition; they were uprooted and destructured, and feel that, though they made many sacrifices for Pakistan, they were betrayed by the Westernized and/or feudal classes there. They thus feel more insecure than other categories of the population, and see India as trying by every means to destroy Pakistan; they also want to take revenge for the massacres of Partition. In our sample we also found a Punjabi Christian and a Sindhi Hindu, both of whom had embraced Islam. Before leaving for Kashmir, the first of these had converted his whole family, except his mother, to Islam and hoped that she too would embrace Islam after hearing of his martyrdom. The second recruit had converted several of his friends through his activities of *daawat*.

In their late teens or early twenties, mostly between eighteen and twenty-five years of age, the recruits tend on the whole to be more educated than the average Pakistani and certainly more so than members of other jihadi groups, such the Sipah-e Sahaba or Jaish-e Mohammad. The majority of them have completed secondary school with good grades and quite a few went to college to do their BA or BSc, where they came into contact with the LeT through *daawat* programmes; these led them to attend the big annual congregations the MDI organizes every year in Muridke with a motivational purpose.[35] The proportion of *madrasah*-educated boys is minimal (about 10 per cent), but includes boys who studied in a *madrasah* after studying in an Urdu medium school. The LeT prefers to recruit educated boys as they are more motivated and well aware of what they are doing. They also recruit in Great Britain and to a lesser extent in the United States and Australia among college students and young professionals of Pakistani background.[36] Some of these boys are simply looking for adventure, others resent the racism of Western society or feel that they belong to neither society and find a sense of belonging and comradeship in a jihadi group. The LeT also boasts of rehabilitating drug addicts and petty criminals.

Why do Pakistani Teenagers Join the LeT?

Apart from spiritual incentives, which I shall analyse later, emotional incentives play an important part in recruitment. Every Pakistani is subjected from childhood to propaganda on Kashmir, in school as well as in the family and through the official media. The cumulative effect of this propaganda has a strong impact on teenagers, who see every day on TV Indian soldiers beating Kashmiris and hear the most horrible stories of children burnt alive or slaughtered in front of their mothers, who are then forced to drink their blood, and especially stories of girls and women raped by Indian soldiers in front of their menfolk. All this evokes the horrors of Partition, for which they want to take revenge; they also feel a strong obligation to rise and defend the 'honour of their mothers and sisters'. In his study of martyrdom among Muslims, Farhad Khosrokhavar (2005) notes that the appeal to honour that becomes a leitmotif in jihad against the enemy justifies the commitment of the future martyrs, both to legitimize their choice towards their parents and to confirm in their own eyes the soundness of this choice. But there is also an 'addictive' dimension, in that the activities, especially the military training periods, are very exciting for teenagers and empower them in a highly class-based and also largely gerontocratic society. Furthermore, the aspect of comradeship with boys their own age should not be underestimated.

Joining the LeT is also a safety valve for surplus manpower: joining a jihadi movement gives young boys who cannot afford to migrate to the West or to the Gulf and are socially frustrated a substitute identity and compensates for their frustrations. In this respect, financial incentives should not be overlooked either; the militants engaged in *daawat* work receive a monthly salary from the LeT and fringe benefits, which are quite attractive for young unemployed boys. Being a martyr is, in addition, an opportunity for lower-class boys to become famous and be remembered for their military actions and also, through death, to gain a privileged status for themselves and their families. The religious legitimacy endows their death with a sacrality that hides its suicidal dimension. For, interestingly, the increase in the number of candidates for martyrdom coincides with an upsurge in the number of reported suicides of teenagers and young adults; these suicides are generally the result of unemployment, poverty, family conflicts or arranged/forced marriages.

But a good number of the martyrs in our sample had also joined the LeT after getting married, or when they had found a stable job, indicating that they could leave for jihad only after having fulfilled a personal aim – or rather, in a South Asian context, an aim set for them by their natal family. One could add that, once this aim is achieved, they feel dissatisfied with their life, some of them having tried their hand at several jobs, but never finding peace of mind till they came in contact with the LeT. Joining the LeT fills a void and helps them establish a sense of purpose and give direction to their life; they feel that they have finally found the place where they truly belong.

The profiles tell of boys who were different from childhood: they were the perfect sons and brothers, obedient, never giving their parents reason for complaint, never fighting with their brothers and sisters, loving everyone and being kind to all, especially young children; they were also never afraid of anything. The physical descriptions are also interesting: handsome, tall and slim with big eyes, an open face, always smiling, soft spoken and invariably light-skinned – all criteria of beauty in Punjab and also tallying with descriptions of the Prophet Muhammad.

The Training

Recruits are not sent to Kashmir immediately, but only after a long period of training. They first attend an ordinary course (*daura–e amma*), which lasts twenty-one days and focuses on religious education and more precisely on the principles of the *Ahl-e Hadith* school of thought; some attend this course twice. They are then sent back home and resume their former activities, together with engaging in *daawat* work in their neighbourhood, and particularly in recruiting their friends. They remain under the scrutiny of the local LeT leaders, who only accept to send them for the three-month special course (*daura-e khassa*) after assessing their level of motivation. This course aims at demonstrating the superiority of the *Ahl-e Hadith* over the other schools of thought and preparing the recruits to preach (*tabligh*) (Rana 2002: 252). Hafiz Saeed used to say that he did not immediately put a gun in the hands of his recruits, but first gave them a religious education.

Together with the advanced religious training, they receive military training in guerrilla tactics and learn survival techniques in a hostile environment. After attending this programme, they come back completely changed: they keep their hair long, do not shave, wear their trousers (*shalwar*) hitched above the ankles; this body symbolism is said to follow the precepts of the Prophet himself. They also change their name and adopt a pseudonym (*kunia*), which is invariably the name of one of the *Aslaf* (pious ancestors, the Companions of the Prophet and the first generation of Muslims). Their relatives also note a complete change in their personality; the militants themselves claim that, when they come back after the *daura-e khassa*, they have matured both physically (*jismi tor pe pukhta*) and psychologically (*zaini tor pe pukhta*). Once they return from the *daura-e khassa* or, in some cases, other more specialized courses, such as commando training, they are no longer interested in worldly life and do not feel happy at home; their relatives describe them either as silent or as talking continuously about Kashmir and martyrdom and quoting *Hadith* about the rewards awaiting those who wage jihad against India (*jihad-e Hind*): in the poetic words of one of them: 'If you put your finger in the ocean, the quantity of water which will stick to it is this world (*dunia*) and the ocean is the hereafter (*akhirat*).' From now, they think only of the next life, which for them is the only 'real life'. They no longer derive any satisfaction from their worldly pursuits, but only wish to enter the Valley where their oppressed mothers and sisters are calling them for help.

This training is an initiatory ritual and a rite of passage, and the whole process replicates marriage rituals in large parts of Pakistan and northern India – which, because they are similar to Hindu rituals, are considered *bidaa* (sinful innovations) and rejected by the *Ahl-e Hadith* school in normal wedding contexts. Here, the *daura* is the engagement (*mangni*); the 'launching' into Kashmir is the *nikah* (the signing of the marriage contract); martyrdom is the *shadi* (the consummation of the marriage with the *houris* in Paradise); and the funeral prayers (*namaz-e janaza*) are the *valima* (the reception given by the bridegroom's family the day after the marriage). This interpretation, which emerged from the testaments and the life stories, is sometimes also given by the would-be martyrs or their loved ones: 'One day, his maternal aunt said: "Abdul Majid, my son, you should get married now." Abdul Majid answered: "Auntie, I have already completed *mangni* [training], when the *valima* will take place after the marriage, you must attend."'[37] The father of a martyr also said: 'On the next day, we invited Abu Asiram's friends for *valima* to celebrate his *shadi* with the houris.'[38] As I shall show later, much other practice involved in Punjabi weddings in Pakistan also plays a role.

All those who have been trained will not go to Kashmir: their determination must be tested at length, in some cases for several years; they go only when their faith is mature and complete – '*pukhta, mukammil*', in their own words. The LeT needs foot soldiers in Pakistan and after training, many boys are engaged in *daawat* work and fund-raising or do odd jobs in LeT offices or camps; sometimes they have to plead with their superiors to get permission to be 'launched into the Valley'. They need to obtain their recommendation (*tazkia*) before they can go and then they again have to wait for 'their number to come up'. Hafiz Mohammad Saeed decides how many mujahidin should be sent to the Valley. The decision depends on the number of deaths that have taken place and also on the requirement and capacity of the organization inside Kashmir to absorb the new fighters.[39]

They also need the permission of their family, which may take a long time if the parents are not yet 'converted' to Salafism.[40] Some families try to delay giving permission in the hope that the boy will change his mind which, of course, never happens. The father may give him money to open a shop and ask him to wait. But the role of the mother is central and this again evokes marriage practice: normally a mother chooses her son's bride, and very few boys would get married according to their own choice and without their mother's active consent. A mother has greater influence on the son than a father and her permission is mandatory even if the father is alive. Significantly, nearly half the martyrs in our sample were the youngest children in their respective families, which probably means that they had been pampered and were the preferred son of their mothers and very close to them. There are many stories of a boy massaging his mother's feet while asking her permission to go to Kashmir and telling his mother that life is held in trust (*amanat*) from God and that it has to be given back to Him. They insist that martyrdom is the best kind of death, and that the Prophet himself always wished to die as a martyr. They ask her to emulate Khansa, an Arabian poetess of the seventh century whose four sons fought in the armies of Islam and were slain in the battle of Qadisiya; they tell her that she will be the mother-in-law of seventy-two *houris*. They also insist that they have to save the honour of their mothers and sisters in Kashmir and ask their mother what she will answer on the Day of Judgement when the Kashmiri women ask her why she did not send her son to defend their honour. They put pressure on their mother, sometimes trying to make her feel guilty by saying: 'You want to prevent me from going to Paradise. I have been waiting for too long. If in the meantime I die in an accident, what will you answer on the Day of Judgement?' Some mothers will only give permission after the boy is married and has a son. But, once mothers have given permission, they are much stronger than fathers – for Punjabis, female power (*sabr*) is the power to endure, to bear hardship, male power is *taqat*, physical strength – and some of them will sell their jewellery to buy their son a Kalashnikov. They pray for his wish to be fulfilled – that he does not come back, is not taken prisoner by the enemy and becomes a martyr – as they want him to be happy.

Apart from the privileges enjoyed by the families of martyrs and the money some of them receive on a monthly basis (see Rana 2002) – poor families of martyrs receive 1,500 Pakistani rupees a month from the Martyrs' and Conquerors' Department (*Shuba-e Shuhada wa Ghazian*)[41] – they also gain great prestige in their community as parents of martyrs, and this is of great relevance in a society where prestige and status are very important. Dreams play an important role as well in persuading mothers to give permission as well as in announcing the martyrdom. In many cases, a few days before the boy 'drinks the cup of martyrdom' (*jam-e shahadat nush karna*) mothers and often maternal uncles see him in Paradise, wearing beautiful white clothes, smiling, surrounded by trees and flowers and drinking milk. Once again, the parallels to marriage rituals are clear: here as in marriage rituals maternal uncles play an important role, both the bride and the bridegroom being escorted to the *nikah* by their mother's brothers. In South Asia, flowers are used as communicators with the divine, and a garland of flowers is placed over the groom's head before the *nikah* ceremony to offer him divine protection. Finally, the symbolism of milk – the female fluid and simultaneously the symbol of purity – is ever present; martyrs ask their parents to give milk to the militants who will come to announce their martyrdom. Similarly, the *khara* (bathing of the bridegroom with milk) in the marriage rituals unites the groom magically with the bride through treatment with milk and achieves his final separation from his mother. The boy is given milk to drink and the barber washes his hair with milk while the bride is bathed only in water. This symbolizes the preparation of the bridegroom for the consummation of the marriage.

Once they enter the Valley of Kashmir, the young men will fight the enemy for several months or even years before they can achieve martyrdom. Their aim is to inflict maximum casualties so that the future generations of enemies will remember and be scared of death.[42] They do not wish to return to Pakistan as *ghazis* (conquerors); this would be resented as a failure, and they may even feel ashamed. Indeed, there is competition between friends about who will be the first one to be martyred. Some complain that they have been waiting for too long, while boys who entered the Valley after them have already been martyred; they feel that God is angry with them and will not accept their sacrifice because their faith is not strong enough, or they reproach their mothers for not praying sincerely enough: 'You do not pray for me. If you had really prayed, I would have been launched already.'[43]

The Reinvention of Death Rituals

Once a *fidai* has become a martyr, the leaders of the LeT go to his home and rejoice with the family; sweets are distributed, the gift of sweets being an important marker of transition throughout South Asia. They give an account of the battle and of the bravery of the martyr, and then the testament is read out. Most martyrs are buried in Kashmir by the local population or by their friends (Bin Muhammad 2001) where their blood purifies the sacred earth that has been soiled by infidel Indian soldiers.[44] In those cases where the dead body is brought back to Pakistan, it is said to be intact after several days, with rosy cheeks and a perfume of roses emanating from it. The martyr's body is not washed before burial, as he is pure. This description of bodies that give out a fragrance of roses on the battlefield, while the corpses of the enemies immediately become rotten, is ever present in the literature about jihad and martyrdom (see Abdullah Azzam's writings), as well as in the accounts of Afghan mujahidin, among others.

When the body is not present, the LeT organizes funeral prayers of the absent (*ghaibana namaz-e janaza*; see Bin Muhammad 2001) in a public arena – for example, in a stadium or in the playground of a local school. Thousands will attend such a ceremony, thus enhancing the prestige of the martyr's family; they often say that never was there such a big gathering in the history of the village or neighbourhood. The *namaz-e janaza* replaces the wedding reception as a source of status and the 'who's who' on the list of attendees is as important as it is for a *valima*. The prestige of the family is enhanced even more when Hafiz Saeed himself or another of the LeT leaders presides over the ceremony. The money normally given on this occasion as *salami* to the newly weds is now given to the jihad fund. During ceremonies organized for women by the family or by the Women's Wing of the LeT[45], it is not uncommon to see martyrs' female relatives donating one of their gold bangles to the jihad fund. Such ceremonies are transformed into political meetings and are privileged opportunities for recruiting new candidates for martyrdom. The father of the martyr pronounces a few words and the testament is read out again – a ritual that inevitably incites other boys to join the LeT. There are many cases in which a father who attended the *namaz- e janaza* of a martyr returned home determined to send one of his sons for jihad. Here too there is a similarity with the 'martyropath families' of Iran, described by Farhad Khosrokhavar (2005), who encouraged their sons to join the *Bassij-e Mustazafin* ('Mobilization of the Deprived'), volunteers for the front during the Iran-Iraq war in the 1980s.

The Testaments

The testaments (*wasiatnamah*) of the martyrs of the Lashkar-e Taiba are mostly short and stereotyped. Contrary to the usual practice in Palestine and Lebanon, they are not available on video cassettes, since the LeT, following strict *Ahl-e Hadith* ideology, rather than the Shi'ite practice of, say, the Hizbullah, considers any representation of a human being as sinfully innovative (*bidaa*). Hence also, there are no posters showing photographs of the martyrs. It is often claimed that all testaments are fake and are written as propaganda by the movement, but this is not necessarily the case. Many models are available both in the textbooks and in the special section devoted to martyrs' testaments in the magazine *Al Daawat*. Each mujahid writes his testament, knowing that it will be read out during the *ghaibana namaz-e janaza* and then published in *Al Daawat* – very few future martyrs mention that they do not wish their testament to be read out in public. All of them start with more or less the same sentence: 'When you get this piece of paper, I shall be in Paradise [*jannat*].' The themes too are always the same: they ask their family to repay their debts and forgive them for any misdeeds. They ask for forgiveness because they did not have enough time to serve their parents, but in exchange their family will be among the chosen ones on the Day of Judgement; they will be proud as he will be waiting for them at the 'door of Paradise' (*jannat ka darwaza*) and will intercede (*sifarish*) on their behalf. According to a famous Hadith, only martyrs can be close to God and intercede for seventy of their loved ones.[46] This redemptive value of joining the LeT and becoming a martyr is constantly emphasized. This argument, as well as the one related to defending the honour of Kashmiri women, enables the martyrs to overcome the sorrow and guilt that they did not fulfil their duty of assisting their parents. The same argument is commonly found in the testaments of Iranian and Palestinian martyrs. Khosrokhavar (2005), for example, cites the will of the martyr Anouar Sakar of Gaza, who wrote to his father, 'Please forget all my mistakes and our disputes. You are an educated man and you know that martyrs act in the interests of their families, so that they may attain Paradise.' The following extracts from LeT martyrs' testaments will serve to illustrate some of the points discussed by me above.

Excerpts from the testament of Abu Moawiya (Sajid Bilal), martyred in Rajauri, south of the Kashmir Valley, on 14 June 2001:

> Dear parents,
>
> When you receive this small piece of paper, I shall be in Paradise, *insha Allah*.
>
> If you love me, I ask you to give a good education to my brothers and not tolerate any satanic activity (*shaitani kam*) in our home.
>
> My dear brother, take good care of our parents. Do not leave my place empty (*meri jagah ko khali nahin chorna*) after my martyrdom and do not let my Kalashnikov fall.

Excerpts from the testament of Abu Jaber (Ansar Abbas, son of Murad Ali), martyred in Thana Mandi, south of the Kashmir Valley, on 21 October 2001:

Dear father,

Keep a beard and ask my brothers to keep a beard. Everybody has to die one day and on the Day of Judgement there will be a reward for every good deed. God will reunite us in his Paradise which is so beautiful that nobody can imagine it and nobody has ever seen anything so beautiful in this world.

My brothers, give a religious education to your children and respect the precepts of Islam. After my martyrdom, take my gun and take revenge for my blood ... Give your children an education that will prepare them to become mujahidin and *hafiz-e Quran*.

My sisters, follow the precepts of Islam, observe *purdah* and do not miss any prayer.

My brothers and friends, go for training to live happily with honour and dignity and attain martyrdom after eliminating the infidels. I pray to God to reunite us on the Day of Judgement in this army of martyrs or *ghazis*. When He sees us, God will smile and He will welcome us in Paradise. My brothers and cousins, if you do not obey God, if you do not take revenge for the martyrs' blood and if you do not protect the honour of your sisters, what shall I answer God on the Day of Judgement? May God save us from seeing on the Day of Judgement our oppressed mothers, sisters and daughters holding on to the clothes of my brothers and pleading with God saying: 'We were being killed and the infidels were ruling over the world but they did not eliminate the infidels and they did not wave the flag of Islam.' May God not count my brothers among the cowards or those who will be sent to hell on the Day of Judgement.

Excerpts from the testament of Abu Abdallah Taibi (Mohib ul Rehman) from Dunyapur, martyred in Doda, south-east of the Kashmir Valley, on 19 January 2002:

Dear father,

Create an Islamic environment in our home. Send my brothers for training, because it will be for you a form of *sadaqa jariya* (permanent voluntary charity giving). On the Day of Judgement, the parents of martyrs will be particularly honoured and a gold crown (*sone ka taj*) will be placed on their head. They will save their loved ones (*apne rishtedar*) from hell and take them to Paradise, provided they did not commit the sin of polytheism (*shirk*).

Life is very short and death can come at any time ... you are very fortunate because your son and your brother died the death which the Holy Prophet wished for himself.

Excerpts from the testament of Abu Abdullah (Mohammad Asif Irfan Bhutta) from Chunian (Kasur district), martyred in Kupwara, northern Kashmir, on 28 August 2000:

My dear brothers,

When the religion of God needs your blood, do not refuse to give it, go for training while pursuing your studies. Do not let my Kalashnikov fall and take

> revenge for the blood of Muslims. Take good care of our parents and make sure that our sisters do not feel my absence.
>
> Dear friends,
>
> Forget about cricket, hockey and all those useless games and enter the field of jihad, make sacrifices so that the Hindu oppressor (*zalim Hindu*) will understand who he dared confront. America is such a big country and it does not have a cricket or a hockey team. Infidels trap Muslims in useless games to divert them from the battlefield.
>
> My dear parents, I could not serve you as I should have done. I made a lot of mistakes, I ask for your forgiveness in the name of God.

The martyrs also address themselves to their mothers and sisters. They ask them to pray five times a day, quoting a Hadith that says that Muslims who do not pray should be treated 'with hatred and animosity for the sake of Allah Almighty', as the abandoning of obligatory prayers is 'an act of great disbelief'. They also ask them to keep strict *purdah*, which in any case, just as in Lebanon and Palestine, the female relatives of the martyrs always keep as a mark of respect towards them. They also insist that they should not cry or show weakness when people come to offer condolences and that they should also prevent others from crying. Some families put up posters on the walls in their neighbourhood asking people not to offer condolences but to come and congratulate them on the martyrdom of their son. Martyrs also ask their mothers and sisters to recite two *nawafel* (supplementary prayers) and thank God and distribute sweets, as people do at a wedding. Once again, we find the theme of marriage, as among Lebanese and Iranian martyrs, in their refusal of sorrow and the identification of martyrdom with festivity. They forbid them to recite *qul* (or *sewom*, the reading of the Qur'an on the third day after death) or *chehlum* (or *chaliswan*, the reading of the Qur'an on the fortieth day following a death), because these rituals are expiatory and intended to beg God's forgiveness for the sins of the deceased and ensure his safe passage to Heaven – rituals described as *bidaa* and which in any case martyrs do not need, since they go straight to Paradise. They also insist that their mothers should refrain from *shirk* (polytheism), which in this context means that they should stop visiting spiritual guides (*pirs*) and the sanctuaries of saints, because God will never forgive the polytheists (*mushrikin*), and it will be impossible to intercede in their favour on the Day of Judgement.

If they are married, they always give permission to their wife to remarry and ask her to educate their children in the spirit of jihad. This too is similar to the case of Anouar Sakar of Gaza, cited by Khosrokhavar (2005), who wrote to his wife, 'I wish that God will grant you children.' Abu Abdul Rehman (Mohammad Ashraf), from Sialkot, martyred on 21 January, 2001 in Akhnoor (south of the Kashmir Valley), wrote in his testament: 'Do not cry. Allah will give you a better husband than Abu Abdul Rehman Ashraf. I give you the permission [to remarry]. I hope that God will reunite us in Paradise. *Insha Allah*, I will intercede for you.'

As for their fathers and brothers, they ask them to pray five times a day and to keep a beard like the Prophet (*Sunnat ke mutabiq*); they should also read the Qur'an together with a translation, in order to understand the text without recourse to exegesis (*tafsir*); this too is in keeping with *Ahl-e Hadith* doctrine. TVs and VCRs should be thrown away, both because of the medium per se and because of the obscenity – music, dance and immorality – they show. Indeed, television sets are ritually destroyed during the annual congregations of the LeT. Martyrs' brothers should refrain from listening to film songs and watching Indian movies, which spread 'Hindu culture' and spoil the minds of children with 'Western ways'; they should also neither smoke[47] nor keep a 'Western hairstyle'. They also ask them to refrain from 'Western games', such as cricket and hockey, which were devised by the infidels to keep Muslims busy and divert them from jihad. Finally, they exhort their brothers (the term '*bhai*' is used to denote both brothers and cousins) and nephews to take revenge for their blood – 'do not let my Kalashnikov fall', it is important to 'show the enemy that the blood of Muslims is not cheap' – and for the crimes perpetrated against Muslim women in Kashmir: 'My Muslim brothers, if you have some zeal (*ghairat*) in your heart, you must come out and defend the honour (*izzat*) of your sisters'.[48]

The Lashkar-e Taiba after the Ban of 12 January 2002

Shortly before the 11 September 2001 attacks, when the United States government was contemplating declaring the Lashkar-e Taiba a 'terrorist organization', Hafiz Saeed sent a letter to the U.S. Senate in which he insisted that the LeT's activities were 'focused only on Kashmir to win freedom for Kashmiri people from Indian occupation according to their aspirations, and to protect them from the brutalities of the Indian army'. But, giving in to American and Indian pressures, President Musharraf banned the LeT in his landmark speech of 12 January 2002. The LeT, which had anticipated this measure, had transferred its infrastructure and many of its militants to Muzaffarabad (in Azad Kashmir), and at the end of December 2001 had elected a new council (*majlis-e shura*), consisting of twelve Kashmiri members, some of whom were originally from Indian-administered Jammu and Kashmir,[49] and a new leader, Maulana Abdul Wahid Kashmiri. Before he was placed under house arrest on 30 December 2001, Hafiz Saeed ostensibly reshaped the MDI into a missionary (*tablighi*) organization named Jama'at ul Daawa Pakistan, completely separated from the LeT, and announced that he would devote himself to education and social welfare activities with the aim of reforming Pakistani society. Yahya Mujahid, spokesman for the Jama'at ul Daawa, was reported as saying: 'We handed *Lashkar-e-Taiba* over to the Kashmiris in December 2001. Now we have no contact with any *jihadi* organisation. We, the *Jamaatud Dawa*, are only preachers' (Rana 2004a). In

July 2004, the Jama'at ul Daawa reportedly split 'with violent clashes likely over party assets. The breakaway faction, which has taken the name Khairun Naas ... consists largely of members of the banned ... LT. Some of them have taken an oath to kill Haifz Muhammad Saeed' (Rana 2004b).

Till then Jama'at ul Daawa was building for itself a support base spread over the whole of Pakistan. The Khidmat-e Khalq ('Service of the People') cell of the organization has become very visible, setting up two *Taiba* hospitals in Muridke and Muzaffarabad (Azad Kashmir), fifty-one dispensaries and mobile medical camps for needy patients in poor areas and in the Afghan and Kashmiri refugee camps: 'We are a welfare organisation and working on various projects in health, education, provision of clean drinking water, advancing financial help to orphans and families of those martyred in *jihad* in Kashmir and Afghanistan'.[50] Al Daawa Medical Mission, which had so far focused on the urban poor now developed its activities in the least privileged areas of Sind (Tharparkar, bordering India) and Baluchistan (the Makran belt), with the dual aim of countering the activities of NGOs and of fulfilling a religious duty (Jamal 2003). According to Hafiz Saeed, NGOs have hidden agendas that aim to weaken faith in God and the spirit of jihad. 'These NGOs are working on an anti-Islam agenda and after the invasion of Afghanistan and Iraq by the U.S. and European countries, their agendas have been exposed.'[51]

However, after keeping a low profile for a short time, the LeT again started its activities, as could be expected, this time under the name Pasban Ahl-e Hadith (Guardians of *Ahl-e Hadith*), but it is still known as Lashkar-e Taiba. Its offices were closed or turned into Jama'at ul Daawa offices, which did not stop recruiting mujahidin for the LeT, but remained operative in Azad Kashmir under the pretext that the ban was not enforceable there. Indeed, the annual congregations held as usual in November 2002 and again in October 2003, in a place called Markaz Yarmuk in Pattoki (one of the *madrasahs* of the movement), rather than at the headquarters of Muridke, where the government had banned it, attracted tens of thousands of people, including a sizeable number of women. The Jama'at ul Daawa is not targeting only the youth; it is giving equal importance to 'converting' women, since without them it cannot realize its dream of establishing the kind of society it wants to create in Pakistan and elsewhere (Jamal 2001). A separate enclosure was reserved for the mothers and sisters of martyrs and they were treated with utmost respect. The website of Jama'at ul Da'awa Pakistan encouraged women teachers and students to attend in large numbers, but also instructed them not to travel without a close relative who fell within the incest barrier (a *mahram*), not to bring children or elderly or sick women along, to be simply dressed and not engage in unnecessary conversation during the journey. The website of the movement still preaches jihad (see Rao et al. and Sikand, this volume, for more details) and the magazine *Al Daawat*, which is available in the better bookshops in Islamabad, has not changed its content. Notably, the section on martyrs and martyrdom continues to occupy a dominant position in the magazine. According to its January 2003 issue, 292 fedayeen attained martyrdom in 2002, while 1,783 Indian soldiers 'were sent to hell'. The LeT claimed responsibility for 118 operations in 2002, including twenty-three fedayeen operations. Some reliable sources estimate that, between January and June 2003, the LeT recruited more than 3,350 young men in the age group eighteen to twenty-five (see SFG 2004).

Hafiz Saeed was arrested on 31 December 2001 and released on 31 March 2002. He was again detained on 15 May 2002 and released in November 2002 by the Lahore High Court, after being kept in unacknowledged detention for six months (he was apparently in an ISI safe house for his own security). Soon after, he married a young Kashmiri widow as his second wife 'as an act of charity' and again started calling on Muslims to wage jihad in Kashmir, since 'oppression against Muslims has not ceased' (in *Al Daawat*, December 2002). After the Indian general elections in 2004, he issued a statement saying, 'From Bihar to Bengal and from Uttar Pradesh to the Hyderabad Deccan, Muslims have become active and soon the idea of secularism will die in India.'[52] At the same time, the movement has opened new schools and dispensaries, mostly in Pakistan's Sind province, and has started investing on a big scale in real estate in Sind. Although the Jama'at ul Daawa was put on a watch list in November 2003 for violating the ban on fund-raising, it did not stop collecting funds, especially during Ramadan (Rana 2003b).

All this also illustrates the ambiguity of President Musharraf towards the jihad in Kashmir. According to Pakistani authorities, the LeT is an 'authentic jihadi movement', which means a group preoccupied only with jihad in Kashmir, a group that controls its militants, does nothing against the Pakistani government and represents no threat to internal security. Hence, the government, in its turn, sees no reason to interfere in its activities. Moreover, the LeT has been instrumentalized by the Pakistani government in order to maintain a certain level of tension in Kashmir; it is a way of channelling the frustrations of young men by directing them against a foreign infidel target. Aware, like his predecessors, that every initiative susceptible to be interpreted as abandoning the 'Kashmiri cause' would amount to political suicide, President Musharraf is always careful to distinguish between 'terrorism' – a term he uses to denote essentially religious extremism and sectarian violence between Sunnis and Shias, which has led to hundreds of deaths in Pakistan since the early 1990s – and 'jihad', i.e., the conflict in Kashmir. Although some have begun to question especially the economic costs of this conflict, this distinction is widely shared in Punjab (the population of Karachi, for example, is less concerned with Kashmir), even by certain liberal intellectuals who sometimes express their admiration for these mujahidin who are prepared to sacrifice their life for a 'sacred cause'. After the beginning of the rapprochement between India and Pakistan the LeT mujahidin were compelled by the Pakistani intelligence services (the ISI) to keep a low profile, but, simultaneously, their international links came to light more clearly and a process of deterritorialization was started. The arrest in March 2002 of the Arab militant Abu Zubaidah in a LeT safe house in Faisalabad, a centre of Pakistani Islamists, put the spotlight on the links between the LeT and Arab militants linked to Al Qaida. Similarly, in September 2003 Indonesian and Malaysian students linked to the Jemaah Islamiyyah were arrested in Karachi from the Jama'at ul Dirasat ul Islamiya, a *madrasah* that is affiliated to the Jama'at ul Daawa. It was also reported that students arrested in the Philippines in October 2003 had received training in LeT camps. Western converts and people of Pakistani origin settled in the United States and Australia who had been trained in LeT camps in Azad Kashmir were also detained in 2003.[53] Some sources claimed that LeT fighters had been detained in Iraq in early 2004, and Hafiz Saeed reacted to the assassination of Sheikh Ahmed Yasin in Gaza by threatening to take revenge in India, 'as the Yahood and the Hunood [Jews and Hindus] are two sides of the same coin' (Nkrumah 2004).

Conclusion

The ambiguity of the Lashkar-e Taiba is plain for all to see: it promotes transnational activities in the name of jihad against infidels anywhere in the world where Muslims are perceived to be oppressed, and aims at creating a new deterritorialized identity (i.e., the *ummah*) based on its understanding of Islam. It rejects all cultural particularities, as these are perceived as dividing Muslims and having a negative influence on ritual practice. But my study demonstrates that, as is the case with every jihadi movement in Pakistan or elsewhere in the region (Afghanistan, Central and South-East Asia), local considerations always prevail over global ones. The jihadi movements have to some extent islamized a nationalist struggle but, notwithstanding the presence of foreign delegates in the congregations and the rhetoric about the oppressed Muslims of Palestine, Burma, Chechnya and the Philippines among others, the main objective of the LeT recruits waging the Kashmiri jihad is to complete the unachieved Partition of 1947 and integrate Kashmir into Pakistan, rather than waging a global jihad. The mujahidin are more concerned with liberating Kashmir from Indian occupation and through martyrdom gaining a place for themselves and their families in Paradise than with waging jihad in distant lands. Even though the context is different, the motivation of the martyrs is similar to that of Palestinian or Lebanese martyrs – to liberate a sacred territory from foreign infidel occupation, to purify it by their blood and to protect the honour of Muslim women.

The martyrs of the Lashkar-e Taiba belong to the category of 'classical martyrs', described by Farhad Khosrokhavar (2005), in that they want to create a nation that seems impossible to achieve. Belonging to this highly structured movement provides a substitute identity and a feeling of moral superiority for young men who feel despised by the Westernized elite of their country and marginalized in a society they consider impure and corrupt and where they do not see any opportunity for upward social mobility. Through their martyrdom, they wish to enter the 'community of the chosen' in the beyond (*akhirat ki zindagi*), which for them constitutes the 'real life' (*asli zindagi*), while eliminating a maximum of enemies.

Notes

This chapter is a revised version of a paper first read at the Wocmes Conference in Mainz in September 2002. It was also presented at the Pakistan Workshop in the English Lake District in May 2003 and at the seminar on the Transmission of Knowledge in Peripheral Islam at the EHESS in Paris and has benefited from the insightful comments of the participants. I am particularly grateful to Aminah Mohammad-Arif for her editorial comments on a draft version of this text. A slightly different and abridged version in French has been published in Mohammad-Arif and Schmitz, 2006. All translations from Urdu are mine.

1. Hafiz Saeed regularly insists on this aim and describes Kashmir as 'the gateway to India'. For instance, on 18 February 1996, he said in the Lahore Press Club: 'The jihad in Kashmir will soon spread to entire India. Our mujahidin will create three Pakistans in India.' (The 'three Pakistans' are Kashmir and the two independent homelands for the Muslims of North and South India: Hyderabad and Junagadh.) This was also expressed by Mohammad Khaled, in charge of finance for the Multan office of the LeT, in an interview with Mohammad Amir Rana: 'Our aim is the whole of India and then Israel's turn will come. We only want the disintegration of India' (Rana 2002: 249); see also Raman (2000).
2. The *madrasah* of Deoband was founded in 1867 to reform South Asian Islam according to the 'fundamentalist' heritage of Shah Waliullah. The Barelvi traditionalist movement, characterized by the cult of the saints and devotion to the Prophet Muhammad, developed from the 1890s as a reaction to Deoband.
3. For more details about this movement, see Abou Zahab and Roy (2004), and the special report by Zaigham Khan in *The Herald* (Karachi), January 1998.
4. The personal history of Hafiz Saeed is highly relevant for understanding his world view. He belongs to the Gujar community, seen as inferior in Punjabi society, and, although he claims to be Kashmiri, he migrated with his family to Pakistani Punjab in 1947 at the Partition of India from what is now the Indian province of Haryana. Thirty-six members of his clan were murdered during the journey to Sargodha. He received religious education from his mother and his maternal uncle. He then did his MA in Arabic at Punjab University and joined the Islami Jamiat-e Tulaba, the student wing of the Jama'at-e Islami. He studied in King Saud University in Saudi Arabia for two years (1978–80) before returning to Pakistan and joining the Engineering University in Lahore as a lecturer in Islamic Studies. After returning from Saudi Arabia, he joined the Abdul Rasul Sayyaf *Salafi* group and participated in the Afghan jihad. For details see interview in *Nida-e Millat*, 22–28 March 2001, quoted in Rana (2003a).
5. Abdullah Azzam was assassinated in Peshawar in November 1989. For details about his biography see Cooley (2000), Bergen (2001) and Kepel (2002).

6. An elitist group founded by Nazir Hussain and Nawab Siddiq Hasan Khan of Bhopal in 1864, which recognizes only the Quran and the Sunna, rather than the various schools of Muslim jurisprudence (*fiqh*) as sources of law. Its base of support is the urban lower-middle class, especially traders. For some details, see Metcalf (1982).
7. Official Saudi funding practically stopped because of the links between the LeT and Osama bin Laden. The LeT joined the International Islamic Front for Jihad, created by bin Laden in 1998 in the wake of the American missile attacks against Afghanistan.
8. Hafiz Saeed. Interview in *Takbir* (Karachi), 12 August 1999, pp. 37ff.
9. According to the Markaz, the eight objectives of jihad are: to end persecution and tumult; to enforce the Islamic world order; to force the infidels to pay a tithe (*jizya*); to protect the weak and the oppressed from repression; to avenge the millions of Muslims who were and are being slaughtered in various parts of the world; to punish those who have broken covenants made with Muslims; to restore to Muslims possession of 'Muslim territories' now occupied by infidels (e.g., Spain, India, '*Bait ul Muqaddas*' (Jerusalem), 'Turkistan' (the present central Asian republics)); to defend and protect Muslims who are continuously facing offensives from infidels all over the world. For details, see Bin Muhammad (n.d.).
10. '*Jihad* culture spreading world over, says *Lashkar* chief'. *The News*, 3 December 2000.
11. For details about the concept of jihad as reinterpreted by the MDI, see Sikand (2001a, this volume, and 2007) and Bin Muhammad (n.d.)
12. Along with the Punjab Governor and two Punjab ministers, Mushahid Hussain Sayed, the then Federal Information Minister, visited the headquarters of the MDI in Muridke in April 1998 'to bring them out in the mainstream and make them an ally in our fight against sectarianism ... It is not a sectarian organisation and is not a source of domestic destabilisation'. *The Friday Times*, 24–30 April 1998.
13. The name (model schools) of this school network is very similar to the names of much sought-after and expensive private English-medium schools. See Jamal (2002).
14. Dr Zafar Iqbal also ran the network of free dispensaries that were set up by the *Markaz* and expanded from 2002 by Jama'at ul Daawa (see below). Education and health care are sectors in which the Pakistani government invests little.
15. The head of the education department at the MDI said: 'We do not live in mosques and *madrassas*, we must live and work in society' (Jamal 2002).
16. For details on the content of textbooks published by Al Daawat Press, see Jamal (2002) and Shehzad (2002).
17. Ninety-five in the Punjab (60 for boys and 35 for girls), 30 in Sind, 12 in Azad Kashmir, 14 in the NWFP and 1 in Baluchistan. Fees vary according to the financial means of the families, those who cannot afford to pay being exempted (Rana 2002: 242). The MDI also runs eleven *madrasahs* and two science colleges.
18. The Kunar province of Afghanistan, also close to Pakistani territory, had for a long time been a stronghold of the *Ahl-e Hadith* school of interpretation. In 1985 Maulana Jamil ul Rahman, educated in the Panjpir *madrasah* in north Pakistan, formed a strict *Salafi* party, the Jamaat ul Daawat ilal Quran wa Ahl-e Hadith, and increasing numbers of Arabs came to fight in its ranks. The links developed during the Afghan jihad between the Arabs and the Lashkar-e Taiba were reactivated after 11 September 2001, when Lashkar-e Taiba militants helped Arabs to leave Afghanistan and harboured them in Faisalabad or in Karachi.
19. Interestingly, they belonged to Okara, Bahawalpur, Karachi, Lahore and Faisalabad (Rana 2002: 235f.).

20. Deobandis follow the *Hanafi* school of jurisprudence, while *Ahl-e Hadith* recognize only the Qur'an and the Sunna. Sipah-e Sahaba (Army of the Companions of the Prophet) and Jaish-e Mohammad (Army of Mohammad) are Deobandi groups; the former was an anti-Shia group, while Jaish-e Mohammad waged jihad in Kashmir. Both were banned in January 2002 but are still active under new names.
21. The Indian government sent airborne troops into Srinagar on 27 October 1947.
22. This is published monthly from Lahore by the MDI (known as Jama'at ul Daawa since December 2001).
23. The term 'launching' is used by the LeT even in its Urdu texts; the Indian authorities use the term 'infiltration' to describe the same phenomenon.
24. Their involvement in the massacres of Sikhs in Chhatisinghpora is disputed. Sikhs in Kashmir have remained neutral in the conflict and at least on the surface enjoy fairly good relations with Muslims in Kashmir despite the massacres at Partition; see also Note 28.
25. In the spring of 1999, a combined force of Pakistani troops and several hundred militants crossed the line of control that separates the Indian and Pakistani armies in Kashmir and seized strategic mountain positions in the Kargil region in Indian-held Kashmir, where they fought off Indian assaults for two months. It was feared that the conflict could lead to a nuclear war. Pakistan had to withdraw in July 1999 under American pressure.
26. Ibn Taimiya (1263–1328), a fundamentalist theologian who promoted Hanbalism, a school of thought that recognizes only the Qur'an and the Sunna as sources of law, has been the intellectual guide of Sunni Islamist movements since the 1970s.
27. According to the LeT, 253 of its mujahidin were killed in 1999, 289 in 2000 and 312 in 2001. The numbers were much lower in the preceding years.
28. 'Today, by the grace of Allah, the successors of the mujahidin of Balakot, the sons of Mahmud Ghaznevi and the *fidai* of Lashkar-e Taiba reached the Red Fort waving the flag of jihad' *Al Daawat*, February 2001. The mujahidin of Balakot were the followers of Syed Ahmed Barelvi.
29. See the long interview Hafiz Saeed gave to the *Qaumi Digest*, an Urdu monthly published in Lahore, January 2002.
30. MDI's textbooks describe infidels as cowards by nature: 'When a mujahid attacks, they scream out of terror.'
31. '*Fidai hamle qurun-e awali se tasallul ke sath thabit hain*' (*Fidai* operations are attested without interruption since the first centuries [of Islam]). Abdul Rehman Makki, *Al Daawat*, May 2001.
32. Life story of Abu Okacha (Tayeb Abbas) from Rahim Yar Khan, date of 'martyrdom' unknown, *Al Daawat*, September 2001.
33. These interviews were conducted in a village of Muzaffargarh district (south Punjab) by Zaigham Khan, a Pakistani anthropologist, in the context of his research on death rituals. I am grateful to him for giving me access to some of the taped interviews.
34. This is also true of members of the Deobandi jihadi groups, such as Sipah-e Sahaba and Jaish-e Mohammad. Most of the militants who join these groups belong to muhajir families settled in central and south Punjab.
35. Apart from this military aspect, the annual congregations provided an opportunity for social networking and promoted the concept of *ummah* through the participation of foreign delegates.
36. 'Fed up with West, I'm off to *jihad*', *Sydney Morning Herald*, 30 April 2004.

37. Life story of Abu Umair (Abdul Majid), from Sharaqpur (Sheikhupura district), 'martyred' in Islamabad (District Anantnag, Kashmir) on 12 June, 2001, *Al Daawat*, September 2001.
38. Statement of Abu Asiram's (Abu Bakr Asim) father. He belonged to Faisalabad and was 'martyred' on 11 July, 2001 in Doda (Banihal, Kashmir), *Al Daawat*, September 2001.
39. See Zaigham Khan in *The Herald*, January 1998.
40. This is however, contrary to what Abdullah Azzam says in his will. On several occasions he emphasizes that those who go for jihad do not need anyone's permission; yet, in the South Asian context, parents' permission is de facto indispensable.
41. According to the LeT, in 2001 175 families were receiving a monthly allowance; others receive monetary help to clear debts. Trainees also receive compensation for injuries and help to find a job.
42. Khosrokhavar (2002) has discussed the concept of the 'martyr on the offensive, animated by the desire to suppress the enemy through religiously legitimated violence', as opposed to that of the 'defensive martyr' of early Christianity.
43. Letter from Abu Okacha to his mother, *Al Daawat*, September 2001.
44. In fact, Indian soldiers are always present at their burial and often also help bury them.
45. The Women's Wing is headed by Umm Hammad, who compiled testaments and life stories published in *Al Daawat*.
46. Quoted by Tirmizi, among others:

> The *shahid* is given seven special favours by Allah – 1) All his sins are forgiven at the first spurt of his blood; 2) he sees his place in Paradise as soon as he is killed; 3) he is saved from punishment in the grave; 4) he is saved from the great terror on the Day of Judgement; 5) on his head are placed a crown of honour and a jewel which is better than this whole world and all that it contains; 6) he is given the power of intercession for seventy members of his household; 7) he is married to seventy-two of the most beautiful virgin women of Paradise (*houris*).

47. This is in reference to the following hadith: 'Every intoxicant is forbidden and every forbidden thing will lead you to hell' (*har nasha haram hai aur har haram chiz jahannam mein lejaegi*). See also '*Kya ye bhi haram*?' (Is this also forbidden?) Fatwas (religious edicts) delivered by Sheikh ibn Baz and Sheikh Mohammad bin Saleh al Athimin (Saudi theologians), Dar ul Andalus, May 2001.
48. '*Ae mere musulman bhaio, jin ke sine mein ghairat hai to wo apni behnon ki izzatein bachane ke lie zarur niklein.*' Testament of Abu Huraira (Mohammad Afzal) from Gujranwala, martyred in July 2000 in Lipa.
49. The names given by the media on 25 December 2001 were as follows: Abdullah (Anantnag), Haji Azam (Poonch), Muzammil Butt (Doda), Mohammad Umair (Baramulla), Chaudhry Abdullah Khalid (Bagh), Rafiq Akhtar (Muzaffarabad), Aftab Hussain (Kotli), Faisal Dar (Srinagar), Chaudhry Yusuf (Amirpur), Maulana Saif ul Qari (Baltistan), Raja Irshad, advocate (Muzaffarabad) and Masud Lone, advocate (Muzaffarabad).
50. Mian Muhammad Asif, in charge of public relations for the Jama'at ul Daawa Peshawar zone, in *Daily Times*, 18 November 2003.
51. 'Foreign NGOs weakening people's faith: Hafiz Saeed', *Daily Times*, 2 May 2004.
52. 'Jihad the only way to win Kashmir: Hafiz Saeed', *Daily Times*, 25 May 2004.

53. The so-called 'Virginia jihad' case in the U.S.A. and the arrests of students of Pakistani origin in Australia.

References

Abbas, A. 2002. 'In God We Trust', *The Herald*, January.

Abou Zahab, M. and O. Roy. 2004. *Islamist Networks: The Afghan-Pakistan Connection*. London; Hurst; New York: Columbia University Press.

Ahmed, E. 1998. The Conflict Within, *Dawn*, 5 February.

Bergen, P.L. 2001. *Holy War Inc.* London: Weidenfeld and Nicholson.

Bin Muhammad, A.S. n.d. *Jehad in the Present Time*. Lahore: Dar ul Andalus. (published in English).

———. 2001. *Shaheed ki Namaz-e Janaza*. Lahore: Dar ul Andalus.

Cooley, J.K. 2000. *Unholy Wars*. London: Pluto Press.

Jamal, A. 2001. 'Setting an Even Bloodier Agenda', *The News*, 22 April.

———. 2002. 'From 'Madrassa' to 'School'', *The News*, 15 December.

———. 2003. 'The Message Spreads', *The News*, 10 August.

Kepel, G. 2002. *Jihad*. Cambridge Mass.: Harvard University Press.

Khosrokhavar, F. 2005. *Suicide Bombers: Allah's New Martyrs* London: Pluto Press.

Metcalf, B. 1982. *Islamic Revival in British India: Deoband 1860–1900*. Princeton: Princeton University Press.

Mohammad-Arif, A. and J. Schmitz (eds). 2006. *Figures d'Islam après le 11 Septembre: Disciples et Martyrs, Réfugiés et Migrants*. Paris: Karthala.

Nkrumah, G. 2004. 'Outright Condemnation', *Al Ahram Weekly*, March, 25–31.

Puri, B. 1995. 'Kashmiriyat: the Vitality of Kashmiri Identity', *Contemporary South Asia* 4(1): 55–63.

Racine, J.-L. 2002. *Cachemire : Au péril de la guerre*. Paris: Autrement.

Raman, B. 2000. *Lashkar-e Taiba: Its Past, Present and Future*. South Asia Analysis Group (SAAG), paper No. 175, 25 December.

Rana, M.A. 2002. *Jihad-e Kashmir wa Afghanistan: Jihadi tanzimon aur mazhabi jamaaton ka ek jaiza* (The Kashmir Jihad and Afghanistan: A Survey of Jihadi Outfits and Religious Organizations). Lahore: Mashaal Books.

———. 2003a. *Jihad aur Jihadis: Pakistan aur Kashmir ke aham jihadi rahnumaon ka taaruf* (Jihad and Jihadis: Directory of the Main Jihadi Leaders in Pakistan and Kashmir). Lahore: Mashaal Books.

———. 2003b. 'JD Continues Raising Funds Despite Ban', *Daily Times*, 19 November.

———. 2004a. 'Jammatud Dawa Splits', *Daily Times*, 18 July.

———. 2004b. 'Jammatud Dawa has no Global Network or Ambitions: Mujahid', *Daily Times*, 25 May.

SFG. 2004. *Cost of Conflict Between India and Pakistan*. Mumbai: Strategic Foresight Group.

Shehzad, M. 2002. 'Church of the Poison Mind', *The Friday Times*, February, 14–20.

Sikand, Y.S. 2001a. 'Changing Course of Kashmiri Struggle: From National Liberation to Islamist Jihad?' *Economic and Political Weekly* 36 (3. January): 20–26.

———. 2001b. *The Muslim Rishis of Kashmir*. Bangalore: Himayat Trust.

———. 2002. 'The Emergence and Development of the Jama'at-i-Islami of Jammu and Kashmir (1940s-1990)', *Modern Asian Studies* 36: 705–51.

———. 2007. 'Popular Kashmiri Sufism and the Challenge of Scripturalist Islam (1900–1989)'. in A. Rao (ed.), *The Valley of Kashmir: The Making and Unmaking of a Composite Culture?* Delhi: Manohar.

Zutshi, C. 2004. *Languages of Belonging. Islam, Regional Identity and the Making of Kashmir*. London: Hurst.

Part III

Organizing, Encouraging and Dissuading: The Uses of Kinship, Gender and Religion

Chapter 7

Is War Gendered? Issues in Representing Women and the Second World War

Elaine Martin

Violent conflict, especially in the form of war is, and has always been, gendered. By gendered, I mean that male/female identity has existed as a category by which roles in war have been determined. As Gisela Bock has observed: 'Gender refers not only to the relationship between sexual difference and similarity but also to sexual hierarchy and power' (Bock 1998: 96). This is not to say that the roles of women and men in war have been static: quite the contrary. Yet gender issues have informed the changes as well as the maintenance of certain elements of the status quo. The editors of *Behind the Lines: Gender and the Two World Wars* write in their introduction, that 'war must be understood as a *gendering* activity, one that ritually marks the gender of all members of a society, whether or not they are combatants.' They continue:

> The implications of war for women and men are, then, linked in symbolic as well as social and economic systems. During total war, the discourse of militarism, with its stress on 'masculine' qualities, permeates the whole fabric of society, touching both women and men. In doing so, it draws upon preexisting definitions of gender at the same time that it restructures gender relations. When peace comes, messages of reintegration are expressed within a rhetoric of gender that establishes the postwar social assignments of men and women. (Higonnet et al. 1987: 4)

In the earliest accounts of war in the Occident, which stem from Biblical sources and texts from classical antiquity such as the *Iliad*, the division of gender roles is unmistakable: men go forth into battle as warriors, while women encourage them, watch from the ramparts, tend to the corpses, mourn the dead and become 'spoils of war' if on the losing side – as victims both of rape and of potential enslavement. Exceptions, such as Penthesilea, Judith or, later, Jeanne d'Arc, serve only to prove the rule. While these constitute the broad lines of the traditional configuration 'men-women-war', even these early examples raise complex questions of interpretation, which recur throughout the history of military conflict. Interpretation is closely linked with how war is recorded and represented. Intimate knowledge of war can be communicated only through language and images, both of which are restricted. As soon as one attempts to narrate or show, in any way, the experience of war, one necessarily enters the realm of interpretation.[1] Even direct combatants can relate the experience only from the (limited) perspective of the individual. There is no such thing as an 'objective' war, only representations. There is, of course, a political valence ascribed to such narratives or images, because those who win the war simultaneously win the right to represent that war for posterity and thus – through the act of interpretation – to influence the future. For this reason it is important that women's voices be heard as well as men's.

Germany in the Second World War represents, for several reasons, a unique development in the history of women's evolving roles in war. First, civilian populations, rather than being involved in warfare merely as 'collateral damage', were specifically targeted for the purpose of overall demoralization. Secondly, women were implicated as enablers of especially pernicious policies, such as forced sterilization, euthanasia and genocide, and furthermore, the civilian population was embroiled in the internal war against so-called enemies of the German state. All of these factors contribute, albeit in different ways, to a blurring of traditional divisions between soldiers and non-combatants, between victims and perpetrators, between pacificist, nurturing women and bellicose, aggressive men. Most importantly, the Second World War also split women as a group internally, that is, within the aggressor nation, into two groups: the 'normal', 'Aryan'', bystanders/followers/collaborators/ perpetrators versus the victims of these perpetrators, who as a corollary of their victim status lost their 'Germanness' or German identity: Jews, prostitutes, members of religious sects such as Jehovah's Witnesses, Gypsies, socialists, communists, and others. In this essay I want to focus on those women who belong to the bystander/co-complicit/perpetrator category and who could be called victims only to the extent that they were also victims of Nazi sexism and of the war. Despite the vast amount of research on National Socialism, which Christa Wolf refers to as 'the rows of book spines in the libraries [that] no longer measure in yards, but in miles' (Wolf 1980: 171), I think that what ordinary German women did and what was done to them in the Second World War emerge most revealingly from their own writings.[2]

An extensive body of texts, most of them autobiographical, written by German-speaking women as well as French, British and women of other nationalities, has come into existence in the years since the first of them appeared in the 1970s. Texts by German women about the Second World War are trebly interesting: they represent the voices, not of the winners, but of the losers; their perspective is one of non-combatants; and, due to the hypermasculine and sexist ideology of the National Socialists, women's self-image was informed by both victimization and guilt. In the 1980s and 1990s I interviewed twenty women who had lived through the Hitler era and subsequently wrote about the experience, for the most part autobiographically. The interviewees ranged from resistance fighters to housewives, from working-class socialists and communists to five members of the aristocracy. None of them was Jewish, but three were persecuted by the Nazis for political reasons (Lore Wolf, Lina Haag, Anni Wadle). Several were in the Hitler youth group for girls (BDM, Bund deutscher Mädel), and two admitted openly to youthful enthusiasm for the Nazis and consequent leadership roles in the youth group (Renate Finckh, Carola Stern). Most of the women were in their formative years as adolescents or young adults during the Nazi years, but some were older. All of them felt compelled to write about what they had experienced. For some it was an explanation for their children, for others it was an act of atonement; for some it was an attempt to set the record straight, and for yet others it was an act of self-therapy or self-healing. This variation within a group that would nominally, at least, be considered cohesive because of a shared 'Aryan' identity already suggests a certain unacknowledged complexity, a certain reductionism in speaking of 'women'.

At first glance, the task of summarizing women's roles in the Third Reich and Second World War would appear to be quite straightforward: we are considering a fixed time period of only twelve years, and a single country, Germany; the players are Germans – either Nazis or the victims and opponents of Nazis; and the focus group, women, is clearly defined. But these assumptions, it turns out, are quite misleading. In reality, for example, the ideas, the behaviours and the value system that led to National Socialism developed long before Hitler seized power in 1933, and the effects of the Nazi period have endured long past 1945, into succeeding generations of both perpetrators and victims. As concerns location, fascism and its policies of imperialist expansionism, racism, militarism and authoritarianism involved most of Europe, the Soviet Union, parts of Africa, and the United States, as well as Germany's Axis partners, Japan and Italy – not to mention, after 1945, South American countries, which became the destinations of choice for former Nazis. The Second World War was truly a conflict that involved almost the entire world. Similar to this expansive geographical involvement, not all participants – willing and otherwise – were Germans. We must consider at the very least Poles and other East Europeans, Russians, the French and the populations of other occupied Western European countries. If we interpret involvement in the war and the Holocaust not as an opposition of Nazis and non-Nazis (the latter as distinguished from the few active anti-Nazis), but rather as a continuum ranging from absolute victim to absolute perpetrator, the groups at both ends of such a range are clear, but the middle may be considerably less so. Just as there were many levels of perpetrators, so too there were many categories of opponents and victims, some of which overlapped. To the obvious category of Jewish victims should be added, for example, socialists, communists, homosexuals, oppositional religious sects, Gypsies and resistance fighters. To complete our process of deconstruction, even the apparently obvious category of women is fraught with potential difficulty: which women? From which social or economic class? From which political orientation? From urban or rural environments? Jewish or Gentile? Gisela Bock writes: 'Among ordinary women in National Socialist Germany, where 35 million women lived by 1939, we find perpetrators, victims, followers, bystanders of racism and the Holocaust, and deplorably few resisters and rescuers' (Bock 1998: 85). To understand completely what women did and what happened to them in the Third Reich and the Holocaust, we would have to reconstruct, one by one, the lives of millions of women.[3] This is, in fact, the approach of the various Holocaust Witness Projects that have been under way for some years (Baumel 1998). Since nothing similar exists for non-Jewish women – those who would likely be bystanders or even perpetrators – one turns to their autobiographical accounts or fictional works as well as interview materials.

The women writers whom I interviewed largely fall into the middle of a victim–perpetrator continuum, in a category that might be called either *Mitläufer* (passive participant) or *Mittäterin* (co-complicit).[4] As 'Aryans', the women in this group were not targeted for annihilation, and the political victims were, unlike their husbands, not tortured, although they were imprisoned and abused. But, if they were not victims, neither were they strictly perpetrators. Even the two in the Bund deutscher Mädel have the excuse of extreme youth; it is difficult to know at what age children should be held solely responsible for their acts. The Nazi/anti-Nazi continuum is equally fraught. Most of the women in my group were neither party members nor members of the Hitler youth group. On the other hand, only three actively opposed the regime; the others seem to have taken the path of least resistance or to have made compromises and accommodations.

Elie Wiesel, the Holocaust researcher, said once in a television interview, 'I don't understand the victims, and I don't understand the killers. But the victims are my problem, and the killers are yours' (quoted in: Day 1980: 183–84). I disagree, however, with his fundamental unyoking of the two, and would argue instead that the two must be studied together. This unwillingness to study victims and perpetrators separately has been seconded by several Holocaust scholars as well. Judith Tydor Baumel writes, for example, that 'one cannot fully examine and appreciate the experiences of Jewish women during the Holocaust without understanding those of their half-Jewish, quarter-Jewish and non-Jewish counterparts during the same period' (Baumel 1998: 3). Joan Ringelheim takes the parallel a step further by pointing out that patriarchal values cut across the boundary between Aryan aggressor and Jewish victim. 'It has been difficult to confront,' she writes:

> the fact that Jewish women were victims *as Jewish women*, not only because some Jewish men exploited Jewish women, but also because Jewish men could not protect women and children from the Nazis. In other words, it has been too difficult to contemplate the extent to which gender counted in the exploitation and murder of Jewish women, and the extent to which the sexism of Nazi ideology and the sexism of the Jewish community met in a tragic and involuntary alliance. (Ringelheim 1998: 345)[5]

Both perpetrator and victim arose from the same social system, from a *Weltanschauung* based on patriarchy, authoritarianism, militarism, racism, sexism and anti-Semitism. Thus it is necessary to study not only victim and perpetrator together but also sexism and racism. Gisela Bock argues: 'Not only did racism shape the historical expressions of gender, but gender also shaped the historical expressions of racism' (Bock 1998: 96). In her interpretation, the two seem inextricable, as does the fascist world view that connects them. These linkages have been explored in numerous literary works, of which a few examples will suffice. Texts such as Robert Musil's *The Confusions of Young Törless* (*Die Verwirrungen des Zöglings Törleß*, 1906) Heinrich Mann's *Professor Unrat* (1905) and Günter Grass's *Cat and Mouse* (*Katz und Maus*, 1961) revealed the pre-First World War fascist tendencies of a military boarding school, pre-war oppressive relations in a public boys' school and authoritarian teacher-pupil relations in the NS era respectively. Centuries of anti-Semitism in Europe made it possible for the Nazis to scapegoat the German Jewish population. Centuries of authoritarian culture prepared people to obey without questioning. Centuries of monarchy prepared people to accept a strong man, a dictator. In his play *The Investigation* (*Die Ermittlung*, 1965), Peter Weiss's 3rd Witness' makes the following observation:

> Many of those who were destined
> to play the part of prisoners
> had grown up with the same ideas
> the same way of looking at things
> as those
> who found themselves acting as guards
> They were all equally dedicated
> to the same nation
> to its prosperity
> and its rewards
> And if they had not been designated
> prisoners
> they could equally well have been guards
> We must drop the lofty view
> that the camp world
> is incomprehensible to us
> We all knew the society
> that produced a government

> capable of creating such camps
> The order that prevailed there
> was an order whose basic nature
> we were familiar with
> For that very reason
> we were able to find our way about
> in its logical and ultimate consequence
> where the oppressor
> could expand his authority
> to a degree never known before
> and the oppressed
> was forced to yield up
> the fertilizing dust
> of his bones. (Weiss 1966: 125)

Weiss suggests in these lines that anyone who did not intervene in the society that 'produced a government capable of creating such camps' was complicit, although, in one reading, this would include the oppressed. Given the long history of anti-Semitism in Europe, perhaps Weiss is, indeed, saying that active resistance to anti-Semitic belief and deeds needed to have occurred much earlier, long before the National Socialist regime came to power. The 'logical and ultimate consequence' seems to refer here to the development of fascist seeds that grow into concentration camps and that, in retrospect, should have been recognizable and preventable.

Virginia Woolf, in her 1938 essay *Three Guineas*, was one of the first to take the additional step of identifying the connection between fascism and a patriarchal value system, a system that linked the denigration of women to a general oppression of the Other, coupled with military aggression and imperialism. Woolf observed in a now-famous passage: '[The daughters of educated men] were fighting the same enemy that you are fighting and for the same reasons. They were fighting the tyranny of the patriarchal state as you are fighting the tyranny of the Fascist state' (Woolf 1938: 102). Summarizing Woolf's analysis in *Three Guineas* , Susan Sontag notes that '[it] was regarded as too obvious to be mentioned': 'that war is a man's game – that the killing machine has a gender, and it is male' (Sontag 2002: 83). Several of the post-Second World War women writers describe oppressive patriarchal father figures: for example, Eva Zeller in *Solange ich denken kann* (1981) and Margarete Hannsmann in *Der helle Tag bricht an; ein Kind wird Nazi* (1982). In her autobiographical novel, Hannsmann says: 'There was no devil more pitiful than Father. Many years later, in a dream, I chopped my father to pieces with an ax' (1982: 33) In our 1991 interview, when I asked Hannsmann whether she envisioned writing about her father again in future works, she replied: 'I won't go down into that cellar again.' Of particular interest in investigating the patriarchy-sexism link is the extent to which sexist attitudes towards women might prove to be a necessary factor in creating a militarist environment and in producing the resultant 'warrior' mentality. Writing in an anti-war pamphlet, *Women and War*, in 1915, British pacifist Helena Swanwick noted: 'Militarist states always tend to degrade women to the position of breeders and slaves. In all these ways the possibility of war, the preparation for war, the militarist basis of States (whether 'civilised' or 'uncivilised') affect the position of women and affect it altogether evilly' (quoted in Bell and Offen 1983: 270–71). The First World War-influenced analyses of Swanwick and Woolf identified an important ideological connection that is still of concern. In his 1997 article, 'Women in the Warrior Culture', Richard Rayner quotes Madeline Morris, a law professor at Duke University in the United States and special consultant to Secretary of the American Army Togo West on harassment issues: 'there is a set of attitudes – including hypermasculinity, adversarial sexual beliefs, sexual promiscuity, acceptance of violence against women, hostility toward women and sex-role stereotyping – that is correlated with rape and the proclivity for it'. She further says, 'substantial anecdotal evidence suggests that this constellation of attitudes is enshrined in the military culture, which not only emphasizes toughness, self-sufficiency and dominance but also paints a particular vision of masculinity as a basis for group identity. The culture tends, through training, jokes, drill chants and songs, to cast women as sexual targets' (Rayner 1997: 29). After providing additional examples, Rayner concludes: 'at one level the military's, any military's, existence is perhaps subconsciously *predicated* on the kind of aggression associated with rape; remove that, and you don't have an army' (Rayner 1997: 29). Nazi-era Germany had prepared women to accept patriarchal and sexist attitudes, to make sacrifices for family and Führer, and even to commit acts that under a non-wartime legal structure would be crimes.

Gisela Bock, a scholar of the National Socialist era, has described some of the ways in which women were actively complicit with the regime and its policies. First, 'many women reported presumable sterilization candidates to the "state doctors" who had the task of searching for the hereditarily diseased'. Secondly, women were among the perpetrators in 'the killing of inmates of psychiatric asylums (perhaps two hundred thousand were put to death by 1945)'. Thirdly, '[i]n 1933, the League of German Woman Doctors was among the first women's organizations to exclude Jewish members'. Fourthly, large numbers of women worked as camp guards, most of them coming 'from a lower-class background' and having been 'factory, office, or domestic workers'. Survivors of the camps testified that many women were as brutal as the men. And finally, '[m]any denunciations were made by women, [although] they were clearly a minority' (Bock 1998: 87–90). Gisela Bock summarizes the effect of this collaborative behaviour thus: 'What is important…is that Gentile women, just like Gentile men, were likely to provide the Nazi bureaucracy with the information needed to render dictatorship and persecution effective' (Bock 1998: 90). In this same essay, Bock raises another aspect of National Socialism and the Second World War that was unique in terms of women's traditional wartime roles up to that point. As Bock explains it: 'National Socialism tried, with some success, to do away with the traditional separation between the private and the public sphere, between the personal and the political. In principle, and often enough in practice, the personal and private was to exist and function exclusively for the benefit of the public and political, for the Volksgemeinschaft and the race, in the specific context of a dictatorship' (Bock 1998: 91). Thus the traditional intermediaries of parents, partners, spouses and families were removed; the German woman was expected to subordinate all other allegiances to the state, personified by the Führer.[6] This 'collapse of private space' as Bock calls it, had the consequence of isolating individuals, breaking the bonds of motherliness and nurturing behaviour, and severing feelings of connectedness and responsibility. If the state takes responsibility for everything, then the individual has none. No responsibility means no guilt.

This phenomenon of being not-guilty-because-of-victimization has been encountered by several scholars of the National Socialist era, in particular by the German sociologist Annemarie Tröger, who conducted numerous oral history interviews with men and women who lived in Berlin and Hanover during the Second World War.[7] In Tröger's words, '[w]ar is often seen as a natural disaster, a catastrophe. This common metaphor is ambiguous; it expresses … the feeling of being completely delivered over to forces beyond one's control … it conveys, implicitly, a political message: there is no collective or personal responsibility for war; it just "breaks out", is not prepared for and not declared' (Tröger 1987: 298). In addition to denying the cause/effect aspect of war and preferring to consider it a huge non sequitur, many women, according to Tröger, played the victim card. In a traditional definition, a victim is a sufferer or someone sacrificed to conditions beyond one's control. Religion, as Tröger notes, also plays a part:

> The religious and popular symbol of the victim absolves the victim of responsibility and guilt. A victim of the war cannot be responsible for it. In the postwar German understanding, this notion is carried even further: as a victim one cannot be held responsible for fascism. This is certainly one reason that interviewees brought up the war as soon as the uncomfortable issue of National Socialism was raised in the interview. (Tröger 1987: 299)

Since women in Germany received the vote only in 1918 one could lend some credence to the claim that conditions leading to fascism and to the National Socialist regime had been put into play long before women had a political voice. It is also true that more women supported the regime after the war began, perhaps from a desire to support the troops (their sons and brothers) and because the government had tightened controls against dissenters. As Christabel Bielenberg wrote in her autobiographical work *The Past is Myself* (orig. 1968): 'In a regime such as Hitler's there could be no standing on the sidelines, but there were also no rules to the game; each to his own conscience, that silver thread which must run through people's lives, ruling how far they should go and no further' (Bielenberg 1986: 98). I interviewed Bielenberg, who died in 2003 at the age of ninety-four, in Tullow, Ireland, in June 1988. When asked about the particular contribution of her story as a foreigner living in Nazi Germany, in Berlin throughout the war, she replied:

> I think I tell the story of an ordinary person with a liberal upbringing being plunged into this situation of a dictatorship. I challenge anybody who has not lived under a dictatorship to understand what it is like, or how they would react themselves. I feel the importance of the story is just that: the story of the simple person brought up liberally, and what drives you ultimately into opposition. (Bielenberg 1988: 24)

Bielenberg's question of how one would react under a dictatorship is quite provocative. It is answered one way or another by every writer who attempts to describe or reflect upon the Nazi years. Why girls or young women were attracted to National Socialism has numerous explanations. As Melitta Maschmann points out in *Fazit* (orig. 1963), Hitler's seizure of power corresponded with the puberty stage of many who later wrote about their experiences. 'At this age', she notes, 'one finds life, which consists of homework, family outings and birthday parties, to be petty and shamefully devoid of meaning' (Maschmann 1983: 9). Like countless others in her cohort she wanted to escape her 'childish, narrow life and attach [her]self to something that was large and important' (Maschmann 1983: 9). She heads up brigades to remove Poles from their homes and replace them with German emigrant families, not allowing the Poles to take their belongings. She talks in retrospect about wearing 'moral blinders' (Maschmann 1983: 138) vis-à-vis the crimes she committed against the Poles and claims that it took her twelve years after the war to achieve an 'inner detachment' ('innere Ablösung') from National Socialism (Maschmann 1983: 214).

Numerous writers and thinkers have speculated on the cause of human violence and war, notably Sigmund Freud in his famous epistolary exchange with Albert Einstein in 1932 ('Why War?'; 'Warum Krieg?'). Einstein posits in his letter that people are roused to a warlike mentality because 'people have within them a lust for hatred and destruction' (Einstein and Freud 1994: 27). Freud concurs with Einstein's hypothesis, arguing: 'We assume that human instincts are of two kinds: those that conserve and unify, which we call "erotic" (in the meaning Plato gives to Eros in his Symposium), or else "sexual" (explicitly extending the popular connotation of "sex"); and, secondly, the instincts to destroy and kill, which we assimilate as the aggressive or destructive instincts' (Einstein and Freud 1994: 31). In an intriguing essay on Christa Wolf's *A Model Childhood*, Ruth Waldeck reflects on how Freud's theories might manifest themselves in a personal narrative from the Nazi era. Waldeck traces the source of 'the unspeakable' ('das Unsagbare') in Wolf's book and determines that it is 'one's own pleasure in cruelty' ('die eigene Lust an der Grausamkeit', Waldeck 1990: 301). Waldeck pursues a passage in which the protagonist, Nelly, feels 'the raging desire, finally, to be able to hit soft flesh' ('die wutschäumende Lust, endlich in weiches Fleisch schlagen zu können', Waldeck 1990: 301). Freud changes Einstein's terms of 'Might and Right' to right and violence, and claims that '[c]onflicts of interest between people are resolved, in principle, by recourse to violence'. He later speaks specifically of war, saying, 'when a nation is summoned to engage in war, a whole gamut of human motives may respond to this appeal; high and low motives, some openly avowed, others slurred over. The lust for aggression and destruction is certainly included; the innumerable cruelties of history and daily life confirm its prevalence and strength' (Einstein and Freud 1994: 28, 31).

Several women writers have addressed the question of violence or force in terms similar to Freud's. Simone Weil, in her essay 'The *Iliad* or the Poem of Force', (1940–41), writes:

> Perhaps all men, by the very act of being born, are destined to suffer violence; yet this is a truth to which circumstance shuts men's eyes. ... The man who is the possessor of force seems to walk through a non-resistant element; in the human substance that surrounds him nothing has the power to interpose, between the impulse and the act, the tiny interval that is reflection. Where there is no room for reflection, there is none either for justice or prudence. Hence we see men in arms behaving harshly and madly. (Weil 1986: 193)

Virginia Woolf concurs in a passage in *Three Guineas*, in which she links the use of force to a critique of the educated classes:

> the finest education in the world does not teach people to hate force, but to use it ... education, far from teaching the educated generosity and magnanimity, makes them on the contrary so anxious to keep their possessions, that 'grandeur and power' of which the poet speaks, in their own hands, that they will use not force but much subtler methods than force when they are asked to share them ... And are not force and possessiveness very closely connected with war? (Woolf 1938: 29–30)

While Freud attributes natural aggression to all human beings, Simone Weil's references to the use of force concern combatants in the Trojan War, all of whom, for her purposes, are male. Similarly, when Virginia Woolf criticizes the educated classes, she means men, since women were denied university educations.

In addition to the unresolved question of whether violence is gendered, many German women's accounts of the Second World War explore the possibility that National Socialist ideology influenced them, if not to commit violence, at least to accept it. The gender solidarity that one might have expected from the German women's movement, which resulted in, among other things, suffrage in 1918, was destroyed by the NS world view, which split women into two groups, desirable and undesirable, as described earlier.

This division was further exacerbated by differences of class and political orientation, both of which dominated over gender as the basis for group identity. German aristocrats, in general, allied themselves rather with other European aristocrats than with like-minded Germans of lower social classes. This phenomenon is described by several writers from the upper classes, but especially compellingly by Marie Vassiltchikov, a 'White Russian princess', who found herself in Berlin during the war years and wrote about this period in her *Berlin Diaries, 1940–1945* (1987). At the other end of the social spectrum, women from socialist and communist circles, such as Lore Wolf, Anni Wadle or Lina Haag, failed to identify with women from the bourgeoisie. Rent asunder by racial differences as well as religious, ethnic, political and class distinctions, women did not exist during the Nazi era as a unified, gender-based group. And yet, as Gisela Bock points out, 'gender difference and gender hierarchy continued to play a prime role in German society at large.' 'The fact', she continues, 'that for the Nazis race as a *political* category was more crucial than sex should not blind us to the importance of gender as a *historical* category' (Bock 1998: 96). From this, one can see that gender differences, already long a part of German society, remained intact, but were contained within the political, ethnic, religious, racial and class groups. It would be another thirty years before women would again have the chance to bond across lines of (other) group identity.

Notes

1. For a comprehensive consideration of the history of photojournalism and war and of photographic depictions of violence and death, see Sontag (2002).
2. I take the term 'ordinary women' from Gisela Bock's usage in her essay 'Ordinary Women in Nazi Germany; Perpetrators, Victims, Followers, and Bystanders' (Bock 1998).
3. This calls to mind the effort of the *New York Times*, which memorialized the victims of the 11 September attacks by publishing their biographies, several at a time, every day in the paper throughout the months following the disaster.
4. For a more comprehensive discussion of various terms to designate different levels of guilt and responsibility, see Martin (2000).
5. One reason for the relative invisibility of gender as a category in Holocaust research, a topic that Ringelheim pursues further in her essay, might be the reluctance to criticize, in any manner, those who survived extreme hardship or to denigrate the memory of those who perished. Accusing Jewish men of sexist or patriarchal behaviour towards Jewish women would thus not be possible. The sanctity of Holocaust victims and their immunity to criticism is an issue that has been raised in other contexts. Art Spiegelman, for example, in his cartoon-style biography of his survivor-father, *Maus*, openly criticizes his father but at the same time expresses guilt for doing so (see especially vol. 2, 1986).
6. Gertrud Scholtz-Klink, 'National Women's Leader', said, in a speech to the Nationalsozialistische Frauenschaft in 1935: 'through marriage we consciously

become mothers of the nation; that is, we understand and share every national requirement laid upon German men, and that, therefore, as wives we must unconditionally become the companions of our men – not merely in personal terms, but in all national requirements' (quoted in Bell and Offen 1983: 379).

7. Eva Zeller said several times in our May 1986 interview: 'I always have the alibi of extreme youth' (Ich habe immer noch das Alibi Jugend).

References

Baumel, J.T. 1998. *Double Jeopardy: Gender and the Holocaust*. London, Portland, Oreg: Vallentine Mitchell.

Bell, S.G. and K. Offen (eds). 1983. *Women, the Family, and Freedom. Vol. 2, 1880–1950*. Stanford: Stanford University Press.

Bielenberg, C. 1986. *The Past is Myself*. London: Corgi (orig. 1968).

———. 1988. Personal interview. Tullow, Ireland, 31 May. Unpublished manuscript.

Bock, G. 1998. 'Ordinary Women in Nazi Germany; Perpetrators, Victims, Followers, and Bystanders', in D. Ofer and L.J. Weitzman (eds), *Women in the Holocaust*. New Haven: Yale University Press, pp. 85–100.

Day, I. 1980. *Ghost Waltz*. New York: Viking Press.

Einstein, A. and S. Freud. 1994. 'Why War?' in A. Kaes, M. Jay and E. Dimendberg (eds). *The Weimar Republic Sourcebook*. Berkeley: University of California Press, pp. 25–34.

Grass, G. 1961. *Katz und Maus : eine Novelle*. Neuwied: Luchterhand.

Hannsmann, M. 1982. *Der helle Tag bricht an: ein Kind wird Nazi*. Munich: dtv.

———. 1991. Personal interview. Stuttgart, 28 May. Unpublished manuscript.

Higonnet, M.R., J. Jenson, S. Michel and M. Collins Weitz (eds). 1987. *Behind the Lines: Gender and the Two World Wars*. New Haven: Yale University Press.

Martin, E. 2000. 'Victims or Perpetrators? Literary Responses to Women's Roles in National Socialism', in E. Frederiksen and M. Wallach (eds), *Facing Fascism and Confronting the Past: German Women Writers from Weimar to the Present*. Albany: State University of New York Press, pp. 61–82.

Mann, T. 1905. *Professor Unrat, oder das Ende eines Tyrannen : Roman*. Munich: Langen.

Maschmann, M. 1983. *Fazit: Mein Weg in der Hitler-Jugend*. Munich: dtv (orig. 1963).

Musil, R. 1906. *Die Verwirrungen des Zöglings Törleß*. Wien: Wiener Verlag.

Rayner, R. 1997. 'Women in the Warrior Culture', *The New York Times Magazine*, 22 June, 24–56.

Ringelheim, J. 1998. 'The Split between Gender and the Holocaust', in D. Ofer and L.J. Weitzman (eds), *Women in the Holocaust*. New Haven: Yale University Press, pp. 340–50.

Scholtz-Klink, G. 1935. 'Speech to the Nationalsozialistische Frauenschaft, 10 September 1935', reprinted in: *Der Parteitag der Freiheit 1935, Offizieller Bericht über den Verlauf des Reichsparteitages mit sämtlichen Kongressreden*. München: Zentralverlag der NSDAP Eher, pp. 165–69, 171–72. Excerpt reprinted in S. Bell and K. Offen (eds), *Women, the Family, and Freedom. Vol. 2, 1880–1950*. Stanford: Stanford University Press, pp. 378–81.

Sontag, S. 2002. 'Looking at War: Photography's View of Devastation and death', *The New Yorker*. 9 December, 82–98.

Spiegelman, A. 1986. *Maus: a Survior's Tale (2 Vols.)*. New York: Pantheon.

Swanwick, H.M. 1915. *Women and War*. Pamphlet no. 11. London: Union of Democratic Control, pp. 1–11. Excerpt reprinted in S. Bell and K. Offen (eds), *Women, the Family, and Freedom. Vol. 2, 1880–1950*. Stanford: Stanford University Press, pp. 1–11.

Tröger, A. 1987. 'German Women's Memories of World War II', in M. R. Higonnet et al. (eds), *Behind the Lines: Gender and the Two World Wars*. New Haven: Yale University Press, pp. 285–99.

Vassiltchikov, M. 1987. *Berlin Diaries, 1940–1945*. New York: Knopf.

Waldeck, R. 1990. '"Heikel bis Heute": Frauen und Nationalsozialismus: Überlegungen zur weiblichen Selbstdefinition als Opfer anhand von Christa Wolfs Roman *Kindheitsmuster*', in L. Gravenhorst and C. Tatschmurat (eds), *Töchter Fragen NS-Frauen Geschichte*. Freiburg im Breisgau: Kore, pp. 293–308.

Weil, S. 1986. *Simone Weil: An Anthology*. Siân Miles, ed. London: Virago Press.

Weiss, P. 1966. *The Investigation*. Trans. J. Swan and U. Grosbard. Woodstock, Ill.: Dramatic Publishing. (*Die Ermittlung*. Frankfurt am Main: Suhrkamp, 1965.)

Wolf, C. 1980. *A Model Childhood*. Trans. U. Molinaro and H. Rappolt. New York: Farrar, Straus and Giroux. (orig. *Kindheitsmuster*. Berlin, Weimar: Aufbau-Verlag, 1976.)

Woolf, V. 1938. *Three Guineas*. New York: Harcourt, Brace and World.

Zeller, E. 1981. *Solange ich denken kann*. Stuttgart: DVA.

———. Personal Interview. Munich, 15 May. Unpublished manuscript.

CHAPTER 8

JUDGING BY AESTHETICS: 'DUE CARE' IN THE MANAGEMENT OF 'COLLABORATION' IN THE FIRST PALESTINIAN INTIFADA

Iris Jean-Klein

Introduction: 'Due Process' in 'Due Care'

Concentrating on the First Palestinian Intifada (1987–91/92),[1] this essay treats a sphere of liberation activism which few studies address – handling 'collaboration with the enemy' in the running of such movements.[2] Although there are no precise figures – human rights watchdogs working in the area were aware but looked the other way, for the same reasons that anthropologists have averted their eyes – estimates by Palestinian academics and 'civil society' organizers (see below) indicate that hundreds of Palestinians, if not numbers in the four-digit range, were killed and injured by activists in this popular national uprising against Israeli occupation, in connection with accusations made against them that they were agents working for the Israeli occupiers. Commenting in hindsight, progressive sources have mooted that the phenomenon only picked up momentum during the third year of the Intifada (in 1990), and signalled the demise of the 'mass-based civilian uprising' as it was being transformed 'by Israel's anti-insurgency strategy' into a 'militarized underground movement of armed youth primarily interested in rooting out alleged collaborators' (see, for example, Hammami 2000: 17). In other words, the progressive avant-garde are in retrospect proposing that a burning concern with 'collaboration' was not a normal part of running this uprising (indeed, that a militaristic ethos had not gone hand in glove with civilian or civic-oriented forms of activism) and that it signalled the abandonment of civic responsibility and discipline.

This has not been my understanding, which I report in this chapter; nor was it the predominant view even among progressive academics and intellectuals at the time, which I shall also come to, but will also not share entirely.[3] I am not suggesting that undisciplined behaviour did not occur, much of it in the domain of 'managing collaborators' (although I am sure that cooperative administration, for example, experienced their version of this problem). What I shall argue is that for many activists, most of the time, containing the problem of 'collaboration' summoned the greatest amount of care and discipline, and was also understood in this way: as a context for demonstrating their own and their movement's discipline, and thus, their morality and justness.

I approach the subject ethnographically, mainly through the actions and understandings of grass-roots activists who were supporting, with varying degrees of ideological conviction and formality of association, the secular 'movements of committee associations' (*harakat lijan*). My analytical approach consists, first, of a readiness to see *process* – social process has its own standards and thus comprising something like 'due process' – in these activities. Furthermore, I capture process descriptively by concentrating on the material forms through which a sense of due process, or its equivalent, was experientially mediated – made to feel real – for the activists themselves. I suspend my own moral judgement, and aim instead for analytical empathy with the methods activists relied on in judging ethics and morality. They concentrated on the persons who facilitated or directly participated in the judgement and execution of someone else as a 'collaborator' (numerous terms designated this positionality: *madsus*, *hasus*, or *ᶜamil* are just some of them). My analysis does not aim to give the perspective of known collaborators – those who made themselves known in this capacity – but something of this subjectivity is refracted in the actions and discourses of activists that I try to recount.

A focus on aesthetic form seems highly appropriate in this case, and the current essay is an expanded explanation of why. As we shall see, such a concentration mirrors the knowledge practices of the activists themselves: it was very much how 'justness' (*ᶜadala*ᵗ) was performed and known or recognized – actually seen – to exist. To anticipate my main argument, pro-nationalist Palestinians derived assurance that judgements of persons as 'collaborators' and corrective or punitive actions against them were just from evidence that aesthetic exactitude prevailed in the course of action taken. From this, i.e., from form or pattern in action, they trusted that honourable conduct and morality prevailed. A sequence of honourable conduct in social animation was intrinsically incapable of being unjust. Observations of aesthetic exactitude, which instantiated morality, centred attention on the frameworks, manoeuvres and techniques that were being exercised.

The remarkable fact here is that the 'means', the material and corporal channels – I stress that I do not mean this in any instrumentalist or 'tool'-like sense of the term 'means', but in purely aesthetic terms and as a matter of accounting for recognition – mattered more to people than any outcome of their application or the ends being pursued. The morality of effects and of the end was guaranteed by the appropriate exercise of the esteemed forms, which simply never failed. People's exercises were thought fallible, but not the forms. (We shall see that the actors were aiming to become themselves tools – were subjects arranging themselves into frameworks and contexts that were poignantly animating these forms.) In short, this approach places a huge amount of epistemological trust in what I have called mediums, methods and 'frameworks' – by which I mean something slightly different from my activist informants, who at the time used the term *nuthum* (sing. *nitham*) mainly to refer to one kind of 'order' or register, namely, active party-political 'frameworks'. That is one of the reasons why 'frameworks' or mediums organize and stand in the foreground of this account.

There are other remarkable aspects of 'process'. One could not presume to know in advance what counted as a medium or method, or what situations and, generally, what information, were 'relevant' to it. This is one of the key questions my account addresses. I had considered giving a list of tell-tale 'signs' or significant actants – pointing to 'things' such as concepts, spaces, relationships and relationship operations, speech patterns, modes of dress, attitude, organizational frameworks and 'morality frames', etc. – but then realized that this was precisely the approach that I was arguing would not work. Morality was taken to be not inherent in a specific domain but in its mode of animation and so was an issue that extended (in the way it was enacted) across all thinkable 'frameworks' that were socially effected and thus 'relevant': kinship, friendship, committee activism, religious practice; the home, the workplace, the street, the shops, etc. Thus it would not make any analytical sense to treat one or several domains of practice as a/the main 'moral framework'. One needs to imagine the various domains, conversely, as (a) frameworks that were first of all not given separately, but needed first to be effected as separate domains, and (b) fields that materialized morality in diverse ways, each phrasing the challenges of the historical moment in its own unique way. The moral framework is aesthetic exactitude and discipline. It is this I signal when, in the end, I refer to this as an 'aesthetic regime' of ethics and justice.[4] Now imagine the range of work entailed in demonstrating moral subject and justness of action – socially or ethnographically.

This is the chain of causality I am going to present, then, as I track the form in which something like 'due process' materialized in the understanding of activists. Justness was contingent on certainty of knowledge (*ᶜaqidaᶦ*); certainty and truth in turn were artefacts – or artefactual moments – of morality; and morality materialized around 'honourable conduct' which, whatever different social actors understood the contemporary expression to consist of, invariably knew itself as an aesthetic discipline: continuous performance of a concern with and aptitude for measure and exactitude in matters of personal presentation and relationship conduct – in the entire range of one's social movements. Anthropologists are not theoretically unfamiliar with the principle of aesthetic authority. For example, Riles (2001) has recently shown in her analysis of document practices that the authority, respect or persuasive force that some documents command is more a consequence of the information they convey through their aesthetic design – the ways in which design 'channels attention' – than linked to their descriptive contents. In observing grass-roots Palestinian activists and how they organized efforts to 'deal with collaborators', we see another ethnographic instantiation, of an order that self-consciously gives great priority, or indeed great authority, to the activity of socially materializing (i.e., animating) divine or/and politically utopian forms of design as a form of instantiating truth, justice and dignity (see Mahmood 2001).

What I have said, about 'due process' materializing around observations of aesthetic and moral conduct, anticipates what I want to make explicit next. The 'relevant' aesthetic and morality were not only, or even mainly, those of a person accused of collaboration; they were primarily those of the activist or network of activists handling an accusation and accused party. That is to say, the process became moral and just by virtue of the fact that the activists handling the case were conducting themselves as disciplined and moral subjects in and through these processes. The correct outcome, including the necessary certainty about the accused person's collaborative subjectivity, 'followed' from the extent to which the activists were practising aesthetic exactitude in the procedures and also 'in themselves'. By dubbing the process 'due care', I am marking this aspect: the correspondences between understandings of processes as just or unjust and the extent to which activists who were making and acting on a case were seen (and knew themselves!) as paying attention to – minding – their own moral integrity. '*Der balak*!', 'Be careful!' mothers and sisters always reminded youths as they were heading out of the house, and meant not only that they should be wary of onslaughts they had not asked for or elicited, but to avoid laxity of self-care in meeting all challenges, those they sought and those that sought them.

There are other elements of process that are indicative of what I call a 'cross-subjective' knowledge and value economy (see Jean-Klein 2000, 2003). For instance, the relevant time frame for observing morality – it is analytically apt that the English term 'observation' has dual connotations of 'watching someone else carefully' and 'own careful adherence to a code', because both were facets of 'due process' – was not limited to moments when an activist or network was actually working on a case (which would have been difficult to discern and to disentangle from other cases and activist moments). It gathered up universal and global knowledge of the person. Observation took in the time before, during and after handling a case. The 'contexts' that were relevant to observing morality were wide-ranging, tracking knowledge of relevant persons' conduct in as well as outside political activism, for example, in the context of familial relationships, at work, and so on. Specifically, everyday social performances, which all, or many, could 'see for themselves', informed on political dispositions that needed to be hidden (for reasons of operational expediency), while visible or socially 'established' aspects of political and nationalist-activist conduct (what people took for indications of an activist disposition in others, and/or an 'infrastructure' of consensus about their tendencies) fed back information that drew out knowledge about everyday social and personal dimensions – which needed to be concealed for reasons of propriety (and by virtue of their proper concealment, refracted 'hidden' political virtues). And so forth. This was still not the full extent of the cross-subjective and recursive information and value economy that mediated the articulation of honourable (and dishonourable) and dignified subjectivities, however. For observation also did not stop at the subject or persons of main interest (the presumed activist, collaborator, martyr, man, woman, household, committee association, etc.). Relevant information about their moral and political disposition was sought in other subjective locations – in the visible conduct of other people or associations who were 'close' relations, who in a sense 'made' and were made by them. Specific 'close' persons and networks thus served as sources of information, as alternative bodies for sounding out or 'echolocating', as Wagner (2001) so aptly terms it, a disposition that was difficult or impossible to see/know otherwise, in and of itself – not just because it might be hiding or the entire body had been removed, but because nobody (or few bodies) possessed all the information relevant to knowing its 'own' range of values in themselves, inherently. Thus, for instance, neighbours and comrades in a movement would try and 'see' the actual value of an incarcerated or hospitalized youth (i.e., a youth who was not available for direct observation) by observing particularly closely the mother's or a sister's personal and social conduct, which were taken to correspond to or as being congruent with the absent youth's, in addition to hearing narrative testimonials and reports from female kin persons. People also sought information about a boy's likely disposition in a father's or brother's behaviour and demeanour, but did not expect a direct moral correspondence, only an 'infrastructural' semblance. Cross-subjective echolocation had application beyond establishing political and activist identities; for example, it was used in the animation of individuals' unique gender identity (see Jean-Klein 2000).

The breadth and depth of observation on the basis of which the morality of subjects was established are indicative of another, more fundamental aspect of this economy of truth and identity making that is also analytically of great importance here. The social or moral value of persons (or of spaces, concepts, types of relationships, objects, and so forth) was not permanently stored within or inscribed into them. Performances and their effects did not stick or linger. Often, social analyses take it for granted that such entities are material artefacts (storehouses, memorials) of creative, productive or otherwise 'valuable' social processes. However, here they are better conceptualized as the inverse – channels through whom/which values were continuously exercised and in this way were given corporeality. Social 'permanence' was the effect of constant repetition of social-corporeal instantiation (and staying true to form, which anthropologists gloss as 'tradition', requiring a lot more effort, creativity and design than common social science understandings of 'tradition' concede). The value of subjects and entities, too, only became evident ('revealed') in such 'social movements' – which could consist as easily of concern with appropriate dressing patterns, relationship habits and patterns in social self-conduct as of the promotion of 'social progress' by caring about a committee (which usually came back to these issues anyway). It was then that their role in performing values became clearly apparent: were they or were they not apt animations of these values, or clearly making efforts appropriate to their age, gender, education, rank, experience?

In an inert state, the value of most subjects, objects and concepts was 'unclear' or 'un(fore)seeable'. This was exactly how activists and other Palestinians described persons suspected of collaboration (and voiced their suspicion of them): as 'unclear' (*mish wadih, mish zahir*) or 'dirty' (*wisikh*); or, indeed (as female suspects were often described), as 'always sitting' or 'just sitting', or (as men might be described) always seen standing about or hanging around inside houses. By describing another person as sociable, appropriately sociable, and (hence) 'clear' (*wadih, zahir*) and clean (*ndhif,* which also implied purity), on the other hand, a speaker testified that s/he knew the referent to be morally upright; sound (*salim*); stable or consistent, and in that sense reliable (*amana*); active; and so forth. It was how a hero (*batal*, pl. *abtal*) might be described, or a martyr (*shahed*, pl. *shuhada*). That was the main difference between activism and collaboration, not any perception of one as 'organized' while the other was not. In fact, the way in which activists were conceptualizing 'collaboration' during their detection, correction and/or persecution imaged collaborators as 'equally' organized, sociologically speaking. However, collaborators' organizing gave a 'negative' image, or figure-ground reversal, of activist organizing in many respects, as I go on to show. The distinguishing feature about collaboration was a lack of moral equivalence, of the highest degree. Collaboration instantiated a subject position that lacked entirely moral intent in its social animation, that was fully content not to make itself out to be subservient to the animation of any morality. (Those collaborating openly with the Israeli occupation were not even themselves claiming that they were performing an 'alternative' morality or collective agenda.) As such, 'the Leagues' of collaborators (known as 'the village leagues') were not only classed as morally inferior, but as an animation of the worst imaginable, barely still human form of (still) mindful behaviour: mindful abstention from subjective and intersubjective performances of morality. (Someone who was found or known to be weak of mind, *habl* or *habla*, for example, was excused or forgiven, although s/he still needed to be socially contained. The offence was to be of sound mind – the more educated the worse the offence – but not to make an effort to participate in the human performance of a particular morality.) Collaboration moved knowingly against the will of the 'Highest Command' – which for some was the UNLU (United National Leadership of the Uprising) and the PLO, for others it was God, and for many it was both – by virtue of aiding a powerful enemy who moved against the masses and organizations that were representative of, intent on witnessing, these widely esteemed bodies. Just as collaboration was not taken to be unorganized or chaotic, it was not seen as external and irrelevant to activist and social organization: it kept activists and decent folk generally alert and mindful, and everybody was thought to have the potential for it. The question was whether one would manage to control it, contain its outbreak or defer its breakthrough in the current generation.

Only a few exceptional figures were understood as being intrinsically perfect and complete in their own design, and therefore as intrinsically and unequivocally fixed in both their value and virtue, even outside their animation. They existed prior to animation and, in fact, were taken as an animatory impetus. (It is comparable to the way in which Western secular-liberal discourse at this moment takes 'human rights' for an exception to the operative rule that all values are constructed and as such arbitrary.) Persons stood between object-status and divine (or politically utopian) design in this respect in that, although they started off minimally (or, rather, multiply) defined, they also could and were supposed to aspire towards singular and permanent definition through consistent value performances into death. Death seemed like a point of relative closure, the only closure, and in that sense was 'home'.

This particular economy poses challenges for the ethnographer if she assumes the main objective of her analysis, or the only available methodological starting point, is the stable classification of a network, domain or entire field according to its intrinsic morality. Efforts to give an account of 'due process' are turned into an infinitely expansive task by its aesthetic (and aesthetic focus). It would seem to require, or to excuse, coverage of an immense range of situations and infinite number of movements. Obviously, the frameworks for action in terms of which I cull the first half of my account (I concentrate increasingly on instantiations of activist and collaborative subjectivities in the latter parts) are not intended as a complete set. However, it should also be clear now that, regardless of what our impressions are in reading or seeing these materials, they are not just 'background'. They are the material textures of discipline and truth. (Perhaps I should stress, equally, that the divisions as such were not seen as given by activists or others in this field.)

It is now clear how my understanding will digress from reports taking the view that the concern which nationalist activism in the First Intifada showed with 'rooting out collaborators' indicated a loss of civil discipline. There remains for me to consider briefly reports written during the Intifada by pro-nationalist and progressive intellectuals who at the time endorsed an ethos of militancy, and my disagreement with them. These reports had championed the opposite extreme position, which overstated the role and authority of formal political organizations in administering 'due process' (for example, Nassar and Heacock

1990: 200f.; Peretz 1990: 90; Yahya 1990: 94–95; see also Tessler 1994: 847ff.). Specifically, these sources were pointing to specialized 'security and justice committees' and/or 'strike forces' within the four committee-movements that were active. To cite from an account by two sociologists:

> Part of [the committees'] role consists in ferreting out and pursuing collaborators … Hundreds of collaborators have repented under pressure from the masses; dozens have been killed through the procedures set up by the committees and their strike forces; hundreds more have been deterred from filling the void and becoming collaborators. The collaborators are … shamed by visits to their families; their names are written on walls; stories circulate about them; unknowing persons are warned to stay away from them. Usually this is enough. They repent in the presence of a religious figure and representative sections of the society and the intifada, notably the shebabs [*sic*] and the popular committees. Early in the uprising, they surrendered their weapons if they had any, which were then publicly destroyed … In the case of those who fail to repent, further pressures are mounted against them, this time through the family and local notables … Those who make deals with the strike forces in the presence of only their families are … more likely, if not carefully monitored, to return to their previous activities. (Nassar and Heacock 1990: 200–1)

While I am arguing that actions taken in respect of 'collaborators' were not aesthetically formless, sociologically undisciplined and morally unprincipled, I do not therefore take the view that only actions in the framework of these political organizations and their task forces counted as organized. Nor, evidently, do I see ethnographic justification for the common view that such political organizations stood on their own, autonomously, without benefiting somehow from parallel frameworks and registers. Even the existing reports, while they seek to foreground committee organisations, mention other actors and actants (Latour 1996, 1999; Law 1999) – 'families', 'local notables' and 'the masses' or crowds (*al-jamahir*). I think I have made it amply clear that process – which we now understand as equivalent to a particular aesthetic in action – was animating and 'crossing' diverse frameworks and discrete subject positions. In this view it would also not make any ethnographic sense to suggest that 'killing collaborators' was mainly a male performance.[5]

Frameworks and Channels of 'Due Care'

'Kinship' (Asab and Qaraba^{t})

Many features of observed Palestinian social organization in the West Bank in the late 1980s and early 1990s were forms of social and political organization that one finds widely distributed across the Arab world, but, of course, they reflected the region's unique political history, notably the establishment of a Zionist state, Israel, in this region.

Two forms of kinship association were socially relevant and working in conjunction or in constant tension with one another. One form materialized around patronymic associations: corporate groups based on putative genealogical kinship, specifically, on patrilineal descent and named after an apical male 'ancestor' (or an influential historical character). In terms of their sociological substance, these associations – referred to as *hamayil* (sing. *hamula*), if they were village-based 'clans', as English accounts commonly render them; and as *dyur* (sing. *dar*), if they were town-based and influential 'dynasties') – have always incorporated differently related persons and families besides patrilineal kin and agnates, notably, subjects known in the anthropological literature as 'clients'. More interesting than this fact is that the social actors themselves, Palestinians, do not conceal it, but on the contrary, make it constantly explicit (see Cohen 1965; Antoun 1972). Thus, men who 'stand together in one line' (*yasuffu ma*^{c} *ba*^{c}*ad*: see Cohen 1965: 138) and are 'owners of [the same] blood' (*ashab*^{u} *il-dam*) – in other words, those who form the genealogically genuine core or backbone of such associations – are kept conceptually distinct from 'contingent' parts or partnerships, such as clients and other associates, albeit not always in name – which is precisely the level or form in which they are usually 'incorporated': one name, but not one blood.

In contemporary social and political organization in the West Bank, 'tribal aggregates' (*asha'ir*), which had been historically significant, had been reduced in their numbers and lost their space for enacting contiguity and relevance, not least on account of the establishment of Israel in 1948 and the massive Palestinian population and leadership flight it precipitated. The Israeli state's entrenchment had also precipitated a third social form in addition to the village-town dichotomy (and challenging these forms): the refugee camps. In any event, the breadth and depth of most socially active agnatic and patronymic kinship associations or 'families' in Palestinian towns, villages and camps in the 1980s and 1990s were at the level of fractions of vaster hypothetical entities (if one imagines them through anthropological designs of lineage segmentary systems, they are sections and branches).

While a politics based on this form of kinship was ideologically rejected and even directly targeted by avant-garde progressives organizing in the Intifada – committee organizers and activists kept saying they were 'gently' eradicating patriarchy, and using the struggle against Israeli occupation as an instrument for championing this 'cause within a cause' – the other form that was socially relevant, known in the anthropological literature of the wider region under the term 'practical kinship' (*qaraba*^{t}, lit. 'closeness'; see H. Geertz 1979), was admitted, so to speak, and even invited to play an 'active' part in progressive political organizing, even though (perhaps because) it worked with, in the sense that it was subservient to – practically feeding or animating

– patronymic associations. In reality, activists were drawing knowledge and other resources from both forms. For example, ethnographically it seemed as though political organizations were taking over ownership and manipulation of paternalistic authority from the descent-based associations (Jean-Klein 2000).

Networks of *qaraba*^{t} were what Palestinians implied when they spoke of 'house(hold)s' (*byut*, sing. *bayt*) and families (^{c}*a'ilat*, sing. ^{c}*a'ila*^{t}). Most households were two- to three-generation deep and, like 'clans', lineage associations and dynasties, were comprised of a genuine core (the *ahl il-bayt* or actual owners/members of the household) and friends or loose associates, who lent social substance and/or motivation to the corporate subject at the centre – who in turn needed to labour to attract and hold the attention of 'associates'. (This foreshadows or shows 'cross-subjectively' the internal composition of committee organizations. They also featured, at all levels, real members (*a*^{c}*da'*, sing. ^{c}*udu*) – those who had signed up as members of the political party to which the committee was formally affiliated – and 'friends' (*asdiqa'*) – those who participated in activities on an ad hoc basis.) Unlike the 'core' of lineage associations, networks of contemporary practical closeness were drawn 'bilaterally'. That is to say, the persons at the core were of one blood (*damm*) and/or from the same womb (*rahm*). (In so far as 'FBD' or *bint* ^{c}*amm* marriage continued to be a burning interest, if not actually preferred and common enough in practice still, husbands and wives were actually also of one blood, and conjugal interactions conceivably set the partners socially apart, estranging them somewhat, instead of 'confirming' or repeating an unstable form of genealogical closeness (between the set of brothers who were the spouses' fathers), as anthropological interpretations of this pattern have tended to assume.)

If there was ideologically a bias where the house(hold) (*bayt*) and its circle of 'close' ones was concerned, it was in favour of the *sitt-il-bayt*, the mistress of the household, whose diligence and organizational aptitude were credited for its smooth functioning and sound reputation. A *bayt* was invariably associated with the name of the woman in charge of running it, in conversational references, for example, as when speakers specified households by affixing the woman's personal name or, if she had a son, her teknonym: *Bayt* Randa. The range of associates of a household implied by *qaraba*^{t}, whom family members identified as persons '*min il-bayt*' (parts of our house/hold), or as 'folk who are well-known to us' (^{c}*ullaf*, sing. *ulf*), tended also to be relations for which the *sitt-il-bayt* was responsible. She was somehow the 'reason' for them: if not the original cause, then the nurturer of them, through choreographed transactions with them, including exchanges of food. Apart from kin on both sides, the male and female household head's, these informal associations always included neighbours (*al-jiran*, sing. *jar*/^{at}) with whom one regularly interacted – a certain degree of neighbourly association was detailed in local custom – and the close colleagues (*zumala*, sing. *zamil/a*^{t}) and friends of household members. Male proprietorship was not socially forgotten, however. It was marked in parallel, in the alternative reference, *dar*, which unlike the term *bayt*, was always coupled with the name of the male head of household, if there was one. *Dar* thus signified 'dynasties', lineages of some stature, as well as the 'hard' material resources with which women and youths animated households.

'Closeness' was materially grounded in precisely choreographed social interactions and transactions (exchanges of food, gifts, information, blessings, visits, etc.). The fact that people persisted in these exchanges even during curfews speaks powerfully to their significance. I would suggest that such exchanges were a way of practically demarcating a cluster of 'close' relations which one could properly attend to, while cutting off (or leaving 'inert') a vast number of other connections one virtually had or could potentially practise, but preferred not to actualize. Relations were, after all, units of information on oneself and as such were better not had in excess of what one could properly attend to, with appropriate discipline. Associations of closeness that nationalist Palestinians cultivated in the First Intifada showed that many were editing their active kin relations, friendships and neighbourhood circles (see Strathern 1996) with a view to contriving, at that time, networks of nationalist-political consensus. Relations with people whose company one had previously enjoyed but who, when the time came, demonstrated a lack of nationalist interest or commitment (or too much of it, making them a liability) had often been allowed to fall inert. One still exchanged greetings with them when one met them in the street, but did not visit their houses, except, perhaps, on religious 'high festivals', and on these occasions gave out as little information as possible. Not to do so would have amounted to abstention in excess and shown a lack of etiquette. 'Kin' who were widely suspected of counter-nationalist activity, or of another form of immoral conduct, were as likely to be cut off. One kept out of their path, had endless reasons for being remiss in visits that would have been 'due', and, if these people came calling, one tried to block their entry. However, this required thought and social acrobatics; for instance, to avert or withhold visits (as in receiving or making visits), one needed 'good', that is, socially plausible and just 'reasons', or else one was 'creating a question mark' around one's own social decency. To say that there was a question mark around someone – *ʿaleihi/ha ʿalamet su'al* – was another way of saying that someone was socially and politically suspect. I witnessed on numerous occasions just how far out of their way people went in order to block a relative and collaborator suspect's entry to their home without seeming to be in breach of hospitality etiquette. It was a challenge.

Segmentary kinship has fuelled considerable debate in anthropology in the past, over an issue that was occasionally referred to as kinship 'amoralism'. I raise this because activists in progressive organizations seemed to validate such a model when they used patrilineal kinship as an epistemological frame for mapping 'collaboration' in relation to activism. They were totally in agreement with the anthropological verdict: kinship simply did not determine identity or trust, although it was a starting point.

The analytical concern of anthropologists had centred around the fact that, although genealogy featured as the main principle of social and political organization, it continually 'failed' as a mechanism for predicting loyalties. Boundaries kept shifting and changing, associations merging and splitting up. The principle as such did not prescribe or inscribe a field of actors at all. It was plainly a mechanism – consisting of the rhetorical adjustment of 'the' apical lineage ancestor – with which men could try and summon, as they saw need or aspiration, a 'task force' of variable genealogical 'depth' and social expanse. The unit of mobilization did not become permanently 'tied', and an association brought together by a man's and his supporters' rallying call would disaggregate again after or outside its practical deployment. The principle reproduced itself every time, but not a particular network that had been mobilized by means of it. What has astounded observers especially is that 'even' closest genealogical connections, those which are described as 'morally obligatory' (*lazim*; see also Antoun 1972) among the practitioners themselves, are not written in stone. As Bourdieu (1977: 53–58) stressed, relations between brothers are simultaneously the linchpin of an agnatic group and the places where they will potentially divide into units that compete and possibly oppose and fight each another (see also Cohen 1965; Antoun 1972). The bottom line is that associations formed by means of this principle are not units of lasting or 'blind' mutual trust – without constant observation. (The most trustworthy entity here is actually the actant, the instrument, more than any momentary artefact of its use.) This is what anthropological analyses have found so incredible, and what makes outside observers on the whole also extremely suspicious of this form and especially of modern movements that seem to be performing it.

Palestinian activists, who were, of course, aware that kinship was not determining, paid careful attention to patterns of moral character reproduction (and its failure) in the lines of known activists and/or collaborators. There circulated many precedent cases of splits in conversations among activists and in their formal instruction by cadres. According to these, large patronymic associations (*hamayil* and *dyur*) typically instantiated moral opposites: one branch (*fasil*) or line had a clean patriotic track record, and another was 'unclear' (either inconsistent or unknowable) or even had a known and established reputation as 'dirty' – made up of known collaborators and/or of common criminals (thieves and/or drug dealers). It was as if the point of the narratives was to remind everyone that a dual character potential lay in every line, body or material infrastructure, regardless of its 'background', and that a sound genealogy or track record was no reason for complacency. The point at which the character split was reported to have occurred, typically, involved a pair of brothers two or three generations earlier, of whom one turned out to be a great activist or the ancestor of one. I should also say that the period to which these accounts were pointing to (two to three generations earlier) was when the Israeli regime was actively nurturing the formation by Palestinians of non-

PLO-affiliated organizations, the so-called Village Leagues. With great regularity, these narratives sounded a warning against agnatic kin beyond the first degree. But the degree alone was never the full story: activist lore dwelt considerably on the contingent circumstances that had elicited a character definition – this way or the other, either repeating or deviating from the genealogically established tendency.

An often-cited case was the *hamula* of the collaborator who in 1989 helped the authorities hunt down and assassinate the seventeen-year-old activist for the PFLP in the Ramallah area, Yassir Abu Ghosh, whose courage and self-sacrifice had become legendary even before his 'martyrdom' (as his death became commemorated). It was widely recalled, when mentioning this 'big collaborator' (*madsus kbir*), that his father had been the second cousin of a renowned PFLP activist, Muhammad al-Khawaja, who in a sense was the 'father' of the PFLF in the West Bank: he was widely credited with bringing PFLP ideas to the territories after 1967. and was 'martyred' in 1976. Initially, the high-ranking activist's second cousin (and present-day collaborator's father) had been forced into collaboration, activists recalled. The Israeli 'Civil Administration' had blackmailed him with recordings they claimed they had that proved he had sexual relations with a Jewish Israeli 'dancer' (this insinuated that the woman had been a prostitute). The man later married his Jewish girlfriend, who converted to Islam so that they could be married, and collaboration became the couple's way of life. However, the couple raised their son, the present-day collaborator, as a Jew, people always pointed out. (His mother's conversion was not recognized in Jewish law; thus, her children would have also counted as Jewish.) But he also converted to Islam later in life, in order to marry a Muslim girl.[6] Again, this couple collaborated in their collaboration: reliable witnesses had seen the woman participating in the hunt for the young hero. The fact that the husband and wife were acting together and like one another – their failure to differentiate from each other – was itself taken as testimony of their lack of morals and failed humanity.

Committee Associations

This organizational framework can be quickly sketched, because I give a detailed account of the salient features and manoeuvres elsewhere (Jean-Klein 2003) and, as I argue there, because committee organizing repeated many of the aesthetic features that were prominent in kinship activity, some of which I have indicated in the previous section. Rather than repeating the entire analysis, then, I concentrate, after providing some background, on a few aspects that strike me as particularly relevant to the way in which 'due care' in respect of dealing with 'collaborators' was exercised.

At the time I am discussing, there were four active and distinctly named committee movements or 'frameworks' (*nuthum*): the 'mainstream' movement Fatah and the three 'progressive' movements of the PFLP, the DFLP, and the

PCP. The four 'party-acronymic movements' – I refer to them by this unusual term in order to signal that they were organized in a fashion that in many matters of aesthetic organization recalled patronymic associations – featured an identical range of specialized committee units that mirrored social and occupational specializations by gender, age, education, and so on, and which were also influential in the organization of social activity outside, or besides, political activism. Every movement also had a unique ingredient in its instantiation of the usual elements, however (see Hasso 1998, regarding the DFLP). (One can compare the similarity with that in the composition of patronymic associations and *byut*, which also showed variation within the limits of a common pattern.) Every movement featured at least one, some as many as three, professionalized public service-providing committees which provided 'alternative' or emergency health care, economic development and/or education (Barghouthi and Giacaman 1990). Each movement furthermore had its own 'federation' (*ittihad*) of women's committees (*lijan an-nasa'iy*); student movement; trade union and workers' associations; security committees and strike forces (*quwat dariba*); and networks of pupil councils and youth clubs. These were the consistent forms. The specialist units of all movements carried out almost identical tasks, regardless of the movement they were enacting and the unique ideology that provided the unique framework, and name, for joining in action. Units of 'strike forces' harnessed the energies of male teenage youths from lower-income neighbourhoods, camps and villages. According to contemporary accounts this sector was charged, mainly, with responsibility for militant actions such as engaging occupiers in street clashes, enforcing adherence to UNLU decrees in public spaces – and 'guarding' the community against crime and collaborators. Student councils were the forum for educated youths of diverse class backgrounds, though youths from wealthy houses were sent abroad to study by their parents. Trade unions reflected a more mature variety of male activism, in part university-educated, but more to the point, gathering together greater social maturity, political experience and mental discipline (*aqliy*). Union activists held greater organizational authority in the movement than members of the strike forces, and partly held or tried to hold social authority over the latter.

The 'women's committees' of all four federations were internally organized according to the participants' status as 'members' or 'friends', and by differences in their capacities based on age, marital status, class and membership rank. Unmarried committee participants (*banat*, lit. girls) were commonly trained in cooperative work and inducted into political visiting, which was mainly the form in which organizational recruitment, networking and intelligence work linked to the detection and verification of collaborators proceeded. *Banat* were also groomed for participation in street actions with *shebab*, the male youths of their movement's strike forces. The activist routines of educated and higher-ranking cadres and planners of women's committees revolved around organizing academic conferences and craft exhibitions bringing together distant chapters; writing newsletters and project-funding applications; and delivering public speeches. Women's committee organizers encouraged women from villages, camps and lower-income neighbourhoods with little formal education to expand their own 'spontaneous' (*afwiy*) actions. They were called upon to extend their maternal sensibilities to all active youth – for example, by intervening in the arrest of *shebab* during street demonstrations; and some were regularly invited to perform on theatre stages – to recount at committee-sponsored political festivities the victimization of members of their families, most often their sons, by arms of the Israeli regime.

Many forms of women's deployment, especially that of 'mothers', were predicated on a practical understanding that the mother-son relationship, and the relationship between girls and their brothers were special. Whereas relations between brothers anticipated a split or break at some point, in these cross-sex relations a separation was nearly impossible to accomplish, even if one needed or wanted to; it anticipated difficulties in making the necessary or 'ideal' divisions. (Each of the two relationships had its own unique potentialities and challenges; the 'stickier' one was not regarded as intrinsically more valuable and moral than the other, as for example in Western and feminist evaluations of maternal closeness.) I am here mainly commenting on issues of information and value economy. The image of the mother on the stage allowed ethnographic glimpses of her in her 'capacity' (or in her status, since she did not need to make special efforts to have this value) as an alternative source of information on the disposition of her son who was not present and would not have been clearly visible 'in himself' even if he had been present. Similarly, cross-siblings provided supplementary views on each other and, through the quality of their relationships, back on themselves. Ethnographic glimpses of this lateral refraction were occasions when the girls functioned as 'witnesses' of the *shebab* – among whom many girls had a brother – in demonstrations, or in prison (where the girls with their mothers and aunties visited them), whose collective conduct the girls reported to 'the community' during their social visiting rounds.

The principle – and actual instances – of familial cross-subjectivity, which is another name for the process I have just described (see Jean-Klein 2000, 2003), featured not only in women's committee organizing. It was repeated in the grammar of transactions between women's committee units, on the one hand, and strike forces and trade union activism, on the other. In the same way that a mother or a sister fed a son or a brother information to which he had no easy direct access, and the other way round, so were these committee units or their activists working together in assembling, circulating, cross-correlating and verifying information about activists and 'collaborators'. In this way, partners in subjectivity extended the observational capacities of each other beyond each subjectivity's limits, as much as each extended the other's social body surface for others to observe.

However, one should not unduly overstate the 'expansive' effect; it should be clear now that fractional subjectivities equally set definitional limits on what each could seem to be. The expansion of the body and field of activity was what added a narrower or more precise definition of value. There is also a danger that one overstates one single value, the positive one, of this 'partnership', when it should be clear that the magnification (definitional limitation) was not always desired, socially or personally, although it was, of course, not in the subjects' own powers to suspend or control it. What I am getting at is the risk of concentrating on isolated partnerships, not anticipating or seeing the 'betrayal' that would take place during second and third forms of cross-subjective exercises. I mean 'betrayal' of individual subjects, not of the subject position or the social cause, which were morally 'affirmed' by the discipline that the tension of a second cross-subjective association 'added'. I mean to say that mothers and sons, brothers and sisters and their equivalents in committee organizing (women's committee units and strike force units, for example) acted not only as a source of information 'for' one another (filling in informational gaps for and/or about their partner to the extent that was in that partner's own interest); at moments when they were accountable to/with other partners – when women's committees acted with union activists who were concerned about the free spirit of youths in the strike forces – they acted as a form of 'intelligence' for another authority: in the name of the father, the lineage, or the movement elders (for example, the trade unions), or the cause – on shebab. As such, they were, at these alternate turns, a form of discipline.

Scholarship on Palestinian political organization concurs that the 'key role' in the uprising played by the mass organizations that had formed in the West Bank in the late 1970s and 1980s consisted not of their mobilization of the masses per se, but in the extent to which they seized and 'channelled', as key organizers put it, energy that was already aroused and spreading 'like fire' – brought out by other, better established and more impassioning frameworks. As if elaborating on what these analyses left unsaid, grass-roots activists often expressed their conviction that mass mobilization and preservation of the mobilizational momentum were in critical ways accomplished by customary means, namely, by blood retribution. The events surrounding the outbreak of the Intifada were cited in evidence. Spilling the blood of a Palestinian was a sure way to get other Palestinians going, they explained. This conviction was reiterated every time news of yet another Israeli atrocity against Palestinians was making the rounds. The Israelis did not understand, they said, that in spilling the blood of a Palestinian they were causing the blood of other Palestinians and Muslims to 'boil,' and then there was (ideally) no stopping them from seeking retribution – it was then their moral obligation. When veteran organizers of trade unions and women's associations often, albeit in whispers, expressed concern about the *shebab* – their own as well as generally speaking – being difficult to keep in check (see also Jad 1997) or on the end of a strict chain of command, they were expressing both fear of total anarchy – mobilization running riot – and fear that a competing organizational framework might gain control over them.[7]

The close cooperation between women's committees and strike forces, I would argue, did much to keep these youths 'organized' in the terms of committee structures. This was visible, for example, in the visiting to injured, incarcerated and recently released activists and their families, to which so much women's activism was essentially dedicated. Specifically, their 'supervisory' role transpired from the information they were gathering and relaying in conjunction with it. They were always finding out as much about or on 'their own' activists and *shebab* as they were finding out for or from them. Some of the information they gleaned, not all of it, they passed on, at their discretion, to older male activists in unions and other bureaucratic capacities – whom they would get to do something about it in this way. This type of information relay was controllable and controlled.

'Religious Traditions'

So far in my discussion I have bracketed the 3 per cent 'strong' Christian minority[8] among the largely Sunni Muslim Palestinian population in the West Bank as far as the organisation of everyday sociality and activism in the Intifada were concerned. Members of both religious communities enacted the same forms and patterns of everyday relations, including the patterns of kinship I have described. Networks of practical kinship were also not segregated, especially in the hetero-religious towns and villages of the south-central West Bank, where the Christian minority has been concentrated and Christians and Muslims have long formed one habitus. However, religious difference was not blurred by conjoined cultural practice. Moreover, as members of each sectarian community kept to their 'own' distinct ritual cycles, it seemed as though the ritual practices of Christians were 'following' those of Muslims, if one considered style of enactment rather than content of belief. Visiting, commensality and the bringing of gifts of food, clothes and blessings according to carefully observed protocols of kinship and neighbourly obligations, as established by local custom (*taqlid* or *ta^cruf*), gave definition to key events in both cycles. On the second day of Easter, for instance, Christian Palestinian men were morally bound to visit their sister, taking gifts of money and clothes for her children and a gift of meat, which the woman would prepare on the day. Among Muslim Palestinians, this was a customary form of cross-sibling exchange marking *ᶜId al-Adha*, the Feast of Sacrifice (see Rosenfeld 1974).

When I speak of the form of one community following that of the other, I am suggesting that similar social practices, including much reciprocal exchange, did not make the positions and dispositions of the two sectors identical – not in everyday social life, and not in the political movements. I begin with *qarabaᵗ*. There it was evident that the position of Christian families was in a sense subsidiary, although not exactly subaltern. For example, Christians were more concerned about duly – in accordance with 'local' custom – participating in their Muslim neighbours', friends' or colleagues' life cycle and religious rituals. Muslims were much less worried about being remiss in their attendance of their Christian neighbours' rituals. They were also much less knowledgeable about their non-Muslim compatriots' ritual customs than the other way round. It thus seemed that, while Muslims could comfortably go about their life without knowing much about the orthodoxy and ways of their Christian neighbours, colleagues and comrades, the inverse was not the case. Many Christians I met had a strong sense that they were not in a position not to care about or to trespass on sensitivities out of ignorance.

While networks of *qaraba* were 'intermingled' (*muhtaliṯ*), the same did not hold for descent-focused associations. Patronymic associations were ethno-religiously exclusive or 'pure'; or such purity was valued by the majority of Muslims and Christians. This may have reflected the fact that denominational exogamy was procedurally complicated by personal laws that required that one of the spouses convert, most often the non-Muslim partner.[9] In any case, interfaith marriages remained rare in the regime of party-endogamous marriage the progressive movements were encouraging.

The way in which Christian and Muslim Palestinians contributed to the nationalist movements presented similar patterns to their 'joint' animation of a single habitus in everyday life: together, but not quite from the same positions or with identical dispositions. The distribution of activists over the four movements reflected this fact. Among Christians it was more likely that support for a particular movement was ideologically impelled, and that the impelling ideology and entire activist disposition included an anxiety about the divide. Many confessed to me concern about political programmes that championed nationalism in the name of one – the Muslim – religious tradition. These were propagating a theocratic state, which would at best make Christians into second-class or special-status citizens. Christian Palestinian nationalists were for these reasons categorically more inclined towards activism in progressive frameworks (the PFLP, the PCP or the DFLP); they championed more decidedly than Fatah a secular nation-state programme. They would not have felt 'at home' in the Fatah movement – 'It is not for me/people like us!' some said when I asked if they would consider it. There was no obvious activist position for culturally conservative nationalist Christian Palestinians.

One might compare the position and insecure sense of rightful belonging among Christian Palestinian activists with those of a bride in her husband's lineage group. A bride or wife could also have greater or lesser status in the new household she entered, depending on whether or not she had married into her father's brother's line and was not among 'strangers', as women in and around Ramallah often said if they had moved away from their patrilineal kin after marriage. Furthermore, however, a wife's position in a house of 'strangers' usually improved with due performance: if she helped to strengthen her husband's lineage and name, notably, by having sons who would carry on the family name. Grass-roots activists in committee organizations who were

Christian seemed particularly keen to establish their equal commitment and courage, while Christian Palestinians who were not active were more anxious than similarly inactive Muslims compatriots about not wanting to be involved, and Muslim activists paid particular attention to Christians and their obedience to UNLU guidelines (see Jean-Klein 2001). On the whole, then, Christians were more conscious than Muslims of a two-tiered or 'double' system of political surveillance: from the occupying regime and its collaborators, and from zealous Muslim nationalists.

In both domains, Christians and Muslims were manipulating the same core concepts, just as they were enacting the same relationship forms. For instance, the concept of martyrdom (*shahada*ᵗ) (see Johnson 1982; Jean-Klein 1997, 2000) had practical resonance for both Christian and Muslim activists, and for those in the progressive movements as well as those in Fatah. (The relevance of differences in content, which we are all aware exist, fluctuates; it had been easy to overlook in the phase of the struggle under discussion, and I am certain many of the progressive avant-garde have since 2000 regretted having also extensively utilized the concept and ethos in promoting their progressive agendas.) Still, Christians and Muslims were not contributing in equal shares, or with equal authority, to the conceptual resources that structured the activist universe they inhabited together. Muslims were more at home in and had a greater sense of authentic identification with and ownership over them. Christians were living these concepts by approximation – I mean, in a comparative and perhaps 'loaned' sense. A word I often heard used was '*zay*' ('like' or 'similar to') and '*bi hal*' ('in place of'); and particularly often from Christian activists explaining what seemed a key concept in kinship or in political activism: 'They…' or 'Most people here…' or 'The Muslims believe [x, y, or z]', they would start an explanation. Then, 'we/Christians don't believe/do [x, y, or z], but we have something like that'. Differences in ownership of or relations to shared intellectual resources by Christian and Muslim activists resembled differences in social ownership between full members and associates or friends in patronymic associations, in networks of *qaraba*ᵗ, or in committee movements. 'Shared' or, rather, universally binding and accepted standards of ethics and principles of justice could, then, in most, though not in all, cases be traced analytically to the Islamic and Palestinian Muslim tradition.

What is significant, perhaps, is that activists from one as likely as from the other religious position judged the killing of collaborators on the basis of formal rightness-cum-righteousness – seen from an 'intersubjective' though predominantly Muslim perspective. Cases of executions I knew or heard told of included Christian as well as Muslim Palestinian activists in the role of perpetrators. Christian Palestinians were also not disproportionately represented among those acting or being treated as collaborators. If Christians, or Muslims, expressed 'doubt', then this, too, was on matters of principle, as I am trying to explain here.

Local Custom

The might or force of Islamic orthodoxy, in administering 'Islamic justice' (^{c}*adala*^{t}) for example, so far as non-Muslims or aspiring secularists among nationalist activists were concerned, was mitigated by the officially established influence of 'local custom' (^{c}*ada*')[10] – a required contingent supplement, or counterpoint, to the Islamic legal codices (the shariah and the Hadith), albeit by terms stipulated within them. Focusing on this 'pre-given' resource, Muslims and Christians had, apparently, equally immediate and authentic relations of social ownership, just like lesser educated (or 'ignorant') and learned persons, or women and men. I said 'apparently' because the credence that is given to local custom as a necessary counterpoint with which moral human action must bring revealed law into engagement ('challenging', and so delineating it – *tahaddah*, one of the Arabic words meaning 'to challenge', is derived from the same root as the noun 'limit' and the verb 'to delineate') itself stems from and is authorized by the Islamic tradition. The very distinction into two sources of knowledge and the demand that they be made to engage continually – under the supervision of special technical provisions that are set out in the legal manuals – is a distinguishing feature of the Islamic legal tradition (see Messick 1993). Thus, while superficially it looks as though through 'local custom', a 'voice' was accorded to the non-Islamic national constituency, a closer look at this 'alternative' form returns one to the prior and, in terms of transmission, more highly prioritized aesthetic to which an alternative was sought. It was the same as when one turns to 'closeness' in the realm of kinship, in the hope of finding an alternative or antidote to patronymic association, in other words, a form of association with a more democratic and participatory inclination, maybe with a subversive streak, as progressive organizers were doing.

The Islamic legal tradition carefully specifies the rules of engagement between Islamic revealed law and other knowledge – presumably to protect the integrity of what must remain the principal authority. The following are examples of institutional and procedural forms (see Messick 1993: 179–81) that resonated in the procedures by which Palestinian nationalist activists, Christians and Muslims, tried to contrive certainty about persons' moral and, thus, their political disposition: '*ijma*^{c}' (consensus), which is in many other settings vested in or 'confirmed' by a formally elected body (a specially constituted committee or council of judges, learned men or respected notables); witnessing (*shehada*^{t}) and the 'collective responsibility' (*far<u>d</u> kifaya*^{t}) of the community to bear witness to the character of an accused person, an event, or to a widespread 'critical' condition or understanding; and *tazkiya*^{t} (verification of the justness of the witness, based on one's own personal experience of them or by their reputation according to consensus). There was one activist concept that Christian Palestinians could imagine was a form that duly represented a contribution from their tradition: the concept of confession (*i^c^tiraf*) and of the confessor (*mu^c^tarif*). It was a virtue (as in the religious orthodoxy) in so far as it described the 'admission of sin' by someone accused of collaboration, but a dreaded political disgrace and possibly also a 'crime' of honour (punishable by party expulsion), which every activist thought himself capable of committing under pressure from the Israeli authorities and feared – the release of information by activists about their own and their associates' actions.

Moving across Frameworks: Observations of Honour

> Like 'social honour' (*ihtiram, sharaf*) and 'justness' (*^c^adala*), the inverse, established notoriety and, more technically, the status of 'sinner'/'unjust' (*fasiq*), are products of collective attribution and somewhat relative in content. (Messick 1993: 180)

In this section I expand on honour as the main form through which activists, and the majority of Palestinians, stated their own moral value and saw it in others. I agree with Messick (see above) that if one judges 'honour' by its content, it is relative. In fact, it would ideally be that, in the social actors' own view, in so far as they self-consciously strive to bring it in line with 'consensus' and in this way to guarantee that the value is a contemporaneous, contingent and continuously active inflection of morality. However, I would stress that the form in which honour was practically instantiated and assessed, including the role of consensus, was not relative. 'Honour' also functions in this section as an analytical medium for illustrating further the functioning of 'local custom' – in which the honour/shame code features as the main subject – and the emphasis on aesthetic discipline in action in the articulation of 'due care'.

Activists of all orientations, and both Christian and Muslim Palestinians, shared aspirations of social honour (*ihtiram, ^c^ird, sharaf*). Furthermore, although progressive activists stressed that their organizations were trying to establish a fresh consensus, in a critical sense the progressive activist consensus did not diverge radically from principles set out in the unwritten body of standards of correct conduct that is colloquially referred to as the 'code of honour' or *masa' il-^c^ird wa-sharaf* (literally, 'the way' or 'progress' of '[two forms of] honour'; see Cohen 1965: 135).[11] Ample ethnographic work on this subject establishes the centrality, in all known localized versions of the honour code, of two things: (a) family-based corporate ownership of this 'property'; and (b) sexual modesty, especially of female members, as its highest expression. These two components are so recurrent that they allow the conclusion that they belong to the stable elements that consensus labours under all circumstances to preserve. Even the progressive Palestinian women's committee organizations in the Intifada, which championed alongside national liberation a 'social revolution' focused on class and gender liberation, gave renewed credence to the value of honour and to these apparently 'hard' components. High-ranking organizers, cadres and associates of women's committees set out 'to show to all' (*li kul in-nas*) that girls and women were capable of leaving the house – for the good reasons of making up for the loss of earnings incurred by the detention or injury or death of a male household member, or to contribute political-patriotic work – without compromising their own and their families' honour. Nobody would have dreamed of suggesting entirely unchannelled and undisciplined movement and social interaction. That would have been considered *haram* – a sinful trespassing on a sacrosanct form. When a mother admonished her daughter who was setting off to visit a friend's house, to attend a committee meeting or to participate in a demonstration, '*Der balik*!', 'Be careful!', she meant: 'Mind your movements, where you are seen, who you speak with, sit with, walk with, the state of your dress …', all such things as well as, 'Don't get yourself arrested!', 'Don't get into a demonstration without having planned to!' and so on.

Activists thus also shared a consensus about the appropriate ways of assessing and, indeed, of going about changing an established consensus on 'honour'. They often referred to the need 'to convince others' ('*aqta*ᶜ*ah an-nas*) by setting a personal and practical example, rather than with verbal pedagogy. 'One must convince other people', or, 'We have to be very careful; not everyone is convinced [*mu*ᶜ*aqid*] yet!' It was said to me, for instance, by the mother of an incarcerated youth during our prison visit to him, in explaining why it was important that the mothers of prisoners showed solidarity with their sons, on this occasion, by trilling at the end of the visiting hour and in this way celebrating and cheering them (see Jean-Klein 2001). The woman recognized that her husband's family risked injury to its sound reputation (*sum*ᶜ*a*) because of her son's imprisonment. This was due to the fact that the grounds for it were not 'clear' to most people, or 'still not understood' by many, she explained; or they might 'not care about' (*ma behimhum*) understanding the grounds. She meant, the majority were not making the necessary distinctions activists were making: between political imprisonment and imprisonment for 'common crime', or between going on political (and morally productive) visits and 'just sitting'. The main point is that the preferred 'new ways' that committee activists were promoting (which they more consistently rendered as necessary, *lazim*, than as a matter of desire) – pride in a boy's imprisonment or in a daughter's active visiting and her addressing a social circle during these occasions, 'as if' she were already married, all 'framed' partly in terms of foreign political concepts and ideas – were not yet widely enough agreed as valid contemporary performances of honour for activists to feel secure in their own moral standing as they stepped out of or 'left' the previous consensus – which in itself was perfectly right. It meant that 'in the meantime' they needed to act 'carefully' – with consideration: 'fighting the occupation militantly and our own society gently' was a credo one often heard activists reciting. 'Gently' meant by setting a practical example that reassured sceptics that the new movements were not compromising personal and family honour or the honour code.

Persons and associations (*byut*, *dyur*, *hamayil*) were unofficially ranked according to how much of this ephemeral property, honour, they 'had': how consistently they in their own personal biography and their genealogical and lateral relations had managed to demonstrate discipline. In principle, everyone who clearly followed the 'way of honour' to the best of their subject-specific abilities (age, gender, education) was equally honourable. But there was this principle which, although the progressive movements were currently challenging it, was still widely agreed – that some categories of persons were 'by nature' or 'by God' differentially equipped with implications for 'standing firm' on one's own, without external supervision or guidance (never without support): men were more capable of being steadfast on their own than women; adults more than children; and those of 'noble genealogy', for example those with direct links to the Prophet Muhammad or to a renowned nationalist activist and martyr, more than those without such a genealogy. Such attributes had the power of an infrastructure that laid down tendencies, they were not a guarantee.

The challenge about 'honour' as a basis for ranking the social and, indeed, human value of persons and associations is that it is not a tangible, or durable, 'property' of persons and associations. It marks not at all an attribute so much as a disposition[12] that becomes manifest in the way subjects handle themselves in challenging new circumstances. The specific craft that needs to be demonstrated time and again, across a myriad of situations, is the ability to properly channel *nafsiy* (energy) – as manifest in the desire for food and drink, or in sexual urges and other human passions (rage *or* care) – which is in some measure necessary for human, social and political progression of 'process', and yet is potentially detrimental to sociality, human spirituality, and the aspired polity: when it is expressed in excess, in the wrong place, at the wrong time – in other words, without discipline. The implication, on which I now concentrate, is that in this regime the subject is never 'closed'. This can be good news or bad news.

Collaborators: Organization without Principle

In my introduction I said that activists and other Palestinians talked about and acted towards 'collaborators' as organized, but as lacking direction and principle in their organization. In this section I want to expand on this. Activists recognized different ranks of collaborators, just as there were different ranks of activists and of martyrs.[13] Some 'collaborators' were better 'established' and more committed to collaboration that others. They were 'formally' established members, only in this case not of nationalist movements but of the Village Leagues, and thus of 'alternative organizations' that were alternative not to Fatah (as the progressive organizations imagined their alternative status) but to the entire 'tribe' of PLO-sponsored ones. The Israeli military-cum-Civil Administration started nurturing these in the late 1970s, by very similar means to those the progressive committee movements were using in efforts to mobilize, and recruit new rank-and-file associates: by making available to 'willing individuals and families' 'development funds' to boost the social influence they clearly lacked.

The Israeli campaign also made economic class a variable in the distribution of collaboration, by calculating that rural populations felt particularly resentful of PLO-sponsored nationalist programmes (because the latter had tended to involve mainly urban professional and intellectual elites). Thus, the Israeli campaign had targeted village-based *hamulas*, and focused on what it considered notables, not commoners. (The progressive organizations in the 1980s were also concentrating on camps and villages, but they focused on 'the masses'.) Palestinians who became League members were all from rural backgrounds.

Collaboration that was 'organized' through League membership or contemporary equivalents, just like their nationalist-activist counterparts, the 'mass organizations', functioned also with unaffiliated participants or helpers while they themselves were subservient to a 'higher authority', their Israeli patrons and regime, who provided them with protection, or the means to protect themselves (arms), and other privileges: such as not impounding their vehicles, giving them construction licences to build extensions to their houses, and so on. (Mass organizations, in their turn, were subservient to, or 'arms', of the PLO and/or affiliated parties based outside the territories. Committee associations also received some funds from their parties (Carapico 2000; Hammami 2000); and families of prisoners and martyrs were entitled to collect small PLO pensions that compensated them for the loss of income from these activists.) Associates working under the patronage or protection of 'big collaborators' (this was the term used for this category of established collaborators) were residents in towns or in camps who were deployed (by means I shall discuss) to sniff out and inform on activists and to recruit further informants. Like their committee-associate counterparts, these supporters were often hesitant or 'innocent' participants acting without a full understanding of what they were a part of, or knowing but caring little for the 'cause'.

A great deal of activists' daily attentiveness to 'collaboration' concentrated on associates, rather than on known and high-ranking collaborators. Quite simply, the latter were (a) considered too set in their ways to 'turn them around' and (b) too well protected and thus technically difficult to reach. Big collaborators were heavily armed and/or moved in groups and with Israeli army personnel on those rare occasions when they came out of their villages and circles. (Popular activists regarded the reclusiveness and cliquish emergence of these persons as evidence of their trepidation and thus of their cowardice and low morals.) With regard to them, the challenge was to persevere in observation, with a view to catching them during those moments when they were alone, or few, or unarmed, just long enough to land a 'hit' – and at that moment be ready to act. It was the sort of task a 'big fighter' (to become a big martyr) would be charged to undertake. Social observation concentrated on spotting the moment and keeping those who were charged informed.

Rank-and-file nationalist activists dealt with rank-and-file informers, focusing initially on educating them. One expected a readiness among associates to change their ways, because activists knew of the ruthless recruitment strategies using moral blackmail. Many were presumed to have succumbed, understandably, to pressure that, unless they cooperated, they and/or others close to them would be harmed – morally as well as, if not more than, physically. However, the fact that they could at one point be held hostage to threats of this kind showed they had cared about their morality, many activists reasoned. Increasingly coercive means were used when what were first assumed to be loose and perhaps unknowing or unwilling associates continued their work, and especially once they could be linked to a known activist's demise. Activists were prepared to take 'confessions' from such people and then, in exchange for a pledge that they would change their ways, to 'vouch' for them in the face of evidence, in this way liberating them from the hold the Israeli regime and/or established collaborators had on them. Officially it might well have been a 'strike force' unit or even some higher committee that was 'in charge'. To say this is, in a way, stating the obvious, given that activists were always eclipsing or surrendering their own authority over their acts by casting themselves – not just in representational terms, but literally – as instruments or tools of a 'higher will'. It was invariably the PLO, the UNLU, 'the society', 'the family', 'the *umma*^{t}', or God, at whose behest and call they were acting. Procedurally, however, the administration of warning was, just like intelligence relay, channelled through 'common' forms such as circles of neighbours, women's visiting rounds, committee delegations, and others. To single out 'strike forces' would be to isolate and reify one of multiple frameworks. They delivered the 'strike', as the name says, but no one assumed that the strike comprised the entire process, or even the most critical part.

A provisional sign that someone had been pressured into collaborating with the Israelis or with a big collaborator, was that the person or couple was economically struggling to get by despite the alleged collaboration. They were 'clearly' not selling their services. Real collaborators were noted for their unconcealed, if not demonstrative, consumption of material benefits they were earning. League members were notorious for flashing the guns and vehicles or forms of 'protection', including legal immunity[14], which they often had. Demonstrative consumption, at a time when nationalist activists were practising demonstrative restraint in their consumption habits (Jean-Klein 2001), then became 'clear signs' of a firmer commitment that went beyond force of circumstances. It included 'careless' criminal behaviour, such as burglary and drug trafficking, without worries about being seen (e.g., in broad daylight), and thus 'clearly' without concern about legal or moral consequences. Living reasonably well, without an apparent source of income and despite the occupation, was also taken as a sign. Many a male collaborator suspect was pointed out to me by nationalist activists – with a view to guiding me in guarding myself – as 'a common criminal' (*mujrim*), 'a drug dealer' (*tajir/ ᶜamil muhaddirat*) and a 'burglar' and 'thief' (*saariq*, or *harami*). On request I would get at least one extensive case elaboration. These occupational descriptions were saying: 'their collaboration is in the process of being confirmed.'

The biographical details of suspected or known collaborators often included marriage to an older woman – the difference being great enough to say 'she could have been his mother', insinuating the worst form of incest. In several cases the woman was the widow of a known collaborator, making the marriage a clear sign. But this was only one of several ways in which cross-sex familial relations – the mothers, sisters and wives of known 'collaborators' – were indexically co-implicated, whereby it was difficult to establish the direction of causality, that is, who the original source of compromise had been. In all cases, activists also knew biographical circumstances surrounding these female relations that signalled a blatant failure to demonstrate sexual modesty, if not outright moral corruption. Minimally, these female relations were depicted as negligent in their performance of their maternal and other relationship duties – 'not acting like a mother' although they had offspring; or not acting like a neighbour should. Just as the standing of someone as clear and clean was deduced from associative movements – whom people visited, who visited them, which places they frequented and which not – so were 'suspects' of moral and political laxity confirmed in time by their associational movement, or its invisibility. If someone was openly fraternizing with Israeli soldiers and/or Village League members and their known associates, at checkpoints or in cafes, restaurants and kebab-stands (eating and drinking with them), and entertained them in their houses, while no decent people were ever called to join or no one could see and say clearly what was going on at these meetings, then these observations became to weighty circumstantial evidence – *dalil aqliy*.

The Partial Definition of Subjects and Subjectivities

Judging by these processes, honour and dishonour were *not* presumed to be dispositions that were determined by genealogy (blood, name or genes). Subjects were thought to be sufficiently 'open' to make it feasible that they might 'fail' to confirm the genealogically established tendency – good or bad – by not repeating it, not transmitting it down the line. Genealogical ancestry (*'asl*) and common 'blood' (*damm*) created a solid basis in the shape of a series of antecedent demonstrations that endowed the individual with a specific 'original' tendency – not unlike the infrastructure of a state (*buniye tahtiye*) which the movements said they were preparing 'for a state' and which was meant to foreshadow or 'incline' towards the progressive, democratic state. The conduct of a father, for instance, who channelled *'asab* (the enduring part being transmitted), was but a possible version of oneself, seen once.

From the undefined space that was there in each individual, waiting to meet with contemporary and extraneous materials and to initiate what 'remained to be seen again', there emerged an imperative to give the offspring of collaborators the benefit, or detriment, of 'doubt' (*irtab*). This was especially the case with regard to children of a collaborating mother, and more so if the father was either not known (i.e., not familiar – thus he could have been anybody, possibly a sound man) and/or he was known and seemed 'clean' – he had divorced the woman, and not the mother but the father's family had mostly seen the children through their upbringing. Activists were looking for signs that the established habits of the closest 'contingency' – of the mother and of sisters – might possibly be repeated, but also for signs that they might not come. While trying not to treat the children as 'determined', activists also tried to act as a positive contingent influence. Lack of certainty about repetition became a source of hope in one direction, while in another it was a source of anxiety over loss. 'Everyone can be turned around' (*kul wahad/wahde yimkin bi[t]hawwa,* or *yimkin tit/yitharrak ila al-wara'*), activists often said, and included themselves. However, some characters were more firmly established than others by virtue of their own 'track record' (*sajjal* or *dawan*); they could take a risk for others: vouching for a repenting suspect, or practically witnessing against the stream of popular suspicion, if they felt certain that a suspicion was ill-founded, by paying visits to that person.

The ways in which activist lore cast continuous efforts by the Israeli intelligence with their 'clients' and helpers to corrupt the local population, including activists – and what one could see of corruption practices – implicated the same forms which activism was observing. If female sexual modesty was the surest human expression of honour, it made sense that sexual entrapment should have been the form in which forcible recruitment was imagined and often attempted.[15] The Israelis, with the help of Palestinian collaborators, manipulated a host of other elements of social etiquette (*ta^{c}aruf*) in efforts to force the hand of unwilling and steadfast subjects, for instance, imposing visits on their targets and in this way feigning visiting patterns which, by their calculations, would convince others that a particular person was 'close' with them, and had been 'turned around'. There were many stories about Israelis feigning a social visit to the house of someone they wanted to incriminate.[16] For this reason, activists were usually suspicious of circumstantial evidence that was too apparent, self-pronouncing, and especially in such cases were inclined towards rigorous cross-checking. A single demonstration or testimony was not accepted as sound evidence. In sound activist practice, it invited closer attention and further information gathering over a longer time and broader range of sources. And, if the activists were not acting soundly, then the doubt or suspicion fell back on them.

Aesthetic Discipline in Action: the Demonstration of Intent

One important motif is still missing in my account of the aesthetic in action on which, I have argued, nationalist and activist Palestinians focused when judging whether or not an assassination (*ightiyal*) or killing (*qatl*) or lesser forms or punishment were 'just'. It is the emphasis that was placed on seeing intent (*niya*ᵗ) on both sides: the collaborator's, to harm the movement – Village League membership alone would have been widely accepted as a 'good reason' for burning someone's car, but not for executing him[17] – and the assailant's (*al-mughir, muᶜtadin*), to exact retribution for actual, precisely tractable damage that concerned him directly. In many cases I heard discussed, someone who was 'reliable' (*amana*) by current consensus had seen an established collaborator assisting in the physical chase of an activist, or the collaborator had been overheard bragging about his/her direct involvement in a case. S/he had thus 'confessed'. However, as I said, proof of the collaborator's intent to block or harm a movement and one of its activists was only half the justness; it further required two things – (a) proof that the collaborator's killing was organized by appropriate relationships; and (b) proof that the assailant had been professionally focused, which would have meant mental and emotional composure. The second condition was in part met via the first, the rightness of the relationship that pertained between assailant and 'victim', meaning the ones injured or killed. (The term 'victim', like others, had no intrinsic moral charge.) Ideally, the identity of the assailant 'followed' the identity of the collaborator's victims, a good reason for needing named cases of betrayal. Vice versa, the name of a victim always pointed at a specific circle of persons who had 'good reasons' to exact retribution, in fact, a socio-moral duty (*wajib*) to do so. I was not aware of any female assassins; and the reason lay probably within these requirements: female persons were not among those who were morally obliged to seek retribution – as they are not regarded as 'owners of the same blood'. In the remainder, we shall see that the assailant's disposition was deduced from the composure with which he had been seen, by a reliable chain of witnessing, heading into the duty-cum-mission. The composure was the contingent element the assassin added to the 'right' structural conditions.

Most activists counted 'strike forces' among legitimate relationship contexts for an execution. But I do not think one should judge this way of thinking too hastily as linked to popular perceptions of these forces as an arm of an abstract and detached bureaucratic machinery. This is what is insinuated in the few academic accounts that mention 'collaboration', which without exception (or much description of process) attribute the entire area of responsibility to 'strike forces' (Nassar and Heacock 1990; Peretz 1990; Yahya 1990) qua 'security and justice committees', borrowing in advance from the anticipated state's presumed legitimacy as established in Western democracies in using violence to control violence. But neither the state's legitimacy nor the impersonal administration of violence was established. Had 'the masses' of people read and believed these accounts by progressive intellectuals, they would have thought 'strike forces' an inappropriate, if not illegitimate, 'form'. As it was, *shebab* who were active in the same strike forces or another branch of the same movement in which the victim was suspected or widely known to have acted were thought to be 'like' relatives (*ahl, 'asab*) who had suffered the loss of their own (association's) blood through the actions of the collaborator; and sometimes they were 'twice' related. Thus they were not so much 'within their rights' but under a duty to exact retribution for the loss of 'their' blood. If this has the ring of the functioning of blood retribution, then it was that, either by analogous extension (by activists and patriotic Palestinians themselves) or, in a sufficient number of cases I was aware of, literally. (Blood retribution was after all underwritten by customary law and endorsed in Islamic orthodoxy where patronymic kinship practice was concerned.) In retrospect, it often turned out that the assailant had been someone politically and socially 'close' to an activist who had been betrayed, injured or killed by that collaborator. More important for this analysis is that the relations that did or did not pertain between the assassin and the accused collaborator was a burning interest to people when they considered the act after the fact.[18]

Blood retribution provided a framework for identifying the proper relationship that rendered the killing disciplined, rightful and moral. But not only was the morality of the perpetrator thus left intact, it was often enlarged through such acts, which were considered 'missions' (*muhammat*, or *ᶜamaliyat, aᶜmal*). Such operations followed 'orders from above' (*awamir min fowq*) which, in addition, reiterated what were already 'orders' issuing forth from kinship obligations; they also carried similar risks to going into battle (and thus demanded as much courage and discipline). Big collaborators were armed, often had bodyguards and lived in houses that were heavily fortified (see Nassar and Heacock 1990: 200–1).[19] An assailant, even if he was masked, could be identified either by the 'victim' him- or herself (often the person struck did not die instantly) or by collaborator witnesses. The assailant then became a high-priority 'wanted' person (*matlub*) and, until his inevitable capture, would lead a fugitive life.[20]

An assassination carried out by an unrelated and disinterested person – someone whose own circle or association had not been harmed, who acted without 'social reasons' – stirred disquiet. I only heard of such cases where, as a result, the assassin himself came under suspicion of being an agent for the Israelis (who had their reasons), or was rated less than that: not part of any greater movement or higher cause (not even just a wrong or inferior kind). To kill without a social reason, *bidun sabab* – neither impelled by, nor reiterating established configurations of specifiable (in that sense accountable) social and/or spiritual duties to 'return' damage done to oneself and so to redeem one's own lost blood and honour – was what collaborators were characteristically accused of doing. They harmed people who had not harmed them.

It would also not, I think, have been acceptable for a young male activist assailant to 'hit' a female collaborator. I never heard of such a case. In fact, I never heard of a female collaborator's 'assassination', not even rumoured. The violent deaths of female collaborator suspects were invariably attributed to the Israelis or to another collaborator and rendered one of their typical 'dirty deeds'. Mostly, it seemed, reputed female collaborators managed to get 'themselves' killed – by a stray bullet (misfired by an Israeli or male collaborator) or through another kind of 'accident'. One might speculate that killing a female person would have had semblances of the appropriate reaction of a young man in honour-killing his sister. In fact, the only thinkable 'good reason' for a cross-sex killing by male hands that was honourable (which is not to say it was not also affectively dreaded) was an honour killing – which restored the 'victim' and the perpetrator back to a state of honour. It is possible that a deed like this was out of the question because it would have had the effect, not of socially cutting that person out, but, on the contrary, drawing her closer – an enactment of kinship between activist and collaborator suspect. Almost certainly it shows that the principle of equivalence had a hand in the process, which is another stable aspect of the process of honour in all contexts where it is known to function. It demands that a challenge be directed at persons of equal status and rank (or higher) – like against like, man against man, big activist against big collaborator, and so on. Women were 'hit' with social network death instead. First, activists of the 'strike forces' cut from underneath them a main resource – source and reason – through which their social activity was constituted: they usually received a blow in the form of losing a collaborator brother, son or husband due to assassination. And then they were 'alone', as it was said of them. The actions, or rather the non-actions, by other women practically spelt out the effect: they withheld the normally due show of social and emotional solidarity with them, which was a way of pronouncing the intent to end all social interaction.

While the social discipline provided by well-established tracks of kinship obligations did much to inflect corrective or retributive actions as moral, if not heroic, they needed to be supplemented or confirmed by the 'right' disposition of the assailant as he embarked on the mission. Self-discipline was displayed, among other things, in the executioner's considered ritual preparation for such a mission. It implied focus of mind, composure and purity of intent (*niya*ᵗ). But it was mostly not directly observable by others who acted as communal witnesses. Such preparation unfolded mostly in lonely practices or among intimates (*'ulaf*): in the home and with closest family, and in the company of immediate comrades who were part of the same cell. Both were reliable witnesses potentially, but comrades could not testify beyond a narrow and exclusive circle, as their delivery would have made their own activism too clear. It was mainly the mother's narrative of the boy's conduct, confirmed by her own conduct and reputation, that acted as the medium for 'echolocating' (Wagner 2001) the youth's firm and focused posture as he anticipated and entered into the engagement. The following is an example.

One week after the notorious collaborator nicknamed *al-ᶜIjl* ('Veal') was shot dead, an Israeli sniper positioned on the rooftop overlooking a busy commercial street of Ramallah shot and killed a youth who had been 'wanted' for the killing by the Israelis.[21] With the news of the boy's death, there started to circulate among activists of the same movement in the wider local area accounts about the boy's anticipation of his death since the day he had made the 'hit' (about which no one had any doubt). In the first instance, the stories came from women who had heard it from the youth's mother when they went to congratulate her (*hanna', ᶜashan bihannuha*) on her son's martyrdom and to 'feel with' her. It was said that during a visit home in the period in which he was 'wanted', the youth had instructed his mother concerning the clothes in which he wished to be buried when his time came: black trousers, a black T-shirt and his *kuffiyeh*. Members of the 'popular' PFLP-associated strike forces in the Ramallah area considered these colours the uniform of their movement at the time. On the day he was shot, the boy's mother would later report, 'he had to have known they were getting close to him'. The boy had asked her for clean black clothes and took his time over the morning prayers. This was an informed premonition, by the woman's account: several of her son's 'friends' (his political associates, one presumed) had been arrested during the preceding days. In these circumstances one prepared oneself, as one expected that at least one of them would break during his interrogation and 'confess'. The following is an excerpt from an account I heard of the mother's account of events subsequently on the day:

> They [Israeli army and intelligence] came to their house in the early morning. His mother said she was still praying inside the house when Captain Jadaᶜun suddenly stood in the door, asking her where her son was, because he was looking for him. 'Well,' she said to him, 'he is looking for you too, because he vowed to God that he would kill two people before he dies: al-ᶜIjl and you. I was just praying that Allah may grant him success'! Captain Jadaᶜun left with his head bowed [this notion suggested he was impressed by his enemy's, the mother's and the son's, posture]. Later they found [the youth] walking in the centre of town. One of his friends was with him, she said. They hit him twice; one bullet in the hip, one in the head. – It is said [by sound persons who were 'close', everyone understood] that his mother was ululating from the roof of their house when they brought her the news [in a display of triumph and joy. The last part of the woman's conduct was not reported by her; it would have been a form of boasting her own stoicism and compromised her credibility].

Conclusion: the Global Range of the Aesthetic of 'Due Care'

The practice of 'due care', as I have described it, spanned diverse 'frameworks' and subjectivities forming themselves into frameworks, facilitating the social exercise of morality, conceived in terms of honour. Differentiations in respect of the frameworks' epistemic and social 'charge' – encapsulating differences in motivation, disposition and agential capacity – centred on gender; age or 'degree' of social maturity (*darajat*); genealogical-cum-economic 'class' (*tabaqa*ᵗ); political-cum-militant 'rank' (*ruqba*ᵗ, pl. *arqab*); formality of organization (the difference between networks constituted around the objective of statehood and those that had the purpose of exercising kinship solidarity and familial closeness); and, to some extent, religious affiliation (e.g., the 'combined' deployment of the epistemologies of confession and of witnessing). All these played a unique part in detecting, monitoring, establishing, trying to set straight or to demobilize, and, if these attempts failed, to 'strike' (*daraba*) and finish 'collaborators'. Differently charged subjects and frameworks played a key role during different moments of a strike, which (like marriage and much else) was a drawn-out sequence of exchanges (see Battaglia 1990). The distinctive figures (subjectivities and frameworks) were re-constituted in the exact process of their deployment (in this case, the process of managing collaboration). Deployment both built on partially preconceived differences and, by exercising them, confirmed them – giving momentary firmness to distinctive form, returning it as 'steadfast' following its collaborative engagement across differences: either in the form of challenge and retort, or as mutually presenting and reciprocally evidencing. Steadfastness, or *sumud*, featured at various moments in this process, and was one of those very rare concepts that had stable, positive value (as well as being historically consistent in its currency), as an active, that is to say, an intentional, effort-rich and resourceful form of 'keeping still'. In conclusion, I would now like to suggest that the 'relationship' which we thus saw pertaining between different frameworks and subjectivities is perhaps also an appropriate way analytically to conceive of the working together of local (*ahliy*) and extraneous, Western knowledge resources in the process of 'due care'. I offer it, first, as an alternative to the aesthetic of hybridity and, secondly, as a way of conceptualizing the engagement between activism and its 'enemies' – collaboration was only one of several forms the exercise of enmity might take – as necessary (*lazim*) and constitutive of activist integrity and distinctiveness.

Scholarly analyses that commented on Palestinian progressive movements' handling of 'collaboration' at the time of the uprising, without thinking twice cast this line of action as 'halfway between the traditional and the modern system of justice' (e.g., Nassar and Heacock 1990). They implied a hybrid form between 'popular' or historically established justice practices – the use of *wusta* (or *wasita*), a customary procedure for settling disputes by using third-party 'go-betweens', was typically pointed to – and aspects that had been uplifted more recently from 'outside', either from other revolutions[22] or from procedures of 'criminal correction' in Western democracies. Evidently, these arguments were anticipating by a few years the social science trend of giving due recognition and legitimacy to 'alternative modernities'.

My argument, that activists found in 'due care' something like 'due process', did not suggest such a thing. In fact, I hope to have made it clear that the notion of 'in-betweenness' is simply not an appropriate aesthetic for describing this process. It misses entirely the critical importance which activists attributed to making and guarding a range of clear subject-divisions that were also instrumental in drawing out unique and/or difficult knowledge – knowledge that was secret or sacred, in and of itself impossible to access or unable to appear – and in eliciting distinctive agency-cum-activism from others. Different 'frameworks' (and I am now including subjectivities that were aspiring to be effective channels and mirrors of values larger than themselves) had the effect of 'extraneous' motivation for others they were intermittently 'partnered' with or challenged by.

Supplementation, if that is indeed the right word to depict the 'relationship' between differentiated collaborative entities, did not work by adding on or bringing in or together, but by providing a source of tension that had the ineluctable effect of challenging and drawing out the momentarily more highly valued, or prioritized, frameworks. Hybridity would have been a show of human failure to differentiate between equally 'relevant' (procedurally speaking) but separately and differentially positioned agents and actants, one of which was conceived of as being 'permanent' and enduring (as well as worthy of endurance) and the other as a valuable resource in the process of transmitting the first but as contingent and purely matter serving the confirmation, literally, of a more highly prioritized partner. That was the difference in 'power' that pertained between these positionalities, as seen between Muslim and Christian Palestinians, male and female agency in the home, lineage members or committee members and their respective affiliates, senior persons and youths, local/traditional and global or revolutionary knowledge and procedure, kinship- and state-focused interests. (One notices that the gender difference is unique in exactly the same way as that between moral humanity and divinity according to Muslim conceptions: it is the 'hardest', in the sense that the partner in the contingent position cannot, in these cases, aspire to convert to the status or join the membership of the steadfast subjectivity.) Perhaps, this is also the way in which anthropologically to think 'together' activist organizing and its enemies?

Notes

I am thankful to Marilyn Strathern, Tony Crook and Annelise Riles for the intellectual stimulation they provided for the kind of analysis I attempt in this essay (for which I take full responsibility); to Gabriele vom Bruck, Yasir Suleiman, Eyal Ben Ari and Tony Good, for their thoughtful comments on early drafts of the paper; and to audiences, first of all at the workshop at Cologne University, and at seminars subsequently at St Andrews University (Scotland) and at Cornell University, where a draft of this chapter was presented. Special thanks go to Amy Levine for her considerate notations.

1. An overview of the historical development of the conflict and of Palestinian political organizations is provided many existing studies and is not repeated here (see, for example, Jean-Klein 2003).
2. The few existing studies on this topic consider allegations of 'collaboration' by non-democratic and authoritarian regimes against suspected activists in oppositional movements (see, for example, Stephen 1999). Such studies do not track processes of truth verification (presumably because the analysts are politically cynical about 'process' from the start) or perceptions of 'justness' of accusations and punitive or retributive actions. A noteworthy exception, on both counts, is Starn's ethnography (1999) of the politics inside an Andean protest movement. The current essay looks at 'collaboration' as it is problematized and addressed by activists in a national liberation movement.
3. Please refer to Jean-Klein (1997, 2000, 2001, 2002, 2003) for detailed accounts of the fieldwork methodology on which the observations here are also based.
4. My use of 'aesthetics' here follows closely Riles's continuation of Bateson's interest in information contained within form – at the level of 'the patterns which connect' (Riles 2001: 185ff. citing Bateson 1980: 8, 2000). I am especially partial to Strathern's (1991: 10) definition of aesthetics, as 'the persuasiveness of form, the elicitation of a sense of appropriateness'.
5. The distribution of responsibilities and moralities that I am suggesting here contradicts many feminist studies and their conclusions about the role of 'gender' in armed conflicts, which have tended to portray women's activism predominantly in a bridge-building capacity (see Ridd and Callaway 1989; Aretxaga 1996; Cockburn 1998; Werbner 1999; Werbner and Yuval-Davis 1999; Sharoni 2001). The consistent bias in the reporting of that literature has created the impression that such an orientation is quasi-natural; this impression is not entirely dispelled by the analytical links that are made with 'maternal sensibilities'. The current analysis is closer to the fresh stream of research that is considerably less inclined towards postulating and defending a gendered dichotomy of moralities (see, for example, Kandiyoti 1991: 429; Keppley-Mahmood 1996; Butalia 1997, 2001; Cockburn, 2001: 20–21; Moser and Clark 2001; and, most exceptionally, Rommelspacher 1999). However, I think of my analysis as diverging from both streams in the sense that it does not try at all to pass moral judgement or to moralize, but instead asks, ethnographically, how such judgements are being made: how morality is practically known and made known.
6. By Jewish law, neither the mother's nor the son's Jewish identity were recognized as being annulled by these conversions. The ceremonials, their officers or the subjects themselves do not have the authority to do so.
7. The point I am trying to stress is that the form 'mass organizations', which the scholarship on the evolution of Palestinian nationalist-political organization presents as a solution to specific organizational challenges, was also potentially a liability, if one reads between the lines of these accounts. This relates back to my point that any entity or concept could be animated in either a positive or a negative value – that their moral value was only 'added' or completed during moments of their animation (see Strathern 2004, regarding the value of 'property').
8. Christian Palestinians were affiliated to fifteen different denominations, the largest of which were the Orthodox (c. 20,000), Latin (17,000) and Greek Catholic (3,000) communities.
9. The legal arrangement inside the Occupied Territories of matters of personal status (birth, marriage and death) was, from the time of Ottoman rule, placed under the jurisdiction of

independent religious authorities. The Ottoman regime had introduced the *millet* system with the intention of granting to ethno-religious minorities in the dominantly Islamic empire partial communal autonomy; neither the British nor the Israeli authorities dissolved it. In this regime, civil marriage was not an option, so that interfaith marriage required that one of the spouses undergo a formal conversion. While conversion did occur in the West Bank in the 1980s and 1990s, it was rare and socially difficult. In practice, it meant the divorce of the converting spouse from her/his family and 'community'. More often it was the bride who officially converted, and, in the cases I heard of, almost exclusively from Christianity to Islam rather than the other way round. A Muslim bride could practically not convert (and live) unless she was an orphan. Basically, her affiliation and identity were not hers to renounce, to leave or 'shake off'. At most, people could try and 'arrest' or be remiss in the practical exercise of their part in their affiliation. My analysis shows how such 'properties' were jointly held and custodianship over one's own part had implications for 'connective' subjects and vice versa.

10. Region-wide and in this setting, local custom is conceptualized in terms of a wide range of vocabulary: tradition (*taqlid*), 'the customary' (*al-muᶜtad*), 'the known, familiar' (*al-mashhur, al-maᶜaruf*), or by a key summary term for all, *ᶜurf* (often translated as 'common knowledge' or 'accepted custom'). See Messick (1993: 179–80).
11. The lingering social relevance of the concern resonates powerfully in the momentous historical event that is the mass flight by thousands of Palestinian Arabs in 1948–49 from the areas inside the fledgling and expanding Jewish state. There was widespread fear that soldiers of the advancing Zionist-Israeli armies were planning the mass rape of Palestinian women. These circumstances compelled a separation of what had been entwined priorities in the previously prevailing attitude, which a popular proverb captured thus – '*Ardi, ᶜirdi* ('My land is my [fem.] honour') – and another proverb stated thus: *Ma' illu 'ard, fish ᶜindu ᶜird'* ('He who has no land, has no [fem.] honour'). Not to have *ᶜird* clearly was unthinkable. In 1948, masses of Palestinians felt compelled to act according to the motto, '*Al-ᶜird qabl al-'ard*', 'Honour before land' (see Warnock 1989: 22–23), and to make 'honour' transportable. 'For many Palestinian men, saving their women from rape was more important than defending their homes or showing bravery and defiance,' one commentator explains (Warnock 1989: 23). The leadership in the Palestinian Liberation movement that had formed by the 1960s was evidently cognizant of the social poignancy that a concern with this intangible and insecure property still had, also for the masses of Palestinians who were living in the territories occupied by Israel in 1967; and reckoned it could as easily be the source of charge as it could be an Achilles' heel of national resistance (see Warnock 1989: 23). In any case, the new national leadership started to promote a second reversal, ostensibly returning to the older version of the saying but now carrying forward the movement's return agenda. Organized nationalist discourses began to promote the slogan, 'Land before honour', *al-'ard qabl l-ᶜird* (see also Sayigh and Peteet 1986: 118). Palestinians in the Intifada frequently cited this motto, and made practical efforts to make a temporary reversal of priorities into a social reality: national-territorial sovereignty (which was taken as the contemporary equivalent of *ᶜard*) before, if not in place of, personal/familial honour (which was to be replaced with activist expressions of political honour). Most activists and people I knew, however, had practically reverted back to attempts to perform both values (see my account of 'honour' below) and thus in a disciplined fashion, simultaneously. It was a challenge.

12. In this respect 'honour' was much the same as 'kinship' and other social properties; '*wusta*', for example, designated an outstanding *ability*, to be proved again and again, to mobilize the necessary actors and other resources to get a specific job done, rather than a secure 'store of connections', as analytical renditions into English tend to presume as a matter of fact.
13. All three–martyrs, activists or 'fighters', and collaborators – were assessed and ranked according to 'firmness' and formality of their commitment to action. Palestinians (and, as we have recently seen, also foreign nationals acting in solidarity with them) who became casualties of the political situation but had not been self-consciously 'heading into action' at the time of their death were described as 'also martyrs' or 'like martyrs', and often as 'innocent' (*bari', jahil*; fem. *bariyat, jahlet*). 'Innocence' spelt a lower grade (*darija*ᶜ) of morality, which derived from a low degree of mobilization and discipline. Specifically, 'innocent' said that the deceased had not been on a mission, not formally integrated (and inducted) into one of the movements as an activist, and hence had been unlikely to be heading towards death with deliberation or readiness or on higher orders (under direct instruction). Innocent martyrs were like 'unknowing', unaware, incidental committee associates, their martyrdom comparable with 'spontaneous' (*cafwiy*) manifestations of progressive-nationalist activism, which was unwitting or unintended in its activist effects. In the present case, the subjects accidentally entered the house of martyrdom. Into this category fell many children and elderly people. Even if special cemeteries for martyrs had existed at the time, which was not the case (the occupying regime disallowed them, just as it blocked special funeral processions for martyrs; but people marked graves of great martyrs in other ways), the bodies of 'innocents' would probably not have been buried there. They were special resting places for the 'true' martyr (*shahid haqiqiy*) – *haqiq* resonated here with accurate, precise, focused, destined, etc. – and 'great martyr'(*shahid kbir*).
14. People frequently discussed, in their daily conversations, others known to them who were apparently engaging in burglary without making significant efforts to conceal such criminal activity. Among the discussants were often 'victims' of such crimes, and the people they pointed a finger at were socially as well as politically estranged relatives – often a second cousin, or a great-uncle on the father's side. The burglars, who were thus known, were often not arrested, not charged, not sentenced or did not have to serve a full sentence, and these developments or phases in a 'case' were the substance of these conversations. To my mind, these observations and conversations mirrored the great extent to which discussions of political detainees' and prisoners' cases were the stuff that fuelled conversations among 'activists' – people who one knew to be activists with relative certainty on the basis that they constantly had these interests and also had the necessary information and conversational skills to keep them meaningful, current and running. There is also independent evidence that Israeli authorities offered known criminals legal immunity in exchange for intelligence service (Black and Morris 1991).
15. As one academic account has described Israel's 'dirty strategies' in suppressing the Intifada:

> 'Photographs of young girls were taken in compromising positions and then used later to blackmail the subjects into collaboration. Women were warned not to frequent beauty parlours where they did not know the owners, in case hidden cameras had been installed in dressing rooms or drugs were used on unsuspecting victims' (Black and Morris 1991: 472–73).

In many Muslim societies photographs of women are considered indications of their moral laxity, all the more so when they are photographed 'uncovered' and together with men. Cadres were forever warning activists about the need to be cautious about visiting places where this was said to notoriously happen (beauty parlours or dressmakers').

16. The Israelis would act as if a person had become an informer after s/he had visited the civil administration office (to receive a licence or a permit) or following interrogation. For example, soldiers would pay the person a conspicuous 'visit' during the early evening hours, bringing copious amounts of liquor, staying for several hours and generally making it look as though this was a friendly and welcome social call. Other attempts were made to co-opt persons by publicizing false charges, and by some of the same means that Palestinian activists used to name and shame collaborators, such as public lists or graffiti (see Tessler 1994). The expectation was that such gestures would invite ostracism or revenge from fellow activists, which would force the person to reconsider his/her earlier refusal to collaborate. The culture of activism deployed the same forms right back, for example also using visiting patterns to confirm suspicions – shown when Palestinians suddenly refrained from visiting – and/or to clear people from accusations — by instituting demonstrative visiting activity.
17. One might take note here of the correspondence between this position and the rejection by the Tripoli-born Islamic legal reformist Rashid Rida's (1865–1935) of the traditional Islamic view of apostasy, wherein the Muslim who was found to reject Islam should be necessarily put to death. His radical alternative suggestion was that only those apostates should be condemned to death who revolted against Islam and were thus a threat to the *umma*ʿ (the community of the faithful), not those who quietly withdrew (see Hourani, 1989 [1983]: 237).
18. Nationalist Palestinians were also all the time observing and judging by these standards the conduct of Israeli soldiers and the commanding officer leading them, for example during a night's raid on their home and neighbourhood, while serving in Palestinian prisoners' supervision and administration, or at a checkpoint. Credit was given where credit was due. For example, Palestinians might speak with resentment, but nonetheless with respect (as an equal), of a commander in the army for acting in a 'civilized' or 'cultured' (*adabiy*) manner, not losing his cool, not showing fear, in control of his soldiers. Other stories ridiculed young Israeli recruits serving in the West Bank, who had allegedly wetted their uniform trousers when, during the search of a home they were startled by the unexpected presence of (and well-timed hiss from) an old grandmother, who had simply refused to clear out. (Invariably, in these stories, a neighbour arrived on the scene just in time to witness the shameful moment and set the narration in motion.) Those who had shown a lack of discipline, for instance, smashing a place out of all proportion, considering the deed the youth they were trying to arrest could possibly be accused of, perhaps also hitting women and children in the house, became living proof of the animality or lack of human quality of the occupiers. 'Dogs!' (*Killab*!) soldiers or collaborators who inflicted damage in a chaotic, unpredictable and unjustified manner were often referred to or called to their faces. Enemies were not presumed to be categorically inhuman nor was there need to dehumanize them in order to fight them to the death; in fact, the inhuman enemy made for a pitiful challenge.
19. Activists used in a few cases handguns taken off 'collaborators', but more often used knives, screwdrivers and other such easily available tools that required close-up contact with the victim.

20. It was part of customary kinship practice, too, for kinsmen of a man who had killed another of a different patronymic association to go into hiding for the duration of the 'period of the boiling blood' (*fawaran ad-dam*), to escape the kinsmen of the victim, who were now expected to try to exact retribution. (See Cohen 1965: 139, 186–87.)
21. Israeli sources claimed the youth had been shot 'in the course of a demonstration'. But I can vouch personally that there had been no demonstration in the area at the time. (My statement is lodged with Al Haq, the Society for Law in the Service of Man.)
22. To quote, '[Activity against collaborators] has historically also marked [other] experiences of rapid social transformations as well as liberation struggles directed against an occupier' (Nessar and Heacock 1990: 200–201).

References

Antoun, R.T. 1972. *Arab Village: A Social Structural Study of a Trans-Jordan Peasant Community.* Bloomington, Ind.: Indiana University Press.

Aretxaga, B. 1996. *Shattering Silence: Women, Nationalism, and Political Subjectivity in Northern Ireland.* Princeton, NJ: Princeton University Press.

Barghouthi, M. and R. Giacaman. 1990. 'The Emergence of an Infrastructure of Resistance: the Case of Health', in J.R. Nassar and R. Heacock (eds), *Intifada: Palestine at the Crossroads.* New York: Praeger, pp. 73–90.

Bateson, G. 1980. *Mind and Nature: A Necessary Unity.* London: Fontana.

———. 2000 (1972). *Steps to an Ecology of Mind.* Chicago: University of Chicago Press.

Battaglia, D. 1990. *On the Bones of the Serpent. Person, Memory, and Mortality in Sabarl Island Society.* Chicago: Chicago University Press.

Black, I. and Brian Morris. 1991. *Israel's Secret Wars. The Untold History of the Israeli Intelligence.* London: Hamish Hamilton.

Bourdieu, P. 1977. *Outline of a Theory of Practice.* Cambridge: Cambridge University Press.

Butalia, U. 1997. 'A Question of Silence: Partition, Women and the State', in Ronit Lentin (ed.), *Gender and Catastrophe*: London, New York: Zed Books, pp. 92–109.

———. 2001. 'Women and Communal Conflict: New Challenges for the Women's Movement in India', in C.O.N. Moser and F.C. Clark (eds), *Victims, Perpetrators or Actors? Gender, Armed Conflict and Political Violence.* London: Zed Books, pp. 99–114.

Carapico, S. 2000. 'NGOs, INGOs, GO-NGOs and DO-NGOs: Making Sense of Non-govermental Organizations', *MERIP* 30(1): 12–15.

Cockburn, C. 1998. *The Space Between Us: Negotiating Gender and National Identities in Conflict.* London: Zed Books.

———. 2001. 'The Gendered Dynamics of Armed Conflict and Political Violence', in C.O.N. Moser and F.C. Clark (eds), *Victims, Perpetrators or Actors? Gender, Armed Conflict and Political Violence.* London: Zed Books,pp. 13–29.

Cohen, A. 1965. *Arab Border Villages in Israel.* Manchester: Manchester University Press.

Geertz, H., 1979. 'The Meaning of Family Ties', in C. Geertz, H. Geertz and L. Rosen (eds), *Meaning and Order in Moroccan Society.* New York: Cambridge University Press, 315–391.

Hammami, R. 2000. 'Palestinian NGOs since Oslo: From NGO Politics to Social Movements?' *MERIP* 30(1) (No. 214): 16–19.

Hasso, F. 1998. 'The "Women's Front": Nationalism, Feminism, and Modernity in Palestine', *Gender and Society* 12(4): 441–65.

Hourani, A. 1989 (1983). *Arabic Thought in the Liberal Age, 1798–1939*. Cambridge, U.K.: Cambridge University Press.

Jad, I. 1997. 'Patterns of Relations within the Palestinian Family during the Intifada', in S. Sabbagh (ed), *Palestinian Women of Gaza and the West Bank*. Bloomington: Indiana University Press, pp. 53–62

Jean-Klein, I. 1997. 'Palestinian Militancy, Martyrdom and Nationalist Communities in the West Bank during the Intifada', in J. Pettigrew (ed), *Martyrdom and Political Resistance*. Amsterdam: VU University Press, pp. 85–110.

———. 2000. 'Mothercraft, Statecraft, and Palestinian Subjectivity during the Intifada', *American Ethnologist* 27(1): 100–27.

———. 2001. 'Domestic Nationalism and Resistance: the Two Faces of Everyday Activism in Palestine during the Intifada', *Cultural Anthropology* 16(1): 83–126.

———. 2002. 'Alternative Modernities, or Accountable Modernities? The Palestinian Movement(s) and Political (Audit) Tourism During the First Intifada', *Journal of Mediterranean Studies* 12(1): 43–80.

———. 2003. '"Into Committees, Out of the House?" Familiar Forms in the Organization of Palestinian Committee-activism during the First Intifada', *American Ethnologist* 30 (4): 556–577.

Johnson, N. 1982. *Islam and the Politics of Meaning in Palestinian Nationalism*. London: Kegan Paul.

Kandiyoti, D. 1991. 'Identity and Its Discontents: Women and the Nation', *Millennium* 20(3): 429–44.

Keppley-Mahmood, C. 1996. *Fighting for Faith and Nation: Dialogues with Sikh Militants*. Philadelphia: University of Pennsylvania Press.

Latour, B. 1996. 'The Trouble with Actor Network Theory', *Soziale Welt* 47: 369–81.

———. 1999. 'On Recalling ANT', in J. Law and J. Hassard (eds), *Actor Network Theory and After*. Oxford: Blackwell, pp. 15–25.

Law, J. 1999. 'After ANT: Complexity, Naming, and Topology', in J. Law and J. Hassard (eds), *Actor Network Theory and After*. Oxford: Blackwell, pp. 1–14.

Mahmood, S. 2001. 'Feminist Theory, Embodiment, and the Docile Agent: Some Reflections on the Egyptian Revival Movement', *Cultural Anthropology* 16(2): 202–26.

Messick, B. 1993. *The Calligraphic State: Textual Domination and History in a Muslim Society*. Berkeley: University of California Press.

Moser, C. and F. Clark (eds). 2001. *Victims, Perpetrators or Actors? Gender, Armed Conflict and Political Violence*. London, New York: Zed Press.

Nassar, J. and R. Heacock. 1990. 'The Revolutionary Transformation of the Palestinians under Occupation', in J. Nasser and R. Heacock (eds), *Intifada: Palestine at the Crossroads*. London: Praeger, pp. 191–206.

Peretz, D. 1990. *Intifada: The Palestinian Uprising*. Boulder, Colo.: West View Press.

Ridd, R. and H. Callaway (eds). 1989. *Caught Up in Conflict: Women's Responses to Political Strife*. London: Macmillan.

Riles, A. 2001. *The Network Inside Out*. Michigan: University of Michigan Press.

Rommelspacher, B. 1999. 'Right-wing "Feminism": a Challenge to Feminism as an Emancipatory Movement', in P. Werbner and N. Yuval-Davis (eds), *Women, Citizenship and Difference*. London: Zed Books, pp. 54–64.

Rosenfeld, H. 1974. 'Non-hierarchical, Hierarchical and Masked Reciprocity in an Arab Village', *Anthropological Quarterly* 47(1): 139–66.
Sayigh, R. and J. Peteet. 1986. 'Between Two Fires: Palestinian Women in Lebanon', in R. Ridd and H. Callaway (eds), *Caught Up In Conflict: Women's Responses to Political Strife*. London: Macmillan, pp. 106–37.
Sharoni, S. 2001. 'Rethinking Women's Struggles in Israel-Palestine and in the North of Ireland', in C.O.N. Moser and F.C. Clark (eds), *Victims, Perpetrators or Actors? Gender, Armed Conflict and Political Violence*. London: Zed Books, pp. 85–98.
Starn, O. 1999. *Nightwatch: The Politics of Protest in the Andes*. Durham: Duke University Press.
Stephen, L. 1999. 'The Construction of Indigenous Suspects: Militarization and the Gendered and Ethnic Dynamics of Human Rights Abuses in Southern Mexico', *American Ethnologist* 26(4), 822–42.
Strathern, M. 1991. *Partial Connections*. ASAO Special Publications No. 3. Savage, Md.: Rowman and Littlewoods.
———. 1996. 'Cutting the Network', *Journal of the Royal Anthropological Institute* (NS) 2, 517–35.
———. 2004 'Transactions: an Analytical Foray', in E. Hirsch and M. Strathern (eds), *Transactions and Creations: Property Debates and the Stimulus of Melanesia*. Oxford: Berghahn, pp. 8–109.
Tessler, M. 1994. *A History of the Israeli-Palestinian Conflict*. Bloomington: Indiana University Press.
Wagner, R. 2001. *An Anthropology of the Subject: Holographic Worldview in New Guinea and Its Meaning and Significance for the World of Anthropology*. Berkeley: University of California Press.
Warnock, K. 1989. *Land Before Honour: Palestinian Women in the Occupied Territories*. London: Macmillan.
Werbner, P. 1999. 'Political Motherhood and the Feminisation of Citizenship: Women's Activism and the Transformation of the Public Sphere', in P. Werbner and N. Yuval-Davis (eds), *Women, Citizenship and Difference*. London: Zed Books, pp. 221–46.
Werbner, P. and N. Yuval-Davis (eds). 1999. *Women, Citizenship and Difference*. London: Zed Books.
Yahya, A. 1990. 'The Role of the Refugee Camps', in J. Nassar and R. Heacock (eds), *Intifada: Palestine at the Crossroads*. London: Praeger, pp. 91–106.

CHAPTER 9

ISLAMIST MILITANCY IN KASHMIR: THE CASE OF THE LASHKAR-E TAIBA

Yoginder Sikand

Let not the enmity of any people make you swerve to wrong and depart from justice. (Holy Qur'an 5: 8)

Introduction

The emergence of radical Islamist groups in Kashmir over the last decade has added a new dimension to the ongoing conflict in the region. It has led to a rapid transformation in the terms of discourse in which the conflict is represented, by India, by Pakistan and by many Kashmiris themselves. The current stage in the Kashmir conflict can be dated to 1989, when the Jammu and Kashmir Liberation Front (JKLF) inaugurated an armed uprising against Indian rule. By the mid-1990s, however, the JKLF had been increasingly taken over by Pakistan-based Islamist groups. The wiping out of many of its cadres in confrontation with the Indian armed forces, the withdrawal of Pakistani support and the growing realization of the need for peaceful, as opposed to military, means for the eventual resolution of the Kashmir dispute seem to be among the major reasons for the gradual decline of the JKLF as a military force in Kashmir, despite the fact that its goal of an independent Kashmir still commands the support of many Kashmiri Muslims.[1] On the other hand, military and other forms of support from the Pakistani establishment, from private jihadist groups in Pakistan and elsewhere, in addition to a passionate zeal for what is seen as a 'holy' cause, account, in large measure, for the gradual takeover of the armed struggle in Kashmir by militant Islamist groups, mainly based in Pakistan and led, for the most part, by Pakistani nationals.

Despite the active involvement of Islamist groups in the ongoing struggle in Kashmir, little has been written about them from a scholarly and detached point of view. This chapter seeks to provide an account of the ideology, organization and development of one of the leading Islamist groups active in Kashmir today, the Lashkar-e Taiba. Of the several Pakistan-based Islamist groups active in Kashmir today, the Lashkar is, by far, the best organized, best trained and most heavily armed. From the mid-1990s, this once little-known group has emerged today as the most serious challenge to the Indian armed forces, being responsible for several attacks in Kashmir, killing a large number of Indian soldiers as well as civilians, both Hindu and Muslim. This chapter looks at the emergence of the Lashkar as a key player in the present stage of the Kashmiri struggle. Owing to the relative paucity of published material, the essay relies heavily on the official Internet website of the Markaz Daawat wal Irshad (Centre for Invitation and Instruction), of which the Lashkar is the armed wing.[2]

The chapter is divided into three main sections. The first looks at the origins of the Lashkar in the specific South Asian context, tracing its understanding of Islam and jihad to the emergence of the Ahl-e Hadith (The People of the Prophetic Tradition), an Islamic reformist movement, in the subcontinent. We then look at the ideology of the Lashkar, seeing how it seeks to fashion armed jihad as a means for the 'liberation' of Muslims from what it sees as 'oppression' and to advance its own stated goal of establishing the 'supremacy' of Islam, as it understands it, as a global ideology. The second section examines the involvement of the Lashkar in Kashmir, seeing it as emerging out of a broader Islamist movement in the region, the roots of which go back to the early years of the twentieth century. The concluding section of the article looks briefly at how far the Lashkar has been able to actually establish itself among the Kashmiri Muslims. In assessing its ability to do so, a distinction is stressed between, on the one hand, its military engagements against the Indian armed forces and, on the other, its ability to impose its own vision of Islam as the accepted version.

The Lashkar: Early Origins

The Lashkar is the military wing of the Markaz Daawat wal Irshad, with its headquarters at the town of Muridke in the Gujranwala district in Pakistani Punjab. The Markaz was established in 1986 by two Pakistani university professors, Hafiz Muhammad Saeed and Zafar Iqbal. They were assisted by the late Abdullah Azzam, a close aide of Osama bin Laden, who was then associated with the International Islamic University, Islamabad. Funds for setting up the organization are said to have come from Pakistan's dreaded secret services agency, the Inter Services Intelligence (ISI) (Ali 2002: 199).

The Markaz is affiliated to the Ahl-e Hadith school of thought, a reformist Islamic movement, which had its origins in early nineteenth-century north India. The founders of the Ahl-e Hadith, men such as Maulana Nazir Husain (1805–1902), Nawab Siddiq Hasan Khan Bhopali (1832–90) and Maulana Sanaullah Amritsari (1870–1943), believed that they were charged with the divine responsibility of purging popular Muslim practice of what they saw as 'un-Islamic' accretions and borrowings from their Hindu neighbours, regarding these as 'unlawful innovations' (*bida'at*), and as akin to *shirk*, the sin of associating anything with God. They insisted that Muslims must go back to the original sources of their faith, the Qur'an and the Hadith, the traditions of the Prophet, and abandon all beliefs and practices not sanctioned therein. They called for Muslims to abide strictly by the Islamic law (shariah) and to abandon 'imitation' (*taqlid*) of the traditional schools of Islamic jurisprudence (*mazhab*, pl. *mazahib*), attempting to refashion the worldwide Muslim community in the mould of the Companions of the Prophet. The *'ulama* of the Hanafi *mazhab*, representing the vast majority of the Muslims of South Asia, entered into bitter conflict with the Ahl-e Hadith on the matter of *taqlid*. The latter defended their opposition to *taqlid* on the grounds that the schools of jurisprudence had developed more than two hundred years after the death of the Prophet, and that, therefore, the Companions of the Prophet did not follow *taqlid*. Since, they argued, Muslims should follow the model of the Companions, there was no need for them to 'blindly follow' the schools of jurisprudence, for this would be tantamount to 'personality worship' of the founders of the *mazahib*, a heinous sin. Further, they claimed, the Hanafis had fabricated numerous hadith to prove the claims of their *mazhab*, and quoted a hadith to the effect that 'he who fabricates hadith shall be thrown into hellfire' (Meeruthi 2000: 3; Amritsari n.d. : 8). Besides attacking the Hanafi *'ulama*, the Ahl-e Hadith directed their attention to bitterly critiquing Sufism, which they saw as a 'wrongful innovation', for, they argued, it had no sanction in the practice of the Prophet and his Companions (Naim 2002: 21). Every 'wrongful innovation', they insisted, was a heinous sin, the punishment for which was damnation in hell. They stiffly opposed the adoration of the Prophet as a superhuman being as well as the devotion to the saints and the cults centred on their shrines that are an integral part of popular Sufi tradition in South Asia, seeing this as a deviation from the practice of the Prophet and the early Muslims. Faith in the powers of Sufi preceptors and the widespread belief in the Sufi saints as intermediaries with God were condemned as akin to polytheism. So, too, was the belief in the supernatural powers of the Prophet and of his being ever-present and all-seeing.

Given the immense popularity of the Sufi traditions and the influence of the Hanafi *'ulama* among the Muslims of South Asia, it was hardly surprising that the Ahl-e Hadith faced stiff opposition, being banned from worship at mosques and condemned as apostates and enemies of Islam. For their part, the Ahl-e Hadith appeared to have revelled in controversy, not losing any opportunity of attacking their Muslim opponents for what they branded as their 'un-Islamic' ways. Being engaged in constant conflict with other Muslims, drawing clear lines of division between themselves as the only truly Muslim group and the rest, seems to have played a crucial role in the development of a separate Ahl-e Hadith identity.

Confrontation with other Muslim groups created an atmosphere conducive to militancy, and the Ahl-e Hadith saw themselves as carrying on in the long tradition of jihad, which they accused other Muslims of having abandoned. The founders of the Ahl-e Hadith claimed the legacy of the early nineteenth century jihad movement led by Sayyed Ahmad Barelvi and Isma'il Shahid against the Sikhs in the Punjab. In the failed revolt of 1857 against the British, several Muslim *'ulama* associated with Ahl-e Hadith-style activism played a role in leading uprisings at some places. After 1857, while some Ahl-e Hadith leaders accommodated themselves to British rule and devoted themselves to peaceful preaching, others continued to carry on violent struggles against the British in the North-West Frontier Province, till they were finally crushed by the end of the nineteenth century. Although from the early twentieth century onwards the Ahl-e Hadith, as a whole, gave up the path of violence in the face of British arms, an Ahl-e Hadith scholar writes that they 'refused to accept the supremacy of the British and the Hindus' and vowed to carry on the struggle through other means to 'convert India into an abode of Islam (*dar-ul islam*) through jihad' (Yusuf 2000: 54).[3] While they desisted from entering into violent confrontation with the British, their opposition to Sufism and to the Hanafis brought them into conflict with many traditional Muslims, which sometimes took violent forms (Meeruthi 2001: 32). However, they were doomed to a marginal existence owing to their vehement opposition to popular Muslim practice, and hence were not able to emerge as a mass movement. Rather, they remained an elitist group, characterized, as Barbara Metcalf writes, by a sense of 'moral superiority' and 'self-righteousness', tinged with 'a certain harshness', and with a small following among urban Muslims, particularly in north India (Metcalf 1982: 283).

The Ahl-e Hadith in Pakistan and the Rise of the Lashkar

Since the Lashkar has its headquarters in Pakistan and most of its fighters in Kashmir are Pakistani nationals, the role of the Lashkar in Kashmir must be seen in the context of the growing salience within Pakistan itself of the Ahl-e Hadith, to which it owes allegiance. Following the creation of Pakistan in 1947, the Ahl-e Hadith began making gradual progress in the country, establishing mosques and *madrasahs* of its own. It had to face stiff resistance from traditional Sufis, for its opposition to Sufism and *taqlid*. It tended to have a more visible presence in urban areas, its strict scripturalist literalism appealing to groups such as urban traders who were not tied down to local Sufi shrines.

Although the Ahl-e Hadith still has a limited following in Pakistan, from the 1980s onwards it was able to make considerable inroads in Pakistani society. A number of factors have combined to make for this: firstly, the growing appeal of scripturalist Islam as a result of the rapid expansion in the number of *madrasahs* or Islamic seminaries in the country in recent decades, many of which are sponsored by the Saudis and preach a conservative and yet militant form of Islam that has a close resemblance with that of the Ahl-e Hadith; secondly, the active sponsorship and patronizing of such *madrasahs* by the Pakistani state, under and after General Zia-ul Haq (d. 1988); and thirdly, the Afghan jihad against the Soviets, which saw a great expansion of resources for groups such as the Ahl-e Hadith, with massive amounts of aid, in the form of money and arms, pouring in from Saudi Arabia and other Arab countries. Many Ahl-e Hadith and other Sunni *madrasahs* emerged at this time as training grounds for militants active in the Afghan jihad. After expelling the Soviets from Kabul, these mujahidin turned their attention to fresh pastures, Kashmir being one of them. Thus, from being a relatively minor group in Pakistan's Islamic landscape, the Ahl-e Hadith grew, by the end of the 1980s, into a major force, with scores of *madrasahs* all over the country, particularly in the Punjab and the North-West Frontier Province, and several newspapers and journals articulating its vision of an Islamic revolution.

Along with other Islamist groups, the Ahl-e Hadith immersed itself in the jihad in Afghanistan. In 1986 it set up the Markaz Daawat wal Irshad, based in a sprawling 160–acre campus at Muridke, a town some 30 kilometres from Lahore, to train mujahidin to fight the Soviets. As the Markaz's activities rapidly grew, it was decided to divide its work into two separate but related sections: the educational and the jihadist. Thus, in 1993, the Markaz established its separate 'jihadic and warfare' wing, the Lashkar. The Lashkar later set up four training centres in Pakistan and Afghanistan, where 'thousands of mujahidin from all over the world are being trained'. Markaz authorities claim that the militants produced at these centres have played a leading role in armed struggles, first in Afghanistan, and then in countries as far afield as Bosnia, Chechnya, Kosovo, the southern Philippines, Kashmir and 'in other areas where Muslims are fighting for freedom'.[4] All Muslims, it believes, are members of one global community. Oppression of Muslims anywhere makes it incumbent on Muslims everywhere to assist them, if necessary through active engagement in violent conflict with their non-Muslim opponents.[5] As the Lashkar case so strikingly illustrates, one of the characteristic features of some contemporary Islamist movements is precisely this global agenda, a marked contrast with the local or national scope and ambitions of Islamist movements in the past.[6]

According to one report, in recent years the spread of the Markaz/Lashkar in Pakistan has been 'phenomenal', and today it has some five hundred offices all over the country, most of them in Punjab, which operate as recruitment centres for would-be mujahidin.[7] At its Muridke headquarters, the Markaz runs an Islamic school and university, most of whose students are local Pakistanis, with some from both Pakistan-administered Kashmir and Kashmiris from the Indian-ruled part of the state, and several Afghans and Arabs. Established in 1994, several hundred students have already graduated from the school. Scores of smaller schools run on the same lines have been set up in various other parts of Pakistan, and by mid-2001 their number was said to be almost 130, with some 15,000 students and 800 teachers on their rolls.[8] Young boys of the age of eight are taken in and are given a twelve-year training, which includes the standard Islamic disciplines, taught from an Ahl-e Hadith perspective, English, Arabic and science, as well as the handling of weapons and techniques of armed combat. A strict military atmosphere is enforced. Students must wear military uniforms, abide by military discipline and 'properly assimilate the commandments of their theologians and military instructors that their future profession – as mujahidin – will be in great demand in the Muslim world on the threshold of the new millennium'.[9] Students from different countries and ethnic groups live together, and every effort is made to discourage ethnic differences. They must wear the same clothes, speak the same language (Urdu, Arabic). Names that might suggest local, clan, tribal or caste origins must be discarded.[10] The only identity that should matter to them is of being Muslim, ethnic differences being seen as working to divide and weaken the worldwide Muslim *ummah*.

At its four training centres, would-be mujahidin are given rigorous military training. This is of two kinds: first, a short twenty-one-day course, the *daura-i 'ama* ('general course'); and secondly, a three-month intensive course, the *daura-i khasa* ('special course'), geared to guerrilla warfare, in which trainees learn how to handle small arms as well as survival and ambush techniques.[11] These courses, it is claimed, 'change the course of life' of the trainees completely', and a sign of this is said to be that they 'no longer shave' and 'wear their *shalwars* (baggy trousers) above their ankles, as enjoined by the Prophet Muhammad (peace be upon him)'.[11] They are fired with a passionate zeal in what is said to be a 'holy' cause, beingwilling to sacrifice their lives and attain 'martyrdom' for it. Families whose sons die in battles with the Indian forces are said to celebrate and rejoice at their deaths, rather than mourn, for they are confident of their securing a place for themselves in heaven.[11] This has particularly crucial implications for how Kashmiri Lashkar activists see themselves. If, traditionally, Kashmiri Muslims were depicted as 'cowards', 'passive' or 'mild' and lax as far as religious observances were concerned, at least compared to their Pathan and Punjabi Muslim neighbours, they are now sought to be made 'true', 'brave' and 'fearless' Muslims, fired by the zeal of would-be 'martyrs' for the faith.

The Ideology of the Lashkar

Like other Islamist groups, the Markaz/Lashkar sees Islam as a perfect, all-embracing system (*nizam*). Islam is said to govern all aspects of personal as well as collective life, in the form of the shariah. For the establishing of an Islamic system, an Islamic state is necessary, which will impose the shariah as the law of the land. This is seen as 'the solution to all our problems'.[12] If such a state were to be set up and all Muslims were to live strictly according to 'the laws that Allah has laid down', then, it is believed, 'they would be able to control the whole world and exercise their supremacy'.[13] Since the laws have already been laid down by God, there is no room for human beings to exercise their judgement in creating fresh legislation. Hence, democracy, in the sense of a system where people make their own laws, is condemned as completely un-Islamic.[14] Since Islam is seen as the very antithesis of nationalism, it demands the establishment of one universal Islamic state, ruled by a single *khalifah*. Thus, the present division of the Muslims into many nation states must be overcome. Since 'the *ummah* is one', it follows from this that 'the system of *khilafah* [Caliphate] does not recognize the physical borders or the independence of one Muslim country from another'. Hence, 'the state is one, the army is one, the flag is one, the budget is one, etc.'[15]

The struggle for the establishment of the Islamic state can take various forms, peaceful as well as violent. Islam, the Lashkar admits, is 'a religion of peace and harmony', and seeks to 'eliminate mischief and disorder, and to provide peace, not only to Muslims but also to the entire humanity'. However, Muslims are commanded to take to armed struggle, or jihad, to defend their co-religionists suffering from the oppression of others. Such a situation is said to prevail over much of the world today. While jihad in defence of Islam and of Muslims labouring under oppression is presented as a liberation struggle, it is also seen as a means for Islam to 'prevail on this earth', for Islam is seen as the only true religion.[16] Armed jihad must continue 'until Islam, as a way of life, dominates the whole world and until Allah's law is enforced everywhere in the world'.[17] Since Islam is meant for all peoples, the Islamic State must spearhead a movement to spread the Islamic 'ideology' all over the world. In the course of this struggle, it is 'expected' that it will encounter 'conflict' with other states and their ideologies. The conflict can be resolved through peaceful diplomacy, but, if that fails, then the only course left open for the Muslims is armed jihad. In this sense, the Markaz/Lashkar believes, jihad is 'the foreign policy' of the Islamic state. This does not, however, mean that force can be used to coerce others into accepting Islam. Rather, jihad is seen as providing them with the 'security that comes from the application of Islam', while leaving them free to follow their own religion or to become Muslims.[18]

The subject of armed jihad runs right through the writings and pronouncements of the Markaz/Lashkar and is, in fact, the most prominent theme in its discourse. Indeed, its understanding of Islam may be seen as determined almost wholly by this preoccupation, so much so that its reading of Islam seems to be a product of its own political project. Being born as a result of a war (in Afghanistan), fighting for a holy cause has become the very raison d'être of the Lashkar, and its subsequent development has been almost entirely determined by this concern. The contours of its ideological framework are constructed in such a way that the theme of armed jihad appears as the central element of its project. In the writings and speeches of Markaz spokesmen, jihad appears as violent conflict (*qittal*) waged against 'unbelievers' who are said to be responsible for the oppression of the Muslims. Indeed, it is projected as the one of the most central tenets of Islam, although it has traditionally not been included as one of the 'five pillars' of the faith. Thus, it is claimed that 'There is so much emphasis on this subject that some commentators and scholars of the Qur'an have remarked that the topic of the Qur'an is jihad.' Further, a Markaz statement declares, 'There is consensus of opinion among researchers of the Qur'an that no other action has been explained in such great detail as jihad.'[19]

The global jihadist programme of the Markaz presents itself as a 'liberationist' project, basing itself on widespread feelings of discontent and suffering of sections of Muslims who see themselves as being persecuted by Western-oriented elites in their own countries, as well as by the 'West' more generally. The greatest problem of the Muslims, says Hafiz Muhammad Saeed, head of the Markaz, is their 'subjugation to the West'.[20] Thus, the Markaz is reported to have gone so far as to call for a jihad against the U.S.A.[21] 'All Muslims', the Markaz believes, are oppressed today, by such 'enemies' as the Hindus, the Jews or Christians. 'Wherever you look, you will find that non-believers are everywhere trying to enslave Muslims and destroy them,' it argues. Hence, Muslims must form a 'solid bloc' to defend themselves from these 'enemies', and if all peaceful means fail they must resort to armed jihad for their liberation.[22] This Muslim bloc must be led by both Pakistan and Saudi Arabia, and have its headquarters at Mecca. It must aim at forming a pan-Islamic union based on strong trade, education and defence links, including a joint military command. Mujahidin from various Muslim countries would be trained to undertake jihad against unbelievers if peaceful means to put an end to oppression of Muslims fail. However, the Markaz insists, jihad is to be directed only at military and not civilian targets. It is contrasted with other forms of war that are pursued for purely worldly concerns, and is described as 'the act of supreme sacrifice to preserve human rights bestowed by Allah'.[23] Jihad is thus a means for challenging 'oppression' and of establishing the rule of Islam.

Jihad is seen as the secret of Muslim power in the past when much of the known world was under Muslim rule, and it is argued that when Muslims 'abandoned jihad and other injunctions they began to degenerate'.[24] In Markaz/Lashkar discourse, jihad is projected as a religious duty binding on all Muslims today. Thus, it is claimed that the prevailing global situation warrants all Muslims to be involved in some way or other in jihad against non-Muslim 'oppressors'.[25] In this grand enterprise there are different roles for different people to play. Those who are ordered by the *khalifah* to fight must do so, while others may be required to assist the mujahidin by supplying them food, arms and other supplies, providing medical assistance, looking after their families in their absence or even simply by exhorting others to participate in the war.[26] Thus, every Muslim, man or woman, must be mobilized to assist in the struggle in some form or the other, and if any Muslim has 'never intended to fight against the disbelievers', his or her faith 'is not without traces of hypocrisy'.[27] Those believers who have the capacity to participate or assist in the jihad but do not do so are said to 'be living a sinful life'.[28] On the other hand, Muslims are promised that they would receive great rewards, both in this world and in the hereafter, if they were to actively struggle in the path of jihad. Not only would they be guaranteed a place in Heaven, but they would also 'be honoured in this world', for jihad is also 'the way that solves financial and political problems'.[29]

The Jihad in Kashmir and India

The Markaz sees its active involvement in the armed struggle in Kashmir as only one stage of a wider, indeed global, jihad against the forces of disbelief, stopping at nothing short of aiming at the conquest of the entire world. As Qari 'Abdul Wahid, former *amir* of the Lashkar in Indian-administered Kashmir, puts it, 'We will uphold the flag of freedom and Islam through *jihad* not only in Kashmir but in *the whole world*.'[30] Likewise, Nazir Ahmed, in charge of the public relations department of the Markaz, declares that, through the jihad the mujahidin have launched, 'Islam will be dominant all over the world, *Inshallah* (God willing).'[31] This war is seen as a solution to all the ills and oppression afflicting all Muslims, and it is claimed that 'if we want to live with honour and dignity, then we have to return back to jihad'.[32] Through jihad, it is believed, 'Islam will be supreme throughout the world'. [33] The mujahidin are promised that, with the launching of the global jihad against all the 'unbelieving oppressors' of the world, 'The day is just round the corner when Islam will prevail in this earth, *Insha Allah*.'[34]

In Markaz/Lashkar discourse, the conflict in Kashmir is seen not as a territorial dispute between India and Pakistan, but as nothing less than a war between two different and mutually opposed ideologies: Islam, on the one hand, and disbelief [*kufr*], on the other. This is portrayed as only one chapter in a long a struggle between the two that is said to have characterized the history of Hindu-Muslim relations for the last 1,400 years, ever since the advent of the Prophet Muhammad.[35] The Prophet is claimed on the basis of a hadith to have singled out India as a special target for jihad. 'Whosoever will take part in *jihad* against India', Markaz leader Muhammad Ibrahim Salaf claims that the Prophet had declared, 'Allah will set him free from the pyre of hell.'[36]

The Markaz/Lashkar sees the roots of the Kashmir problem as lying in its Muslim rulers having been replaced, first by the Sikhs and then by the Hindu Dogras through British assistance. With India (the 'Hindus') having taken over Kashmir in 1947, a long and protracted reign of bloody terror is said to have been unleashed on the Kashmiri Muslims. This is seen as a direct and logical consequence of the teachings of Hinduism itself, because, it is alleged, 'the Hindus have no compassion in their religion'.[37] Hence, it is the duty of Muslims to wage jihad against the 'Hindu oppressors', for 'it is the Hindu who is a terrorist'.[38] All Hindus are tarred with the same brush, described in such essentialist terms as 'terrorists', 'traitors', 'cowards', 'enemies', etc., these powerfully echoing widely shared sentiments among Pathan and Punjabi Muslims of Hindus being 'weak' and 'slavish', having been subjected to 'Muslim' rule for centuries, and of being 'crafty' and 'cunning', probably owing to Hindu near-monopoly of trade and commerce in India. This also builds on Pathan sentiments of 'manly honour', 'chivalry' and 'bravery', which Hindus are supposed to lack, being allegedly 'effeminate' and 'cruel'. Thus, Hafiz Muhammad Saeed declares: 'In fact, the Hindu is a mean enemy and the proper way to deal with him is the one adopted by our forefathers ... who crushed them by force. We need to do the same.'[39] India is a special target for the Markaz's mujahidin. According to the *amir* of the Markaz, Hafiz Muhammad Saeed, 'The jihad is not about Kashmir only. It encompasses all of India'.[39] Thus, the Markaz sees the jihad as going far beyond the borders of Kashmir and spreading through all of India. The final goal is to extend Muslim control over what is seen as having once been Muslim land, and, hence, to be brought back under Muslim domination, creating 'the Greater Pakistan by dint of jihad'.[40] Thus, at a mammoth congregation of Markaz supporters in November 1999, Hafiz Muhammad Saeed declared, 'Today I announce the break-up of India, *Inshallah*. We will not rest until the whole of India is dissolved into Pakistan.'[41] On the same occasion, Amir Hamza, senior Markaz official and editor of its Urdu organ, *ad-Da'wa*, thundered: 'We ought to disintegrate India and even wipe India out.'[42] Those who take part in this anti-Indian jihad are promised that 'Allah will save [them] from the pyre of hell', and 'huge palaces in paradise' await those who are killed in fighting the 'disbelieving enemies'.[43]

This project for the disintegration of India, followed by its takeover by Pakistan and the establishment of an Islamic state in the entire subcontinent, is sought to be justified by an elaborate set of arguments that use the rhetoric of liberation. Thus, instances of human sacrifice, untouchability, infanticide, the oppression of the 'low' castes by the Brahmins and the suppression of women in Hinduism are described in great detail, and on this basis it is sought to be shown that such a religion as Hinduism should not 'be allowed to flourish'. In Markaz literature, the mass slaughter of Muslims by Hindu chauvinist groups, often in league with the Indian state and its agencies, and the growing wave of attacks on other marginalized groups in India, such as the 'low'-caste Dalits, Shudras and Christians, are presented in stark colours, and the point is forcefully made that such a country 'where non-Hindus are not allowed to exist', should be broken up. The Markaz/Lashkar poses as a 'champion' of not just the oppressed Muslims of Kashmir or India but even of the 'low'-caste Shudras and Dalits. It sees itself as having a divinely appointed mission of saving the Shudras from Brahminical tyranny. Thus, it says, 'It is incumbent upon us to save the Shudras of India ... from the clutches of Brahmins', and insists that 'the Brahmin Authority' must be 'ransack[ed]'. Although it claims that its jihad is aimed only against 'the tyrannical government and the army' and that 'nowhere do the *mujahidin* target non-Muslim or innocent people', there are reports that speak of Lashkar fighters being involved in the killing of several Hindu villagers in Jammu, Kashmir and in neighbouring Himachal Pradesh.[44]

The Lashkar's Involvement in Kashmir

Roots of Islamism in Kashmir

The emergence of the Lashkar as a powerful military force in Kashmir must be seen in the context of the emergence of an Islamist constituency in the region, a process that can be traced back to the early years of the twentieth century. A major development in Kashmir at this time was the establishment of the first branch of the Ahl-e Hadith in Srinagar, in 1925, by Sayyed Hussain Shah Batku, a Kashmiri student of the Madrasa Miyan Sahib in Delhi, a seminary set up by one of the pioneers of the Ahl-e Hadith in India, Maulvi Nazir Hussain. On his return to Kashmir after completing his education, Batku began directing his attention to attacking what he saw as 'un-Islamic' and 'Hinduistic' practices and beliefs associated with the popular Sufism of the Kashmiri Muslims. Batku is said to have 'raised a storm of controversy' for his critique of customary practices which he condemned as 'un-Islamic', such as visiting Sufi shrines, imploring Sufi saints to intercede with God, keeping fasts on particular days dedicated to various saints and reciting litanies (*aurad*) in the mosques. This is said to have seriously 'aggrieved the leading theologians of Srinagar'. The leading Hanafi *'ulama* of Kashmir are said to have issued several fatwas against him, branding him as 'an apostate and an infidel' and as the *dajjal* (Anti-Christ), subjecting him to a 'social boycott' (Wani 1997: 35–6). Among the other notable pioneers of the Ahl-e Hadith in Kashmir were Maulana Anwar Shah Shopiani (d. 1969), Maulana Ghulam Nabi Mubaraki (1902–80) and Sabzar Shah. Anwar Shah was a close disciple of Batku, and played a major role in spreading the message of the Ahl-e Hadith in Srinagar and Shopian. He also undertook missionary tours to outlying regions of the state, including Bhadarwah (Doda) and Ladakh. Like Anwar Shah, Maulana Mubaraki was a trained *'alim*, a prolific writer and a powerful orator. He edited two Ahl-e Hadith journals, *Tauhid* and *Muslim*, and wrote extensively against the Ahmadis, the Shia, the Arya Samajists and the Christian missionaries, all of whom he saw as bent on the extirpation of Islam from Kashmir. He served as the president of the Ahl-e Hadith *jama'at* in Kashmir for several years, as well as the Imam of the Ahl-e Hadith Jam'ia mosque in Srinagar. Unlike Anwar Shah and Mubarakpuri, Sabzar Shah was not a trained *'alim*, although he is said to have 'grasped the fundamentals of Islam and wedded himself to the cause of the Ahl-e Hadith'. In order to convey the message of the Ahl-e Hadith beyond the relatively narrow circle of middle-class Kashmiris, to which it had been largely restricted, he would roam the streets of Srinagar in the garb of a peddler selling soaps, combs, pins, bangles and toys. To his customers, mostly women and children, he would invariably speak about the 'strict monotheism' of the Ahl-e Hadith and would fiercely denounce 'shrine worship and other polytheistic practices'. For this, it is said, he was beaten on numerous occasions, but, it is said, he refused to relent. (Wani 1997: 36–7).

In the face of great opposition, the Ahl-e Hadith managed to make a small, yet significant number of converts, mainly in the towns of Srinagar, Islamabad (Anantnag) and Shopian. In 1923, in order to coordinate the efforts of individual activists and to 'face the determined challenge posed by the *mullas* of Kashmir', a central organization, the Anjuman Ahl-e Hadith Jammu and Kashmir, was established in Srinagar, with one Haji Muhammad Shahdad as its president. The establishment of the organization 'came as a thunderbolt' to the traditional Hanafi *'ulama* and Sufis of Kashmir, who are said to have now 'declared a virtual war' on the Ahl-e Hadith. Several Ahl-e Hadith activists were physically attacked; a social boycott was instituted against them; they were turned out of their localities; and, being branded as apostates, they were refused entry into the mosques, following which they had to set up their own separate places of worship.[45] Leading Hanafi *'ulama* issued *fatawa* declaring them to be non-Muslim renegades.

Despite the zeal of its activists, the Ahl-e Hadith singularly failed to develop a mass following in Kashmir (Khan 2000: 133). Several factors may account for this. First, its stern opposition to the 'blind imitation' of the schools of jurisprudence brought upon it the wrath of the traditional Hanafi *'ulama*, who exercised a significant influence in Kashmir. Secondly, its hostility to Sufism, which it branded as an innovation not sanctioned by the practice of the Prophet, could hardly win the hearts of many Kashmiris, given the strong influence of popular Sufism in the region. For their trenchant criticism of popular practices associated with the shrines and cults of the Sufis, the followers of the Ahl-e Hadith were branded by the Kashmiri *'ulama* as *kafirs* (unbelievers) and *munkar-i auliya* ('deniers of the friends of God'), this greatly limiting their appeal to the Kashmiri Muslims. Thus, the Mirwai'z of the Khanqah-i Mu'alla, one of Kashmir's most important Sufi shrines, denounced the Ahl-e Hadith as the *dajjal* (Anti-Christ). One Hanafi *'alim* issued a fatwa declaring that no Muslim should marry a follower of the Ahl-e Hadith, and nor could the corpse of an Ahl-e Hadith follower be buried in a Muslim graveyard. Other *'ulama* declared it impermissible (*haram*) for Hanafi Muslims to pray along with Ahl-e Hadith followers. For their part, Ahl-e Hadith Imams condemned Kashmiri Hanafi mosques as 'little better than temples', because of the practice therein of reciting litanies (*aurad*) aloud before the congregational prayers (Khan 2000:138–51).

The Ahl-e Hadith's advocacy of a stern, legalistic understanding of Islam brooked no compromise with deeply rooted local cultural traditions, many of which it did not hesitate to brand as 'Hindu' or 'un-Islamic'. This naturally limited its appeal among many Kashmiris. In addition, the Ahl-e Hadith focused most of its efforts in the towns of Kashmir, almost completely neglecting the countryside, where most Kashmiri Muslims lived. It confined itself, by and large, to stirring religious controversy and preaching, not providing any significant social services that might have made for a larger following. Further, internal differences contributed to the weakening of the movement. In 1940, it split into two rival groups on the issue of *qabl-i zawal*, or on whether the Friday congregational prayers could be offered between 11 a.m. and 12 noon (Wani 1997: 41).

Writing in 1997, Wani noted that the Ahl-e Hadith has not been able to 'take deep roots in the [Kashmir] valley' (Wani 1997: 41). Rather, it remains a largely elitist phenomenon, with its core support base among a limited section of the urban lower middle and middle classes, roughly the same core support base of competing groups such as the secular nationalist JKLF and the Islamist Jama'at-e Islami. Although Ahl-e Hadith thus failed to establish a mass base for itself in Kashmir, it did provide fertile soil for the emergence of other Muslim reformist trends from the 1930s onwards, inspired by its efforts at purging the popular Kashmir Muslim religious tradition of elements that were deemed to be 'un-Islamic'. These trends, in turn, played a significant role in preparing the ground for radical Islamist[46] groups, including the Lashkar. Of particular importance in this regard was the emergence of the Jama'at-e Islami. Established in 1941 by Sayyed Abul 'Ala Maududi and organized as an independent organization and political party in Kashmir in 1952, the Jama'at-e Islami is now a major force to contend with in the region.[47] Like the Ahl-e Hadith, the Jama'at-e Islami sought to combat 'un-Islamic' practices, but, unlike it, it abstained from directly attacking the Sufi tradition and refrained from branding other Muslims as apostates or deviant. In contrast to the Ahl-e Hadith, the Jama'at was not opposed to Sufism as such but only to those practices and beliefs associated with popular Sufism, which it saw as 'un-Islamic'.[48] Its advocacy of an Islam based on the model of the Prophet's Companions and its opposition to what was seen as local 'un-Islamic' customs, such as prostration at the graves of saints, beseeching them for help, keeping fasts or holding feasts on special days dedicated to them, made for a growing appeal to a class of educated, particularly urban, Kashmiri Muslims, who were influenced by Muslim reformist currents from outside. Unlike the Ahl-e Hadith, which devoted most of its energies simply to preaching and entering into controversies with its Muslim opponents, the Jama'at gave great stress to modern education, setting up scores of schools where secular as well as religious subjects were taught. Its social services, combined with its resolute opposition to Indian rule, won it considerable support among many Kashmiri Muslims, disillusioned with the politics of the ruling National Conference for what they saw as 'selling out' the interests of the Kashmiris to India. For many young Muslims belonging to this class, the Jama'at's understanding of a socially engaged Islam was seen as an attractive alternative to popular Sufism, which was branded as 'other-worldly', 'superstitious', 'corrupt' and, above all, 'un-Islamic'. It is primarily among this constituency that the Ahl-e Hadith's vision of Islam, which the Lashkar represents, derives its greatest support in Kashmir today. Owing to their shared commitment to a radical understanding of Islam, the Lashkar seems to have been able to win over the support of several Kashmiris associated with or sympathetic to the Jama'at-e Islami, thus making for a broader appeal for the Ahl-e Hadith than it previously enjoyed.

The Lashkar in Kashmir

As in the case of the other Pakistan-based militant groups now active in Kashmir, the Lashkar's direct participation in the Kashmir conflict dates back to the end of the Afghan war in 1992, in which an estimated 1,600 of its militants are said to have participated. After the Soviet withdrawal from Afghanistan, the Lashkar shifted its attention to Kashmir to 'help the oppressed and innocent Kashmiris who were undergoing Indian aggression for the past fifty years'.[49] In this, it was assisted by the Jama'at-e Islami of Pakistan and the Inter-Services Intelligence (ISI), the powerful Pakistani secret service agency, both key players in the Afghan jihad.[50] Raman, an Indian political analyst, writes that from 1992 onwards, the Pakistani authorities began sponsoring militant Islamist outfits, including the Lashkar, to undertake what it called a jihad in Kashmir, instead of channelling such aid directly, in order to escape being branded as a 'terrorist state'. Raman calls this the 'privatization of jihad', and remarks that the patronage given to these groups must be seen as a reflection of the growing fear of mass support of the JKLF and its advocacy of an independent Kashmir, which went fundamentally against Pakistan's own perceived interests.[51] The Islamists were seen as a far more reliable ally, for all of them are fiercely opposed to nationalism, and, therefore, insist that Kashmir must join Muslim Pakistan, this being seen as but the prelude to a grand unity of all Muslims. With various militant Islamist groups, many of them Pakistan-based and led by Pakistanis, now being liberally assisted by the Pakistani state, assistance for the JKLF began drying up. Presumably, the Indian authorities must have seen this new situation as being to their advantage, as it meant a serious division in Kashmiri Muslim ranks.

The Lashkar is said to have first entered Kashmir in 1990 (Singh 1996: 128) sending in a number of its trained activists, most of whom were Pakistani nationals. It then 'upgraded' its jihad there in 1993, when its militants attacked an Indian army base in Poonch. In 1994, following the laying down of arms by the JKLF, the Lashkar began sending large numbers of its fighters into Kashmir, most of them from outside Kashmir, mainly Pakistanis, Kashmiris from Pakistan-controlled Kashmir and Afghans. The year 1996 witnessed a major shift in the Lashkar's Kashmir strategy, with greater attention being paid to the border districts of Jammu, particularly Rajouri and Poonch, areas dominated by non-Kashmiri Muslims such as the cattle-grazing Gujjars and Bakkarwals, ethnically related to the Punjabi Muslims, as well as Doda. Reports suggest that some of the mass killings of Hindu villagers in these areas have been its handiwork, with the aim of engineering an exodus of the Hindu population of these areas so as to make its task easier.[52] By mid-2001, the Lashkar claimed, it had killed 14,369 Indian soldiers in Kashmir, losing in the process 1,016 of its own men.[53] In mid-1999 India and Pakistan almost came to war after Pakistan-based militants, believed to have been backed by the Pakistani army, occupied certain strategic heights in the Kargil sector in the Ladakh region in the remote northern part of Kashmir. The four principal militant groups taking part in this operation, all Islamist and manned mainly by non-Kashmiris, were the Harkat ul-Mujahidin, the Tehrik-i Jihad, al-Badr and the Lashkar.[54] These groups together formed a joint military command to coordinate their military operations against the Indian army.[55] The Lashkar contingent consisted, among others, of several students from its college at Muridke, led by one 'Abdur Rahman 'Abid, a graduate of Madinah University.[56] The Lashkar force was joined by some two hundred militants from the Nuristan province of Afghanistan, the first time that such a large number of Afghan fighters had entered Kashmir in recent years.[57]

The Pakistani attempt to enter Kashmir through Kargil, however, failed, and under pressure from the West, the then Pakistani Prime Minister, Nawaz Sharif, appealed to the militants to withdraw from the heights they had captured. The militants reluctantly obeyed what they saw as Sharif's capitulation to the U.S.A., but announced what they called 'the second stage' of the Kashmir jihad – taking the battle against the Indian army right inside the Kashmir Valley itself, in order, as Zaki ur-Rahman Lakhvi, the *amir* of the Lashkar, put it, 'to avenge' the atrocities unleashed by the Indian army on the Kashmiri Muslims. According to the *amir* of the Markaz, Hafiz Muhammad Saeed, in this second phase 'the *jihad* would spread all across Kashmir. It would spread to every peak, every forest and every path'.[58] As part of this new strategy, the Lashkar came up with a new means of attack – suicide bombers, which it named 'Ibn Taimiya Fida'i ('Faithful') Missions', in memory of the medieval Arab Islamic scholar who crusaded against what he saw as un-Islamic practices, and to whom the Ahl-e Hadith owes much of its inspiration.

The successful attack by a *fida'i* mission on the Indian army headquarters in Srinagar in November 1999, in which several Indian soldiers were killed, came as a great boost to the morale of the Lashkar fighters, smarting under their forced withdrawal some months earlier from the Kargil heights. In the wake of the attack, Hafiz Muhammad Saeed declared before an audience of an estimated three hundred thousand people in Muridke in November 1999 that his fighters could now 'strike anywhere in India', threatening even to target the

Indian Prime Minister's office if India did not stop its aggression against the Kashmiri Muslims and vacate Kashmir. The jihad, declared the Hafiz, was not now limited simply to freeing Kashmir from Indian control. Rather, he stressed, it was aimed at 'liberating' India itself.[59] He revealed that the Lashkar was now planning to extend its activities beyond the borders of Kashmir deep inside India.[60] Some 50,000 Pakistani youth are said to have responded to this appeal to join the grand anti-India crusade. That this was no empty boasting was made clear in a Lashkar attack on an Indian army post at the Red Fort, the very heart of Delhi, in December, 2000, in which several Indian soldiers are said to have been killed.

The Limits of Jihad: Its Implications for Kashmir, India and Pakistan

The development of the Ahl-e Hadith in Kashmir, from being a marginal group, fiercely opposed by many Kashmiri Muslims, to emerging, in the form of the Lashkar, as the most formidable element in the ongoing armed struggle in the region, poses crucial questions regarding the actual level of support for the Ahl-e Hadith's own vision of Islam in Kashmir. Given the limited support for the Ahl-e Hadith in Kashmir prior to the outbreak of the armed struggle in 1989, it appears that its emergence as a major actor in the region is largely owing to the role of the Lashkar in taking on the Indian army. The support for the Lashkar in Kashmir, limited though it might be, must, then, be seen as essentially a result of its stern opposition to Indian rule rather than as representing any considerable acceptance of its theological vision. In assessing the Kashmiri Muslim response to the Lashkar's involvement in the region, a clear distinction needs to be made between how many Kashmiri Muslims would probably approve of the Lashkar's military strikes against Indian soldiers and army installations, on the one hand, and how far they might accept its understanding of Islam and its ultimate agenda, on the other. Many Kashmiris, and not necessarily all supporters of a 'Wahhabi' sort of Islam, might well support the Lashkar in its willingness to take engage the Indian army. On the other hand, the consistent opposition of the Lashkar to any negotiated settlement of the Kashmir issue, insisting that the only solution to the question is carrying on with the jihad until the region finally merges with Pakistan, certainly limits its potential support base.[61] The fact that the Lashkar is almost entirely in the hands of Pakistanis and Kashmiris from Pakistan-controlled Kashmir and that it refuses to recognize the possibility of an independent Kashmir means that it has a very limited appeal to those Kashmiris who support an independent, sovereign state, which, however, neither India nor Pakistan seems willing to accede to.

A further obstacle in the path of the Lashkar in Kashmir is its own understanding of Islam, rigid, regimented and vehemently opposed as it is to

Sufism. 'Sufism', the Lashkar insists, 'has been designed jihad with no other purpose than to dampen the spirit of jihad'.[62] Since jihad is seen as integral to Islam, Sufism is regarded as 'un-Islamic'. The Lashkar's vehement opposition to Sufism, in line with the Ahl-i Hadith position on the matter, seems at striking odds with Kashmir tradition, where Sufism is still deeply rooted. The history of the spread of Islam in Kashmir is virtually synonymous with the missionary efforts of various Sufi orders, most notably the Kubrawi, the Suhrawardi, the Qadri, the Naqshbandi and the Rishi. Until today, Sufism remains the dominant form of Islamic expression in Kashmir, and the vehement opposition to it from Islamist groups that see it as 'un-Islamic' has registered little success. Indeed, defenders of the cults centred round the Sufi saints have not hesitated to brand the 'Wahhabis'[63] as 'un-Islamic' and 'enemies of the faith' in turn. Until such time as Sufism remains dominant in the region and continues to play a central role in the definition of Kashmiri identity, there seems little hope for groups such as the Lashkar to see their understanding of Islam win popular acceptance. The Lashkar is even less likely to find warm support among the Shias of the region, who form the majority in the Kargil district of Ladakh and are a sizeable minority in the Kashmir Valley, for the Shias are seen by the Ahl-e Hadith as non-Muslim 'heretics'.

If the odds seem so heavily weighted against the Lashkar in attempting to win support for its own vision of Islam among the Kashmiri Muslims, it can still continue to play a major role in escalating the conflict in the region, making it even more difficult to resolve the issue. The Lashkar insists that dialogue with the 'disbelievers' is prohibited in Islam, and that hence the only way ahead is through armed jihad.[64] This intransigence has serious implications for all three parties to the Kashmir dispute – India, Pakistan as well as the people of Kashmir. While carrying on with the armed strikes in order to inflict maximum damage to India might suit the short-term interests of the Pakistani establishment, it might, as some commentators have warned, have major consequences for Pakistan's own future, the full implications of which do not seem to have been appreciated by the managers of Pakistan's Kashmir policy. It is quite possible that the growing strength of groups like the Lashkar might mean that Pakistan, too, could soon be engulfed in civil war, with armed groups seeking to take over the country in the name of establishing an Islamic order.

The Lashkar, for its part, insists that it will not stop with its jihad in Kashmir, but, rather, regards it as but the beginning of a greater struggle to establish an Islamic state in all of South Asia, including both India as well as Pakistan. It has repeatedly condemned what it sees as 'un-Islamic' forces within Pakistan, demanding that there should be a 'total enforcement of Allah's shariah' in the country.[65] The Pakistani ruling elite are accused of 'disbelief', taking the name of Islam while at the same time refusing to establish an Islamic system in the country. There is every fear that if the Pakistani state were to enter into some sort of agreement with India on Kashmir, armed Islamist groups active in Kashmir today might turn their attention inwards and seek to carry on with their agenda at home through armed struggle. Hafiz Muhammad Saeed, the *amir* of the Markaz, himself hints at the possibility, cautioning that, 'As soon as we start to fight the disbelievers, we are sure to stop fighting among ourselves. But if we persist in keeping from *jihad* against the enemy, we are bound to go on fighting among ourselves'.[66] Pakistani political scientist Eqbal Ahmad, sensing the very real threat of militant Islamist groups, many of them active in Kashmir today, plunging Pakistan into a bloody civil war, warns his countrymen, 'The chickens of *jihads* once sponsored by imperialism and the [Pakistani] state have been coming home to roost. Afghanistan threatens to become a metaphor for the future'.[67] Ahmad's appeal seems to have fallen on deaf ears, for the Pakistani establishment seems oblivious to the consequences of its continued patronage of groups such as the Lashkar, which today have become so powerful as to be, in the words of Minhas, a Pakistani analyst, quite 'unmanageable'.[68] The implications of the Lashkar's determination to carry on with what it calls a jihad against India pose serious questions for India, too, faced as it is with the growing threat of Hindu militancy, targeted primarily against the country's large Muslim population. As mentioned earlier, the Lashkar views its involvement in Kashmir as merely a prelude to a grand war against India, aiming at nothing less than the merger of India into a 'Greater Pakistan'. It sees itself as crusading on behalf of India's Muslims, who are said to be labouring under great oppression at the hands of militant Hindu organizations and the Indian government.[69] Leading Markaz spokesmen have appealed for Indian Muslim leaders to launch an armed struggle against India.[70] Not many Indian Muslims would, however, seem to be receptive to the appeals of the Lashkar to launch a jihad against the Hindus. With a Hindu right-wing government in power in India and the growing challenge of Hindutva fascism, voices calling for peace and dialogue with the Hindus seem to prevail over those insisting on confrontation and conflict.

The Crisis in Afghanistan and the Lashkar in Kashmir

The American reprisals against the Taliban following the 11 September 2001 attacks on the World Trade Center and the Pentagon were fiercely opposed by Islamist groups, including the Lashkar. In the wake of the attacks, the Lashkar is said to have dispatched several of its armed volunteers to Afghanistan, to supplement the 600 Lashkar special guards who had earlier been specially appointed as personal security for Osama bin Laden.[71] The Lashkar viewed the American assault on Afghanistan as the launching of a new 'crusade' by the 'Christian' West against the Muslim world. One of the principal aims of the attacks, it claimed, was to destroy Pakistan's nuclear capabilities.[72] The head of the Markaz warned Pakistani President General Pervez Musharraf not to cooperate with America, and issued a thinly veiled threat, calling for defiance of the government if it continued to toe the American line.[73] The head of the fatwa section of the Markaz, Mufti 'Abdur Rahman, issued a fatwa claiming it a binding duty on all Muslims to help their Afghan co-religionists. If Pakistan's rulers supported America, he laid down, this would be treated as a gross violation of Islam, and they would be considered as 'rebels and traitors of Allah and His Prophet'. If a group of Muslims is attacked by 'unbelievers', the fatwa said, 'the entire Muslim community must help it, even through war'. In the ongoing 'war between Islam and disbelief', as it described it, it declared, 'it has become obligatory for all the Muslim states in the interest of the dignity of Islam and the Muslims to ... forge unity in their own ranks and send their armies to support jihad and the mujahidin'. [74]

Under pressure from the Americans, Musharraf was forced to take action against some militant groups based in Pakistan and active in Afghanistan, including the Lashkar. Several leading Lashkar activists, including the head of the organization, Hafiz Muhammad Saeed, were arrested, only to be soon released. Careful not to embarrass Musharraf, and to win his support for its continued involvement in Kashmir, the Markaz reorganized itself in December 2001, setting up two separate wings. The first, christened as the Jama'at ud-Da'wa , was to focus on *tabligh* or Islamic missionary activism and on 'political and reformist activities'. The other, which would retain the name of the Lashkar-e Taiba, would devote itself to jihad, which would remain confined to Kashmir alone. In other words, jihadist activities of the Lashkar in other parts of the world were to be stopped, and the resources of the organizations directed to Kashmir. In the face of charges that the mainly Punjabi Pakistani Lashkar activists in Kashmir had taken over the movement and had, in the process, marginalized the Kashmiris, a new central committee of the Lashkar was set up in late December 2001, which consisted entirely of Kashmiris, from both Pakistani- and Indian-administered parts of the state, and headed by a little-known Kashmiri Islamic scholar, 'Abdul Wahid. This promoting of Kashmiris within the central apparatus of the organization was also intended to rebut charges of the militant movement in Kashmir being an externally inspired and directed one, and not an indigenous 'liberation' struggle.[75] Significantly, alongside this, the radical anti-American rhetoric was toned down in the Markaz's official website, probably under pressure from Musharraf. However, despite Musharraf's insistence that Pakistan was taking all possible steps to prevent the entry of militants into Kashmir from its territory, Lashkar activists continue to cross over into Kashmir and their military engagements with the Indian armed forces show no sign of letting up.

Conclusion

The continuation of the armed conflict in Kashmir has resulted in untold sufferings for the Kashmiris, and has also diverted scarce resources from desperately needed development work to an unprecedented arms build-up in the region. An entire generation has grown up in Kashmir for whom killings are a daily affair. It is increasingly becoming clear to many, including the Kashmiris themselves, that the only possible long-term, viable solution to the vexed Kashmir issue is through a negotiated agreement between India, Pakistan and the people of Kashmir that satisfies all parties to the dispute. Armed conflict can only mean a further tragic loss of life and continued destruction. Given this, it appears that, if groups such as the Lashkar refuse to read the signs of the times, they might be threatened with further marginalization. Already muffled voices within Kashmir's pro-Pakistan Jama'at-e Islami, in addition to pro-independence Kashmiri nationalist groups, have been calling for peaceful dialogue, and it seems, one hopes, a matter of time before other Islamist groups begin to veer round to seeking a resolution of the dispute through peaceful means (Sahni 1999: 132).

In this context, the refusal of certain Islamist groups in Pakistan and Kashmir, such as the Lashkar, on the one hand, and militant Hindu groups in India, on the other, to consider a negotiated settlement of the dispute, based on the aspirations of the Kashmiris themselves, is the greatest hurdle in the path of establishing peace in the region. With any move towards peaceful negotiation of the dispute ruled out on the grounds that entering into agreements with 'disbelievers' is forbidden in Islam, the Lashkar insists that the jihad must continue until its logical culmination – the break-up of India and its absorption into a 'Greater Pakistan'. While this seems an obviously vain and dangerous hope, it is a vision, one must recognize, that inspires thousands of Lashkar activists, leading them on to even sacrificing their lives, to kill or to be killed.

The Lashkar has been able to carve for itself a presence as a major actor in the Kashmir conflict less because of the appeal of its ideology than owing to its engagement with Indian armed forces in the region. The 'Islamization' of the conflict has had crucial implications for the way in which numerous Kashmiris have come to see themselves. The image, long internalized, of Kashmiris as 'passive' 'cowards' has been forcefully challenged by gun-wielding militants. The tolerant, rich and vibrant Kashmiri Sufi tradition has come under great strain, as new forms of understanding Islam have emerged, stressing conflict, armed jihad and martyrdom. If Kashmir was one of the few parts of South Asia that were spared the frenzy of Hindu-Muslim violence in 1947, it was owing, in large measure, to the deeply embedded Sufi traditions of the Kashmiris. Today, with traditional Sufism being under threat from competing understandings of Islam, and with unrelenting assaults on Muslims in India at the hands of Hindu chauvinist groups, Kashmir's indigenous religious resources of conflict management and inter-community dialogue seem powerless to pose any major challenge to the politics of religious hatred. In the meanwhile, the toll of innocents, sacrificial victims at the altar of communal strife, continues to mount.

Notes

1. The JKLF abandoned the path of military struggle in 1994, believing that the struggle for Kashmiri independence should be carried out using non-violent means.
2. The Markaz's website can be accessed on www.markazdawa.com. However, the contents of the site are constantly changed, and many articles quoted here have been removed, particularly after the incidents of 11 September 2001.
3. For this purpose, some saw the need for cooperating with the Hindus to overthrow the British, and hence several Ahl-e Hadith *'ulama* joined the Indian National Congress (Bari, 2001: 147–48).
4. A Brief Introduction to the Markaz and the Lashkar, http://www.lashkertaiba.net/introduction/introduction.html. These four centres are the Mu'askra-i-Taiba, the Aqsa, the Umm al-Qurra and 'Abdullah bin Ma'sud.
5. A fierce advocate of pan-Islamism, the Markaz/Lashkar seeks to unite Muslims all over the world into one solid bloc. It is said to be part of Saudi dissident Osama bin Laden's 'International Front for Jihad Against the U.S.A. and Israel ('Badamibagh and After', http://www.saag.org/notes/note46.html).
6. I owe this point to Francis Robinson.
7. 'Lashkar-i-Taiba: The New Masters of Kashmir', http://jammukashmir.com/insights/insight9808.html
8. http://www.markazdawa.org/English/organization/education.htm
9. http://www.homestead.com/kashmirstory/jihad2~main.html
10. Names are also probably changed to conceal their actual identities. A radical uniformity is sought to be imposed by giving the recruits a common Arabic title of Abu ('father of'), after which an Arabic name is added.
11. 'Allah's Army: Mujahideen-e-Lashkar-e-Taiba', http://members.xoom.com/_xmcm/markazdawa/lashkar.html
12. 'Implementation of Shar'iah is a Cure-All', http://www.dawacenter.com/magazinevoiceofislam/feb00/democracyvsislam.html
13. Speech of Hafiz 'Abdur Rahman Makki, http://www.dawacenter.com/ijtimah/mak.html
14. Hafiz Muhammad Saeed: 'Neither Despotism Nor Democracy in Islam', http://www.dawacenter.com/magazinevoiceofislam/nov99/editorial.html, p. 2.
15. 'Democratic System vs. Islamic Polity', http://www.dawacenter.com/magazinevoiceofislam/feb00/democracyvsislam.html
16. 'Voice of Islam', February 2000, http://www.dawacenter.com/magazinevoiceofislam/feb00/editorial.html, p. 2.
17. 'Jihad in the Present Times' [part I], http://www.dawacenter.com/jihad/jihad001.html, p. 2.
18. 'Jihad: the Foreign Policy of the Islamic State', http://www.dawacenter.com/magazines/voiceofislam/sept99/jihad.html, p. 1.
19. 'Jihad: The Foreign Policy of the Islamic State', http://www.dawacenter.com/magazines/voiceofislam/sept99/jihad.html, p. 2.
20. Hafiz Muhammad Saeed: 'Jihad is the Only Solution', http://www.dawacenter.com/magazines/voiceofislam/feb00/seminar.html
21. B. Raman: 'Osama Bin Laden: an Up-Date', http://www.saag.org/papers/paper25.html, p. 3.
22. 'Radio al-Jihad', http://www.marazdawa.org/radio/news.htm.

23. 'What Jihad Means in Islam', http://members.xoom.com/_xmcm/markazdawa/jehad.htm, p. 2.
24. http://www.dawacenter.com/magazines/voiceofislam/dec99/ijtima.html
25. Jihad in the Present Times [part iii], http://www.dawacenter.com/jihad/jihad003.html, p.3.
26. Ibid.
27. Ibid., p.5.
28. Ibid., p.7.
29. Hafiz Muhammad Saeed: 'Khutbah Jumu'ah', http://www.dawacenter.com/ijtimah/khutbah-e.html, p. 1.
30. http://www.dawacenter.com/magazine/voiceofislam/dec99/ijtima.html
31. 'Jihad is the Only Solution', http://www.dawacenter.com/magazines/voiceofislam/feb00/seminar.html
32. 'Speech by Qari 'Abdul Wahid Kashmiri', http://www.dawacenter.com/ijtimah/kashmiri-e.html
33. 'Speech by Abu Sa'ad Shabbir Ahmad', http://www.dawacenter.com/ijtimah/shabbir-e.html
34. 'Voice of Islam', February 2000, p. 2, http://www.dawacenter.com/magazines/voiceofislam/feb00/editorial.html
35. http://www.dawacenter.com/magazine/voiceofislam/dec99/ijtima.html
36. http://www.dawacenter.com/ijtimah/Isalaf-e.html, p. 1.
37. 'Kashmir: The Forgotten Jihad', http:www.dawacenter.com/kashmir/kashmir.html, p. 1.
38. 'Radio al-Jihad', http://www.marazdawa.org/radio/news.htm
39. Hafiz Muhammad Saeed: 'No More Dialogue on Kashmir', http://www.dawacenter.com/magazines/voiceofislam/sept99/editorial.html
40. 'Hafiz Muhammad Saeed's address to the Takmil-i Pakistan Conference', http://www.markazdawa.org, p. 1.
41. Hafiz Muhammad Saeed: 'Khutbah Jumu'ah', http://www.dawacenter.com/ijtimah/khutbah-e.html., p.1.
42. Ibid.
43. 'Speech by Muhammad Ibrahim Salafi', http://www.dawacenter.com/ijtimah/Isalafi-e.html.
44. Ibid
45. Ahl-e Hadith followers generally worship in separate mosques all over South Asia, many of them refusing to pray behind Imams belonging to other Muslim groups. Their practice of *amin bi'l jahr* (announcing amen aloud) and *rafa-i yada'in* (lifting the hands to the ears before genuflecting in prayer) clearly distinguishes them from the Hanafis. On numerous occasions, Ahl-e Hadith followers have been forcibly expelled from Hanafi mosques.
46. Islamism as understood here is a political ideology committed to the setting up of an Islamic state, inspired by a vision of Islam as an all-embracing ideology.
47. For details, see Kashmiri (n.d., 1984).
48. Several leading early Jama'at activists hailed from Sufi families known for their piety and scholarship. Senior Jama'at leader, Qari Saifuddin, translated and published the works of the leading Kashmiri Rishi, Hazrat Nuruddin Nurani, presenting him as an orthodox Muslim, in contrast to the image of him as having been an unorthodox Sufi and a proponent of syncretism.
49. 'Allah's Army', see note 11.

50. 'Are the Talibans Coming?', http://www.kashmir.force9.co.uk/editorials.htm
51. B. Raman: 'Kashmir: After Ten years of Militancy', http://www.saag.org/papers/paper44.html
52. 'Lashkar-i-Taiba', see note 7.
53. http://markazdawa.org/English/magazines/voice/april2001/eleven%20years.htm
54. These groups all share a common commitment to an Islamist vision. Some of these groups are clearly sponsored by the Pakistanis, who, it seems, feel that the existence of multiple groups would make them more dependent on Pakistan. A united movement, it would appear, might pose serious challenges to Pakistani control and manipulation.
55. 'Kashmiri Militants Fighting Indian Advance', http://www.ummah.org.uk/kashmir/news/advance.htm
56. 'Kargil: The Graveyard of Indian Troops', http://www.dawacenter.com/archives/tour.html
57. 'Militants Say Over 200 Afghans Deployed in Kashmir', http://www.rawa.org/kashmir.html
58. 'Kashmir Militants Start "Round Two" Of Struggle', http://www.asia2000.org.nz/news/NL1392432000.html
59. 'Kargil: the Graveyard of Indian Troops', see note 56.
60. 'Ijitma Coverage By Indian Newspapers', http://www.dawacenter.com/ijtimah/indiannewspapers.html.
61. 'There is no negotiated settlement in Islam,' a Markaz statement insists, adding that, 'there should be no deal with the disbelivers [as] [t]here is no way the disbelievers will allow Islam to prevail; 'Kashmir, the Forgotten Jihad', http://www.dawacenter.com/kashmir/kashmir.html, p.1.
62. 'Jihad in the Present Times' [part v], http://www.dawacenter.com/jihad/jihad005.html, p. 3.
63. A term used to refer to the followers of the eighteenth-century Arab Muhammad ibn 'Abdul Wahhab, who vehemently opposed Sufism, branding it as 'un-Islamic'.
64. Hafiz Muhammad Saeed: 'Hizbul Mujahideen Should Not be Deceived by India's False Promises', http://www.markazdawa.org/english…_vislam/August2000/editorial.htm, p. 2.
65. Hafiz Muhammad Saeed: 'No More Dialogue on Kashmir', http://www.dawacenter.com/magazine/voiceofislam/sept99/editorial.html, p. 2.
66. http://www.markazdawa.org/english/jihad/present1.htm
67. Eqbal Ahmad: 'Jihad International Incorporated', http://www.sangat.org/review/islam/jihad.html, p. 4.
68. Saeed Ahmed Minhas: 'Sectarianism and Deeni Madaris in Pakistan',http://www.sangat.org/review/Islam/minhas.html, p. 1.
69. http://www.markazdawa.org/English/newsandmedia/news/english/index.htm, p. 1.
70. http://www.markazdawa.org/English/newsandmedia/news/english/index.htm
71. http://markazdawa.org/English/newsand media/jtimes/200220_4/014.htm
72. http://markazdawa.org/English/magazines/voice/200110/Pak%20is%20real%20target.htm
73. 'Lashkar-i-Taiba Chief Urges Muslim Ummah to Rise, Stand Shoulder to Shoulder with the Afghans', Jihad Times, 26 October 2001, http://markazdawa.org
74. Mufti Abdur Rahman: 'The Decree in Support of Osama bin Laden and Afghanistan', http://markazdawa.org/English/magazines/VOICE/200220/page2.htm
75. http://markazdawa.org/English/index.html

References

Ali, T. 2002. *The Clash of Fundamentalisms: Crusades, Jihads and Modernity*. London & New York: Verso.

Amritsari, S. n.d. *Ahl-i Hadith Aur Islam*. New Delhi: Dar-ul-Kitab.

Bari, S.A. 2001. *Azad Hindustan Mai Muslim Tanzimey: Ek Ja'iza*. New Delhi: Institute of Objective Studies.

Kashmiri, A. n.d. *Tarikh-i-Tahrik-i-Islami Jammu Aur Kashmir: Aghaz-i-Islam Se 1947 Tak. Srinagar*: Department of Publications and Publicity, Jama'at-i-Islami of Jammu and Kashmir.

Kashmiri, A. 1984. *Tarikh-i-Tehrik-i-Islami Jammu Aur Kashmir:1947 Se 1970 Tak. Srinagar*: Department of Publications and Publicity, Jama'at-i-Islami of Jammu and Kashmir.

Khan, B.A. 2000. 'The Ahl-i Hadith: A Socio-Religious Reform Movement in Kashmir', *The Muslim World*, 90: 137–57.

Meeruthi, A.M.S.A. 2001. *Akabir 'Ulama-i Ahnaf Ke Bhuley Bisrey Fatawe*. Delhi: Dar ul-Kitab Islamiya.

Meeruthi, S.A. 2000. Foreword, in H.S. Yusuf (ed), *Tehrik-i-Jihad, Jama'at Ahl-i-Hadith Aur 'Ulama-i-Ahnaf*. Delhi: Dar ul-Kitab Islamiya.

Metcalf, B.D. 1982. *Islamic Revival in British India: Deoband, 1860–1900*. Princeton: Princeton University Press.

Naim, A. 2002. *Bar-i Saghir Mai Agar Wahhabi Na Hotey*. Maunath Bhanjan: Ahl-i Hadith Academy.

Sahni, S. 1999. *Kashmir Underground*. New Delhi: Har-Anand Publications.

Singh, B. 1996. *Sulagta Kashmir*. New Delhi: Voice of Millions.

Wani, M.A. 1997. *Muslim Religious Trends in Kashmir in Modern Times*. Patna: Khuda Bakhsh Oriental Public Library.

Yusuf, H.S. 2000. *Tehrik-i-Jihad, Jama'at Ahl-i Hadith Aur 'Ulama-i Ahnaf*. Delhi: Dar ul-Kitab Islamiya.

Part IV

The Inscription of War in Mediated Worlds

Chapter 10
In the Combat Zone

Marilyn B. Young

In the aftermath of U.S. victory in the first Gulf War, the first President George Bush was optimistic that the country had 'kicked the Vietnam syndrome'. But the syndrome continued to manifest itself in the popular imagination of war. The Rambo series had tried to reverse the verdict of defeat, but it left standing the public conviction that Vietnam was not a good war. Despite a victory intended to vanquish the memory of Vietnam, the only notable movies made about Desert Storm – *Courage Under Fire* (1996) and *Three Kings* (1999) – were haunted by it. The first, in its insistence that post-Vietnam America must have heroes, underlined their absence. The second, in its sardonic consideration of the American victory in the Gulf, recalled its earlier defeat. It is a telling comment on the current Iraqi war that *Three Kings* was rereleased in autumn 2004.[1]

Three Kings opens with black and white text informing us that the war is over even as a soldier shouts the question: 'Hey! Are we still killing people?' No one seems to know the answer. The soldier peers through the scope on his gun, sees an Iraqi on a distant hilltop, white flag in one hand, weapon in the other. Before either the audience, or the soldier, can tell whether the man intends to shoot or surrender, the American fires and the man falls dead. 'Congratulations', his buddy says. 'You got yourself a raghead. I didn't think I'd get to see anyone shot in this war'. We next observe one of those interviews with the troops that, like ads for the military, punctuated television coverage of the first Gulf War. Both the press and the troops who so enthusiastically performed for them are mocked: 'They say you exorcised the ghost of Vietnam in [this war with its] clear moral imperative', the reporter informs the soldiers, who readily agree: 'We liberated Kuwait'. The rest of the movie makes deadly fun of this answer. 'I don't know what we did here', George Clooney's Special Forces officer bitterly complains to a friend, 'just tell me what we did here'. 'Do you want to occupy Iraq', the friend answers, 'and do Vietnam all over again'? One can be certain that that line, when audiences hear it again in the context of the second Gulf War, will have a deadly resonance.

In effect, the first Gulf War, as *Three Kings* presents it, is Vietnam all over again. There is no clear moral imperative; on the contrary, Shi'ites and Kurds are cynically encouraged to rebel against Saddam Hussein and then abandoned to their fate. Even the bad guys drive the point home: 'Do [*sic*] your army care about the children in Iraq?' one of Saddam's Republic Guard soldiers, pausing in the act of torturing an American captive, asks. 'Do your army come back to help the people? … My son was killed in his bed. He is one year old. He is sleeping when the bomb come … Can you think how it feels inside your heart if I bomb your daughter?' Individual Americans, like Clooney, through their honesty, virility and disregard for authority, redeem the country's honour, but only in opposition to, or apart from, the government, never in support of its stated aims. In this, *Three Kings* is a sardonic retelling of what Pat Aufderheide (1990: 84) has described as the 'noble-grunt' Vietnam war movie. The enemy are not Vietnamese or Iraqis but rather 'the cold abstract forces of bureaucracy and the incompetence of superiors'.

For the past few years, the only refuge for the righteous fighting man has been the Second World War.[2] It was, unsurprisingly, the first point of reference for George Bush in the immediate aftermath of 11 September 2001 (as it had been for his father, on the eve of Desert Storm): the attack was another Pearl Harbor; the enemy was fascist, totalitarian, a spoke in an 'axis of evil'. Only in the Second World War, the film historian Thomas Doherty (1993: 271) pointed out, can Americans find 'the consolation of closure and the serenity of moral certainty. For Hollywood and American culture the Second World War would always be a safe berth'. Fought for an unquestionably just cause, ending in total victory, the Second World War could be reliably invoked to remind Americans of their own best selves. Vincent Canby (1998) observed that movies about Vietnam had made war itself seem bestial; *Saving Private Ryan* made war 'good again'. This was war as men of Stephen Spielberg's generation played it on the street when they were boys: storming beaches, house-to-house fighting, sharpshooters in doorways, vulnerable human beings against tanks, always outnumbered.[3]

No one can identify with a B-52 and, as Michael Sherry (1987) pointed out long ago, we rarely witness bombing raids from below. Ground combat is much more satisfying. The camera always faces out against the enemy, or inwards at the grievous wounds enemy fire causes. The individual soldier fighting for his life is the victim of war; those he kills, since they are so evidently bent on his destruction, are the perpetrators of violence. His innocence is ours. Spielberg's achievement went beyond nostalgia. By enabling identification with the individual combat soldier, his Second World War epic extended a pardon to soldiers everywhere. On the large and small screens of the country, a handful of heroes fight off the enemy horde (variously, Germans, Japanese, Iraqis, Somalis, Vietnamese), Second World War tropes mixing freely with those of old-fashioned westerns. While Ryan's war has nothing to do with contemporary American high-tech military tactics, *Saving Private Ryan* established a useful paradigm. The tight focus on the situation of the combat solider is inherently dramatic and, by screening out everything save the immediate context in which he fights, recent war movies, wherever they are set, serve as all-purpose propaganda instruments. The Vietnam war movies of the late 1980s similarly kept the focus on the individual fighting man, erasing history and politics in favour of 'an emotional drama of embattled individual survival' (Aufderheide 1990: 86). But the differences are crucial: in *Platoon, 84 Charlie Mopic, Full Metal Jacket*, and *Casualties of War,* the mission is explicitly meaningless, the officers useless or worse, the men abandoned by authority, the struggle a civil war. 'We didn't fight the enemy', the hero of *Platoon* concludes, 'we fought ourselves and the enemy was us'. The mission in *Saving Private Ryan* is assumed to be good, the Germans are the enemies, and who wouldn't want to fight under Tom Hanks?

So attractive, in retrospect, is this old-style ground war that HBO made it into a ten-hour series based on the book credited to Stephen Ambrose, *Band of Brothers*. I watched only one-third of the episodes; after that the rituals of male bonding become wearying. It is not that one missed the presence of women, since, except for sex, everything women do was competently handled by men, who cared for each other as tenderly as any woman could. The often gentle universe of *Band of Brothers* reinforces the manifest content of the series: once upon a time America was very, very good. Magically, its old goodness constitutes an ongoing goodness as well, if only Americans can be brought to remember and cherish the good past. Like the Cold War movies of the 1950s – and in direct contrast to the late Vietnam war movies – *Band of Brothers* and *Saving Private Ryan* revel in a 'sentimental militarism' that relies not on ideology, but on faith in benevolent male authority (see Appy 2001: 94).

Something more interesting is going on in *Band of Brothers* than this filiopious history. At the very end, a defeated German general is allowed to address his massed troops, now, like himself, prisoners of war. He tells them how proud he is of them and how well they have fought, with what courage and bravery. The listening Americans are moved: he has described their war as well as his own. War stories written from inside out vary by geography but the story they tell is always the same: death, fear, brotherhood. Bravery, courage, the capacity to commit atrocities, are not determined by the cause in which they are displayed. 'It's about the man next to you', one of the characters in *Black Hawk Down* says. 'That's all it is'. The flat statement that one kills and dies for the man next to you never leads to the obvious question: what are both of you doing there? Some historians, like Gerald Linderman (1997), have written the inside story of war with attention to its contradictions, as tragedy rather than heroic epic. Contemporary war movies, from *Saving Private Ryan* to *We Were Soldiers,* follow Ambrose's lead. They abstract war from its context, leaving it standing on its own, self-justifying, impervious to doubt, a fact of nature.

The Pacific theatre has been a less popular location in which to revisit the Second World War; perhaps jungle warfare recalls Vietnam too directly.

Terrence Malick's *Thin Red Line* was a resounding box office failure, in part because, as Neil Gabler (2002: 4) pointed out, in its sharp caricature of the indifference of military authority to the lives of the troops, it was the 'last of the Vietnam-era movies'. Jerry Bruckheimer chose a safer subject, the attack on Pearl Harbor. The only way to watch *Pearl Harbor* is on video, with your finger poised over fast forward. The product of U.S.$127 million worth of special effects, *Pearl Harbor* is oddly dated. The computer graphics look as unreal, in their high realism, as the tiny galleons that fought on the Spanish Main in Hollywood's days of yore; the love story is faithful to the genre as it was practised in the 1940s magazine *True Romance*; the acting is silent-movie grandiose, the sentiments are neo-Hallmark. The only surprise is that the film-makers, intent on a happy ending to the carnage of Japanese-wrought destruction, offer us only Doolittle's raid on Tokyo, rather than Hiroshima.[4]

Hollywood nostalgia for the Second World War is not only about doing an end run around Vietnam or salvaging war as a fruitful human activity. It is also intended to hold a mirror to our own corrupt times. In the fat, soft days before the recession and 11 September 2001, the generation that fought the Second World War was praised, in antique slang, as 'the greatest'. Succeeding generations could aspire to being good, maybe great, but by definition they could not be the greatest. 'It is as though', Ian Buruma (2001) wrote after seeing *Pearl Harbor*, 'we should feel nostalgic for times when dying for the nation was called for. We are supposed to believe that people at war were better human beings, and we should be more like them'. The film-makers, Buruma concluded, were not cynical but something worse: 'I have a feeling [they] are deeply sincere. They believe in their own spectacle ... So who needs reality? Just sit back and enjoy the show. Until the next war. And then we die, ingloriously'.[5] Though not, Buruma should have added, in the movies.

Having waved the flag for so many years before 11 September 2001, Hollywood's first reaction was to put the industry at the disposal of the government.[6] Less than a month later, forty Hollywood executives made the pilgrimage to the White House for a two-hour discussion with Chris Henick, deputy assistant to the president, and Adam Goldman, associate director of the office of public liaison. Leslie Moonves, president of CBS, explained their mission: 'I think you have a bunch of people here who were just saying, "Tell us what to do. We don't fly jet planes, but there are skill sets that can be put to use here"'. With its usual relaxed attitude toward historical accuracy, the *New York Times* stated that, while 'not new to Hollywood', such patriotic sentiments had been 'rarely in evidence since World War II'. But in one particular, the reporter, Jim Rutenberg (2001: B-9), had it exactly right: the Second World War was the 'era to which executives are now looking for guidance'. More specifically, 'several people who had attended the meeting referred, as models for cooperation, to the director Frank Capra'. Others hoped to produce contemporary versions of movies like *Mrs. Miniver*, although comparing 11 September to the blitz seems a dubious comfort.[7]

There was a clear need both 'domestically and internationally to tell the story that is our story'.

On 8 November 2001, a smaller group of Hollywood executives responded to an invitation from Karl Rove, senior White House adviser, for a more focused and 'high-powered' discussion of how Hollywood might help the war effort. While denying any interest in making propaganda films, the executives reiterated their desire to add a new chapter to Capra's *Why We Fight* series (Lyman 2001a). Meanwhile, the *Los Angeles Times* reported that Sylvester Stallone, who has had extensive experience in recycling the Second World War themes through new wars, was working on a script that would parachute Rambo into Afghanistan to fight the Taliban. Actually this would be Rambo's second visit to the country; in 1998 he fought with the 'Afghan Warriors' previously known as 'Freedom Fighters' (Harlow 2001).

The meeting with Rove took place in Beverly Hills and included not only high-powered movie executives, but representatives of the networks, labour unions and Cineplex owners. Movie content, all agreed, was not up for discussion. However, Rove did suggest that Hollywood could help clarify certain issues: 'that the war is against terrorism, not Islam ... that this is a global conflict requiring a global response, and that it is a fight against evil rather than a disagreement between nations'. In addition, the movies could join in issuing a 'call to service' to all Americans and 'aid in the process of reassuring children and families in these uncertain times'. Jack Valenti, president of the Motion Picture Association, was pleased by the 'seamless web of unity' created at the meeting: 'It was really quite affectionate to behold' (Lyman 2001b). The affection was mutual. Hollywood and Washington, Rick Lyman reported, had come 'closer together' and 'political sniping over issues of violence and vulgarity' had 'virtually ended'. After all, who, other than Jerry Falwell, would want to join Osama bin Laden in an attack on American pop culture? (Lyman 2001c).

Television had a minor role in the Korean War and was blamed for losing the Vietnam War. Things went better in the Gulf. High-tech war, war as a video game, played well. The entire population had the experience of being in the nose cone of a missile as it descended towards its target and all but those on the ground were spared what happened next. Through over a month of bombing and a week of ground fighting, no estimates of Iraqi losses were ever offered, nor did the press demand them. The result was a televised war relatively innocent of dead bodies: a war that, except for the bombing of a Baghdad air raid shelter and the repeated shots of desperate oil-soaked cormorants, would not spoil one's dinner. By the end of the war, it had become possible to take the enemy as not people, but machines; the tanks, buses and cars that jammed the highway out of Kuwait City seemed to have fled on their own, so that their charred hulks contained no human remains. There was thus an apparent, visual purity to the U.S. victory that successfully masked its savagery. It seemed difficult to imagine what greater service the news media could offer a warring state.

That was before the second Gulf War. Reporters had merely been contained in the first Gulf War. This time, they were drafted. The embedded press corps, by and large, fulfilled its punning name. At one point in the war, the TV talk show host Charlie Rose conducted a telephone interview with Frederik Balfour, a *Business Week* correspondent who was embedded in the Third Infantry. Balfour had opposed the war before it began, but now riding along with the troops, dependent upon them for his protection, he found it was impossible not to feel part of their 'cause'. Rose next asked Colin Soloway, *Newsweek* correspondent with the 101st Airborne Division, if he'd been able to go along on any Apache helicopter missions. No, Soloway explained regretfully, Apache helicopters only have seats for the two pilots. Still, he was able to view the video tape when the helicopters returned to base and the pilots were glad to 'walk him through' whatever engagement they had conducted. The television audience did not get to see the tapes – any more than they had during the first Gulf War.

The government script for the second Gulf War was a mix of the Second World War and the fall of the Berlin Wall. Television news dutifully depicted the liberation of Baghdad, Iraqi joy and the toppling of the outsize statue of Saddam Hussein. But the script seemed to end there and what happened next, the chaos, looting, vandalism, followed by isolated acts of sniping and then full-scale rebellion, have brought the country forcibly back to its memories of Vietnam. Unlike Vietnam, however, images of the ongoing wars in Afghanistan and Iraq have been carefully rationed. Restrictions on accompanying the troops are reinforced by the evident danger to newsmen when they do.

In the immediate aftermath of 11 September 2001, films whose themes were too close for comfort, like *Collateral Damage*, about a terrorist attack, were delayed, while movies about old wars were advanced. The chair of Paramount explained why *Black Hawk Down,* about the intervention in Somalia, would appear on local screens sooner than expected: 'It's about the sacrifices that soldiers make so the rest of us can be safe'. Mark Bowden, who wrote the book on which the movie is based, pronounced himself well satisfied with the treatment. 'Many people read *Black Hawk Down* as an argument not to use military force', Bowden told the *Times* reporter, 'which I never intended. … This movie says that we have the capability of doing this kind of thing. It's ugly and it's terrible, but we have these very brave young men who do this, and we need to use them now and then' (Masters 2001).

Black Hawk Down begins with a scrolling text informing the audience of the humanitarian purpose of the U.S. intervention – famine relief – a purpose that could not be fulfilled as long as the evil warlord Aidid controlled the capital, Mogadishu.[8] The film wisely skips the unopposed 'made-for-TV' amphibious landing on the beach at Mogadishu (see Shalom 1993).[9] Instead, it focuses entirely on the effort to rescue the crew of a helicopter shot down in the course of a mission to snatch several of Aidid's key lieutenants from their meeting place in the crowded city. The small band of troops is besieged by thousands and thousands of armed and apparently crazed Somalis (called, throughout the movie, 'skinnies', a reference to the famine, though in fact, most of the Somalis look more like stereotypical muscled boys in the hood). There are no references to the constant and indifferent use of excessive force so that, as Alex de Waal concludes in his article, 'U.S. War Crimes in Somalia', by the time of the rescue mission 'literally every inhabitant of large areas of Mogadishu considered the U.N. and U.S. as enemies, and were ready to take up arms against them' (de Waal 1998). But then, as Jerry Bruckheimer explained, 'We never set out to tell that story. We wanted to make a film about what these young guys were sent out to do and what they did to survive' (Carter 2002).

Initially, the makers of *Black Hawk Down* considered drawing an explicit connection between U.S. withdrawal from Somalia and the growth of Al Qaida, but dropped the idea because they thought 'the connections were apparent' (Elder 2002). A special screening of the movie was attended by Vice President Cheney, Secretary of Defence Rumsfeld, Deputy Secretary of Defence Paul Wolfowitz, Secretary of the Army Thomas E. White, assorted generals and Oliver North, identified in the Army News Link as a 'political analyst'. Ridley Scott told the audience he had made the movie to 'set the record straight'. He wanted to disabuse the public of the notion that the military had 'messed up on Somalia', when in fact 'it was heroic in a very unstable part of the world'. White agreed: the movie reflected the 'values of valor and self-sacrifice' of the military in its current war against terrorism and indeed throughout its history (Burlas 2002). Yet, with all its patriotic trapping, the implications of *Black Hawk Down* are potentially dangerous to war-makers: what is it about America's good intentions that they go so quickly awry? What, after all, was accomplished by the deaths of one thousand Somalis and eighteen Americans? The implication of the film's ending, that the U.S. should not have withdrawn its troops so precipitously, does not resolve but compounds the confusion. What, other than more dead Somalis and Americans, would continued military action have achieved? Could it be there was something wrong with American intentions?[10]

For all its heroics, *Black Hawk Down* could not erase Vietnam, another war said to have begun with good intentions that went unaccountably wrong. Nor did *Saving Private Ryan* do the job. Giorgio Mariani may be correct in saying that the '"monument" that Spielberg erects to his father's generation ties past and present together in a seamless web, thereby absolving the nation not only from the sin of Vietnam, but also from all the other "mistakes" of the half century separating us from the end of World War II' (Mariani 2000: 4).[11] But this is only generally true. Absolution, to be effective, must be specific. To erase Vietnam, Hollywood would have to go back to Vietnam, where the unravelling of the war story began. In 1941, in an effort to take the bad taste out of the First World War and the powerful anti-war movies that dominated the interwar years, Hollywood released *Sergeant York*, a moving tale of a pacifist turned war hero. 'We can sit in the theater and see [York] go fight a better World War I for us,' Jeanine Basinger has written. Films like *Sergeant*

York, she explained, 'wipe out earlier images and replace them with new ones, appropriate for the times' (Basinger 1986: 100). To create a 'new mythos' for the Second World War, Thomas Doherty (1993: 100) wrote, 'Hollywood had to recast the Great War as a reasonable national enterprise, not as the crazy slaughterhouse depicted in literature and film for the previous twenty years. ... Outright obliteration was a prerequisite'.

To fight this new war, the films, literature and histories of Vietnam must be obliterated. *We Were Soldiers*, in what may be the first of many returns to Vietnam, is the twenty-first century's *Sergeant York.*[12] Like *Black Hawk Down*, *We Were Soldiers* was released ahead of schedule and Paramount was pleased with the test screening: 'The movie has very, very patriotic American values. The audience embraced those values'. Joseph Galloway, who, with Lt. Col. Harold Moore, wrote the book on which the movie is based, was delighted with the film. As he explained to a reporter, 'audiences would be drawn to the story because it is not defeatist about what eventually became the misadventure of Vietnam'. The book, like the movie, is relentlessly patriotic. 'This', the prologue reads, 'is about what we did, what we saw, what we suffered in a thirty-four-day campaign in the Ia Drang Valley of the Central Highlands of South Vietnam in November 1965, when we were young and confident and patriotic'. It was a 'love story', about men 'proud of the opportunity to serve [the] country'. It was also a story about the 'far more transcendent love' that comes to men 'unbidden on the battlefields. ... We killed for each other, we died for each other, and we wept for each other. And in time, we came to love each other as brothers. In battle our world shrank to the man on our left and the man on our right and the enemy all around' (Moore and Galloway 1993: 3–4). The film version makes it also a story about family values, a manly reporter ready to pick up a gun and worthy enemies.

As it happens, Moore's unit, the first battalion, Seventh Cavalry Regiment, First Division, was also Custer's and in the movie, before leaving for Vietnam, Moore is shown thoughtfully leafing through an illustrated account of the battle of Little Big Horn, along with a French book describing what is called the 'massacre' of French troops in a battle along Route 19, near where he will soon find himself fighting for his life. Mel Gibson's brow furrows as he contemplates the fate of the French (a brief scene shows Vietnamese soldiers slaughtering French prisoners) and of Custer's men.[13] The domestication of the Vietnamese enemy, common during the war itself, strikes an odd, discordant note. After all, the Indians, in the last couple of decades of films and novels, have been victims; which would make Moore and his men the executioners, and that can't be right. Still, the scene is crucial, the first of many reversals of the images of the Vietnam War. The victims of massacres in Vietnam, it turns out, were white men. My Lai disappears; there are no burning villages but instead well-armed, uniformed Vietnamese regulars; napalm strikes burn Americans and Vietnamese alike (the B-52 sorties crucial to the battle are never shown); the American commander is everywhere in the midst of the battle, barely protected and always in danger; the Vietnamese commander gives his orders from the safety of a clean, well-kept, underground tunnel complex (in fact, the Vietnamese command post was not sheltered).[14] Americans die in great numbers, but are anyhow victorious over the far more numerous Vietnamese, and a soldier's last words express gratitude that he has sacrificed his life for his country. Gone is the resentment of authority of the Vietnam movies of the late 1980s; in this Vietnam, as in *Black Hawk Down*, no one gets left behind (see Aufderheide 1990: 94ff.).

In these movies, Vietnam has become a war of which Americans can feel proud.[15] The pride derives from the demonstration of courage and the memory of suffering, irrespective of the cause in which the one is displayed and the other endured. Both are proof that the nation, if it would only embrace its heritage, now explicitly including Vietnam, has not gone soft. Ridley Scott, the director of *Black Hawk Down*, decided not to depict the dragging of a dead American through the streets of Mogadishu. Instead, he showed a helicopter pilot, naked from the waist up, his arms outflung, being lifted out of his craft by the mob, a contemporary deposition scene. After watching the film, George Monbiot wrote that the U.S. had cast itself 'simultaneously as the world's savior and the world's victim, a sacrificial messiah on a mission to deliver the world from evil' (Monbiot 2002: 13). Monbiot called it a 'new myth of nationhood'. I am not sure how new it is, but I agree with Monbiot that it 'contains incalculable dangers', and it will be playing on movie screens everywhere in the months and years to come and, more disastrously, in the real world as well.

There is something odd about these recent representations of America's messianic mission. From *Private Ryan* to the *Delta Force* officers in Somalia and Hal Moore in Vietnam, the insistent theme is that Americans sacrifice their lives only for one another. Private Ryan's war, for example, is the obverse of movies made during the Second World War, when the individual had sometimes to be sacrificed for the sake of the mission. Ryan reverses the moral of the story; the lives of a group of men are risked for the sake of a single individual. 'In the new metaphor war movies seem to be presenting', Neil Gabler wrote, 'Americans are no longer distrustful of authority and no longer doubt the cause. Rather, we trust each other and see the cause as us' (Gabler 2002). And who can doubt that 'we' are a worthy cause? The legitimacy of the state, incarnate in the nation at war, is vested in the wars the United States has fought and the new ones the Bush administration plans to fight, all of them, once launched, justified by the way they are fought for the 'man on our left and the man on our right and the enemy all around'.

Notes

1. See Waxman (2004). The director, David O. Russell, also plans to release a documentary about the second Gulf War. According to the story, *Three Kings* has

'received belated acclaim for its prescient depiction of the moral dilemmas of the war in Iraq'.

2. One could argue that this has been the case, with interesting variations, since 1945. See Appy (2001) for a particularly interesting analysis of the way Hollywood translated the 'sentimental militarism' of the Second World War films for Cold War use, a translation marked by ambivalence and ambiguity.
3. For an especially eloquent evocation of this culture, see Engelhardt (1998).
4. There are a few good moments in the movie, lines that seem to have wandered in from some other script. It is as if, below the level of consciousness, even Jerry Bruckheimer and Michael Bay had doubts about the enterprise. Early on, a veteran of the First World War remembers fighting in the trenches and fervently hopes no one will ever again have to see what he saw. But the holder of this potentially anti-war sentiment is the brutal father of one of the two boys who grow up to be heroes, and we need not pay it undue attention. Similarly, the Japanese responsible for planning the attack on Pearl Harbor protests when he is praised as a genius. A genius, he says, would have figured out how to avoid war. Obviously a man not destined to win a war, since, as the actor impersonating (one cannot call it acting) Jimmy Doolittle tells us: 'Victory belongs to those who believe in it the most and believe in it the longest'.
5. Buruma (2001) compared *Pearl Harbor* to patriotic Japanese war movies, which, unlike their American counterparts, stressed duty, courage, sacrifice and purity of will rather than the evil of the enemy.
6. Hollywood's response to 25 June 1950, the day war broke out in Korea, was much the same. On 28 June 1950, the Title Registration Bureau of the Motion Picture Association announced it had received five hand-delivered titles from various producers: Korea, South Korea, Crisis in Korea, Formosa and, rather ominously, Indochina. Film Daily boasted of the industry's instant response to the call to battle: 'For the third time in a generation, the awesome shadow of Mars shot full across the American industry … and … the industry fell into line and asked for its marching orders from the government'. More formally, Francis S. Harmon, who had chaired the coordinating committee between Hollywood and various government agencies during the Second World War, returned to act as liaison for the duration of this one (see Detzer 1977: 153; Doherty 1993: 276).
7. The reference to Capra was more precise than the reporter is likely to have realized. Capra, according to Saverio Giovacchini, was chosen by the government because of his 'conservative political background. … The series makes no effort to understand the causes of the war as anything more than an unexplained assault on the world' (see Giovacchini 2001: 150).
8. In fact, the famine had largely abated before U.S. intervention and the targeting of Aidid restored his waning power, transforming him into 'the aggrieved party in a war with UN colonialists' (see Shalom 1993).
9. The landing was pure pr for the Marines. Indeed, the entire operation can be seen as an effort by the Pentagon to demonstrate the need for high defence budgets despite the end of the Cold War – use it or lose it (see also Peterson 2001: 54).
10. In one of the endless migration tales of the American Empire, Sinp Sithavaday, an eighteen-year-old whose family had fled Laos in 1979, found himself in Somalia, a member of the Tenth Mountain Division's second battalion, Eighty-seventh Infantry. Interviewed by his local newspaper, Sithavaday, without directly criticizing the movie, talked about the 'growing hubris' of U.S. troops: 'We thought, we have rocket launchers, night goggles, infrared designators, all kinds of technical stuff. We are the

meanest'. After a few months, he had become dubious about his mission: 'There was a lot of anger at the U.S. They saw us flexing our muscles and killing them'. Like the soldiers sent to Indochina a decade before his birth, Sithavaday complained: 'How can you tell a farmer from a militia member?' (Leslie-Finn 2002).

11. English version on-line at www.acoma.it/n18/inglese/mission2a.htm
12. The passage of time has made the displacement easier. For example, *Coming Home*, a 1978 anti-war movie, was summarized in the 25 February 2002 *New York Times* TV Late Movie listings P. E7 this way: 'Jane Fonda, Jon Voight, Bruce Dern. Strong, stinging triangle of wife and Vietnam vets'.
13. See Hanley et al. 2001. The history of the Seventh Cavalry includes several massacres going the other way: the Battle of the Washita, in 1868, when the Seventh Cavalry ordered a large group of Indians into a constricted area and then slaughtered them; Wounded Knee, in 1890, when the Seventh Cavalry massacred 370 Sioux, many of them women and children; the massacre of Korean villagers in July 1950.
14. The ABC documentary, *We Were Young and Brave*, produced in 1994, is very clear on this point: air power was the deciding factor in the battle. A Vietnamese colonel describes watching, unprotected, as a 'sea of fire' engulfed his troops: 'if you saw it you would think we all died'.
15. This is in direct contrast to the documentary, in which some of the survivors of the battle returned to the Ia Drang along with their Vietnamese counterparts. The mood is elegiac, sometimes bitter, and the overall effect is of the terrible waste of lives, however bravely sacrificed. Moore and Galloway (1993) both accuse the military of stage-managing the post-battle assessments of Ia Drang. 'You can almost date the rot at the heart of the American effort in Vietnam to that week', Galloway insists. By depicting the battle as a victory, the ABC narrator explains, the military 'pulled an unsuspecting nation further into war'. Post-battle newsreels described the Ia Drang as proof that the 'best of the enemy's forces could be stopped dead in their own territory'. Survivors were expected to join in a ghastly charade – clips of which are included – in which Westmoreland congratulated them on their victory. The men are unsmiling and many of them look away, refusing eye contact with the general. The battle itself is brilliantly depicted, using both North Vietnamese and U.S. Army film footage, and the critical commentary of Moore, Galloway and other combatants is far more stark than anything in the movie.

References

Appy, C. 2001. '"We'll Follow the Old Man": the Strains of Sentimental Militarism in Popular Films of the Fifties', in P.J. Kuznick and J. Gilbert (eds), *Rethinking Cold War Culture*. Washington, DC: Smithsonian Institution.

Aufderheide, P. 1990. 'Good Soldiers', in M.C. Miller (ed), *Seeing Through Movies*. New York: Pantheon, pp. 81–111.

Basinger, J. 1986. *The World War II Combat Film: Anatomy of a Genre*. New York: Columbia University Press.

Burlas, J. 2002. '"BHD" Reflects Army Values', *Army LINK News*, 16 January, www.dtic.mil/armylink/news/

Buruma, I. 2001. 'Oh! What a Lovely War', *Guardian*, 28 May (online).

Canby, V. 1998. 'The Horror and Honor of a Good War', *New York Times*, 10 August.

Carter, C.J. 2002. '"Black Hawk Down" Movie Turns Grim Somalia Fight into a Dramatic Tale of Heroism', *Valley News*, 2 February, C1.

Detzer, D. 1977. *Thunder of the Captains: The Short Summer of 1950*. New York: Thomas Y. Crowell.

de Waal, A. 1998. 'U.S. War Crimes in Somalia', *New Left Review* 230 (July/August): 131–44.

Doherty, T. 1993. *Projections of War: Hollywood, American Culture and World War II*. New York: Columbia University Press.

Elder, R.K. 2002. 'The War Stories of BHD', 13 March 2002, http://metromix.com/movies

Engelhardt, T. 1998. *The End of Victory Culture: Cold War America and the Disillusioning of a Generation*. Amherst: University of Massachusetts Press.

Gabler, N. 2002. 'Seeking Perspective on the Movie Front Lines', *New York Times*, 27 January, News of the Week in Review.

Giovacchini, S. 2001. *Hollywood Modernism: Film and Politics in the Age of the New Deal*. Philadelphia: Temple University Press.

Hanley, C.J., Choe, S.H. and M. Mendoza. 2001. *The Bridge at No Gun Ri*. New York: Henry Holt.

Harlow, J. 2001. 'Hollywood Joins the Campaign: Rambo Gets Call-Up as Movies Catch War Fever'; *Los Angeles Times*, 11 November (online).

Leslie-Finn, M. 2002. 'Lyme Man Looks Back on his Tour of Duty in Somalia', *Valley News*, 2 February, C4–C5.

Linderman, G.F. 1997. *The War Within: America's Combat Experience in World War II*. New York: Free Press.

Lyman, R. 2001a. 'White House Sets Meeting with Film Executives to Discuss War on Terrorism', *New York Times*, 8 November, B-8.

———. 2001b. 'Hollywood Discusses Role in War Effort', *New York Times*, 12 November, B-2.

———. 2001c. 'At Least for the Moment, a Cooling Off in the Culture Wars', *New York Times*, 13 November, E-1, E-6.

Mariani, G. 2000. '"Mission of Mercy/Mission of Murder": Spielberg's *Saving Private Ryan* and the Culture of Baby Boomers', *Acoma* 18(Winter), English version online at www.acoma.it/n18/inglese/mission2a.htm

Masters, K. 2001. 'Against the Tide, Two Movies Go to War', *New York Times*, 4 November, p. 6.

Monbiot, G. 2002. 'Both Saviour and Victim', *Guardian Weekly*, 7–13 February.

Moore, H.G. and J. Galloway. 1993. *We Were Soldiers Once … and Young: Ia Drang — the Battle that Changed the War in Vietnam*. New York: Harper Perennial.

Peterson, S. 2001. *Me Against My Brother: At War in Somalia, Sudan, and Rwanda*. New York: Routledge.

Rutenberg, J. 2001. 'Hollywood Seeks Role in the War', *Times*, 20 October, B-9.

Shalom, S.R. 1993. Gravy Train: Feeding the Pentagon by Feeding Somalia', *Z Magazine*, November (online).

Sherry, M.S. 1987. *The Rise of American Air Power: The Creation of Armageddon*. New Haven: Yale University Press.

Waxman, S. 2004. '"Three Kings" Director Plans Documentary on Iraq War', *New York Times*, 16 August, B1.

CHAPTER 11

'VIRTUAL' DISCOURSE AND THE CREATION AND DISRUPTION OF SOCIAL NETWORKS: OBSERVATIONS ON THE WAR IN KASHMIR IN CYBERSPACE

Aparna Rao, Monika Böck, Katharina Schneider and Michael Schnegg

Introduction

Contemporary processes and forms of violent conflict and militarization are closely related to the development of colonialism, globalization and technological change. One of the issues addressed by the workshop at which a preliminary version of this chapter was presented related to the effects of long-drawn out periods of armed violence on social organization. Notably, we asked, how does the social practice of individual and community bonding and networking change in war-torn societies? Obviously, any in-depth study of such behavioural change during actual periods of war is difficult, and it is even harder to ascertain the degree to which such change may translate into new forms of social bonding and networking. A way out is to examine discourses that as Chilton (1987: 8) observed, are 'a part of social action … embedded and facilitated by social and political institutions, and … produced by institutional or individual actors enjoying different degrees of social and political power'. In this chapter we look at discourses – interwoven systems of linguistic and visual symbols and meanings – embedded in the social and political (and economic) field of what has come to be known as the 'Kashmir conflict', facilitated and influenced by the globalized technological institution of the Internet, and produced by a variety of local and transnational individual actors. We seek thereby to understand the relationship between this war –

fought during the last fourteen years between Indian forces claiming to defend the 'integrity' of the Indian state and a variety of local, supra-regional and partly international militias claiming to fight for freedom, Islam or both, and resulting in the deaths of over 70,000 armed and unarmed men, women and children, in many hundred disappearances, kidnappings and numerous rapes, in the flight of almost the entire *c.* 250,000–strong Hindu (Pandit) population of the Kashmir Valley and the migration of several hundred Muslims – and the rupture of pre-war social bonds as well as the creation of new ones. In our effort to grasp these transformed scenarios, we focus on the role of new information technologies in the formation of new ('virtual') communities acting within a conflict as deterritorialized players with clearly spelled-out local goals. We also touch upon the transformation of older networks. Our approach thus reflects a current trend towards multi-sided fieldwork in anthropology, which includes the increasing investigation of 'virtual' communities (e.g., Jones 1997; Hakken 1999; Hine 2000; Morton 2001a; Wilson and Peterson 2002; Bräuchler 2005). The Internet enables extensive networking to reach and/or create social relations and bondings that were almost inconceivable until recently. Indeed, many of these interactions in cyperspace take place among diaspora communities, whose members often draw on their own experiences in the diaspora to play a major role in creating and/or reinforcing symbols, meanings and identities.

In the following we examine in some detail aspects of discourse in a 'virtual' community consisting overwhelmingly of people who consider themselves to be Kashmiris. After some general remarks on the relationship between the media and the state we shall turn to an online community, which in a way resulted out of the ongoing conflict. We trace this community back to its beginnings and then analyse in greater detail the structure of the discourse. We seek to understand the concerns of this community and ask to what extent these are related to the war situation at 'home'.

Embedding Discourse: Some General Remarks on Media and State Hegemonies in South Asia

In South Asia, in addition to the often (self-)censored print media and the propaganda churned out by largely state-owned radio and TV stations, 'patriotic' feature films[1] have long played a role in a country's 'war effort' and it has also been argued (e.g., Mitra 1993) that television has played a central role in the resurrection of Hindu fundamentalism in India.[2] A major difference between the Web and even private TV channels is that the former can be and is used simultaneously and equally as a platform by all conflict parties. This aspect appears especially pertinent when one realizes that over the past roughly fifty years South Asian states have been experiencing several major 'internal' armed conflicts (apart from innumerable riots and at least one state-sponsored pogrom) in addition to some half a dozen 'external' wars. However, for decades most South Asians remained fairly oblivious of these 'internal' wars and armed movements, and, even for those who had more information, access was overwhelmingly limited to the state's perspective. This has changed with greater freedom of the press and with the loosening of the state's stranglehold over radio and TV, but, above all, through increasing access to the Internet.

Indeed, although the role of the Web has been largely neglected by researchers, over the last decade the Internet has been playing a major role in South Asian politics.[3] In many South Asian countries it is also seen to present a potential threat to state hegemony, and the fact that online communities are in many ways locations where conflict-laden 'politics of identities' (Kaldor 1999) are negotiated and spread among a worldwide audience has increasingly come to the awareness of national governments. Summarizing the findings of the recent report published by the 'Reporters Sans Frontières', Verma (2004) notes that in the Maldives, for instance, three persons were imprisoned for posting allegedly subversive topics online, and in Bangladesh 'a new law is on the anvil that seeks to legalize e-mail surveillance', purportedly to 'strengthen national security and the war against terrorism'. In Pakistan also the Internet is closely monitored with U.S. technological help in 'the fight against Al Qaida, which uses the Internet very effectively', and the government of India too has made attempts to ban or regulate certain sites, again with U.S. technological help.[4] One of the most publicized instances in India was when the government banned the entire Windows 95 operating system, following the production by Microsoft of a colour-coded world map showing the different time zones. This map violated Indian laws by marking Jammu and Kashmir as disputed and locating it outside Indian territory. To regain access to the Indian market, the colour coding was removed with the release of Microsoft Office 97.

Producing Discourse: Communication within Conflict

Members of the South Asian diaspora (in particular with Indian origin)[5] claimed their places in cyberspace right from its consolidation in the early 1990s. They have initiated and manage a plethora of often community/language/region-specific discussion forums, which aim at establishing and encouraging contacts among members of these communities, language groups and regions wherever they may reside. These online communities are not only translocal, but also transnational, in both operation and membership. While in the 1990s computer-mediated communication (CMC) was primarily set up by and among the diaspora, now, with improvement in technology and access, increasingly considerable feedback exists between transnational and local communities 'back home', and much of the discourse that takes place online both reflects and constructs the concerns of the transnational, wider society as well as the concerns of those 'back home' (e.g., Appadurai 1996: 195f.). As many scholars have noted for South Asia, migration to the West in particular has greatly impacted their notions of what constitutes their identity (e.g., Jain 1998; Uberoi 1998). Further, new communication technologies have often helped place content and awareness of identity at the centre stage of what Van der Veer (2002: 174, 183f.) refers to as the 'dialectics between nationalism and transnationalism'. In the case of the Kashmir conflict, CMC has played a significant role in negotiating the politics of identities since the conflict turned to armed violence in 1989, which seems to resonate with the local situation and the pressure of migration.

Since its inception the Kashmir conflict has led to drastic changes in communication between individuals, and the last fourteen years of violence have further exacerbated the situation. The division of Kashmir into Indian-administered and Pakistani-administered portions led to numerous Muslim families being split and the flight of several hundred Hindu and Sikh families from Pakistan-administered Kashmir to Jammu and Kashmir. The subsequent fifty years of intermittent conflict made regular communication between them difficult, letters often being opened on both sides of the ceasefire line/LoC[6] and direct telephone connections between the Indian- and Pakistani-administered parts of Kashmir being non-existent. With the beginning of the armed violence in 1989, the exchange of letters grew still more uncertain and ceased altogether in December 2001, following the attack on the Indian Parliament by Pakistani and Kashmiri militants. Thereafter until December 2003, when postal services resumed once again, direct and legal communication between the civilian population on either side of the ceasefire line/LoC was extremely difficult. The situation for Pandit families who fled the Valley in and around 1990 is slightly different: most live dispersed and at least theoretically, many have had access to postal services in India or the West. Only those few who braved all the odds and continued to live in the rural areas of the Kashmir Valley were almost completely cut off from all means of communication for the first few years of the 1990s. In spring 2005, when the efforts to ease political tension between India and Pakistan bore fruit, a bus service was implemented crossing the ceasefire line/LoC and facilitating communication between Kashmir Valley and Azad Kashmir. After fourteen years of disruption, the exchange of messages – and even physical visits – between separated families has now become possible again.

Internet facilities are still not very common in the Kashmir Valley, especially not outside urban areas, but they are steadily increasing. In late November 2002 there were 804 Internet connections and forty Internet cafes in the capital, Srinagar; the towns of Sopore and Islamabad had nearly one hundred connections each. There were six servers in the Kashmir Valley, of which only three functioned, with, however, Srinagar's Kashmir University having two of these. By spring 2003, with the entry of several private firms, faster service and a tremendous drop in prices, the number of connections rose sharply. So did the number of Internet cafes, which had become immensely popular with the urban youth, much to the chagrin and worry of conservative, religious-minded persons, who suspected that these, somewhat like closed public telephone booths before them, were turning into sites of romancing, fixing dates and, worse still, meetings of young men and women. Allegedly, such cybercafes, both in the Valley and to the south in Jammu, the winter capital of the Jammu and Kashmir government, were also used to download and distribute pornography, so much so that raids were conducted and arrests made (Baig 2004). This notwithstanding, as elsewhere in South Asia, CMC was becoming a major vehicle of interaction, especially among the relatively affluent, young and middle-class section of society. This section also has numerous members in the diaspora, and hence it is not surprising that long-distance communication between relatives and friends takes place increasingly, not only via the telephone, but also via the Internet.

Over a decade ago Rheingold (1993: 6) observed that 'people anywhere ... inevitably build "virtual" communities ... as more and more informal public spaces disappear from our real lives'. There can be many reasons for such 'disappearances'. A complete disruption of the earlier public culture in the Kashmir Valley and a powerful diasporic situation are two reasons applicable to the online community we now turn to.

Establishing a 'Virtual' Kashmiri Community: Initiating Discourse in Usenet (1996–97)

The first, and still one of the most important, locations in cyberspace where cultural identities are discussed, constructed and reconstructed is Usenet,[7] in particular the newsgroups under the soc.culture.* -hierarchy[8] (see also Mitra 1997). In 1996, by the time the current armed conflict in Kashmir had been raging for over six years, hot debates were going on in Usenet about the creation of two new newsgroups with the proposed names soc.culture.kashmir and soc.culture.indian.jammu-kashmir. According to Usenet guidelines anyone who wants to create a new newsgroup has to submit a formal proposal (an RFD, i.e., 'request for discussion') to the Usenet community (i.e., to news.announce.newgroups and news.groups) and any other newsgroups or mailing lists[9] related to the proposed topic. In the case of soc.culture.kashmir this proposal (RFD) was cross-posted to soc.culture.indian, soc.culture.pakistan, and a Kashmiri mailing list – the latter we shall introduce below in greater detail. After a period of discussion – during which a name and charter are agreed upon and it has been determined whether the group will be moderated, and if so by whom – a 'call for votes' (CFV) is usually cross-posted among these same groups. Vote gathering and counting are handled by a group of neutral Usenet volunteer votetakers (UVV). Until 1996, debates about Kashmir were mainly carried first by soc.culture.indian (sci) – its Usenet history dating back to September 1986, but its activity not increasing noticeably until March 1989[10] – and then also by soc.culture.pakistan (scp), created in March 1990, incidentally perhaps, shortly after the outbreak of violence in the Valley. Both these groups were, and still are, unmoderated according to the spirit of freedom of speech of early Usenet communities; but as a result they are also often severely affected by heavy traffic as well as by vulgar and obscene postings. In these two nationally marked cyber-territories political controversies between Indian and Pakistani, Hindu and Muslim, Indian and Kashmiri viewpoints were battled out, often escalating into severe 'flame wars',[11] where deliberately hostile and insulting messages are exchanged.

In 1996, paralleling the 'real-life', 'non-virtual' demands for independence, Kashmiri netizens claimed their own autonomous territory in cyberspace too. In the RFD on the creation of soc.culture.kashmir (sck), it was argued that sck should be a moderated group, because of keeping discussion free of spam, flames and profanities, and that moderation would not, of course, be used as an instrument of censorship (message 26 February 1996)[12]. But Indian netizens cast doubt on the ability of these Kashmiris to administer their 'virtual' territory independently in a 'really' democratic way and suspected that 'a fabricated version of reality' would be provided (message 7 June 1996). To keep the group balanced, it was suggested by an Indian Hindu that the proposed moderator – a Kashmiri Muslim – should be assisted by an Indian/Hindu co-moderator – the best person being a Kashmiri Pandit (message 2 March 1996). However, this attempt at salvaging whatever was left of inter-community bonding failed. No such person was found, either because he/she was not willing to act as moderator or because he/she was not acceptable to the Kashmiri Usenet community. A panel of three to five moderators was then suggested that would include representatives of all three political perspectives on the Kashmir conflict (i.e., Kashmir as part of India, as part of Pakistan or as an independent state), and probably also outsiders not involved in the conflict, in order to guarantee balanced discussions. This suggestion was however considered by Indian Hindus as 'close to impossible' (message 15 April 1996), and Kashmiri Muslims were also concerned that 'such a proposition is going to result in a India/Pakistan war amongst the moderation panel' (message 29 March 1996). Finally, soc.culture.kashmir went into the voting process, listing two Kashmiri Muslims as moderators, since all the other suggestions, the proponents argued,[13] would have been a 'humiliation' for the Kashmiri Usenet community. This again led to Indian Hindus suspecting that 'this newsgroup (moderated) will be at the forefront of the propaganda machinery of Islamic Jihadist' (message 25 May 1996).[14]

One of the reasons why moderation became such a big and unresolvable issue in discussions on the creation of sck was that the proposal of soc.culture.indian.jammu-kashmir (sci.j-k) as an unmoderated group was simultaneously in the voting process. As the political battle was already embedded in the name space of these two groups, the process of their creation turned into heavy, and often defamatory, political campaigns against each other. Proponents of sci.j-k were accused of having lobbied very heavily on various Indian mailing lists, thereby making the voting for their group (and by implication rejecting sck) an issue of 'patriotism as if this were some kind of a national battle' (message 19 March 1996). At the end, the proposal of sci.j-k passed with 23,670 votes in favour and 1,803 votes against – a result on a scale never before witnessed by the Usenet community (message 16 April 1996) – and sck failed with 453 'yes' votes and 1,993 'no' votes (message 20 June 1996). This left the Usenet volunteers with a familiar problem innate to their well-meant, democratically oriented guidelines for group creation: those who hold the majority in the Net (which in the case of India also reflects the 'non-virtual' demographic situation and the vastly superior conditions of access to the Internet) can simply outnumber a minority, with the consequence that the latter is denied a forum it finds acceptable.

The victory of sci.j-k was then announced in one of the Indian mailing lists in military terms: 'Indian netizens win cyberwar over Kashmir' – this victory was perceived as important enough to be immediately published in the 'non-virtual' world too, by the national newspaper *The Indian Express* (see message 3 April 1996). The blending of real and 'virtual' disputed territory also becomes obvious in the following comment: 'while India is struggling to hold elections in Kashmir … more than 20,000 Indian netizens swamped electronic polls to keep the troubled state within India' (message 3 April 1996). Choosing the right moderator was obviously not the 'true' reason for voting down sck; this argument could not mask even a fraction of the 'true' aims of this battle, which reflect attempts at safeguarding Indian hegemony. Quite a few members of the Usenet community considered the events surrounding the creation of sci.j-k and sck as unjust, opining in support of sck:

> We can now add Kashmiris who do not agree that the province should be part of India to the shameful list that already includes Ahmaddi Muslims and Macedonians; they will never have a group whose name they do not consider an insult, simply because the same 23,000 Indians who were turned out for this vote would turn out to strike down a group name they consider inacceptable. (Message 17 April 1996)

When a second proposal for creating sck – this time as an unmoderated group – also failed, the support was even more explicit: 'Let them have it. Don't widen the rifts. The following are valid groups: soc.culture.bengali, soc.culture.punjabi, soc.culture.tamil, soc.culture.kashmir – all of the above cultures exist outside Indian borders too' (message 28 March 1997). Since the Usenet community leaves ample scope for subaltern activities, a 'hegemonic' claim established on Usenet territory could be countered fairly easily by finding a 'dissident' Usenet site that was willing to carry the disputed newsgroup, despite the negative voting results. Hence, without making a fuss over it, soc.culture.kashmir was quietly, and so to say 'irregularly', created in April 1996 (message 5 April 1996 on the subject: 'How was this NG created?').[15] Just as soc.culture.indian.jammu-kashmir had been flooded by fanatically Hindu Bharatiya Janata Party-postings immediately after its 'regular' creation, so also soc.culture.kashmir was boarded by cross-posters such as activists of www.ummah.org.uk asking for contributions to jihad funds – or by a strange figure designing himself as Dr Jai Maharaj, a Hindu-centric top cross-poster, well known to the Usenet community.[16]

The Community Reloaded: Recapturing Discourse @yahoogroups.com (2000–4)

Usenet has its own culture or 'spirit', the procedure of creating a new newsgroup being part of this. If someone is deemed not to have the right community 'spirit', then he/she is advised by Usenet volunteers to create a mailing list or an e-group on one of the commercial providers such as Yahoo, where mailing lists or e-groups are not embedded in a wider community. There is, for example, no 'Yahoo community spirit', and no feedback is required from a wider community when creating a new e-group in Yahoo 'territory'. In August 2000 Yahoo introduced a new service called 'Yahoo!Groups', making it more comfortable for users to create and manage their own e-groups by adding some new technical features. Within one year, by August 2001, 136 e-groups were identifiable at http://groups.yahoo.com, simply by keying in the term 'Kashmir'; in May 2004 this number increased to 233. Today almost all the movements and organizations concerned with Kashmir have their own disussion forums. To begin with, there were also a few subregional e-groups (e.g., Zanskar-online, Kupwara-online), but most of these remained either moribund or had very few members.

One of the largest Yahoo e-groups on Kashmir, not ostensibly connected to any organization, was founded as a mailing list in 1995 by Kashmiri students from the Valley of Kashmir studying in the United States.[17] At the time not only was this mailing list involved in discussing the creation of soc.culture.kashmir (see above), but the proponents of sck then became some of its central members, and the lost battle on Usenet turned into the group's myth of origin written down on the group's new home on http://groups.yahoo.com:

> [This discussion forum] soared in popularity only after Kashmiris were denied a chance to establish a moderated Kashmir related *Usenet* newsgroup, called *soc.culture.kashmir*. The huge no vote from the Indians sent a clear signal that current political climate was not right for a neutral public forum on Kashmir. They voted in record numbers to establish a newsgroup under the Indian hierarchy, called *soc.culture.indian.jammu-kashmir*.

After its 'migration' to Yahoo, the size of this community (i.e., registered membership, but not necessarily active in discourse at any point of time) fluctuates minimally – from 407 in February 2001, through 423 in May 2001,

427 in August 2001, 473 in October 2001, 431 in July 2002 and 465 in November 2002 to 447 in February 2004 and 599 in July 2005. The members are mainly middle-class urban Sunni Muslim male professionals (students, faculty members, engineers, doctors, etc.) and businessmen, aged between roughly twenty and forty-five, from the Kashmir Valley, some living there, but most of them outside it. A few young Kashmiri Hindus living in the Valley until around 1990 – some of whom were ex-neighbours or classmates of certain Muslims in this community – are also members; so too are some men from Pakistan-administered Kashmir (Azad Kashmir and Northern Areas), living either there or in Europe as migrant workers or professionals. A few non-Kashmiris, either Muslim or Hindu from Pakistan or India, respectively, are also part of this group. For a detailed analysis of the identity of community members who were active in discourse in a sample period, see Tables 11.1 and 11.2 below.

The community is obviously far from representative of all Kashmiri Muslims, but as far as people hailing from the Valley are concerned, it appears to well represent the urban male intelligentsia in terms of family background, religious convictions and professional and political aspirations, and it also seems to mirror mobility patterns.[18] The reader may well ask on what we base our statements about the composition of this community. Very simply, most members refer at some point of time to their (or others' real or alleged) professions, places of origin, religion and mother tongue, thus breaking with an apparently common feature of 'virtual' discourse – anonymity. Anonymity has often been seen as 'one of the most powerful aspects of Internet communication' (Mitra 1997: 77), and can be used to good purpose by breaking down the inhibitions present in face to face discourse. Because one can remain 'faceless' when communicating, identity is often uncertain at best and there may be no means to recognize gender, national origin or ethnic identity.[19] However, being rooted in what Mitra called 'national newsgroups' (Mitra 1997: 58) may automatically lead to more consistent identity performance and a clearer positioning of identity. It is, then, no surprise that in this e-group, which is primarily dedicated to the discussion of Kashmir issues, almost all members engaging in the discourse reveal their politico-religious positions (see Table 11.1 below). They do so either by explicitly identifying themselves (for example as Kashmiri Muslim or Kashmiri Hindu), by giving their full names (and professions, locality, etc.), by implicit positioning via the name chosen – for example, a typically Muslim or Hindu first name, or a surname prevalent only in the Valley – or, again, by choosing a culturally significant 'nick name'[20] such as 'real Kashmiri' or 'proud Indian'. The diaspora situation of most community members and their need and desire to draw on prior experiences of communality in order to establish a sense of community in 'virtual' space (Mitra 1997: 70) may encourage them to present their online identities as 'openly' and consistently as they do. When in 1995 Mitra (1997: 63) analysed the newsgroup soc.culture.indian referred to above, he found that 'the past identities … brought to the network … help the users find their network identity by seeking the congruences that existed prior to entry into … virtual space'. In a somewhat similar manner the members of this e-group seem to find these congruences when sharing memories such as college experiences or when referring to rather harmless pieces of what is considered Kashmiri culture, such as Kashmir-specific funny stories and jokes (see below). Moreover, since they are well aware of the shattered communality 'back home' marked primarily by mistrust and fear, and since they do not wish to reproduce these dangers of the local war-torn situation and split their 'virtual' community, the urge to perform 'authentic' and 'trusted' online identities is all the greater. Attempts to establish 'trust' are made not only through repeated demonstrations of the congruence between 'virtual' and 'real' life identities, but also by producing 'authentic, factual accounts' (Hine 2000: 122) of past and present events in Kashmir and trying to design an acceptable and trustworthy image of a future Kashmir 'beyond conflict'. Before we examine how trust and mistrust compete with each other in the discourse of this e-group, and whether a vision of a trustworthy Utopia beyond war and conflict can be processed successfully, let us first give an overview of its discourse activities.

Browsing Trough Discourse Activities (2000–4)

Although the common interest of all members is 'Kashmir' in some form or shape, topics of discussion vary widely (see, for example, Rao 2004). Broadly, discourse is composed of the following:

- Extracts from news items, mostly from English-language newspapers published primarily in the Kashmir Valley, but also elsewhere. These are distributed mainly by two organizations in the form of newsletters, but also sent in by individuals.
- Dyadic correspondence between individuals – in other words communication addressed to a specific fellow member, which are also forwarded to the rest of the community.
- General mail addressed to the community as a whole.
- Appeals to persons or organizations as fictive participants of the discourse, e.g., Maqbul Butt – the founder of the Jammu and Kashmir Liberation Front (JKLF)[21] – President Bush, Mary Robinson, Kofi Annan, the Organization of Islamic Countries, etc.
- News cross-postings from other e-groups, mainly that of the organization Lashkar-e Taiba (see also Abou Zahab and Sikand, this volume), which distributes its messages as a so called 'bulletin'.
- Cross-postings requesting funding from organizations such as the Jama'at-e Islami Pakistan[22].
- Information regarding websites, books, photographs, TV programmes, etc.

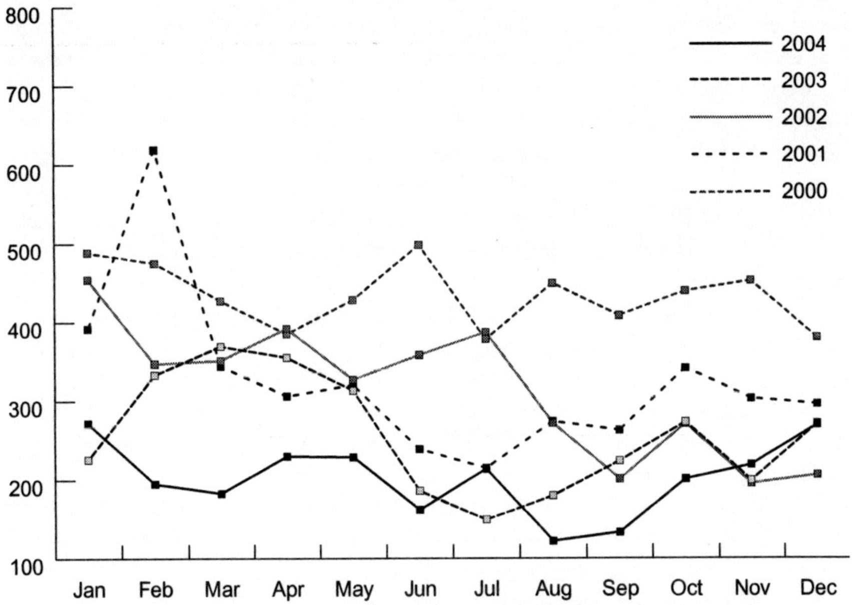

Figure 11.1: *Fluctuation in the number of messages between 2000 and 2004*

There is a fair amount of fluctuation in the number of messages (see Figure 11.1), the maximum (619 messages) being in February 2001, with, surprisingly perhaps, only 263 messages in September 2001.

Zooming In: the Peak of Communication in February 2001

The intensity of communication is one reason why we choose to concentrate on an analysis of the community and its discursive activities in the month of February 2001. But this month was important also because it witnessed a number of major occurrences that were to shape people's lives in the area for some time to come.

One of these events was the third and fourth extensions of the so-called 'unilateral Ramadan ceasefire', initially announced by the Indian government on 19 November 2000. Though rejected by some major militant organizations, such as the Lashkar-e Taiba and the Jaish-e Mohammad,[23] this ceasefire was accepted by the All Parties Hurriyat Conference (APHC)[24] and was also widely considered a preparatory step towards the talks that were held in July 2001 between India and Pakistan, which, however, yielded no outcome. Notwithstanding these extensions, violence continued, and in all about two hundred unarmed civilians, soldiers and militants died in this period. For instance, on 16 February, six demonstrators were killed and twenty-four others injured in the village of Haigam when Indian soldiers fired on some 15,000 persons protesting at the custodial death of Jaleel Ahmad Shah, a District Secretary of the JKLF, and demanding that his dead body be handed over to them. The irony of these cruel killings was that Shah had, a few weeks earlier, led a group of Kashmiri Muslim volunteers to donate blood in the Indian state of Gujarat, which had just experienced a devastating earthquake. In a culture where the symbolism of blood is of such vital importance, this generous donation and Shah's role in it were obviously highlighted and put to good use locally by the JKLF to garner emotional support and 'prove' the insincerity and ingratitude of Indians. But the incidents at Haigam also had severe macro-political repercussions, since they took place in spite of the ceasefire. They also heralded the beginning of a new hold of the Lashkar-e-Taiba over many people in the Kashmir Valley.

The incidents at Haigam immediately found resonance in the online discourse of the community we analysed, triggering a debate about the role of the Indian army in Kashmir. But soon this theme was recaptured by the more general discussion of the political future of Kashmir, which obviously was stimulated by the approaching bilateral talks between India and Pakistan. This theme – addressed under various subjects such as 'Ceasefire', 'Republic of Kashmir', 'Why Kashmir is a Classic Nation' or 'Real Difference between Independent Kashmir and Annexation to Pakistan' – figured most prominently in the discourse taking place in February 2001 and charged the community with high tension. As we shall show below, this tension partly went off in comments about intra-community relations, which rated second in the list of themes communicated in that month (see Schneider 2007). Before we go into greater detail of these discussions, we shall first analyse the composition of the community and the structure of its communication.

Close-up (1): Discursive Actors in February 2001

As already mentioned, only a fraction of the e-group's members are 'active' in discourse at any given point of time. In February 2001, only eighty-four of all the 407 group members participated in communication, as either recipients or senders of mails. As already mentioned above, several methods were used to get to 'know' these actors; to learn yet more about them we used a search engine and keyed in their email addresses. This often led us to guestbooks with detailed profiles and to partly community-specific Internet directories that gave considerable information about their members in a clear attempt at community bonding. In a few cases we also used the domain of their email addresses as clues to their location (e.g., *name*@qatar.net.qa) and profession (e.g., *name*@pop.service.*.edu).

Table 11.1: *Current location and professed religious identity of community members participating in discourse in the sample period of February 2001*

		Religious Identitiy							
		Kashmiri				**Others**			
Location	**Total No.**	**Azad Kashmiri Muslim**	**Kashmiri Muslim**	**Kashmiri Pandit**	**Dogra Hindu**	**Indian Hindu**	**Pakistani Muslim**	**Muslim**	**Christian**
Azad Kashmir	2	2							
Jammu and Kashmir	3		2		1				
India	7		2	3		2			
Pakistan	5	3					1	1	
Australia	1		1						
Canada	3	2	1						
Canada–U.K.	1							1	
Europe	3	1	1					1	
Gulf	8		4				2	2	
Japan	1							1	
Malaysia	1							1	
U.K.	13	2	6				1	4	
U.S.A.	18	1	7	1		3	1	4	1
Unknown	18	2	4			1		11	
Total No.	84	13	28	4	1	6	5	26	1

A detailed analysis of the discourse that took place between these eighty-four persons in February 2001 shows that the majority (forty-six) considered themselves as 'Kashmiri'; however, only five resided in Indian- or Pakistan-administered Kashmir (one of these being the late Maqbul Butt, the founder of the JKLF); the greater number of those considering themselves as Kashmiri (forty-one) lived in the diaspora. Table 11.1 also shows that thirty-four persons lived in the West – most (eighteen) in the United States or the United Kingdom (thirteen), three in Europe. Eight were in the Gulf states, seven in India, five in Pakistan and one to three in various other countries. The location of eighteen members could not be identified. Twenty-eight individuals identified themselves explicitly or implicitly as Kashmiri Muslims, thirteen as Azad Kashmiri Muslims (including one Muslim from Northern Area) and five as Pakistani Muslims. Twenty-six others said they professed Islam, but their ethnic or national identity could not be ascertained. A further six persons identified themselves as Indian Hindus. The lone Christian (President George Bush), is, like Maqbul Butt, a fictive participant in the discourse.

Data set out in Table 11.2 on the professions and religious identity of these actors exemplify the diasporic and class characteristics mentioned earlier for the community as a whole. They show that twenty persons were white-collar

Table 11.2: *Profession and professed religious identity of community members participating in discourse in the sample period of February 2001*

		Religious Identitiy							
		Kashmiri				Others			
Profession	**Total No.**	**Azad Kashmiri Muslim**	**Kashmiri Muslim**	**Kashmiri Pandit**	**Dogra Hindu**	**Indian Hindu**	**Pakistani Muslim**	**Muslim**	**Christian**
Political Activist	26	9	9		1		2	4	1
Businessman	4		1				1	2	
Engineer	9	1	4			1		3	
Journalist	2		1	1					
Lawyer	1		1						
Medical	6		2			1		3	
Scientist	2		2						
Seaman	1							1	
Student	7		2	2		1		2	
Unknown	26	3	6	1		3	2	11	
Total No.	84	13	28	4	1	6	5	26	1

professionals, seven were students and four were businessmen; only one was a worker (seaman), and twenty-six were political activists. The professions of twenty-six members are unknown.

Close-up (2): Network of Communication in February 2001

In an attempt to explore the structure of communication in February 2001, we first listed these eighty-four actors following the time sequence of the messages they sent (sender) and received (receiver). The data concerning the individuals (and some but not all of the organizations[25]) were then translated into a network diagram (see Figure 11.2), which represents the webs of communication as well as the centrality or marginality of various actors in terms of the number of mails posted and received.

Figure 11.2 shows that, out of the eighty-four active members, sixty participated in explicit dialogues in a dyadic fashion. The remaining twenty-four do not show up in this figure as they did not respond to specific messages, but addressed the community as a whole. The size of each node complies with the number of messages exchanged, and the connectedness of a node – which also translates into centrality – corresponds with the degree of integration into the discourse: The more an actor is linked to other actors in communication, the more central he is in the network. Hence connectedness, together with size of nodes, reflects the intensity of communication. It is no surprise that the most central persons (Nos. 61 and 28) are the moderators of

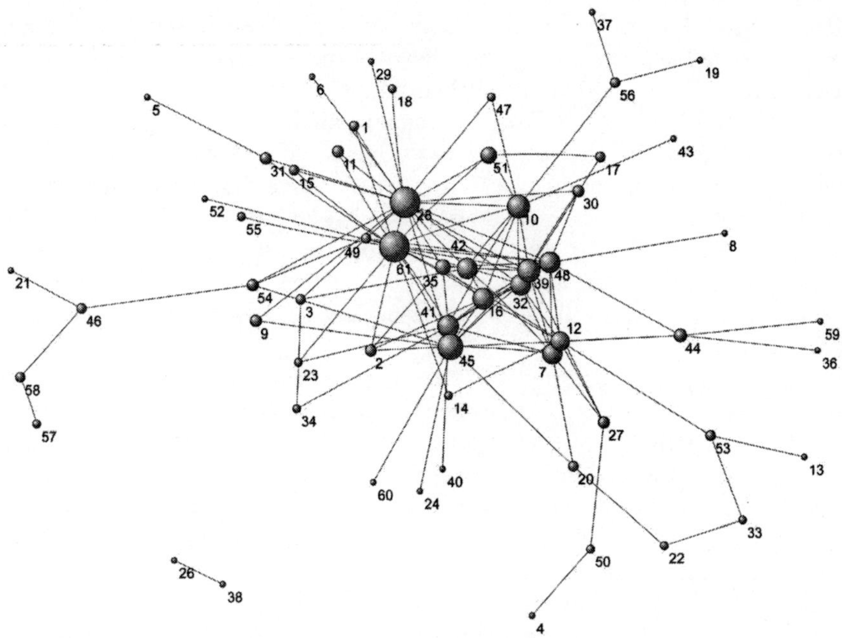

Figure 11.2: *Network of communication in sample period of February 2001*

the e-group, posting and receiving the largest number of messages. A closer look at the religious affiliations of the sixty persons engaging in explicit dialogues shows that fifty-two (85 per cent) are Muslim and seven (11 per cent) are Hindu – as such the percentage of Hindus in this 'virtual' sample is far higher than that in the 'real-life' Valley, even prior to 1990. Although central discourse (marked by the largest and most connected nodes) is dominated by people from Kashmir Valley – also including two Kashmiri Pandits (Nos. 45 and 48) who 'in real life' have been entirely physically absent in the Valley since 1990 – two persons from Azad Kashmir, one from Northern Areas (Nos. 7 and 17, and No. 12 on the central right side in Figure 11.2), and five non-Kashmiris are relatively central. Two non-Kashmiri persons (Nos. 10 and 32 in the centre of Figure 11.2) are Hindus based in India. Person No. 10 successfully hides most parts of his online identity but signs his mailings with a Hindu first name, and this is borne out by his perspectives in various discussions. The other Indian Hindu (No. 32) is a student based in the United States, originally from South India. The Muslim located in the bottom centre of the network (No. 41) is an activist of the Jama'at-e Islami (see Sikand 2002 and Note 22 to this chapter) based in Saudi Arabia. Several community members accuse all three of being 'agents' or 'spies' of Pakistan and India, respectively. Two other Muslims (Nos. 16 and 51) are also fairly central; one

(No. 16) could not be identified reliably, but he displays himself in discussion as an Islamic hardliner close to the views of the Pakistan-oriented Jama'at-e Islami; the other (No. 51) most likely is a Kashmiri; he is based in Britain and was already active in the aforementioned Usenet debate about soc.culture.kashmir.[26] Finally, although one could reasonably expect those who style themselves 'political activists' to be fairly central to communication, we find that 'in reality' most of them are fairly marginal (see Nos. 58, 26, 38, 3, 23, 24, 40, 14, 20, 53, 44, 17, 43, 56 from the left corner to the top right corner in Figure 11.2), with the exception of No. 12 (bottom left side of central network), who calls for the independence of Kashmir from both India and Pakistan.

With having non-Kashmiri 'outsiders' in such central positions of discourse (see Figure 11.2 above), mistrust seems to be embedded directly in the heart of this e-group, threatening all tender efforts to (re-)establish communality. Yet our analysis still turned out as a cohesive, well-connected network, with only a minor fragment of two persons adhering to the same U.S.-based diaspora organization (see Nos. 26 and 38 on the bottom left of Figure 11.2). That almost all actors participating in dialogical conversation are integrated into a coherent network of communication is rather unexpected to us, especially when we take notice of all the animosity and suspiciousness prevailing in the discourse of February 2001. Hence the dangers of splitting the group increase all the more since Kashmiri arguing against the mainstream are suspected of spying for the Indian or Pakistani government, too. Three times in February two men (No. 12 in Figure 11.2, an inhabitant of the Northern Areas of Pakistan, and No. 42, a Kashmiri Muslim from the Valley living in India) were accused of being Indian agents – the only apparent reason being that both express rather nonconformist (though mutually diverging) views on a variety of issues, and are thus obviously in a minority here. One of the men (No. 12) is highly critical of the Pakistani militant presence (i.e., of the mujahidin) in Kashmir and complains of Pakistani repression in Gilgit-Baltistan, thus indirectly attacking the notion of Kashmir as a legitimate part of Pakistan. The second man (No. 42 in Figure 11.2) is also critical of what he terms 'Pakistani interference'; he refers to the relatively large extent of autonomy existing in the Kashmir Valley and compares the violence indulged in by the Indian Security Forces with that of the mujahidin, thereby also qualifying the extreme brutality of the Indian personnel.

Interestingly all these agent accusations come from non-Kashmiri 'outsiders', who themselves were suspected of spying for the Pakistani government (No. 3 and No. 16), and equally the attempts at openly defending the accused are made by an 'outsider' who allegedly is an Indian agent (No. 32 in Figure 11.2). Apparently 'fellow' Kashmiri members do not want to interfere in this dispute. Hence, after a series of such accusatory and counter-accusatory mails, one of the moderators (No. 28) strictly rebukes the accusers for their 'rabid posts' that 'eat our time and energy', and the other moderator (No. 61) more cautiously tried to cool tempers down by starting a 'joke initiative'. This clearly de-escalatory strategy is brought in playfully with: 'Yes, we need some mirch masala once in a while to add some spice to this otherwise sullen forum. ... However, let's be friends and not take comments like these as too seriously. ... Does anyone have any Kashmiri jokes to share with us?' Even the moderators – at least one of them – seem to shy away from dealing explicitly with the issue of agent accusation. Their restraint can be seen as a reflection of the situation 'back home' in the Valley, where accusation of being a *gaddar* (traitor), counter-accusation and the wildest of conspiracy theories in every sphere of life are the stuff of everyday discourse at all levels of society. Within this online community the restraints of Kashmiri members to interfere with these accusations may either be taken as just an expression of weariness or as a reflection and a building block of the silent political conformity expected of all Muslim members of society.

These agent accusations are symptoms of the fragility and brittleness that constantly threaten the attempts at building trust and cohesion among the community members. The 'joke initiative' started by the moderator may not only be taken as a de-escalatory strategy but also as an effort to rebuild an 'authentic' and 'trusted' communality by showing cultural competence through telling (and understanding) Kashmir-specific funny stories. Eleven persons, all Valley Kashmiris, participate in this 'joke initiative'. Seventeen funny stories, whose contents reflect Kashmir-specific themes of everyday living – ranging from marital situations and football in Srinagar through sheep breeding and professional story-tellers to a hospital sojourn connected with Sheikh Abdullah[27] – are recounted over a span of five days, sometimes in transcribed Kashmiri and usually with an English translation. The form and contents of this discourse also point to attempts to return to past values obtaining among the Valley's population, and, although language is not a major barrier since translations are provided, other aspects of culture probably are. But this lighter mood is disrupted by one of the agent accusers, a Pakistani Muslim (No. 3 in Figure 11.2), when, in a quasi-return to the agent theme, he writes under the subject 'Please don't miss the target/jokes':

> Dear freedom loving Muslim brothers ... Indian agents and some of our innocent brothers are talking about Mirch Masala and Jokes ... How we can laugh, when our sisters/daughters/mothers are being raped by Indian security forces. ... Please keep your eyes fixed on the target and write about Jihad talk about Jihad and listen about Jihad ... just struggle for rights.

In his reply one of the moderators (No. 61) justifies the joke initiative thus:

> Humor is an essential part of effective communication. This is one of the tools we can use to get our message across. I am not too versed in the Hadeeth, but is there any evidence that Prophet Muhammad (peace be upon him) disallowed us from

> using such techniques in our Dawah or effective communication? I do not believe so ... Allah commands us to be patient. Yes, we should not dance and sing in light of all the calamity that our people are enduring, but we need to stand firm in our belief, maintain our composure and try our best to bring relief to our suffering people ... The concept of Jihad is only understood by the true believers. This forum, as you know, has many non-Muslim members and may not be the right forum for the discussion of Jihad.

In other words, not only must humorous discourse be justified, but also its defence is embedded in an all-embracing 'Islamic discourse'. While from numerous other mails the said moderator appears to be a devout Muslim, his reply here is an obvious attempt to mediate within a fairly heterogeneous community, while also assuring his critic of his personal religious allegiance – again, a major dilemma characteristic of contemporary Kashmiri Muslim society.

Close-up (3): Discursive Relations between Politico-Religious Groupings in February 2001

The tension within the community arising out of the heterogeneous politico-religious orientations is best illustrated by another view on our communication network (see Figure 11.3). In this analysis we aggregated the dyadic communication between the sixty individuals according to their politico-religious identities. The size of nodes represent the number of messages sent and received as a grouping. The nodes are connected by in- and outgoing arrows, the strength of which represents the number of sent (outgoing arrow) and received (ingoing arrow) messages. Strikingly enough those groupings representing the minorities in the discourse are more or less equally active in posting and receiving messages – displayed by nearly equally sized nodes – although each of them includes a different number of persons: the grouping of the two Indian Hindus (IH in Figure 11.3) displays more or less the same activity as the grouping of Pakistani Muslim (PK in Figure 11.3) comprising more than twice as many (five persons), and this proportion is paralled by the grouping of four Kashmiri Pandits (KP in Figure 11.3) and eight Azad Kashmiris (AKM in Figure 11.3, which also includes the one person from Northern Areas).

Even more meaningful, however, is the flow of communication between the groupings depicted by differently sized in- and outgoing arrows. As expected, the strongest arrows lead off from the strongest grouping – the Muslims from the Kashmir Valley (KM in Figure 11.3), comprising a majority of twenty-five persons, which also includes the moderators as the two foci of communication. Interestingly, the attention of this KM grouping seems to be attracted mostly by Kashmiri Pandits (KP in Figure 11.3), and here the online

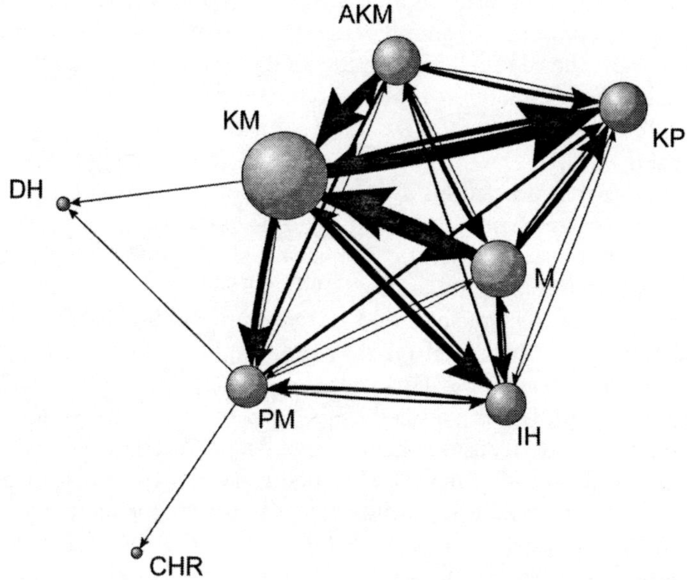

Figure 11.3: *Network of communication in sample period of February 2001, aggregated according to religious identities*

community seems to rebuild bondings which 'in real life back home' had been cut off violently in 1990 (see above). All the more striking, however, is the less notice the KM grouping takes of those coming from Pakistan-administered areas (AKM), whereas the AKM refer to the KM quite strongly (see Figure 11.3). A closer look at the discourse taking place in February 2001 shows that these features of communication reflect not only the cleavages between the politico-religious groupings but also the disagreement about the political future of Kashmir.

The divergent views regarding the politico-religious orientation of the members figure most prominently in a dispute about the news cross-postings of the Lashkar-e Taiba. Several claims for banning these postings where asserted by the Kashmiri Pandits (KP) in this month of February 2001, saying that the forum should not be misused for disseminating propaganda, and stating that these postings contain hardly more than faked information about the 'offline' realities in the Valley: 'I called up Srinagar, but nothing had happened. They [the Lashkar-e Taiba] are trying to create a wedge between us,' argued one of the central Kashmiri Hindu actors (No. 45 in Figure 11.2 above). While in his comment the 'us' still seems to indicate at least a small leftover of inter-community togetherness, the critique of the other central KP actor (No. 48 in Figure 11.2 above) reveals deep cleavages and tension. He provokingly suggested that, if such *'jehadi'* material is posted on the forum, newsletters of the Indian Hindu fundamentalist organizations should also be posted, and he continued in an inflammatory manner: 'Why should Kashmiri Pandits support the so called *jehad* in the Valley? We won't, we are Indian and will always remain Indians … If Muslims are dying in the Valley why should we care – those who live by the gun die by the gun'.

According to Mitra (1997: 62), 'the process of cross-posting makes it much easier to violate the conventions of "neighbourhood", and users can, with great ease, cross into areas where they simply do not belong'. In our case there is obviously dissent over whether the Lashkar-e Taiba legitimately belongs to the 'virtual neighbourhood' (Appadurai 1996: 195f.) of this Kashmiri online community or not. Obviously only the Kashmiri Pandits experienced these cross-postings as an intrusion on the community's sphere, threatening its cohesion, since no single Muslim complained about this to the moderators. These tried to muffle the Pandits' objections, pointing to values such as democracy and freedom of speech, and arguing that any contribution would be allowed in the forum – no matter what political point of view it displayed – provided, however, that it was Kashmir-relevant. One of the moderators whom we already know as devout Muslim (No. 61 in Figure 11.2 above), felt nonetheless urged to rebuke the above-mentioned Kashmiri Pandit for inflaming the discussion by referring to the Lashkar-e Taiba as 'terrorists'. The other moderator (No. 28 in Figure 11.2 above) seems rather desperate about the estrangement of this person and sadly asked: 'it really pains me whenever you talk of "you" and "we". Tell me have we really parted?' Mediating within a heterogeneous community, which 'offline' has already fallen apart and is constantly threatening to do so 'online' too, seems to get rather complicated for the moderators when the notion of a common, 'shared' identity comes into play.

Hence, in the online discourse taking place in February 2001 the attitudes of the Kashmiri Muslims towards 'their Pandit brothers' appear extremely polarized. On the one side, severe acrimony and hatred are displayed, as it is shown, for instance, in a message from one of the central KM actors in the network of communication presented above (No. 39 in Figure 11.2), who abuses the Kashmiri Pandits 'as a race which is bankrupt' by blaming them: 'You betrayed your motherland along with thousands of others who just abandoned it for the sake for Rs. 1,500 a month'. Sporadically such hostilities towards KPs seem to be blending with 'the upper class' as an eponym of 'the enemy'. On the other side, however, there are several Kashmiri Muslims repeatedly working against such splitting tendencies, as is shown, for example, in the complaint of a more marginal person, who is the only Muslim woman[28] participating in the discussion (No. 31 situated towards the top left side in Figure 11.2):

> I have a very uneasy feeling that I have become involved with a group which though doing an applaudable job of bringing Kashmiri minds together is very biased. Whatever, the discussions going thru [*sic*] the group are a sure indication of the

> venom we have against Pandits and the upper class ... The so-called upper class has equally suffered. Maybe materially they may have not (which incidentally, many have), but they too have been part of the misery we all Kashmiris are going thru [*sic*] ... Earlier we were segregated on the basis of religion ... and now the Have and Have-nots. Heyy, for once, do not side track yourself, we should remain focussed on the issue on hand. That is Uniting Kashmiris (irrespective of caste, creed and class).

The wish for inter-community togetherness of at least some Kashmiri Muslims is even more explicitly demonstrated in a posting from one of the JKLF activists (No. 44 situated in the middle right from the centre in Figure 11.2 above), who pointed out the Pandits' contribution to the Kashmiri educational system before their exodus in 1990 and emphatically stated: 'I pray for the day my Pandit brothers and Sikh brothers will be back in my motherland and all of us will not be identified on the basis of religion or caste, but only by our *Kashmiriyat*'.

The Concept of *Kashmiriyat* – a Bonding Agent?

Kashmiriyat – the concept of a distinct Kashmiri identity – evolved in the 1930s when a movement explicitly involving both the Muslim and Hindu intelligentsia agitated against feudal-cum-colonial rule (see Rao 1999b). Informed by spiritual, artistic and linguistic commonalities, as well as drawing succour from vague notions of sociocultural harmony and 'simple lifestyle', *kashmiriyat* seems to represent a 'golden age' of what can be termed 'cultural security'. Many of the politically conscious use the term, though in diverging ways: For Kashmiri Hindus and a few moderate Kashmiri Muslims *kashmiriyat* seems to represent inter-community togetherness. They link this to an allegedly specifically local form of Islam which they think harmonizes with the secular ethos informing the idea – though increasingly not the practice – of the Indian state. For Kashmiri Muslims, feeling betrayed by the political attitudes of most Kashmiri Hindus, *kashmiriyat* developed from a vague longing for political-cum-cultural identity to a form of Kashmiri Muslim identity, both intimately linked to the concept of an independent Kashmir ('self-determination' for Jammu and Kashmir or 'Greater Kashmir') state. Both fundamentalist and militant reformist Muslims in Kashmir reject the term outright, either as negating their aim of union with Pakistan as a Muslim nation (*ilhaq-e-Pakistan*) or else as contradicting the ideals of *ummah* as a 'global Islamic community' (Rao, n.d.). With the exodus of the Kashmiri Pandits in 1990 the concept of *kashmiriyat* died, and gradually the term was then dropped from the official 'offline' discourses of the insurgents and more militant Islamic terminology, such as jihad, took its place (Rao 1999b).

Whether explicitly mentioned or implicitly resonating, it seems to be the concept of *kashmiriyat* which – despite of all the acrimonies and hostilities –

keeps the Kashmiri Pandits integrated in this online community. Furthermore, the notion of *kashmiriyat* still bears some capacity to evoke an integrative project of a future Kashmir 'beyond conflict'. Hence a KM actor rather marginal in the discourse (No. 1 situated towards the top left side in Figure 11.2) passionately argued for the inclusion of Kashmiri Pandits in a future Kashmiri nation:

> I hope that I'll witness the reconciliation of Kashmiri Pandits and Kashmiri Muslims ... I had been to Kashmiri Pandit Refugee Camp recently & all I can say is that I witnessed LOVE and Kashmiri patriotism from these Kashmiris ... I think the greatest obstacle to thinking the Kashmiri nation is that we look for our Self/Identity in the mirrors of India and Pakistan – the split image is psychotic. Many [*sic*] Kashmiri Pandits or Kashmiri Muslims rely on an overidentification with either India or Pakistan ... I don't want to go Kashmir – independent or otherwise – without Kashmiri Pandits.

The message initiating this discussion on 'why Kashmir is a Classic Nation' – again posted by a KM actor rather marginal in the discourse of February 2001 (No. 53 depicted on the bottom right side in Figure 11.2) – implicitly backs an integrative project based on *kashmiriyat* too, when drawing on Sanskrit traditions while giving evidence for Kashmiri identity as constituent of a future 'nation':

> Kashmir has an existing cultural identity in original and can top it up with a common set of principles or goals. Kashmir is a classic nation, because it qualifies as a 'political nation' and as a 'cultural nation' ... It dates back to Laukika era 4225 [i.e., AD1149] and is documented in 7,826 verses of the magnum opus of Pandit Kalhana. It has existed as a 'cultural' nation ever since through centuries and unfortunately lost its moorings as a 'political' nation when the Mughal troops entered the Valley in 1586.

Inspired by this mail, some other members, marginal as well as central to the discourse taking place in the month of February 2001, joined the discussion while adding specific aspects to the picture of a future Kashmiri nation. But a closer look at the statements reveals that most of the criteria mentioned in this discussion are of an exclusive nature. For example, considerations about the concept of a nation as compatible with the concept of *ummah* appear to exclude the Kashmiri Hindus, while evoking the image of a solely Muslim-based 'Greater Kashmir'. However, referring to the 'unique environment' as a 'manifestation of huge natural, almost impassable barricade all around', which designates solely the Kashmir Valley, seems to thwart this argument as it apparently excludes those Kashmiri Muslims living in Azad Kashmir and Northern Areas. This exclusive attitude towards the Kashmiri Muslims living in Pakistan-administered areas is most clearly articulated in the posting of one of the central KM actors (No. 39 in Figure 11.2 above):

> I don't think we can make independent Kashmir with parts of Pakistan controlled Kashmir, for culturally they are different from us. Moreover, they are violent and an unruly race and Kashmiris cannot make with them. For example take those Mirpuris, who are about two hundred thousand alone in Britain ... By sheer force of their money, they will dislodge Kashmiris from Kashmir by buying our property, if at all Azad Kashmir is allowed to join Kashmir to form a country.

While the inclusion of the Kashmiri Pandits remains debatable at least, there seems to be a clearly spelled-out tendency among the central KM actors that the region administered by Pakistan is culturally different and thus should be dropped from the visions of a future Kashmir 'beyond conflict'. The different strength of the in- and outgoing arrows linking the AKM and KM groupings depicted in Figure 11.3 above can be considered a reflection of these observations, since the need of the AKM side to argue is obviously greater than the readiness of the KM side to answer. Exclusion from or inclusion in the project of a future Kashmir is informed once again by the notion of a distinct cultural identity nurtured by the idea of *kashmiriyat*, though the interpretation of the concept depends on the political aims and/or personal experiences of the individual members.

Between Cohesion and Fragmentation: Some Concluding Remarks

'To re-create community through rediscovering communality', as Mitra (1997: 70) puts it, or, in the words of an e-group's member, 'to bring Kashmiri minds together', is – despite all centrifugal tendencies – still a major effort of this online community. In this process of producing cohesion the community reproduces in some parts the local 'offline' situation of the violent conflict. This is best exemplified by their 'online' struggle for autonomy in Usenet, followed by their 'online exodus' and 'online migration' to a new 'cyber home' – events which then became an important part of the community's 'online memory'. Their online discourse reflects both the divergent views and aspirations of the community members when designing a future beyond conflict and the social tensions prevalent 'offline' in the Kashmir Valley. The accusations and insults within the e-group's communication fit into the broad patterns observable in the Valley of rumour-mongering and spreading conspiracy theories, and reflect a conflict-ridden society where clear credibility of sources of information either do not exist or are at least not perceived to exist.

However, there are also tendencies to overcome the situation of a war-torn society by re-building bonds that have already ceased to exist in the local offline reality 'back home'. Even if these re-established bonds appear extremely fragile, and even if their interactions are infused with antagonism and dissent, the members of this network enact their imagined community with quite remarkable tenacity and persistence. In this respect, the concept of *kashmiriyat* may still be considered a bonding agent, acting, so to speak, off the stage and recalling a vision of inter-group togetherness every now and then when the community is on the verge of disruption. The reasons why communication appears as a cohesive network – and not fragmented into disconnected pieces, as we had expected earlier, having in mind the verbal punch-ups and fighting within the group – appear quite simple after all. On the one hand this fighting is battled out in the discursive space of the Internet, which means with no face to face contact with 'the enemy' and no 'physical' damage at least. On the other hand, although extremely heterogeneous in its politico-religious affiliations, the community is still quite homogeneous in its class characteristics (i.e., well-educated middle-class diaspora). And, last but not least, all efforts to heat up the battle can be countered either by the moderators' strategies of cooling down hot tempers or by their administrative power simply not to allow insulting messages to be distributed to the forum.

Notes

1. For *Mission Kashmir* see Inden (2007); also for the Kargil war see Chowdhury 2000.
2. Over the last decade or so, these discourses have been supplemented by texts and images on the Web and increasingly also through DVDs.
3. Its importance even at the level of diplomacy is evident from the manner in which the withdrawal of Sikkim from the official Chinese list of states in South Asia and its map of the region is facilitating the process of normalization of Sino-Indian ties (*Kashmir Times*, 9 October 2003).
4. In July 2003, with the help of CERT (http://www.cert.org/), a Software Engineering Institute run by the Carnegie Mellon University, Pittsburgh, the Indian government designated the 'Computer Emergency Response Team' (CERT-IN) as the authority for blocking Internet sites, in order to prevent cyber attacks on business, defence and government organizations ('India plans cyber defence centre', *BBC News Online*, 20 January 2003). A few months later, CERT-IN invoked the Information Technology Act, 2000, to force nearly four hundred Indian Internet service providers into blocking the Yahoo e-group 'Kynhun' (http://groups.yahoo.com/group/kynhun/) for promoting 'anti-national' news and having links with the banned separatist group Hynniew Trep National Liberation Council (HNLC), a militant group acting in the north-eastern state of Meghalaya. Since the providers could not block that single group, they blocked access to the complete Yahoo site, with the result that thousands of Indian netizens could not access other discussion forums on groups.yahoo.com that are commonly used for sharing information with family and friends and keeping contact among members of the South Asian diaspora. Many of them therefore flooded the CERT-IN's discussion board and called for the ban to be lifted, pointing out the very slippery legal grounds on which the Indian government had issued this order (see 'Outrage over India Yahoo ban', *BBC News Online*, 29 September 2003). This incident sparked off a debate on the freedom of expression and the state's interference in cyberspace, drawing the attention of wider global news- and e-group communities as well as the global

media watch 'Reporters Sans Frontières', who severely denounced the Indian government for arbitrary and ill-founded Internet censorship (see 'Government ban on separatist site blocks access to all Yahoo! discussion groups', 29 September 2003, http://www.rsf.org).

5. According to a Gartner India survey report of 2000, 'the pace of growth in the Indian Internet user community was the highest in the entire Asia-Pacific region – over 3.1 million Indians surfed the Net regularly, that is, at least one hour a week' (*Frontline*, 13 October 2000). Latest data (March 2005) show that the overall figure of users has risen to 39,2 million, a growth of 684% between 2000 and 2005 and an average penetration of the population of 3.6% (http://www.internetworldstats.com/stats3.htm accessed on 8 June 2005). The close positive correlation between the popularity of the Internet and the extent of diasporic population seems to be borne out by statistics available from the otherwise 'socially backward' district of Mallapuram in the Indian state of Kerala, which has both the highest percentage of Internet users (every household having at least one Net-savvy member), and also the maximum number of expatriates (to the Gulf); see *Outlook*, 6 September 2004: 10).
6. The Line of Control (LoC) was originally established in January 1949 as a ceasefire line ending the first war over Kashmir fought by India and Pakistan. Following this declaration Jammu and Kashmir got split into two parts leaving 84,000 sq. km of the territory under Pakistan's control, and the rest (roughly 65 per cent) under Indian control. Conditional to this declaration also was that a plebiscite should be held under UN supervision. In July 1972, after the third Indo-Pakistan war and the formation of Bangladesh, India and Pakistan signed the 'Shimla Accord', which re-established the LoC with minor variations on the earlier boundary. Also part of this accord was the declaration that the Kashmir dispute will be solved through bilateral negotiations and not through a UN-administered plebiscite (see also Rao 1999b). Currently the LoC is still monitored by the UN Military Observer Group in India and Pakistan (UNMOGIP; see http://www.un.org/Depts/dpko/missions/unmogip/).
7. Usenet is a worldwide-distributed discussion system that originated in 1979 as a Unix-based network. In 1995, Deja News was created to provide a more user-friendly interface to Usenet. In February 2001, Google (http://groups.google.com) acquired the Usenet database from www.deja.com, now providing open access to the entire Usenet archive of more than 850 million messages (see also Goltzsch 1997).
8. Usenet consists of a set of newsgroups classified hierarchically by subject under the basic 'big Eight' topics – sci.* (science), comp.* (computer, hardware, software), soc.* (social and cultural issues), humanities.* (philosophy, fine arts, literature, etc.), rec.* (recreation, games, sports, hobbies, etc.), talk.* (debates about current issues), news.* (Usenet-specific themes), misc.* (miscellaneous themes not covered by talk.* such as health, employment, etc.) and alt.* ('alternative' themes, covering all conceivable topics and often controversial themes at the limits of the tolerance of the Usenet community, which did not succeed in passing the procedure for creating a new newsgroup. In the alt.* section the netiquette is more loosely observed than it is in other sections). With the increase of Usenet throughout the world many hierarchies outside these 'big Eight' have been added, ranging from regional/language-specific topics such as de.* (Germany and German-language newsgroups), za.* (South Africa and Afrikaans newsgroups), chinese.* (China and Chinese-language groups) or tr.* (Turkey and Turkish-language newsgroups) to organizations such as solinet.* (German trade unions) or christnet.* (Christian network) and themes of special interest such as biz.* (business products and

services) or hrnet.* (human rights network). For a master list of newsgroup hierarchies see Eisen (1999) or browse http://groups.google.com.

9. In the following analysis we use the term 'newsgroup' to refer only to Usenet specific discussion forums. The terms 'mailing list' and 'e-group' refer to other forms of discussion forums with their own specific technological features: 'mailing lists' describe discussion systems using LISTSERV or MAJORDOMO as platforms. Usually they are accessible only by subscribing as a member (and no archive exists). The term 'e-group' is used here when talking about discussion forums hosted by commercial providers, such as groups.yahoo.com.
10. The activity of newsgroups is traced on groups.google.com counting the number of messages posted per month. In the case of sci the postings increased from zero to eight in the first two years to 205 in March and 925 in December 1989. From 1996 onwards the traffic highly increased with 5,000 to 8,000 messages per month, and it peaked at 16,898 postings in June 1999.
11. 'Flaming on the Internet' – as stated by http://en.wikipedia.org/wiki/Flame_war (accessed on 24 August 2004) – 'started in the Usenet hierarchies. A flame may have elements of a normal message, but is distinguished by its intent. A flame is never intended to be constructive, to further clarify a discussion, or to persuade other people ... Flamers are attempting to assert their authority, or establish a position of superiority. Occasionally, flamers merely wish to upset and offend other members of the forum'.
12. The analysis of the following discussion was done without subscribing as members to the newsgroups mentioned; we exclusively used the archive provided by Google, which is openly accessible to everybody. The messages, quoted in the following paragraphs, can be traced by keying in the subject 'soc.culture.kashmir' and the date quoted to the search engine of http://groups.google.com.
13. The entire process, as also the following reaction, are neat reflections of the extent to which the conflict 'at home' had led to acrimony among individuals who saw themselves as representing their respective communities: 'How many moderated newsgroups out there are forced to have an assortment of moderators chosen from communities other than their own? We feel we should be able to run OUR OWN moderated newsgroup to the best of our ability' (message 18 April 1996).
14. This mirrored the frequently heard view put forth by the Indian government and believed by most Hindus and many Muslims in India that the violent conflict in the Kashmir Valley was purely the handiwork of Islamist and 'jihadi' forces, notably in Pakistan, and found no real resonance among the common people of the Valley. Such notions were fuelled by the fact that in Lahore on 14 August 1990 (Pakistan's independence day) the Afghan mujahidin leader Gulbuddin Hekmatyar together with Ghulam Mohammad Safi of the Hizb-ul Mujahidin declared jihad in Kashmir against the Indian government.
15. This was made possible by Usenet-specific technical features. In Usenet the messages posted on one computer are transferred to other interconnected computer systems via a wide range of networks – but only if the administrator or owner of that site decides to carry the traffic of the concerned newsgroup on its operating system. Hence each Usenet site makes its own decisions about the set of newsgroups available to its users, and these sets differ from site to site. But this also means distribution within more or less limited networks. In the case of sck its limited distribution is probably related to an extreme fluctuation in the number of messages posted per month, rising rapidly to

669 messages in October 1996, dropping back to nearly zero in some months of the years 1997 and 1998, peaking at 1,347 in November 1999 and hovering around zero to 23 postings per month from October 2001 onwards. Groups.google.com ceased to trace the activity of sck in January 2004, but still provides open access to its archive.

16. Through his inexhaustible energy to abundantly cross-post mails on various subjects to various newsgroups (especially to soc.culture.indian) the figure 'Dr Jai Maharaj', who runs his own newsgroup under alt.fan.jai-maharaj, annoyed various Usenetters, and detailed information is given under http://www.vic.com/~dbd/minifaqs/jai.maharaj.miniFAQ for anybody who wants to escape from his harassment.
17. Rao was invited by one of its active members to join this e-group and registered in December 2000. Her role was primarily that of a passive member, though she was not only 'lurking' all the time, but every now and then she also forwarded some press reports found in the Internet or received from colleagues and friends on the Kashmir issue. Registered members have access to the group's archive dating back to December 1999. Rao is grateful to the e-group's moderators for granting permission to use all discussion materials for research purposes. In contrast to the Usenet data quoted above, the postings of this e-group are not openly accessible in the Internet, and therefore we decided to keep the discussions cited in the following paragraphs anonymous. Comparison with the 'real-life' situation in the Kashmir Valley draws on fieldwork data collected by Rao between 1991 and 2003.
18. Both middle-class and wealthy Muslims from the Kashmir Valley have for several decades migrated to the West and the Gulf in search of better job opportunities. Emigration generally intensified in the 1990s due to the conflict (see also Mohammad-Arif 2002: 37), when many more left the Valley temporarily or more permanently to go not only to the West, but ironically perhaps, also in larger numbers than ever before to India. The nature, duration and precise reasons for all this migration – migration as clearly opposed to flight of both Muslims and Hindus – have varied considerably over the last fourteen years and cannot be discussed here at any length. Suffice to say that, in the early years, many families sent their sons out for a variety of reasons: to prevent them from volunteering for the armed movement, to reduce the danger of repression by Indian forces (and, in rural areas, also the risk of forced recruitment by armed militant organizations), and because of the disruption of educational facilities, commercial activities and general life due to the long bouts of military curfew, general strikes called by militant groups and the complete breakdown of normal civilized life. While the less wealthy sent their children to India to study or work, the wealthier, or those with greater influence, sent them to the West or Australia; of an estimated few thousand men outside South Asia, almost 1,000 live in the U.S.A. More conservative families with little wealth but some influence with a member of one of the militant organizations or of a constituent of the All Parties Hurriyat Conference (APHC, see below) tried to send their sons to the Gulf, Iran, Turkey or Cyprus.
19. It has even been suggested that this 'visual anonymity allows for people deliberately to play with their identities and adopt different personae' (Hine 2000: 118). This 'play' has further been seen by some as symptomatic of wider transformations of postmodernist culture involving the fragmentation of the self and the emergence of a new sense of identity as decentred, multiple and fluid (e.g Turkle 1995). However, this sweeping association of the Internet with identity manipulation also has its critics. It was found for example, that many people 'produce quite stable and consistent identity performances' and observed 'high levels of consistency between the identities ...

performed online and offline' (Hine 2000: 119). How identity is constructed online seems to depend on form and 'genre', for it seems that playful identity construction is found mostly in specific forms and 'genres' of CMC, such as Internet Relay Chat (IRC), where it is 'rooted in a unique form of communication that is disembodied, dislocated, anonymous, multiple-simultaneous, and faceless' (Waskul and Douglass 1997), and defined by 'primary "light" interactions with an emphasis on fantasy and play' (Morton 2001b: 68). With its asynchrony and more 'serious' discussions, the e-group we analysed differs from the 'light' and playful mode of interaction in IRC.

20. This is usually practised in IRC but partly also in nationally oriented bulletin boards (see Morton 2001b).
21. The JKLF is the oldest and probably the most popular Kashmiri dissident group tracing back its origins to pre-independence days in 1947 (see Rao 1999b). Internationally it attracted attention in 1971 with an aircraft hijacking by Hashim Qureishi. The group was re-established in 1976 by Amanullah Khan and Maqbul Butt. The latter was sentenced for murder in 1968, broke out of jail in 1969 and was rearrested and then hanged in 1984, largely in retaliation for the murder of an Indian diplomat by another JKLF member in Britain. The JKLF calls for a united, secular and democratic Kashmir. Although credited with the launching of the militant struggle in Kashmir in 1989, it renounced the path of violence in 1995, following the release of its prominent leader, Yasin Malik, from jail. The JKLF now insists that a lasting solution to the Kashmir question can be found only through peaceful dialogue. These above-mentioned leading figures of the JKLF are at the centre of various factions, partly agitating from the Netherlands, Toronto and Great Britain. Various expatriate members of these factions are active participants of the analysed e-group and also contributed to the online discourse taking place in February 2001.
22. The Jama'at-e Islami of Jammu and Kashmir (JIJK) was set up as an independent organization in 1954 and is ideologically close to the Jama'at-e Islami-e *Hind*, which was established in pre-partition India in 1941 by the noted Islamist thinker and activist, Maulana Sayyed Abul Ala Maudoodi (1903–79). Maudoodi considered nationalism, secularism and democracy as decidedly un-Islamic and insisted that it was the religious duty of all Muslims to struggle to establish an Islamic state governed according to Islamic law. Following the Partition of India in 1947, the Jama'at e Islami-e Hind was divided into three organizationally separate bodies in India, Pakistan and Kashmir. From the mid-1960s until 1987, the Jama'at-e Islami of Jammu and Kashmir adopted an ambivalent posture between India and Pakistan, the latter being considered by Maulana Maudoodi as a Muslim state that was yet to become truly Islamic. The JIJK participated in elections held in Kashmir under the Indian Constitution, but from 1990 onwards it has been active in the ongoing militant struggle, supporting Kashmir's accession to Pakistan. In recent years dissensions have arisen within the JIJK between supporters of its chief ideologue, the pro-Pakistani Sayyed Ali Shah Gilani and more moderate leaders, such as Ghulam Muhammad Bhat, the latter favouring a peaceful resolution to the Kashmir dispute, in contrast to the former, who view it as a jihad against the Indian state.
23. In 1995, to press for the release of Masud Azhar, one of its earlier members and main ideologues, a small group calling itself Al-Faran took six Western tourists in Kashmir hostage and beheaded at least one of them; it is believed that most of the others were also killed. In December 1999 Masud Azhar was released by India in exchange for the hostages held on an Indian Airlines plane hijacked to Afghanistan; shortly thereafter,

he founded the militant organization Jaish-e Mohammad (which has no known links with the Jaish-Mohammad now fighting in Iraq; see also Abou Zahab, this volume).

24. To curb infighting, many militant organizations – including the JKLF and the Jama'at-e Islami (see above) – formed the All Parties Hurriyat Conference (APHC) with the common objective of pressing for 'self-determination' and the establishment of a society that is in keeping with Islamic values. As an umbrella group of thirty-four political and religious organizations – some of these are pro-independence, while the rest advocate Kashmir's accession to Pakistan – the APHC was established in 1993 and meanwhile has earned itself the reputation of being extremely corrupt and its major leaders of having ill-gotten wealth. While most of this money comes from Pakistan, some comes from Iran and a great deal from Kashmiri (and Azad Kashmiri) diasporas in the West and the Middle East. When the first round of Indo-Pakistan talks began in 1998 and many Kashmiris demanded that their representatives be allowed to participate, Pakistan said it would speak on their behalf. Pro-independence protest in Kashmir was muffled and a complete strike prevented by the APHC, which in return received a large pay-off from Pakistan. While the ISI and other Pakistani organizations campaign for the APHC both locally and internationally (e.g., through various Internet sites), it should be noted that neither is the APHC homogeneous, nor do all its constituents favour joining Pakistan (Rao 1999a,b).
25. We did not include in this figure organizations that distributed newsletters (i.e., the Markaz Daawat wal Irshad – synonymous here with its militant wing, the Lashkar-e Taiba – which posted thirteen mails and two other organizations with fourty-one and eighty-one news items each) as they posted to the e-group as a whole and none of them received responses either directly or indirectly from other group members. The JKLF-Amanullah Khan faction (with two email addresses) also does not appear in Figure 11.2, because they posted two messages also to the community as a whole and got no response.
26. Altogether nine persons – five in the centre of the discourse (Nos. 55, 11, 18, 61, 51) and four (Nos. 21, 58, 20, 33) on the margins of the network – could be identified as having been involved in the aforementioned Usenet debate.
27. Sheikh Mohammad Abdullah was the charismatic leader of the main political organization of the Kashmiris, the National Conference (NC), founded in 1939 with an explicitly secular and socialist manifesto. As a personal friend of Jawaharlal Nehru, Sheikh Abdullah was at the forefront of the Kashmiri movement against feudal-cum-colonial rule. With the abolition of feudal rule, land reforms were a major step taken by the NC government under him as Prime Minister of Jammu and Kashmir. At that time Sheikh Abdullah's popularity was high, largely because of his adherence to the ethos of *kashmiriyat* – the concept of a distinct Kashmiri identity – which he knew how to combine with the principles of secularism, democracy and social justice, as well as with the demands for 'self-determination' and 'full autonomy'. However, all vestiges of democracy were finally shed in 1953 with Abdullah's dismissal by the Indian government and with his arrest and incarceration on charges of treason until 1968. After his release and re-election in 1975, he could not find much support in the local population again, as he turned out this time to be less democratic than before, but more nepotistic and corrupt. In 1982 Sheikh Abdullah died and his son Farooq Abdullah was appointed Chief Minister of Jammu and Kashmir (Rao 1999b).
28. There is another female person taking part in the discussion of February 2001, she is a Kashmiri Pandit (No. 9 towards the bottom left side in Figure 11.2).

References

Appadurai, A. 1996. *Modernity at Large: Cultural Dimensions of Globalization*. Minneapolis: University of Minnesota Press.

Baig, I.A. 2004. 'Post Raids Cyber Cafés Lose Business', *Kashmir Times*, 7 September.

Bräuchler, B. 2005. *Cyberidentities at War: Der Molukkenkonflikt im Internet*. Bielefeld: Transcript Verlag.

Chilton, P. 1987. 'Metaphor, Euphemism and the Militarization of Language', in P. Joenniemi (ed), *War, Peace and Culture. A Special Issue of Current Research on Peace and Violence* 1(1): 7–19.

Chowdhury, S. 2000. *Despatches from Kargil*. Delhi: Penguin Books.

Eisen, L.S. 1999. *Master List of Newsgroup Hierarchies: A Comprehensive List of Local and Regional Newsgroup Hierarchies*. http://www.magma.ca/~leisen/mlnh/ accessed on 2 November 2005.

Goltzsch, P. 1997. 'Das soziale Paradox der Technik illustriert am Usenet', M.A. Thesis. Hamburg: University of Hamburg. http://minerva.hanse.de/use/0.html accessed on 2 November 2005.

Hakken, D. 1999. *Cyborgs@Cyberspace? An Ethnographer Looks to the Future*. New York: Routledge.

Hine, C. 2000. *Virtual Ethnography*. London: Sage (repr. 2003).

Inden, R. 2007. 'Kashmir as Paradise on Earth', in A. Rao (ed), *The Valley of Kashmir: The Making and Unmaking of a Composite Culture?* Delhi: Manohar.

Jain, R.K. 1998. 'Indian Diaspora, Globalisation and Multiculturalism: A Cultural Analysis', *Contributions to Indian Sociology* (NS) 32(2): 337–60.

Jones, S.G. 1997. *Virtual Culture: Identify and Communication in Cypersociety*. London: Sage.

Kaldor, M. 1999. *New and Old Wars: Organized Violence in a Global Era*. Stanford, Calif.: Stanford University Press.

Mitra, A. 1993. *Television and Popular Culture in India*. New Delhi: Sage.

———. 1997. 'Virtual Commonality: Looking for India on the Internet', in S.G. Jones (ed), *Virtual Culture. Identity and Community in Cyberspace*. London: Sage, pp. 55–79.

Mohammad-Arif, A. 2002. *Salaam America. South Asian Muslims in New York*. Trans. S. Patey. London: Anthem Press. (Orig. French, 2000, *Salam America. L'Islam indien en diaspora)*

Morton, H. (ed). 2001a. *Computer-Mediated Communication in Australian Anthropology and Sociology*. Special Issue, *Social Analysis* 45.

——. 2001b 'I is for Identity: What's in a Name?' *Social Analysis* 45(1): 67–80.

Rao, A. 1999a. Self-Determination in Kashmir: Identity, Islam, and the Search for Justice. *ISIM (Newsletter of the International Institute for the Study of Islam in the Modern World, Leiden)* Issue No. 4: 17.

——. 1999b A Tortuous Search for Justice: Notes on The Kashmir Conflict. *Himalaya Research Bulletin* XIX(1): 9–20.

——. 2004. Debating Religious Practice in Cyberspace: Lived Islam and Antinomian Identities in a Kashmiri Muslim Community, in I. Ahmad and H. Reifeld (eds), *Lived Islam in South Asia: Adaptation, Accommodation and Conflict*. Delhi: Social Science Press, pp. 83–106.

——. n.d. 'Peoples and Cultures of the Kashmir Himalayas'. Typescript.

Rheingold, H. 1993. *The Virtual Community*. New York: Harper Perennial.

Schneider, K. 2007. 'Zwischen den Fronten: Kashmiri Identität, Religion und Gemeinschaft – Beobachtungen zu einem Konstruktionsprozess im Cyberspace', MA thesis. Cologne: University of Cologne.

Sikand, Y.S. 2002. 'The Emergence and Development of the Jama'at-i-Islami of Jammu and Kashmir (1940s–1990)', *Modern Asian Studies* 36: 705–51.

Turkle, S. 1995. *Life on the Screen: Identity in the Age of the Internet*. London: Weidenfeld and Nicolson.

Uberoi, P. 1998. 'The Diaspora Comes Home: Disciplining Desire in DDLJ', *Contributions to Indian Sociology* (NS) 32(2): 305–36.

Van der Veer, P. 2002. 'Religion in South Asia', *Annual Review of Anthropology* 31: 173–87.

Verma, R. 2004. 'Cyber Policing on the Rise across Asia: Report', *OneWorld*, 25 June.

Waskul, D. and M. Douglass. 1997. 'Cyberself: The Emergence of Self in On-Line Chat', *The Information Society* 13(4): 375–97.

Wilson, S.M. and L.C. Peterson. 2002. 'The Anthropology of Online Communities', *Annual Review of Anthropology* 31: 449–67.

Internet Sites

http://en.wikipedia.org/wiki/Flame_war (accessed on 24 August 2004).

http://groups.google.com (accessed on 2 November 2005).

http://groups.yahoo.com (accessed on 2 November 2005).

http://groups.yahoo.com/group/kynhun/ (accessed on 5 May 2004, now dead archive).

http://www.cert.org/ (accessed on 2 November 2005).

http://www.internetworldstats.com/stats3.htm (accessed on 8 June 2005).

http://www.rsf.org/article.php3?id_article=10750 (accessed on 2 November 2005).

http://www.un.org/Depts/dpko/missions/unmogip/ (accessed on 2 November 2005).

http://www.vic.com/~dbd/minifaqs/jai.maharaj.miniFAQ (accessed on 2 November 2005).

Newspaper Articles

BBC News Online 20 January 2003. 'India plans cyber defence centre'.

BBC News Online 29 September 2003. 'Outrage over India Yahoo ban'.

Frontline 13 October 2000. 'Gartner India Survey Report'.

Kashmir Times, 9 October 2003. 'Sikkim Removed from Chinese Official Website'.

Outlook 6 September 2004.

Newsgroups

alt.fan.jai-maharaj

news.announce.newgroups

news.groups

soc.culture.indian

soc.culture.indian.jammu-kashmir

soc.culture.kashmir

soc.culture.pakistan

Chapter 12

Martyrs, Victims, Friends and Foes: Internet Representations by Palestinian Islamists

Henner Kirchner

> The fact that we are Muslims does not mean that we still fight with sword and shield. We have to make use of all the resources and the newest technology.[1]
> (Sheik Nasrallah, spiritual leader of the Lebanese Hizbullah)

Perceptions in the Western media about the Middle East conflict are increasingly determined by 'real-life' (often street) actions by militant Palestinian Islamic organizations such as the HAMAS or the so-called[2] Islamic Jihad. But the actions of these organizations in cyberspace are not as well known and have not been studied by scholars. Following the events of 11 September 2001 the use of the Internet by radical Islamist groups did briefly move into the focus of a sensation-hungry public, but even here attention was drawn only to certain views disseminated through this medium. In sharp contrast to this, the parties involved in the Israel–Palestine conflict and their supporters have paid much greater attention to this medium and its use by their respective opponents. Attempts to destroy online presentations of the 'other side' (so-called 'defacement') show that these are perceived of as part of the infrastructure of the 'enemy'. Such efforts on the side of pro-Palestinian activists can be traced back to uncoordinated initiatives of specific individuals. Other, more organized online militants acting in a 'cyberintifada' in the name of the Palestinians are supranational groups of hackers, such as the WFD (Worlds Fantabulous Defacers), the Silver Lords, Gforce Pakistan, m0r0n, Nightman und Dr. Nuker (also Pakistan). These groups recruited themselves as defenders of the Palestinian cause, but their references to nationalist, moral or humanitarian intentions only seem to serve as a pretext for presenting themselves. For them, the defacement of Israeli websites is more a question of prestige than an act of warfare.

On the Israeli side, on the other hand, 'real' organizations were founded (see Taggert 2001) to destroy the use of the Internet by Islamists or prevent it altogether. The most successful of these organizations is the so-called Online-Haganah[3] named after a Zionist militia in the mandated Palestine from which the Israeli army derived. The choice of this name indicates that cyberspace is conceived of as a future battlefield, especially in low-intensity warfare. The more developed a country is in terms of high-tech, the more vulnerable it seems to be. The technological backwardness and the underdeveloped Internet infrastructure in the Palestinian territories caused by decades of occupation can for once be used as an advantage in this kind of conflict. For a characteristic of cyber conflicts is the kind of weapons used by the antagonists – software, computers and laptops are sold in next door stores and telephone connections turn into equipment for cyber-warriors, and the battlefields are unforeseeable.

In the last few years online presences have developed into strategic resources whose importance is as significant as the pressure on the individuals or groups using them in 'real life' is high. In the following I shall try and examine the intentions connected with the use of websites in Palestine and ask who the target groups are and what the possible implications for the future may be.

The Conflict

The Israeli–Palestinian conflict obviously cannot be presented in its totality and complexity (see also Jean-Klein, this volume). Here I shall focus only on the period just prior to the use of the Internet in the region, and then on events that are closely related to this.

Until the declaration of the so-called principles of Oslo and Washington and the subsequent establishment of a Palestinian autonomy office, the population in the area that had been occupied by Israel since 1967 (Gaza Strip, West Jordan and East Jerusalem) was under the authority of Israeli military and civilian rule. Contact with measures taken by the occupation administration and its personnel could not be avoided in daily life, and this related to almost all spheres, ranging from the election of local representatives to the education system. This was especially true for a great number of workers who commuted daily or weekly to Israel. All forms of autonomous organizations by Palestinians were prohibited and persecuted. This hindered the development of a Palestinian civilian community and had lasting effects on its orientations, since internal conflicts always take place against the background of the confrontation between occupier and occupied. The declaration of absolute national unity as the only way to preserve an independent Palestinian identity was another obstacle on the Palestinian side and inhibited supporters of different ideological tendencies from openly fighting out their internal socio-political disagreements.

These differences came to light for the first time during the First Intifada (1988–91). The so-called 'Islamic tendency' (a description of various Islamist groups, parties, organizations and people sympathizing with them) was able to establish itself in Palestinian society – although weakly at that time – as a competitor to the Palestine Liberation Organization (PLO) and to the United National Leadership of the nationalist powers inside the occupied territories. With the establishment of Palestinian self-administration, the PLO returned as an autonomy office, the Palestinian National Authority (PNA), to some parts of the occupied territories, and nationalist and Islamist groups took on the roles of government and opposition, respectively.[4] The possibility for open activities of the Islamists, especially of the HAMAS, however, was always limited. On the one hand the autonomy office took action against supporters of HAMAS,[5] even using violence. On the other hand, HAMAS had also been under the pressure of severe Israeli persecution. This pressure was intensified after the military branch of the HAMAS, the Izz-ad-Quassam brigades (named after Izz-ad-Din Kassam, an Islamic teacher and fighter against Zionist settlers, killed in the 1936 insurrection), started suicide assassination attempts against the Israeli civilian population in spring 1994.[6]

Despite these conflicts, the period of partial Palestinian autonomy between 1993 and 2000 can be regarded as a time of new departures for the Palestinian civilian population. Especially in the sphere of the media, newly won freedoms were tested and conflicts with the autonomy office over opportunities of reporting were fought out. Topics that the officials surrounding Yassir Arafat wanted to make taboo were the widespread corruption within the PNA, as well as rivalries between Palestinians from the Gaza Strip and the West Bank area, on the one hand, and the so-called 'Tunisians', on the other. The latter were PLO officials who had returned from their exile in Tunisia.[7]

During this period the Internet was exclusively used as a 'one-way medium', i.e., analogous to print and broadcast media. At first, the Internet presence of the Islamist groups, from HAMAS and Islamic Jihad down to local Islamistic initiatives, was restricted to short solidarity websites, which were posted on the Internet by supporters in the Western diaspora. The Palestinian NGOs, like Hannan Ashrawi's Al-Miftah or Palestine Monitor, were the first to discover the opportunities that the Internet provided for their work. International support for groundwork and peace initiatives, as well as for Palestinian educational institutions that had started with the beginning of the Oslo process, made it possible for these institutions and organizations to form. It also enabled them to obtain the financial means to maintain websites and Internet services. These organizations knew how to use the dynamics of the Internet and spread their knowledge and information. Then, in the mid-1990s, Islamists started to benefit from these experiences and opportunities, and with this they became faster and more adaptable than the PNA. Especially the use of the section 'email' for newsletters and mailing lists is of great importance. IAP News (iapinfo@iap.org) from the Islamic Association for Palestine (see below) is a good example.

With the beginning of the second Palestinian uprising, the so-called Al-Aqsa Intifada (the use of the name of the mosque on the temple compound, Masjid al-Aqsa, lends this uprising a religious connotation), the Palestinian civilian population has become almost paralysed, since the conflict has turned into a battle. The Palestine National Authority is paralysed by the retaliatory actions of Israel and the assassinations of Islamists. These killings and attempts to kill are producing a series of 'martyrs'. And the number of 'martyrs' belonging to any organization serves as a measure of its strength and thus its position is strengthened within the internal Palestinian balance of power. Because of their partially clandestine structures they can continue with their activities, militant or social, while the scope of action of the PNA and its president Arafat has literally shrunk to a minimum. During the renewed Israeli occupation the civilian structures of an increasingly autonomous Islamic society have begun to form a major part of the overall Palestinian civilian society.

The Media

The precursor of today's electronic media is the press, which throughout its history had to fight against two factors: the oppressive political regime on the one hand, and illiteracy and poverty, on the other. In the age of global communication this still holds true for the local Arabic-language media. But, besides these local media, there also exist pan-Arabic broadcasting media (like the new satellite TV channels) and the Internet, which has proved to be the newest and fastest-growing medium in Palestine over the past years. In particular, it has turned out to be 'the preferred way of communication of media and institutions when it is important to exchange information in a fast and uncontrolled way' (Reuter and Seebold 2000: 129). The opportunity that the Internet provides in communicating with the Palestinian diaspora without filters or obstacles has certainly been a factor in its popularity. Thus Internet phone calls are far more common here than, say, in Europe or the U.S. Unlike other authoritarian Arab regimes, the PNA was unable to regulate the use of the Internet, even before it was paralysed by the Second Intifada. Therefore a means of communicating existed and still exists that evades jurisdiction, because 'those politically responsible do not yet realize the potential of the Internet' (Reuter and Seebold 2000: 130). The result is that the Internet is even more widely used than in the neighbouring Arab states (Reuter and Seebold 2000: 131). This is especially true of the closely woven net of Palestinian NGOs, which rely on international attention (see Fayyusi 1998: 190; Pauli and Schnegg, this volume). The Oslo agreement of 1993 is the legal foundation for the Palestinian crypto-statehood, the Palestinian National Authority, and the introduction of a Palestinian top-level domain (.ps). Therefore it is the only legal foundation of the electronic Palestinian medium, whose function is seen not only as one of nation-building but also that of eventual state-building.

Hence the Internet confirms the legitimacy of the existence of a quasi-state (Fayyusi 1998: 190f.). Additionally, it is very often the only opportunity to establish and maintain contact with the outside world: 'Using the internet is the only opportunity we have at the moment of seeing anything more than our houses! It is the only way of making a connection with the world'.[8]

However, the technical implementation of any form of Internet use has to pass through the eye of the needle, that is, Israel. This is because of the 'technical predominance of Israel' (Reuter and Seebold 2000: 130) even in this field – in the end, every single Palestinian provider depends on the Israeli state telephone company Bezek: 'The four biggest providers, Palnet, Palestine On.Line, Palestinian Academic Network and Jerusalem Online are explicitly Palestinian foundations, but every single one of them has been brought to life with the help of Palestinians of Israeli nationality. This happened because of capital available and technical formation. They receive their technical equipment from Israel and the U.S.' (Reuter and Seebold 2000: 130). Indeed, measures taken by the Israeli occupation army, such as the sabotage of Palnet facilities by Israeli soldiers on 16 July 2002, illustrate just how vulnerable the Palestinian Internet infrastructure is. Following this destruction, the Internet could not be used via Palnet for several days in the West Bank area. Even institutions such as ministries and universities could not be reached via the Net; for example, the Internet services of Bir Zeit University, which enabled courses to be maintained during phases of curfew, could not be accessed.

Unfortunately, reliable contemporary accounts about the use of the Internet and other media by Palestinians do not exist. This too is because of the political situation – it is impossible to obtain data about Internet use or to conduct a survey under occupation and often heavy fighting – and because one cannot record in what way it is used. However, one can draw inferences. For example, it is estimated that on average about eight readers share one copy of a newspaper. Also it is not unusual for people to exchange at a kiosk a newspaper they have read for a new one. Now, according to an investigation carried out in 1996 by the Palestinian state department, television, followed by radio and newspapers, is the most popular information medium among Palestinians. The Internet does not even figure here (Palestinian Central Bureau of Statistics 1996: 23).[9]

The Islamists – or the 'Islamic Scene

A superficial examination of the Western media does not reveal the number of groups that are active in the Palestinian territories under the banner of Islamism. This is, first of all, a problem of the Western perspective of Islamism. Specific criteria, such as suicide assassinations, are seen as evidence for the Islamist background of any organization. But this ignores the fact that there are a large number of militant groups and various local militias that are driven simply by the wish to resist the occupation. The affiliation of these small groups, formed by young men, with any political tendency is often a result of the local political situation. In a village dominated by Islamists, even secular nationalists or Christians may fight in an 'Islamic' group. In addition, the picture is blurred by the almost weekly foundation of very small local groups; existing groups also change affiliation or only their names. Only a few groups are actually part of one of the greater Islamist organizations such as HAMAS or Islamic Jihad. Only these organizations act in the entirety of Palestinian territories occupied in the 1976 war, and in both of the two separate parts of this territory, the Gaza Strip and the West Bank area. All in all, three organizations (HAMAS, Islamic Jihad and Hizb-u-Tahrir) fit the criteria: a long-term presence in the West Bank and the Gaza Strip and a clear structure as a political organization. In the following, the Hizb-u-Tahrir (Liberation Party), which is also active in Palestinian areas, is not taken into consideration because it is an international organization that focuses on Pakistan, India and other parts of Asia. The remaining two organizations (HAMAS and Islamic Jihad) represent two different understandings of Islamism.

The 'Movement of Islamic Resistance' (Harkat Al-Muquawama Al-Islamiya – HAMAS[10]) derives from the Islamic centre in Gaza, the local offshoot of the Ikhwan al-Muslimin (Muslim Brotherhood), founded with the connivance and indirect promotion of Israel in 1973, who wished to establish a new political force in Gaza in opposition to the secular PLO (Mishal and Sela 2000; Watzal 2001). According to their own accounts the HAMAS was founded as an independent political organization in December 1987 by the leader of the Gaza branch of the Brotherhood, who until he was killed by Israeli forces in 2004 was the spiritual leader of the HAMAS and a national Palestinian symbol, as is Arafat. This foundation was followed by the formation of a military branch, the Kata'ib ash-Shahid Izz ad-Din al-Quassam (Izz-ad-Din-Quassam-brigades)[11] in 1991, because, according to its political leaders, 'Where there is military occupation, there shall also be military resistance'.[12] The HAMAS is strictly organized in separate groups, each led by a consultative council (*Majlis ash-Shura*), and it is said that on the whole the organization has about 3,000 members and more than 80,000 activists at its disposal. It runs a number of social institutions in the education and health sectors, ranging from kindergartens to universities and from basic medical services to hospitals, mainly in Gaza. This has not only created an atmosphere of trust among Palestinians, but also provides its members and supporters with jobs and income. The combination of social trust and economic security lends the *HAMAS* an aura of credibility that is not possessed by any of the other disputing parties, not even the PLO or PNA. The secret consultative council of the HAMAS appoints the political leadership and its international representatives; but it is not supposed to wield influence over the Quassam brigades (its military branch), who act autonomously to the greatest possible extent, because of the great pressure of persecution by Israeli occupation authorities. Until the end of August 1999 their most important base outside Palestine was in Jordan; when, under Israeli pressure, the HAMAS was banned there, Damascus became the seat of this international office. One can only speculate about the financial sources and resources of the HAMAS; they are said to possess about 10 million U.S. dollars.[13] Besides Palestinians in exile, private individuals from the Gulf states are among the donors,[14] but one must also remember that, as Hippler (1996: 7) observed,

> support of the HAMAS by whoever – Israel, Saudi Arabia, Iran, Syria or Libya – does not necessarily mean that the organisation is controlled from outside or that their actions can be ordered or prevented from outside. The HAMAS today is a strong factor of Palestinian domestic policy which can neither be easily ignored nor broken up with a lasting effect through military actions.

Within HAMAS, the members are themselves divided as to the extent of territory that should constitute the Palestinian state, whether 'Palestine' includes all of historic Palestine or only the territories that have been occupied since 1967, and, furthermore, whether a future Palestinian state can coexist with Israel. Shortly before the Second Intifada began, the Israeli political scientists Shaul Mishal and Avraham Sela (Mishal and Sela 2000) concluded that predominantly HAMAS forces are prepared to coexist with Israel when they obtain a Palestinian state. In another study Mishal and Sela (2002) also suggest that the relations between HAMAS and Israel are largely determined by the rivalry between the Islamists and the PLO or PNA.

The second large organisation, the Palestinian 'Islamic Jihad Movement' (Harakat al-Jihad al-Islami – IJM)[15] was founded at the end of the 1970s, after a split from the Palestinian branch of the Ikhwan al-Muslimin (Muslim Brotherhood). At the beginning, its members were mainly students who returned to Palestine from a variety of foreign countries. This organization blamed other Palestinian organizations, nationalist or Islamist, for being far too passive with regard to Israeli occupation, and from the mid-1980s it started assassinating Israeli soldiers and settlers. The IJM is supposed to have only a few hundred members, who operate in independent groups, which give themselves different names from time to time. This contributes to the confusion and is certainly intended. Because of its small number of members and its absolute concentration on the 'military battle', the Jihad Movement does not maintain a network of social institutions. It draws its legitimacy and reputation within the Palestinian population above all from the uncompromising way in which it fights against Israeli occupation. The demand for military action (jihad) has always been stronger in the IJM than in other organizations and the jihad assassinations are regarded by observers as technically superior. Besides Gaza, the city and the refugee camp of Jenin in West Jordan are said to be the main focus of the Islamic Jihad Movement in Palestinian territories. In spite of the deliberate assassination of its leading executives by Israel in the mid-1990s, the militancy of the Islamic Jihad and

Figure 12.1: *Dome of the Rock, Qur'an and weapons – icons not only for Palestinian Islamism (website of the Al-Quds brigades, http://www.kataebaqsa.org, accessed on 12 October 2003)*

its capacity to act have not been hindered, but its political influence on Palestinian society has obviously been reduced. The organization is no longer regarded as a possible alternative to the HAMAS and has no prospects of gaining political responsibility in a post-Arafat era.

Online Presence

Corresponding to the differences in the structure of the organizations and their political approaches in the Palestinian territories, the online presence of the HAMAS and that of the Islamic Jihad Movement are also different when it comes to numbers, amount, design, content and obvious intentions.

The HAMAS, the organization that acts politically as well as militarily, has several websites at its disposal and operates numerous mailing lists. The most important websites as accessed in February 2003 are:

- 'The Palestinian Information Center', http://www.palestine-info.net
- 'Palestine Times', http://www.ptimes.org
- 'Filasteen al-Muslimah', http://www.fm-m.com

Websites of the military branch of the HAMAS – the Izz ad-Din Quassam brigades – are not present on the Internet any more, because they have become targets of attack by pro-Israel activists.

The Islamic Association for Palestine (IAP) and its website http://www.jap.org occupy a special position. The IAP works quite openly in the field of welfare and news concerning the Palestine conflict. It has an office in Palo Alto in the U.S. State of Illinois and employs people on a full-time basis. As numerous personnel connections prove, there are links between the IAP and Islamists from Palestine, but without any exclusive bias towards the HAMAS. The IAP describes itself in the footer of its mailing list as follows: 'IAP is a not-for-profit, public-awareness, educational, political, social, and civic national grassroots organisation serving the American Muslim, Arab and Palestinian communities and dedicated to advancing a just, comprehensive and eternal solution to the cause of Palestine and suffrages of the Palestine people'.[16] IAP avoids being identified directly with HAMAS, but there are indications that the two are affiliated. IAP sells the print version of the HAMAS newspaper *Filasteen al-Muslimah* in the U.S.A. and organizes fund-raising campaigns, such as fundraising dinners for HAMAS charities.

The Palestine Islamic Jihad has basically only one website which was forced to change its domain name several times: 'Neda al-Quds/the Call from Jerusalem', http://www.qudsway.com. While the HAMAS website is completely bilingual (in Arabic and English) and is in parts also provided in other languages (for example, Turkish, Russian, Persian, Urdu, Malay), the Islamic Jihad Movement works exclusively with Arabic texts. If one compares the Arabic parts of the websites with their equivalents in English or any other language, one notices that the Arabic websites are more extensive and have different contents. The menu bars are more extensive and contain more sub categories. The appeals for donations can also be found mostly in the Arabic

Figure 12.2: *Worship of martyrs, www.palestine-info.info, accessed on 12 October 2003*

versions. In other words the multilingual sites of the HAMAS are multiple websites that are meant for different target groups and are therefore designed accordingly.

Online Structures

Some crucial questions regarding the websites of all organizations accused of involvement in terrorist activities are: who operates the websites, who hosts them and who registers the domain name. More than 30 million domain names and information on their registration can be found on Whois.net – Domain Based Research Services (http://www.whois.net). Investigation regarding the domain names that are relevant in this chapter revealed the following:

- Palestine Information Center. The domain name 'palestine-info.net' has been registered for a Lebanese with an address in Beirut since 1988. The registration of the domain is valid till 2011. The provider's seat is in Russia and the computers on which the dates of the websites can be found are in Sweden.
- Islamic Association for Palestine. The person who registered the domain name 'iap.org' is not named by the Public Interest Registry, although IAP is a non-conspiratorial group. Instead, they refer to the provider, which, in this case, is the U.S. Network Solutions Inc. in Virginia. Even physically the website seems to be in the U.S., which is not really surprising in this case.
- Palestine Times. One can observe the same structures as with 'iap.org'. The name of the person who registered the domain is not known. Again the provider is a U.S. firm, this time Domain Bank, Inc. in the U.S. state of Pennsylvania. And again the Web servers are in Sweden, as they are for 'palestine-info.net'. The postal address is a PO box in London.
- Filasteen al-Muslimah. The monthly HAMAS paper (translated as 'Palestine is Muslim') is presented here, and a combination of the previous cases can be found. The domain is registered for a firm address with a PO box in Beirut, there is an Australian provider and the computers with the dates are in Sweden.
- Neda al-Quds. This domain is already a substitute for the first domain of the Islamic Jihad Movement, 'qudscall.com', which was disconnected in 2002. The new website is administered by a provider in Iran ('kanoon.net', Teheran), which registered the site directly at VerSign Inc., the registration authority for domains. Therefore, the true proprietor remains unknown and so does the real location of the Web server. In this case it is not possible to trace further, since the dates are diverted via several anonymous servers.

Hence it can be stated that Islamic organizations take advantage of Western infrastructures in the form of providers, but as soon as one has to name a concrete person in accordance with registration guidelines, they switch to addresses in countries that are beyond the Israeli or U.S. spheres of influence.

Content and Function

Who are these websites really for? According to self-portrayal and press announcements, they are generally meant for all Muslims in the world (the *ummah*), and especially for Palestinians and their relatives. I shall now deal in greater detail with three such sites – Filasteen al-Muslimah, the Islamic Association for Palestine and the Palestine Information Center. Using these examples I shall argue that each of the above-mentioned websites is destined for a specific target group. Filasteen al-Muslimah, the organ of the political leadership of the HAMAS, was originally published as a print magazine and the website restricts itself to presenting the current issue and those published until now in Arabic in a PDF format. The contents of the issues are not translated. The PDF format facilitates the presentation of Arabic texts, especially in terms of printing, processing, duplicating and distributing, since the original layout stays intact. Filasteen al-Muslimah thus seems to be an internal HAMAS website that is only semi-public. This is further indicated by the fact that the URL of this website is seldom distributed and has no links to the organization's other websites.

The IAP website is exclusively in English, and obviously the target group is the Arab American population in the U.S. Hence also the articles available in the 'gift shop' are sold exclusively within the U.S.A. This website is updated almost daily and the articles on current affairs are usually not older than two days. News distribution concerning Palestine seems to be its real purpose; general articles, historical representations or justifications for the use of violence can rarely be found. But the news archives are more extensive and in order to distribute these they maintain a mailing list, which, however, is not used for discussions. Anyone can put his or her name down on this list via the IAP website.

The Palestine Information Center, also a HAMAS Web project, is very different. It constitutes a kind of base for international public relations work, and is hence multilingual in Arabic, English, Turkish, Persian, Urdu, Russian and Malay. The suffering of the Palestinian civilian population is one of the central features in its presentation. Other reports highlight the effects of Israeli occupation and emphasize the resulting right of Palestinians to resist. At first glance it is not evident that this is a HAMAS website, since the link 'HAMAS Movement' or Harakat HAMAS can be found only in the menu bar of the home page. In April 2003 this link was deleted in the English version but was retained in the Arabic one. Other Palestinian organizations are not mentioned.

The link Harakat HAMAS leads to other HAMAS websites, which can be opened as websites within this website. In other words, these are the quasi-

Figures 12.3 and 12.4: *Parallel screenshots of the English and Arabic websites of the HAMAS*

asylum for the HAMAS home page. Originally, the organization had a website of its own with several domains (hamas.org, hamas.net, hamas.com and hamas.co.uk). These domains were, together with the original websites of the Izz ed-Din Quassam brigades, seized by 'American Patriots' and pro-Israeli online activists during an anti-Islam campaign following the events of 11 September 2001. These registered the domain names for themselves, so that the original domain holders could not use the domain names after the registration time of two years.[17] Whoever goes to these websites is welcomed by the note 'hacked and now owned by the U.S.A.'.[18]

There are obvious and major differences between the Arabic and English versions of these sites. Differences in layout and content suggest that there are different editorial teams who design the websites and that they also aim at different target groups. The English version emphasizes the suffering of the Palestinian population and, in order to show this, it uses pictures of victims of Israeli military operations. In the Arabic version the glorification of the militant resistance against occupation dominates. Portraits of 'martyrs' and killed activists of the organization with guns in their hands and in martial poses present a picture of determination, ability to defend oneself and readiness, which is withheld from the users of the English version.

But the differences go beyond the pictorial content. This becomes clear when one looks at the menu bar. While there are general sections like 'Palestinian history', 'Jerusalem' and 'The Al-Aqsa Mosque' in both versions, there are some sections that can be found only in the Arabic version. For example, 'Palestine Today' leads to a current news report in Arabic from which one can get to speeches and statements by HAMAS representatives as well as to speeches by activists given during demonstrations or funerals. There are also a variety of press reports, including some 'clippings' from European and U.S. newspapers that have been translated into Arabic. The user can participate in a small section, the so called 'Reader's Corner', which offers poems about the resistance, as well as reviews of new literature by readers. Other sections that are exclusively for the Arabic audience are 'Political Analysis', extensive audio and video presentations that can be downloaded, a photo archive and a collection of caricatures.

The differences in presentation and content are not the result of attempts at deceiving a primarily Western public; the different versions simply serve different purposes. A Western public is not addressed by the website, nor is it meant to be. The HAMAS proclaims that an end to Israeli occupation can be achieved only by the efforts of Palestinians and the support of Muslims. I suggest that the target group of the HAMAS website in English is the group of second- and third-generation migrants of Arab background in the West. In most cases these feel more at home when reading English rather than standard Arabic. They also handle the new media more naturally and can use the Internet easily and cheaply (see Anderson 1997). This target group that does not speak or read Arabic at all or only poorly nevertheless feels more or less

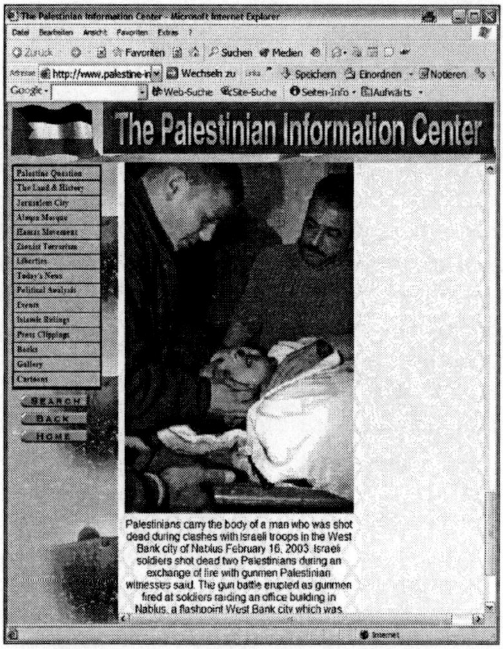

Figure 12.5: *The suffering of victims in the English version*

Figure 12.6: *The emphasis on the so-called 'martyr operations' in the Arabic version*

'Arab' – a phenomenon Anderson (2001) referred to as 'creolized discourses'. The website is seen by them as a good source of information, especially the archive materials and the biographies of the central personalities of the HAMAS (see Howeidy 2001). As opposed to the English version, the Arabic version aims at the Arabic speaking and reading public. These are not necessarily the Palestinians in the occupied territories, whose opportunities to use the Internet are only limited, but the so-called *ummah*, the Muslim ecumenical movement. The emphasis on the Arabic version in contrast to international versions shows that the Arabic-speaking Muslims are seen in some way as being special. Another reason could be that rich citizens of the oil-producing Arab states in the Gulf region are among the sponsors of the HAMAS. Via a network of charity organizations, the HAMAS profits from the readiness of Arabs in the Middle East as well as in the diaspora to donate money.[19] Hence the operators of the website provide these sponsors – and potential sponsors who want to support the militant aspect of the resistance against Israeli occupation – with something like a progress report.

Without there being direct inconsistencies between the two versions, the Arabic language is thus a decisive factor for the type of information and its presentation. It appears, then, that the ability to understand Arabic helps in initiating access to a circle of already initiated users and as a gauge of trustworthiness. Both versions contain presentations of Palestinians as being the sole victims of unjustified violence. The English version further emphasizes their role as victims. Victims and sufferings of the other side are completely left out and partly negated. Both versions also have in common that religious contents play a noticeably minor part. The icons of Palestinian Islamism that can be found on every single website are no doubt religious, but here there is also a fusion of religious and nationalistic arguments and motives as well as criticism of the North-South divide. As Damir-Geilsdorf (2003: 11) observes, 'religious ideas fuse with the rhetoric of the so called Third-World movements, criticism of capitalism as well as demands for political, economical and cultural autonomy. ... The glorifying rhetoric of these Palestinian groups has at the same time a recognizable nationalistic orientation. Very often the reader is not able to find "Islamic" arguments'.

The Arabic versions of the websites place the military struggle and the 'martyrs' who laid down their lives for the cause of the Islamic jihad at the

Figure 12.7: *Logo of the Jihad Islami website, http://www.jimail.com/abrar/index.htm, accessed on 12 October 2003*

centre. This is especially true of the Jihad Islam website, in whose images military macho poses dominate. In addition to pictures of men with weapons one finds glorified biographies that convey the impression – and this is intended – that the entire life of the martyr has been dedicated to the act of martyrdom. Relatives and friends can add their own impressions to these portrayals and the role of the mother is highlighted. These symbolic elements contribute to the creation of martyr cults and Damir-Geilsdorf (2003: 11) notes: 'Only when the death of a martyr is announced in public and a message is conveyed, does he really become a martyr. By his death the martyr sets an example. He symbolizes the fact that the group he comes from is able to defend itself through these measures and does not fear death'. The websites show how one can leave the role of the object/victim behind oneself and become the active subject again – here militant Islamist Palestinians are projected as representative of all Muslims. For, according to the current use of the language, the term 'martyr' applies not only to those who commit suicide assassinations, but to all who die during a battle and even all those who have to suffer Israeli violence – in this way their death makes sense (Damir-Geilsdorf 2003). The explosive effect on the community in the diaspora lies in the success of this approach to become active, to act. Recruitment has not been a major aim of these websites, but events such as the suicide assassination attempt by a British Muslim in Tel Aviv in May 2003 (BBC 2003) and the hijacking of two buses by Muslim migrants in Germany (Seidel 2003b) show that one must not underestimate such propaganda (see also Seidel 2003a). Distorted reports in Western media – often equating cause with occupation and effect with terrorism – further intensify the situation, since Muslims cannot identify with this perspective.

Appeals in Arabic for donations, which mention that the authors pride themselves on their share of the 'militant fight', show that these websites also aim at sponsors, especially from rich oil-producing states in the Gulf region. The costs incurred are listed meticulously: 'The price of a Kalshnikov bullet is three U.S.$. The prices for a Kalashnikov range between 2,000 and 3,500 U.S.$ at the moment. An RPG [a ballistic missile] costs 12,000 U.S.$ and one kilogram of TNT, that is used by our mujahidin brothers costs 100 U.S.$'. On the website of the military branch of the HAMAS, taken from the Internet, reports on technical progress can be found: thus, for example, the ability to construct intermediate-range missiles (Al-Qassam missiles). The rivalry with other militant Palestinian organizations is especially conspicuous. With this they try and present themselves as the better investment: 'With God's help the Shahid Izz ad-Din Quassam brigades were able to raise the number of Zionists killed during martyr operations to 65%'. People are asked to give the necessary weapons to those 'thousands and thousands of young mujahidin in Palestine who defend the dignity of the Muslim community'. It is thanks to the Internet that it is now possible to make anonymous donations and therefore there are no more 'excuses in the face of God'.[20]

Concluding Perspectives

The Internet presence of Palestinian Islamists has gone through an interesting process: from the digital equivalent of a leaflet to an extension of other structures of organization. The reason why the opportunities the medium offers are rarely used to the full and therefore interactivity is not exhausted is the target group (in Arab countries and in the diaspora) and the limited opportunities of the organizations and framework of underground activity. It is the reality of the Internet that there is no contradiction between clandestine and publicly accessible websites, as is also evident in the case of Al Qaida. But the clandestine sets limits for public presentation that even the Internet cannot overcome. Islamic organizations of neighbouring regions that have a secure infrastructure at their disposal, such as the Lebanese Hizbullah (www.moqawama.tv), illustrate opportunities that may be used in the future. Beyond the original function of these websites, which was propaganda, new opportunities to use the medium emerged. While recruitment via the Internet is still an exception, the websites can be used to keep the present and future sponsors informed of the progress made. Another field of research that has to be investigated further is the effect that these websites have on the Muslim community at large and in the Western diaspora in particular.

Websites have become targets for hackers of the opponents because of their infrastructural functions. Especially during the first few months of the Second Intifada, a real exchange of blows between pro-Israeli and pro-Palestinian online activists developed. This development has not continued with its original intensity, but, with the attack on opposing websites and with the use of computer viruses, the borderline between sabotage and cyber-war was crossed for the first time. This transition from online activism to acts of sabotage represents the next step in the explosive force of the Internet.

Notes

1. See the English-language site http://www.moqawama.tv/page2/main.htm, accessed on 22 February 2001.
2. Because the name itself indicates a very idiosyncratic appropriation of Islamic tradition – 'jihad' can, but must not, encompass militancy. Furthermore, 'jihad' is per se Islamic. This pleonasm is thus a conscious strategy that is used in order to magnify the effect.
3. http://haganah.org.il/haganah/index.html, accessed on 8 May 2003.
4. The support for the Islamists within Palestinian society can only be estimated. The Egyptian newspaper *Al-Ahram Weekly* cites the results of a survey according to which there was a support of 29 per cent for HAMAS in February 2003 ('We won't succumb', *Al-Ahram Weekly*, 6 February 2003)
5. One example is the execution of thirteen pro-Islamic demonstrators by Palestinian police forces long before the outbreak of the Second Intifada.

6. The first of these so-called 'martyr operations' followed as an act of retaliation for the murder of praying Palestinians by an Israeli settler during the Ramadan fast of 1994.
7. These so-called 'Tunisians' constituted the exiled leadership of the PLO, loyal to Yassir Arafat, whose headquarters has been in Tunis since 1982, when it was forced out of Lebanon by the Israeli invasion.
8. Palestine Monitor – PNGO Information Clearing House, report in mailing list, 16 July 2002.
9. The PLO has no online presence; only the Autonomy administration has one: www.pna.org. But this site – as well as alternative sites under www.pna.net and www.pna.gov.ps – could no longer be accessed on September 2006.
10. '*Hamas*': Arabic for 'zeal'.
11. The organization is named after a religious scholar who led a guerrilla war against the Zionistic settler movement in 1928 and died as a *shahid*, a martyr, who is admired even beyond Islamic circles.
12. Interview with the HAMAS official Abu Marzuq, in the HAMAS newspaper *Filistin al-Muslima*, August 2002: 20ff.
13. Estimates made by Friedrich Schneider, an economist from Linz, based on calculations of donations, trade, secret service information and underground banking: 'U.S.-Geldwäschefahnder: Im Untergrund verirrt', *Der Spiegel*, 45,2001.
14. The organization is said to have received a single donation of more than 60 million U.S.$ from Kuwait in 1989.
15. Organizations with the same name exist in several countries, such as Egypt and Pakistan, but have no connections. See http://www.stura.uni-leipzig.de/~farao/gruppen/jihad.htm (accessed on 3 June 2003), in German.
16. IAP-Net, mailing list of the Islamic Association for Palestine. This text is the footer under every mail send by the IAP mailing list. By the end of 2003, they shortened it to: 'The Islamic Association for Palestine (IAP) is a national grassroots organization serving the American Muslim, Arab and Palestinian communities and dedicated to advancing a just and comprehensive solution to the cause of Palestine'.
17. This is the regular term for registration; after two years, the domain must be registered again; if not, it will be free for others.
18. This is not a measure taken by the U.S. government. As the additional banner on the website shows, it is an operator of dozens of commercial pornographic websites, and combines business with patriotism.
19. As may be expected, Israeli sources lay special emphasis on this aspect; for example, the Institute for Counter-Terrorism, located at the right-wing end of the spectrum, http://www.ict.org.il/inter_ter/orgdet.cfm?orgid=13 (accessed on 5 October 2002).
20. Appeal for donations to Shahid Izz-ad-Din Qassam Brigades, www.qassam.net, accessed on 3 June 2002, translation mine.

References

Anderson, J.W. 1997. 'Is the Internet Islam's "Third Wave" or the "End of Civilization"? Globalizing Politics and Religion in the Muslim World, USIP Conference on Virtual Diplomacy'. Washington, DC, 1–2 April. http://www.usip.org/oc/vd/confpapers/polrelander.html, accessed on 2 May 2003.

———. 2001. 'Muslim Networks, Muslim Selves in Cyberspace: Islam in the Post-Modern Public Sphere'. Paper prepared for a panel on Public and Private Spheres in Muslim Societies Today: Gender and New Media, Conference of the Japan Islamic Area Studies Project on 'The Dynamism of Muslim Societies', Tokyo, 5–8 October 2001. http://nmit.georgetown.edu/papers/jwanderson2.htm, accessed on 2 May 2003.

BBC. 2003. 'U.K. Bomb Suspects: Muslim Views', BBC News, 2 May 2003. http://news.bbc.co.uk/1/hi/uk_politics/2996141.stm, accessed on 2 May 2003.

Damir-Geilsdorf, S. 2003. 'Die Schwäche in Stärke verwandeln – Selbstmordattentate sind ein modernes Phänomen: Wandel und Erweiterungen des islamischen Märtyrerbegriffs', *Frankfurter Rundschau*, 12 August.

Der Spiegel. 2001. 'US-Geldwäschefahnder: Im Untergrund verirrt', No. 45.

Fayyusi, L. 1998. 'The "Voice of Palestine" and the Peace Process: Paradoxes in Media Discourse after Oslo', in G. Giacaman and D.J. Lønning (eds), *After Oslo: New Realities, Old Problems*. London, and Chicago: Pluto Press, pp. 189–211.

Hippler, J. 1996. 'Ein trojanisches Pferd – Hamas und die Hintermänner', *Freitag*, 15 March.

Howeidy, A. 2001. 'Visiting Hamas', *Al-Ahram Weekly*, 7 June.

Mishal, S. and A. Sela. 2000. *The Palestinan Hamas: Vision, Violence and Coexistence*. New York: Columbia University Press.

———. 2002. 'Participation without Presence: Hamas, the Palestinian Authority and the Politics of Negotiated Coexistence', *Middle Eastern Studies* 38(3): 1–26.

Palestinian Central Bureau of Statistics. 1996. *Culture Survey 1996 – Main Findings*. Ramallah: Palestinan National Authority.

Reuter, C. and I. Seebold. 2000. *Medien und Meinungsfreiheit in Palästina*. Hamburg: Deutsches Orient-Institut.

Seidel, E. 2003a. 'Weder Islamist noch Halbstarker: Der muslimische Opferdiskurs ermutigt zu Gewalttaten', *Tageszeitung*, 28 April.

———. 2003b. 'Verzweifelt und verführbar – Busentführungen: Die unberechenbare, spontane Gewalt frustrierter junger Muslime stellt die Innenpolitik vor ebenso große Herausforderungen wie der islamistische Terror', *Tageszeitung*, 5 May.

Taggert, W. 2001. 'The Digital Revolt: Resistance and Agency on the Net'. NMIT Working Paper, 9 June. http://nmit.Georgetown.edu/papers/wtaggert.htm, accessed on 2 July 2001.

Watzal, L. 2001. *Feinde des Friedens: Der endlose Konflikt zwischen Israel und den Palästinensern*. Berlin: Aufbau Verlag.

Websites and Mailing Lists

haganah.org.il/haganah/index.html, accessed on 8 May 2003.

IAP-Net, mailing list of the Islamic Association for Palestine, etc.

www.fm-m.com, accessed on 21 March 2002 (site is no longer accessible).

www.ict.org.il, accessed on 5 October 2002.

www.jap.org, accessed on 5 February 2003.

www.jimail.com/abrar/index.htm, accessed on 12 October 2003

www.kataebaqsa.org, accessed on 12 October 2003.

www.moqawama.tv, accessed on 22 February 2001.

www.palestine-info.net, accessed on 5 February 2003.

www.palestine-info.info, accessed on 12 October 2003.
www.ptimes.org, accessed on 5 February 2003.
www.qassam.net, accessed on 3 June 2002.
www.qudsway.com, accessed on 8 January 2003.
www.stura.uni-leipzig.de/~farao/gruppen/jihad.htm, accessed on 3 June 2003.
www.whois.net, accessed on 5 February 2003.

CHAPTER 13

MAPPING A CONFLICT IN CYBERSPACE: CHIAPAS ON THE WWW

Julia Pauli and Michael Schnegg

Introduction

How is it possible that a seemingly small, locally bounded conflict has become internationally known and that the Zapatistas, one of its main actors, have received extensive global support? The amount of media attention the Ejército Zapatista de Liberación Nacional/Zapatista Army of National Liberation (EZLN), or Zapatistas for short, has stimulated over the last years is impressive. Several major U.S. newspapers, including the *Washington Post* (Robberson 1995), *Newsweek* (Watson 1995) and *Time Magazine* (McGirk 1999), have reported how 'Mexican rebels [are] using a high-tech weapon' (Robberson 1995) and are 'wired for warfare' (McGirk 1999).

On 1 January 1994 the EZLN stormed and occupied a number of municipalities, including the famous tourist destination of San Cristóbal de las Casas located in Chiapas, one of Mexico's poorest states, and declared war on the Mexican government and military.[1] The actual fighting lasted only for several days. Then, the EZLN retreated into the Lacandon rainforest. Not only was 1 January 1994 the beginning of what the Mexican intellectual Carlos Fuentes (1994: 56) described as the first post-communist rebellion in Latin America. It was also the day the North American Free Trade Agreement (NAFTA) commenced symbolically. The prominent and eloquent EZLN spokesman Subcomandante Marcos verbally connected the two events, identifying NAFTA as the death certificate of the ethnic peoples of Mexico (Ross 1995: 21). On the twelfth day of the conflict the government declared a ceasefire and the uprising was transformed from a 'shooting war into a war of words' (Froehling 1997: 295), 'a war of ink, of written words, a war on the Internet' (Ronfeldt et al. 1998: 70).[2] Reflecting on the nature of this 'cyberwar' (Arquilla and Ronfeldt 1993), which is considered to be the first of its kind (Keenan 2001: 549), Froehling observes that it is characterized by an apparent contradiction: a high-tech medium, the Internet, aids a group of indigenous people who are mostly unaware of its existence (Froehling 1997: 291). In a similar vein Everett concludes her evaluation of the diffusion and use of the Internet throughout Latin America with the remark that she wonders 'how, when and if the people of Chiapas will have opportunity to participate in this "electronic struggle"' (Everett 1998: 391).

So who, then, is doing the virtual fighting? Apparently, the warriors of the Chiapas 'cyberwar' are not indigenous peasants. To understand this puzzle it is necessary to separate the different organizational dimensions of the conflict. Arquilla and Ronfeldt (2001: 174–77) and Ronfeldt et al. (1998: 24–42) have proposed a classification of the movement into three layers. In their view the *indígenas*, the indigenous people of Mayan origin, form the ground layer or social base. The middle layer is composed of what Arquilla and Ronfeldt call the EZLN leadership. Their members are mostly educated middle-class Ladinos with little or no Indian ancestry. The famous Subcomandante Marcos belongs to this layer. Finally, a third layer can be distinguished, consisting of local (i.e., Mexican) and transnational NGOs (i.e., of U.S. or Canadian background). Actors belonging to this layer are the creators of the 'cyber-images' of the Chiapas uprising.[3] It is this group of virtual supporters that we analyse here.[4]

It is crucial not to confuse these different layers. The image of a 'Techno rebel' crawling through the Lacandon jungle with his or her laptop and gun in hand seems to be quite attractive, as demonstrated by some segments of the media coverage of the conflict. Journalists have created images of Subcomandante Marcos using mobile phones to upload EZLN communiqués directly into the Internet. Yet one of the most prominent cyber activists, Harry Cleaver, stresses that no one in the EZLN is online (Cleaver 2000).[5] The 'Zapatista techno myth' is in fact so widespread that outside Mexico the Zapatistas are more likely to be associated with cyberspace than with Chiapas (Russell 2001: 198). Russell (2001) suggests that this kind of representation of the conflict says more about Western perception of the indigenous rebellion than about the uprising itself. Similarly, Froehling (1997: 302) stresses that the way 'traditional media' have covered the use of the Internet by 'indigenous guerrilleros' of the EZLN is more imagined than real. He argues that this action is guided by Western technology fetishization and is more concerned with the promotion of the Internet than with the uprising itself. Another indicator of this kind of perception is the use and function of the website www.ezln.org. This website, which we analyse in some detail below, has so often been considered the official website of the EZLN that the webmaster of the site, a private person named Justin Paulson, felt obliged to post an announcement that the website is 'not an official publication of the Zapatista Army of National Liberation'. The statement appeared despite the fact that the EZLN leadership granted permission to use the domain name 'www.ezln.org' for the registration of this site. However, the webmaster directly addresses journalists in Spanish, asking them not to continue to falsely cite the page as an official representation of the movement: 'Estimados periodistas: La información proporcionada en esta página no representa "la palabra oficial" ni del EZLN ni del Subcomandante Marcos – como algunos de Uds. han reportado en sus notas – a menos de que sea contenida en un comunicado público plenamente identificado como tal.' Interestingly, it seems to be unimaginable for some observers of the conflict that the EZLN does not have an official website.

Whatever the motives of this kind of media coverage might be, the importance of the Internet for the evolution of the uprising cannot be ignored (Froehling 1997: 303; Ó Tuathail 1997; Cleaver 1998a, 1998b; Everett 1998: 391).[6] The virtual supporters have used a number of computer-mediated communication tools to spread their messages (Russell 2001). Our focus will be on the use and linkages of websites. Websites can publish information that 'traditional' media cannot or will not report (Russell 2001: 203). In addition, websites can be easily accessed from any place around the world. Without much investment it is possible to release and archive a huge amount of information. This provides opportunities for creating a collective and public memory of a social movement. As such, the cultural artefacts displayed on websites, mainly texts and images, are of special interest for understanding the genesis of social movements. Of course, websites do not give a complete picture of 'virtual Chiapas'. Cleaver (2000) strongly attacks Hellman's (2000) focus on websites that analyse the virtual aspect of the Chiapas conflict. In his mind it is an error to limit oneself to websites, because these are only 'scattered moments ... drawn out of the continuing flow of information on Chiapas' (http://www.eco.utexas.edu/facstaff/Cleaver/anti-hellman.html). To him, the 'real flow' worth analysing is found on mailing lists and conferences. It is certainly important to analyse newsgroups and related forms of expression, as has been done, for example, by Russell (2001). But why should any investigation be a mutually exclusive approach? Russell concludes her analysis of postings that occurred between 9 and 15 February 1995 on the Usenet newsgroup 'Chiapas95', maintained by Harry Cleaver, with the remark: 'additional forms of CMC such as websites need to be explored. Websites, for example, often exploit a broader range of the Internet's potential than do listservers. Websites incorporate the characteristics discussed here with hypertext links and multimedia graphics to create increasingly innovative media' (Russell 2001: 218).

As mentioned earlier, the EZLN has no official home page, yet there are dozens of websites related to them, their uprising and their messages. We shall try and show that these websites are not isolated from one another, but are part of a specific network structure. This virtual structure has been especially well suited for mobilizing non-state actors and groups around the globe. Subcomandante Marcos demonstrates that he is well aware of the global embeddedness of the EZLN when he writes 'and we learned that these things happened, and that "NO TO WAR!" was said in Spain and in France and in

Italy and in Germany and in Russia and in England and in Japan and in Korea and in Canada and in the United States and in Argentina and in Uruguay and in Chile and in Venezuela and in Brazil' (communiqué from 'Subcomandante insurgente Marcos', 17 March 1995).[7] Given the virtual character of the Chiapas network, the structures we try to trace are not the face to face relations between important political actors involved in the conflict, but the structure of hypertext linkages among the most important organizations in cyberspace. All organizations involved in the electronic Zapatista network analysed here are in one way or another 'pro-Zapatista'. The 'enemy', e.g., the Mexican government or military, rarely uses cyberspace as a battleground. Yet, Ronfeldt et al.'s (1998) description of the conflict as a 'public-relations battle' (1998: 51) is justified. Russell (2001) analyses the different communication channels and the way they are used by different actors. The government seems to prefer traditional media, like television or newspapers, over the Internet. More than for traditional, hierarchical actors such as the Mexican government, the Internet offers new possibilities to organize, communicate and diffuse information for non-state actors such as the virtual Zapatista supporters (Ronfeldt and Arquilla 2001). The Internet thus significantly enhances the bargaining power of these actors, as the course of the EZLN uprising clearly demonstrates. We begin our analysis with the introduction of network concepts applicable for this research and then describe our data and data collection method. We continue with a general description of the virtual actors. An analysis of types of network centrality leads us to the most important actors in the network. Finally, we describe the overall structure of the network of organizations in cyberspace and conclude with general remarks on the virtual success of the EZLN.

Classification of Networks

The concept of 'networks' has become extremely popular among scholars of different fields to understand the increasing use of the Internet by a variety of social movements, rebellions and uprisings (Arquilla and Ronfeldt 1993, 2001; Garton et al. 1999; Ronfeldt and Arquilla 2001). However, only recently have some scholars begun to call for the methodologically sophisticated tools of social network analysis developed over the course of the last thirty years.[8] Social network analysis has evolved from its metaphorical origins to a powerful and flexible set of techniques to study patterns in social organization (Wellman 1988; Wassermann and Faust 1994; Schweizer 1996; Schnegg and Lang 2001). So far, there have been few attempts to use the social network approach to understand the virtual representations and linkages of social or political actors such as the supporters of the EZLN.

Among the many approaches to the description of social networks one concept is especially well suited for the analysis undertaken here, the notion

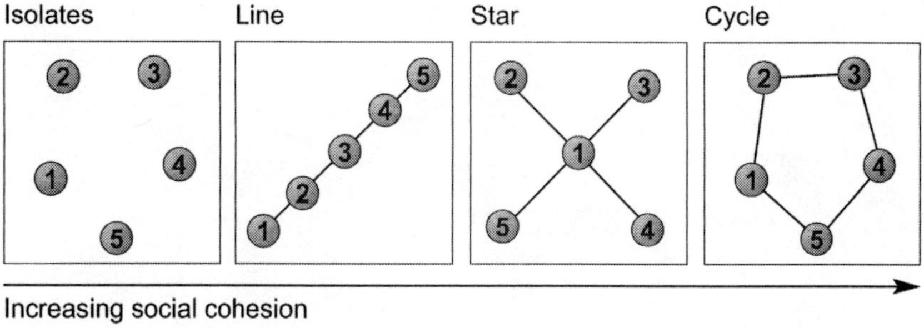

Figure 13.1: *The four basic network organizations*

of social cohesion. The concept has a long intellectual history in the social sciences that dates back to the beginning of the twentieth century and the work of Durkheim. Today, the importance of cohesion as a basic marker of organizational structure is widely accepted in social theory and a range of different measurements have been proposed. From an organizational point of view the concept is easily illustrated by the following four examples, illustrated in Figure 13.1. This Figure shows four types of network organizations: 'isolates', a 'line', a 'star' and a 'cycle'.[9] How do those four organizations differ in terms of their network structure? Most fundamentally, they differ in their degree of cohesion. Cohesion is defined as the density of ties and, more specifically, the potential of a network to resist disconnection (White and Harary 2001). Not being linked at all, the 'isolates' have a cohesiveness of zero. The 'line' is a bit more cohesive, but can still be disconnected by the removal of any single node. The 'star' functions well as long as we do not remove the crucial actor, the head. In contrast, the cycle shown on the right side of the figure is cohesive in the sense that it is the only type that resists disconnection – no matter which node we remove it stays connected. Most organizational structures resemble none of the four ideal types shown in Figure 13.1. Instead, they are a blend of 'isolates', 'lines', 'stars' and 'cycles'. This is where the tools of network analysis become important, for they provide precise measures to determine the cohesiveness of an organization.

Collecting Network Data in Cyberspace

The data we analyse here are the hyperlink relations between seventy-two websites that are very involved in the conflict in Chiapas. The data collection process and the sampling of the network data were divided into three steps. First we identified websites that are linked to the conflict. We used the snowball sampling method, which calls for taking a central node – in our case the website www.ezln.org – and subsequently identifying all nodes that are directly linked to it.[10] These organizations are the units of analysis in our

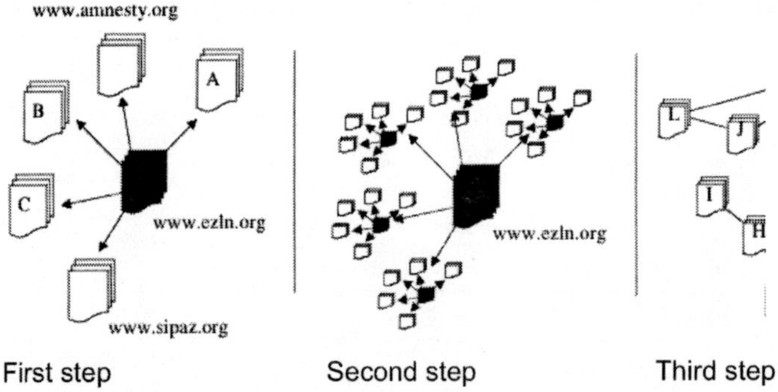

Figure 13.2: *Data collection and network reconstruction*

study. In a second step we traced all linkages that exist between those nodes. In a final step the complete network was reconstructed. Figure 13.2 illustrates the data collection process.

The data collection was done by the software Linklint, which was programmed to extract all hyperlinks found on the specific website.[11] The data were collected in July 2001 and reflect the situation at that point in time. Coding the data turned out to be more time-consuming than anticipated. We had to check each of the long lists of hyperlinks generated by Linklint for the appearance of any of the other seventy-one organizations in the sample. To guarantee the highest possible validity of the data, this coding procedure was done by hand and not by a computer program. At the end of the coding procedure we obtained an affiliation matrix between the seventy-two organizations. Entries in the cells of this matrix tell us about the presence or absence of a link between any of the websites. In addition to the network data we gathered further information about the seventy-two organizations in our sample. Between the end of October 2001 and the beginning of November 2001 we visited all websites and coded each site according to a set of variables. These variables included language, country, type of organization and dominant discourse. Before we move on to analyse the structure of the network we shall introduce the distribution of these variables to give a first impression of the sample.

The Virtual Support Community

The virtual support community can be characterized as international, multilingual and often engaged in more than one 'social struggle'. Table 13.1 gives the distribution of the languages in which the documents have been written.[12] Spanish and English are by far the most prominent languages,

Table 13.1: *Distribution of languages*

Language	No.	%
Spanish	28	38.9
English	28	38.9
French	4	5.6
Spanish/English	4	5.6
Italian	3	4.2
German	2	2.8
Spanish/Japanese	1	1.4
Dutch	1	1.4
Portuguese	1	1.4
Total	72	100.0

followed by French and Italian. German, Japanese, Dutch and Portuguese make up only a very small proportion of the languages used. The discourse is dominated by Spanish, the language of the conflict's national origin, and English, as the most important international language. Yet many documents are written in languages other than Spanish, demonstrating the international orientation of the conflict. The places of origin of the organizations involved in virtual Chiapas further clarify this picture. Table 13.2 shows the distribution of the countries and continents in which the organizations are located. The table shows the dominance of Latin America, followed by the United States and Europe. Within the Latin American cluster the majority of websites are of Mexican origin (84 per cent). In addition we find some linkages to Australia, Asia, Canada and to international organizations, such as Amnesty International, which were not coded as having a single origin. The impression of a strong international orientation of the conflict, which the analysis of the language distribution reveals, finds further support. Whereas Latin America is the most important location by itself for organizations linked to the conflict, the United States and Europe taken together overcome the Latin American orientation of the network.

Table 13.2: *Distribution of countries of origin*

Country	No.	%
Latin America	31	43.1
U.S.A.	18	25.0
Europe	16	22.2
Canada	3	4.2
Worldwide	2	2.8
Asia	1	1.4
Australia	1	1.4
Total	72	100.0

Table 13.3: *Distribution of organizational types*

Organization	No.	%
NGO	33	45.8
Private person	15	20.8
Press	8	11.1
University	5	6.9
Government	4	5.6
Church	3	4.2
Company	2	2.8
Union	1	1.4
Political party	1	1.4
Total	72	100.0

Table 13.3 classifies the organizations according to types. NGOs[13] are followed by private persons and the press as the most important types of organizations. Apart from these we found universities, a few governmental organizations and religious congregations, such as churches, to be influential players. Previous research (e.g., Froehling 1997; Ronfeldt et al. 1998) already indicated the fundamental importance of NGOs in the course of the Chiapas conflict. The virtual support for the EZLN did not develop out of the blue. On the contrary, many of the actors,[14] especially NGOs and several private persons, were already engaged in other kinds of 'social struggles' (Froehling 1997; Ronfeldt et al. 1998: 35–42; Cleaver 2000). As such, the virtual solidarity for the Chiapas uprising was able to use and build upon already existing networks. To understand this process in more detail we coded the thematic discourse on forty-seven of the seventy-two websites. It was more difficult to code the rest of the sites into one of the four categories. The most important discourse found is that against globalization and neoliberalism (33.3 per cent), followed by sites that centre around the conflict (23.9 per cent) and sites concerned with the abuse of human rights (8.5 per cent). NGOs rallying against NAFTA are prominent in the 'anti-globalization' category. On websites that fit this category, the Chiapas conflict, although important, is often one of many examples of the struggle against the spread of 'neoliberalism'. Information on other struggles, such as the IRA conflict or different activities to disturb meetings of the WTO and similar gatherings, can also be encountered on these sites. It is not surprising that most of the 'anti-globalization' websites are not of Latin American origin (only 17 per cent are), but were created in the United States, Europe, Canada or Australia. Contrary to this, the majority (56 per cent) of the websites coded as focusing on the details of the Chiapas conflict are of Latin American origin. Websites that deal with human rights abuses, with the Chiapas conflict as one among others, are again more international in scope. Here no clear pattern regarding the country or continent of origin can be observed.[15] Thus, the virtual network has an international scope in terms of the

languages represented and countries of origin. Furthermore, NGOs are the most prominent type of organization and the discourses concentrate on two dominant themes: globalization and the Zapatista movement. So far, we have covered the aggregation of all organizations involved in the representation of the conflict. Now we shift our focus to individual sites and the structure of linkages among these. First, we turn to the identification of actors who are more dominant and influential than others.

Central Actors in Virtual Chiapas

What is considered as important in everyday language translates into the concepts of centrality in network terms. Two ways to operationalize centrality are the popularity and outreach of an actor (Freeman 1979). The more outgoing ties an actor has, the further and wider s/he can reach others; the more incoming ties an actor has, the more popular s/he is. In the virtual network around the Chiapas conflict the most popular nodes are the website www.ezln.org itself, the site www.ezlnaldf.org, which documented the Zapatista march to Mexico City in February and March 2001, and the site of an independent research institute and NGO, www.ciepac.org. Among the most popular actors, we also find well-known print media institutions such as the influential liberal Mexican news magazine *El Processo* and the newspaper *La Jornada*, which demonstrates how traditional and new media are intertwined in this conflict (Hellman 2000). Among the organizations that reach out the furthest, well-known national and international actors are also present. The actor with the greatest extension is the 'official arm' of the EZLN, www.fzln.org. Two NGOs, www.ciepac.org and www.foodforchiapas.org, and 'the struggle site' by an Irish activist (www.flag.blackened.net/revolt) complement the list of the five sites with the furthest outreach in the network.

More complex notions of network centrality take indirect relations into account. One of these measures, betweenness centrality, identifies those actors that hold strategically important positions – those who are the powers around the throne (Freeman 1979). The results of the analysis recognize the above-mentioned Irish 'struggle site' (www.flag.blackened.net/revolt), the www.fzln.org and www.ezlnaldf.org as the most important actors in the virtual web. Before we go on to determine the degree of social cohesion, we wish to provide some ethnographic impressions about a number of these central actors. Ezln.org has been our entrance point into 'virtual Chiapas'. The number of visitors, 1,000,000 in 2001 as the home page states, indicates that www.ezln.org is a very popular site.[16] In many respects this site is prototypical for other pages in the sample. The visitor is first confronted with a picture of Digna Ochoa, a human rights advocate, who was murdered in Mexico City in October 2001, only a few days before our visit to the site. Digna Ochoa's picture and information on her murder and her political life were found on several websites of the EZLN support network. The immediate posting of her death on the respective websites shows how fast news is made public on highly active websites such as www.ezln.org.

In addition to news and announcements many websites maintain an electronic archive. In these archives the user can find declarations, communiqués and letters of the EZLN and its leaders, most prominent among them the work of Subcomandante Marcos. The archive on www.ezln.org is used as a source for further translations and distributions of these texts. In cases where no translation exists, foreign supporters translate the declarations into their mother tongue. The 'frequently asked questions' section (FAQs) is another feature that can be found on many websites. They offer those who are still unfamiliar with the conflict brief chronicles of the most important events and introduce actors central to the uprising. These representations are often simplified, sometime even naive, and not very reflexive or self-critical.[17] Interviews with Subcomandante Marcos are found on many virtual Chiapas support sites. Often, these are accompanied by photographs of Marcos and his interviewers, for example Gabriel Gárcia Márquez. Some sites contain complete photo galleries. In these galleries photographs of Subcomandante Marcos are very common. Several of his well-known characteristics, e.g., close-ups of his eyes behind a ski mask or pictures of him horse riding and smoking a pipe, are emphasized. Although it is not uncommon to find the question 'Who is Marcos?' accompanied by the answer 'Nobody' on these websites, the majority of texts and photographs indicate a different message. At least in virtual Chiapas words and views of and from Subcomandante Marcos are quite dominant. Ezln.org is an example of a type of website that focuses around the Chiapas conflict. It does not provide information on other 'social struggles'.

The Irish 'struggle site' www.flag.blackened.net/revolt is a typical example of a different subsample of websites. These sites provide information on numerous 'social struggles'. The page is maintained by an Irishman named Andrews, a private person, who is extremely dedicated to fighting 'globalization' and 'neoliberalism' in all its possible forms. Like www.ezln.org, it is an extremely active website, featuring a lot of recent events. It also uses the Internet to archive huge amounts of information.

Ciepac.org represents a third type of sites specifically rooted in the Chiapas network. Centro de Investigaciones Económicas y Políticas de Acción Comunitaria/Center for Economic and Political Research for Community Action (CIEPAC) presents itself as a non-profit organization and research centre with no political or religious affiliations. It is based in Chiapas and the site is published only in Spanish. But the focus is not on Chiapas alone, although one can find a great amount of information on the conflict. Apart from this conflict, more general 'Mexican' issues are covered, such as the threat to biodiversity in southern Mexico. It also provides information on the murder of Digna Ochoa. In addition, it publishes archives with declarations and communiqués by the EZLN, accompanied by information about the development of the conflict and the EZLN. Another common feature of this type of website is the publication of an online journal or bulletin; the CIEPAC bulletin is called 'Chiapas al Día'. Several books are also promoted and can be bought at the online bookshop.

Our description shows two seemingly contradictory tendencies. On the one hand, we find a diverse and multilingual network of organizations from places around the globe that participate in the distribution and publication of information relating to the conflict. On the other hand, the information presented on the websites overlaps to a significant extent. A fixed amount of official declarations, communiqués and letters from the EZLN as well as a number of photographs and interviews are presented on most websites in the same fashion. Thus, many websites resemble each other. We shall show that there is similarity not only in content, but also in structure.

Cohesiveness of the Network

As mentioned earlier, social networks can differ drastically in their degree of cohesiveness. Given the international character of the support network, a low cohesiveness may be expected. Yet the opposite is the case: only 6.9 per cent of the network consists of 'isolates', none of the sites are connected by only a single connection (i.e., represent a 'line') and only 5.6 per cent are 'stars'. All other nodes, almost 90 per cent of the network, are part of the dominant and redundant core of the virtual structure. Figure 13.3 visually underlines the statistical evidence. The virtual network around the conflict is not only dense but also very cohesive. Multiple links make it almost invulnerable to disconnection.

Conclusion

Virtual Chiapas represents a substantial success of communication technology and organizational structure (Castells 1997: 79; Ronfeldt et al. 1998). A set of motivations, a specific capacity to network and an efficient use of texts and images are the building blocks of this remarkable achievement. To conclude, we shall discuss each dimension – motivation, structure and content – in some detail.

What has motivated actors to participate in virtual Chiapas? Why did such a heterogeneous group – international, multi-organizational and multilingual – engage itself in the conflict? Given the diverse backgrounds of the participants, a number of motivations play a role. We now look more closely at those we consider most important, but this is not an exhaustive list. First, a significant number of actors were already involved in other kinds of 'social

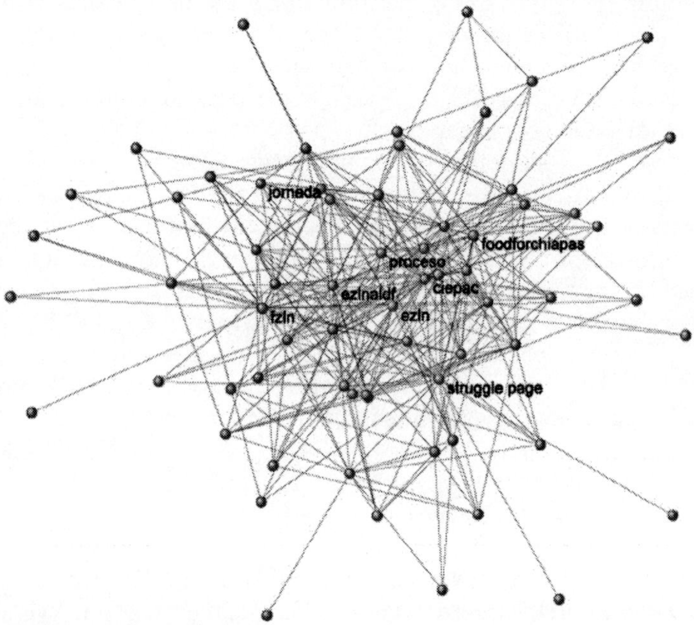

Figure 13.3: *The virtual Chiapas network*

struggles' (Cleaver 1994; Froehling 1997; Ronfeldt et al. 1998). For them, the Chiapas conflict was an addition to and extension of previous efforts. The fact that the beginning of the uprising coincided with the commencement of NAFTA did not have only a symbolic meaning. It was possible to build upon the already existing 'anti-NAFTA' networks and the Central American solidarity networks. Secondly, especially Mexican NGOs involved in virtual Chiapas hoped for a stimulation of the Mexican democratization process through the EZLN uprising – and that effect is generally acknowledged (e.g., Ronfeldt and Arquilla 2001). Thirdly, taking a broader historical perspective, the EZLN uprising had all it needed to be a 'cause célèbre' for a disoriented 'left' – a charismatic spokesman and an apparently just cause (Froehling 1997: 298; Everett 1998: 390). Fourthly, a significant number of NGOs wanted to foster new forms of democracy based on the increased influence and power of civil society actors to counterbalance state and market actors and play a role in public decision-making. The EZLN was perceived as just such an actor (Ronfeldt et al. 1998: 175). Given this diverse set of motivations one may expect a network structure that consists of many disconnected clusters. However, as we have shown, the virtual representation is dense and extremely cohesive. This cohesiveness is an indicator of close relations between the actors. They are linked through multiple channels, which makes it almost impossible to disconnect them. How did such a structure evolve?

The EZLN does not have an official home page. No one in the EZLN is online (Cleaver 2000). Why? One suitable answer might be the remoteness of the *guerrilleros'* daily lives. Yet other Latin American guerrillas acting under similar circumstances are connected to the Internet and maintain home pages (Huffschmid 2003). From a structural perspective it has been a brilliant decision not to have an official website. For virtual EZLN is not just one website that says it all. It is a whole virtual network, a huge 'metapage', spreading similar information in dozens of variations. Due to this structure, once entered, it is difficult to leave the virtual Zapatista universe quickly. This structure is an important reason for the success of the movement. Another important reason is the content of the communicated messages. The network is not only connected through its dense and cohesive ties. Resemblance in content creates one additional moment of connectedness. So does activism, i.e., sharing the experience of mobilization (Hellman 2000). Through a 'collective memory' of EZLN texts and images the different organizations are bound together and a core of ideas exists. Were this not so, the danger of 'virtual fractionizing' would be great. New impetus, in the form of more communiqués, declarations, letters, interviews and photographs, is constantly produced. This constant flow of new web page entries reflects the creativity of Subcomandante Marcos. However, the similarities within the virtual support network do not imply that the actors are interchangeable. Every node in the network maintains its unique character. This explains why several observers have called the ideological make-up of the movement an umbrella, covering a number of causes (e.g., Froehling 1997: 298; Ronfeldt et al. 1998).

Is virtual Chiapas a model for the representation of other conflicts? There is no simple answer to this question. Cleaver (1998b), an activist and analyst of the electronic EZLN support network, speaks of a 'Zapatista effect' reverberating through social movements around the world. However, not every conflict and every social movement may have the properties necessary for a public relations battle as successful as the one fought by Zapatista supporters. What difference does a central and official website make? Will it lead to more clustering within the virtual network? How dense and cohesive will such a network be? Furthermore, how important is a charismatic leader like Subcomandante Marcos? Would there be a virtual Chiapas without him? And, finally, what does a virtual network look like that lacks an extensive 'collective memory' like the EZLN archives? Much more empirical and comparative research is needed on the virtual networks that are created and maintained around conflicts.

Notes

We thank Christine Avenarius, Andrea Kallabis and the editors for their insightful and important comments.

1. See http://www.ezln.org/documentos/1994/index.html for Spanish and English versions of the first declaration which also includes a list of demands, such as land, education, health care, freedom and justice.
2. Froehling (1997) and Russell (2001) describe the timing and use of different forms of computer-mediated communication (CMC), e.g., newsgroups and websites, during the proceedings of the conflict.
3. This does not imply that all actors of this layer can be found in cyberspace, or that the activities of these groups are limited to cyberspace only.
4. Just as in the analysis undertaken here, Ronfeldt and Arquilla do not focus on the connections between the different layers in any detail. However, one has to keep in mind that the different layers depend on one another.
5. Hellman (2000) gives a description of the way the EZLN and its spokesman, Subcomandante Marcos, diffuse their messages.
6. The antecedents and proceedings of the Chiapas conflict are complicated and complex. Due to the more limited nature of our essay we neither present nor analyse any of these. Valuable overviews are given by Collier and Quarantiello (1994), Harvey (1994), Ross (1995), Benjamin (1996), Gilly (1997), and Womack (1999), among others. On the postmodern character of the uprising see the different views expressed by Burbach (1994) and Nugent (1995). Similarly, we shall not address the ongoing debates on the usefulness of cyberspace for political activism or the connections between 'real' and 'virtual' Chiapas (see Hellman 2000 vs. Cleaver 2000; Hellman 2001 vs. Paulson 2001).
7. See http://www.ezln.org/documentos/1995/19950317b.es.htm for a Spanish version of Marcos's statement. A similar awareness can be observed among supporters and sympathizers of the uprising (e.g., Cleaver 1994; Wehling 1995; Dusch 2000).
8. Ronfeldt and Arquilla's (2001) article is an important example of this development. In this article they introduce several tools of social network analysis for the study of what they term 'netwar'.
9. Building upon the work of Evan (1972), Ronfeldt et al. (1998: 11f.) propose a similar, although slightly different, classification. They do not consider isolates. However, their basis for the label 'chain network' is equivalent to our 'line', their 'star or hub network' is also called a 'star' by us, and structures they identify as an 'all-channel network' equal what we call a 'cycle'.
10. As has been said before, www.ezln.org is not the official website of the EZLN, although the EZLN leadership gave permission for the domain name www.ezln.org to be registered for this site. It is debatable whether this website is the most important one. Nevertheless, it is certainly one of the more important sites (see Hellman 2000: note 3) and as such a good entry into the virtual network.
11. Linklint is an Open Source Perl program that checks links on websites: http://www.linklint.org/
12. A few websites offer a translation option. We did not take this into account.
13. Our definition of non-governmental organizations (NGOs) is similar to Ronfeldt et al.'s (1998: 35) definition. Non-profit organizations, private voluntary organizations and grass-roots organizations are all included in this category. However, private persons creating their own Zapatista websites are treated as a separate category.
14. When we speak of a (virtual) actor in this context we mean the organization that maintains the website.

15. Our classification parallels to some extent Ronfeldt et al.'s (1998: 36–42) classification of NGOs involved in the Chiapas uprising. They differentiate between 'specific issue networks', namely NGOs concerned with human or indigenous rights, and 'multiple issues networks', having multiple and more diverse agendas, such as the 'anti-NAFTA' networks. It is interesting to note that a pan-Mayan movement, which also uses cyberspace to spread its messages, is evolving in southern Mexico and Central America. This movement, which Ronfeldt et al. (1998) label a typical 'specific issue network', has hardly any connections to the virtual Zapatista movement we are studying here (see also Ronfeldt et al. 1998: 37).
16. Like all other descriptions, this number refers to October 2001. By the beginning of 2003 this number had risen to 3,000,000.
17. A problematic representation of the 'other', be it 'the Indio', 'the peasant' or 'the Zapatista', is inherent in virtual Chiapas, and a number of scholars have critically treated the subject (e.g., Ó Tuathail 1997: 307; Everett 1998: 390f.; Hellman 2000).

References

Arquilla, J. and D. Ronfeldt. 1993. 'Cyberwar is Coming!', *Comparative Strategy* 12(2): 141–65.

———. 2001. *Networks and Netwars*. Santa Monica, Calif.: Rand.

Benjamin, T. 1996. *A Rich Land, a Poor People: Politics and Society in Modern Chiapas*. Albuquerque: University of New Mexico Press.

Burbach, R. 1994. 'Roots of the Postmodern Rebellion in Chiapas', *New Left Review* 205: 113–24.

Castells, M. 1997. *The Power of Identity*. Malden, Mass.: Blackwell Publishers.

Cleaver, H. 1994. 'The Chiapas Uprising and the Future of Class Struggle in the New World Order'. http://www.eco.utexas.edu/facstaff/Cleaver/chiapasuprising.html, accessed 10 April 2003.

———. 1998a. 'The Zapatistas and the Electronic Fabric of Struggle'. http://www.eco.utexas.edu/Faculty/Cleaver/zaps.html, accessed 10 April 2003.

———. 1998b. 'The Zapatista Effect: the Internet and the Rise of an Alternative Political Fabric', *Journal of International Affairs* 51 (2): 621–40.

———. 2000. 'The Virtual and Real Chiapas Support Network: a Review and Critique of Judith Adler Hellman's "Real and Virtual Chiapas: Magic Realism and the Left"'. http://www.eco.utexas.edu/facstaff/Cleaver/anti-hellman.html, accessed 10 April 2003.

Collier, G.A. with E.L. Quarantiello. 1994. *Basta! Land and the Zapatista Rebellion in Chiapas*. Oakland, Calif.: Food First.

Dusch, S. 2000. 'Theorie des Cyberwar – Cyberwar der Theorie'. http://userpage.fuberlin.de/~ami/ausgaben/2000/8–9–00_7.htm, accessed 10 April 2003.

Evan, W.M. 1972. 'An Organization-Set Model of Interorganizational Relations', in M. Tuite, R. Chisholm and M. Radnor (eds), *Interorganizational Decisionmaking*. Chicago: Aldine Publishing Company, pp. 181–200.

Everett, M. 1998. 'Latin America On-line: The Internet, Development, and Democratization', *Human Organization* 57(4): 385–93.

Freeman, L. 1979. 'Centrality in Social Networks: Conceptual Clarification', *Social Networks* 1: 215–39.

Froehling, O. 1997. 'The Cyberspace "War of Ink and Internet" in Chiapas, Mexico', *Geographical Review* 87(2): 291–307.

Fuentes, C. 1994. 'Chiapas: Latin America's First Post-Communist Rebellion', *New Perspectives Quarterly* 11(2): 54–58.

Garton, L., C. Haythornthwaite and B. Wellman. 1999. 'Studying On-line Social Networks', in S. Jones (ed), *Doing Internet Research. Critical Issues and Methods for Examining the Net*. Thousand Oaks: Sage, pp. 75–105.

Gilly, A. 1997. *Chiapas: la razón ardiente*. Mexico, D.F.: Ediciones ERA.

Harvey, N. 1994. *Rebellion in Chiapas: Rural Reforms, Campesino Radicalism and the Limits to Salinismo*. La Jolla, Calif.: Center for U.S.-Mexican Studies, UCSD.

Hellman, J.A. 2000. 'Real and Virtual Chiapas: Magic Realism and the Left', *Socialist Register*. http://www.yorku.ca/socreg/, accessed 10 April 2003.

———. 2001. 'Reply to Paulson', *Socialist Register*. http://www.yorku.ca/socreg/, accessed 10 April 2003.

Huffschmid, A. 2003. ‚Der Subcomandante greift zur Befehlstaste. Lateinamerikanische Dschungelkrieger im Netz', *Neue Züricher Zeitung*, 4 March. http://www.nzz.ch/netzstoff/2000/nzz00031huffschmid.html, accessed 4 March 2003.

Keenan, T. 2001. 'Looking like Flames and Falling like Stars: Kosovo, "the First Internet War"', *Social Identities* 7(4): 539–50.

Marcos. 1995, Communiqué 17 March 1995. http://www.ezln.org/documentos/1995/19950317b.es.htm, accessed 10 April 2003.

McGirk, T. 1999. 'General Analysis: Role of NGOs. Wired for Warfare. Rebels and Dissenters are Using the Poser of the Net to Harass and Attack their More Powerful Foes', *Time Magazine* 154(15).

Nugent, D. 1995. 'Northern Intellectuals and the EZLN', *Monthly Review* 47(3): 124–38.

Ó Tuathail, G. 1997. 'Emerging Markets and Other Simulations: Mexico, the Chiapas Revolt and the Geofinancial Panopticon', *Ecumene* 4(3): 300–17.

Paulson, J. 2001. 'Global Resistance and the Struggle of Dignity: the Case of Chiapas', *Socialist Register*. http://www.yorku.ca/socreg/, accessed 10 April 2003.

Robberson, T. 1995. 'Mexican Rebels Using a High-tech Weapon: Internet Helps Rally Support', *Washington Post*, 20 February, A1.

Ronfeldt, D. and J. Arquilla. 2001. 'Networks, Netwars and the Fight for the Future', *First Monday* 6(10). http://www.firstmonday.dk/issues/issue6_10/ronfeldt/, accessed 10 April 2003.

Ronfeldt, D., J. Arquilla, G.E. Fuller and M. Fuller. 1998. *The Zapatista Social Netwar in Mexico*. Santa Monica, CA: Rand.

Ross, J. 1995. *Rebellion from the Roots: Indian Uprising in Chiapas*. Monroe, Me.: Common Courage Press.

Russell, A. 2001. 'Chiapas and the New News: Internet and Newspaper Coverage of a Broken Cease-fire', *Journalism* 2(2): 197–220.

Schnegg, M. and H. Lang. 2001. 'Netzwerkanalyse: Eine praxisorientierte Einführung', in H. Lang and M. Schnegg (eds), *Methoden der Ethnographie*. http://www.methoden-der-ethnographie.de, accessed 10 April 2003.

Schweizer, T. 1996. *Muster sozialer Ordnung*. Berlin: Reimer.

Wasserman, S. and K. Faust. 1994. *Social Network Analysis: Methods and Applications*. New York: Cambridge University Press.

Watson, R. 1995. 'When Words are the Best Weapon. Revolution: Information Can Undermine Dictatorship, and the Faster It Flows, the More Trouble They're In. How Rebels Use the Internet and Satellite TV', *Newsweek*, 27 February, 36–40.

Wehling, J. 1995. 'Netwars and Activists Power on the Internet'. http://www.spunk.org/library/comms/sp001518/Netwars.html, accessed 10 April 2003.

Wellman, B. 1988. 'Structural Analysis: From Method and Metaphor to Theory and Substance', in B. Wellman and S.D. Berkowitz (eds) *Social Structures. A Network Approach*. Cambridge: Cambridge University Press, pp. 19–61.

White, D. and F. Harary. 2001. 'The Cohesiveness of Blocks in Social Networks: Node Connectivity and Conditional Density', *Sociological Methodology* 31(1): 305–59.

Womack, J.J. 1999. *Rebellion in Chiapas: An Historical Reader*. New York: The New Press.

Part V

Peace Building at the Crossroads: Appropriations of War, Ambivalences of Interest

Chapter 14

Violence and Peace Processes

John Darby

Introduction

Most of the thirty-eight formal and comprehensive peace accords signed between 1988 and 1998 failed to last more than three years.[1] A ceasefire may initiate a peace process, but it never brings a complete end to violence. The word itself acknowledges that there has been a truce rather than a surrender, and that neither side has abandoned the option of returning to the use of force. At best, a ceasefire may trigger a peace process, which, if completed successfully, will allow violence to diminish and return to forms that can be handled by normal policing and legal procedures. A major obstacle to this conclusion is violence itself and the effect it may have on the process.

There is already a substantial and rapidly growing literature on the relationship between violence, ethnicity and conflict resolution, and on changing patterns in contemporary violence; this has particularly highlighted the shift away from international wars and towards internal violence.[2] We also know more about the optimum conditions for intervention in situations of violence. Hampson's study of five peace settlements, all involving UN involvement, singled out the role of third parties and emphasized the importance of post-accord implementation (Hampson 1996). All these studies have confirmed the central part played by the degree and duration of violence in determining the timing and chances of success for peace initiatives. Mediators have a better chance of success in the early stages of protracted conflicts because 'attitudes and perceptions have not hardened and parties are still willing to talk with each other' (Crocker et al. 1999: 26). As violence increases, it has been argued that coercion by external states may be needed to supply 'the requisite political will and "muscle" required to bring parties to the table and to end violence' (Crocker et al. 1999: 669). In the main, most studies of violence and ethnic conflict have concentrated on how entry points may be found in the conflict cycle for external intervention. Zartman (1989) and Haass (1990: 232) emphasize the importance of taking advantage of the 'ripe moment' when the parties in conflict have reached a 'hurting stalemate' when the costs and prospects of war outweigh the costs and prospects of settlement for the major combatants. The role of violence during peace processes themselves has not been neglected. It is not uncommon for a peace process to be overturned by violence even after an accord has been agreed and is being implemented, as happened in Angola. Stedman has identified the part played by spoilers – dissidents who refuse to go along when militants have gone into negotiation – in disrupting peace processes (Stedman 1997).

The argument advanced in this chapter is that, even when political violence is ended by a ceasefire, it reappears in other forms to threaten the evolving peace process. Three main categories of violence are identified: violence by the state; violence by militants; and violence in the community. They interact with each other, and with the new violence-related issues that emerge during negotiations, and create new tensions and responses. Each has a different effect and different implications for policy-makers. Is it possible to reduce security levels without allowing violence to destabilise the process? How can militant leaders carry their more extreme supporters into a compromise settlement? Can ex-militants be reintegrated into society without addressing the concerns of their victims? How can a culture of violence be changed?

The Terrain of Peace

A peace process is often compared to climbing a mountain, but a mountain range is a better metaphor, and the first peak is usually the ending of violence. All previous expeditions have failed. There are no obvious paths to the top. The climbers, previously preoccupied with the arts of war, are inexperienced in negotiation and must pick up the skills as they go along. To make matters worse, the mountaineering team is composed of people who have previously been at each others' throats, often literally, and who are now roped together. They must now overcome their suspicions and fears to accomplish a common task for the first time. For many, the ending of violence is a sufficient objective. If they succeed a ceasefire may follow. At last the travellers are able to peer over the summit. But they will not see a tranquil panorama of gentle hills. Instead the view reveals new mountains, some apparently more formidable than the one just climbed. It becomes evident that the successful conquest of each new peak requires different skills and different guides. Those who negotiated a ceasefire are not necessarily the appropriate people to negotiate political agreement or to achieve economic regeneration and redistribution.

The only available guidebooks and maps are drawn from descriptions of similar expeditions, so they provide only general and sometimes misleading advice. Peace processes are often regarded as following four phases: first pre-negotiation, often involving secret negotiations, during which the terms of disengagement from violence and engagement in talks are agreed; then the formal ending of violence, usually through ceasefires; next the negotiations themselves, aiming at a political/constitutional agreement; and finally what is often referred to as post-settlement peace-building. Violence affects each of these phases differently. Although the process itself usually follows open warfare between a highly militarized state and guerrilla-type opposition, the level of violence may temporarily intensify during the pre-negotiation phase as combatants try to optimize their negotiating positions. The negotiations themselves are often conducted against a background of quasi-paramilitary violence and the emergence of more extreme dissidents. All of these might be described as process issues, but negotiators also have to confront a new range of content issues, including demands for the early release of prisoners, decommissioning and demilitarization and policing reform. If an agreement is reached, the focus shifts to the reintegration of militants into society and a consideration of their victims.

It would be easier if the mountains to be tackled were ranged in obvious sequence. In reality, unexpected peaks emerge from the mists and demand the immediate attention of the climbers. Each peace process has its own distinctive terrain and its own priorities. In Northern Ireland the decommissioning of weapons became one of the most formidable obstacles, yet it was bypassed at a brisk trot in South Africa. In the Basque country significant reforms in policing and administrative devolution were achieved before inclusive negotiation was possible. So a peace process is rarely a predictable sequence from violence to settlement. There are no clear boundaries between the phases, and the order in which they are tackled may not follow the expected sequence.

The new sources of violence that replace political violence fall into three main, and frequently overlapping, categories: violence by the state, violence by militants and violence in the community. I shall now deal with each of these in some detail.

Violence by the State

The formal ending of violence does not reduce the armoury under the control of the government and its agencies. In the short term, at least, these soldiers and their weapons present two principal dangers, one associated with deliberate illegal actions by governments, the other an incidental consequence of security disengagement.

Just as paramilitary members are divided on the benefits and drawbacks of entering negotiations, so are the governments with which they negotiate. Those responsible for security are characteristically more suspicious of ceasefires and more reluctant to dismantle prematurely the security apparatus assembled to deal with the violence in the first place. As a result, elements within some governments have used ceasefires as an opportunity to undermine and destabilize their opponents, and in others to maximize the government's advantage before entering negotiation. In 1994 the Sri Lankan government, frustrated at what it regarded as Tamil refusal to compromise, introduced a 'war for peace' strategy, which aimed at military victory followed by a settlement. The allegations that successive Spanish governments were conducting a 'dirty war' against ETA were vindicated by the imprisonment of a former minister in 1998; further evidence emerged in 2000 when another senior member of the Spanish Socialist Party and a Civil Guard general were convicted of kidnapping and murdering two members of ETA. In Colombia a State Department report found that 'individual members of the security forces actively collaborated with members of paramilitary groups – passing them through roadblocks, sharing intelligence and providing them with ammunition' (Guttierrez and Torriero 2000). A Human Rights Watch report in 2000 found that half of Colombia army's eighteen brigades had ties with right-wing militias. The persistence of any government in such activities involves a high risk that the negotiations they are intended to anticipate may collapse in distrust.[3]

The management of security disengagement is one of the most difficult aspects of any peace process. If a ceasefire holds, it becomes more difficult to justify the retention of a large and expensive security apparatus and, after a reasonable time has passed, a start is made to dismantle it. Discontent follows, and some disgruntled soldiers may gravitate towards paramilitarism. In South Africa some members of both the state security services and the African National Congress (ANC) were still active in crime syndicates in 1998, according to the Minister of Safety and Security.[4] The sharp rise in crime that followed the 1996 peace accords in Guatemala were 'often the work of members of the existing police force or the army', as well as unemployed ex-combatants.[5] The arrest of members of the security forces for terrorist offences underlines the threat left after all internal wars: that members of an experienced and well-armed force, threatened by downsizing and unemployment and generally demoralized, have the potential to destabilize a nervous peace process, especially in its early months.

Violence by Militants

A ceasefire is never unanimous. It may bring an end to the traditional war between security forces and paramilitaries, but paramilitary organizations are not the monoliths presented by themselves and their opponents. They are complex organisms performing different functions, and their complexity is compounded by misinformation routinely propagated by both the paramilitaries and their opponents. They provide umbrellas for different interests. Their activities may include violence against the state, negotiations with the state, violence against their ethnic, religious or ideological rivals or negotiation with them, wars with rival organizations inside their own community, 'fund-raising' through bank robberies, kidnapping and drug dealing, 'policing' local communities often by force and intimidation, quasi-judicial proceedings and sanctions, even running an alternative civil administration. The diversity allows paramilitary leaders to assume the high moral ground by emphasizing their political and civil roles, while turning a blind eye to murder and other forms of violence. It also helps to explain apparently irrational strategic shifts from war to negotiation, as different elements within the organizations gain temporary dominance.

During peace processes the varied interests sheltering under the paramilitary umbrella diffuse and fragment.[6] Those who wish to continue their pressure through violence are the most uncompromising and often the least disciplined. Others move seamlessly from racketeering and drug dealing for 'the cause' to the same activities for private gain. The organization's *raison d'être* may have ended, but the infrastructure of weapons, control mechanisms, community businesses and status remains in place. Most of all, those whose lives had been linked for years socially, economically and politically to the diverse interests of the paramilitary groups are still linked to them.

Altogether it is possible to distinguish four elements within paramilitary families during peace processes: dealers, zealots, opportunists and mavericks. 'Dealers' comprise those militants, like the Palestine Liberation Organization (PLO) and Sinn Fein, who decide to engage in negotiation rather than war. When the Dealers have persuaded the greater part of their followers to end their violence and go into negotiation, and their opponents have reached a similar position, a peace process has started. 'Zealots' comprise those radicals who pick up the torch they believed has been surrendered by the 'dealers'. There are many examples. The Tamil Tigers systematically assassinated other Tamils who accepted public office in Sri Lanka. 'Zealots' in Israel-Palestine, including HAMAS and Islamic Jihad, continued the struggle they believed had been abandoned by the PLO. These 'zealot' groups are often augmented by breakaway members of the dealing group who feel that their leaders have betrayed the purity of their cause. In essence, 'zealot' violence is carried out by those who remain outside the negotiations from choice or exclusion. Their aim is not to influence the content of a peace agreement. It is to ensure that agreement is not reached or, if reached, is derailed. 'Opportunists' comprise other militant interests who are wary about the peace process, but who may later come round to participation. Some 'opportunists', like the Inkatha Freedom Party in South Africa, accept early in the process that they have no real alternative but to enter talks, and try to optimize the terms. Others, like the Popular Front for the Liberation of Palestine and the Democratic Front for the Liberation of Palestine, may begin as 'zealots' but come round later to seeking involvement in the process. If 'opportunists' join the process, they are in turn likely to suffer defections as their own 'zealots' peel off in an apparently limitless downward spiral. The picture is further complicated by occasional acts of violence by 'mavericks' who carry out unauthorized crimes for personal gain or from habit, especially in the period immediately following the declaration of a ceasefire.

Conceptually these three categories are distinct, and have fundamentally different views of the peace process. In practice there are confusing and shifting overlaps between them. This is not surprising, for two principal reasons. First, their relationships are governed by personal as well as ideological factors, and coloured by the years of 'the struggle' when they were comrades. Secondly, the confusion between the ex-militant factions provides cover that enables the 'dealers' to profess that the ceasefire continues despite their willingness to condone the high level of violence necessary to maintain control within their own communities. Still, the tensions and alliances between these four groups may destabilize a peace process in four principal ways.

A Return to Political Violence

When a paramilitary group agrees to deal, the decision invariably follows an internal struggle. The more disaffected militants may later desert to splinter groups or perform maverick acts of violence. Others will go along with the majority view, but their agreement may be conditional. When ETA (Basque Homeland and Liberty) extended its ceasefire in November 1998, for example, it warned that it would not become permanent without rapid progress on the peace process. The continuing allegiance of militants depends on gaining measurable rewards from negotiation, notably prisoner releases and the dismantling of the security apparatus. These rewards are rarely immediate. Consequently the pendulum may swing back towards the militants.

The pendulum does not swing at a constant rate. In November 1999 ETA ended its ceasefire, alleging that the government was stalling on political talks. The ceasefires also broke down in both South Africa and Northern Ireland, leading to periods of renewed political violence in 1992 and 1996 respectively. The eventual resumption and completion of negotiations in both places suggests that even an unsatisfactory experience of talks may have an impact on the negotiators.

Tactical Violence

The minimum price for a ceasefire is the inclusion of militants in negotiations. For constitutional parties this raises the apprehension that their political surrogates may use the threat of violence for tactical advantage, and that the gunmen outside the negotiating rooms would determine the pace of negotiation. Any acts of violence during a process are taken as confirmation of this fear. The early stages of the Oslo peace process were hampered by Israeli suspicion of the PLO's motives, and later the government regarded HAMAS's atrocities as evidence that Arafat either was unable to control his own people or was colluding with it for tactical advantage.

Throughout the Northern Irish peace process Ulster Unionists warned that Sinn Fein would use violence by the Irish Republican Army (IRA) to remind other negotiators of their power. In 1999 their submission to George Mitchell's review of the peace process claimed that the Republican 'commitment to peace and democracy' can now be seen as little more than a tactic, a means of squeezing as much as possible out of the governments while reserving the right to go back to the 'armed struggle',[7] Indeed, there were occasions during the ceasefire period when the Sinn Fein leaders appeared to feed Unionist fears, as when Gerry Adams drew the attention of a Republican rally to the fact that 'they [the IRA] haven't gone away, you know', an implied threat that the IRA would resume the war if Sinn Fein did not profit during the negotiations. Despite these apprehensions, the unwillingness of Sinn Fein or the Loyalist parties to resort to tactical violence was one of the more remarkable aspects of this peace process.

Spoiler Violence by 'Zealots'

Most revolutionary groups started off as 'zealots', using terror to undermine the government and violence to establish dominance over rival groups. Their initial targets – for the Tamil Tigers in Sri Lanka, for ETA in the Basque Country and for the Provisional IRA – were rival groups from their own community. The need to dominate one's own community continues, and often increases, during a peace process. In Sri Lanka the Tamil Tigers effectively undermined any negotiations by a succession of assassinations of Tamil rivals. In 1998 they murdered the Tamil mayor of Jaffna, having previously killed her husband, and then her successor as mayor. A year later, in September 1999, a Tamil suicide bomber killed himself and the Tamil moderate leader Neelan Tiruchelvam. The Tigers' willingness to eliminate their opponents greatly strengthened their ability to sustain the war but, if they eventually enter negotiations, their own rhetoric makes it likely that new Zealots will break away and attempt to continue the campaign of violence.

Peace processes are particularly vulnerable to 'zealots' in their early years, and their violence often comes from more than one side. The Oslo process, as all other major attempts to start negotiations in Israel-Palestine, had to deal with both Israeli and Palestinian extremists. The killing of an engineer, Abu Ayyash, by the Israeli security forces led to bus bombs in Tel Aviv and Jerusalem. In March 1994 twenty-eight Muslims were killed and forty wounded in a mosque by the Israeli settler Baruch Goldstein. This pattern of violence continued throughout the Israeli peace process. Any prospect of progress attracted the bombers. In 1995 the Israeli Prime Minister Rabin was assassinated.

The South African process was undermined by both white and black dissidents. The ANC and its alliance partners left the peace negotiations in 1992 after the Inkatha Freedom Party (IFP) killed forty-eight people in

Boipatong and twenty-eight marchers were murdered in Bisho during the resulting protests. Surprisingly, given the sharp increase in crime in South Africa during the 1990s, violence by black 'zealots' was relatively well controlled during the period of negotiation, perhaps a reflection of the dominance of Nelson Mandela and the ANC. The main threat from disaffected whites came from Eugene Terre Blanche's resistance movement, the Afrikaner Weerstandsbeweging (AWB), which attempted an occupation of the negotiations venue near Johannesburg in 1993 and, in 1994, 'invaded' Bophuthatswana to assist its President. This shambolic failure effectively ended violence by white 'zealots'.

The emergence of 'zealots' is hardly a novelty in Irish politics. The Irish writer and IRA member Brendan Behan once said that the first item on the agenda for any Republican meeting was 'the split'. The Provisional IRA itself was formed in 1969 after a split from the Official IRA. A new epidemic of splits followed Sinn Fein's signing up for the Mitchell Principles in October 1997. Nor were 'zealots' restricted to the republican family. The growing involvement of the main Loyalist paramilitary parties in the peace process led to the formation in 1996 of the extreme Loyalist Volunteer Force (LVF). All these groups, Loyalist and Republican, attracted dissidents from the more established groups.

Family Feuding: Internal Paramilitary Violence

The ex-militants who enter a peace process are confronted by a number of headaches, as the comrades who had fought with them in the war disperse in different directions. Inability to exercise control within their own communities undermines their position as they enter a negotiation process. The challenges to this control inevitably increase in complexity, not only from 'zealots' and 'opportunists', but from 'maverick' militants who carry out unauthorized crimes for personal gain or from habit, especially in the period immediately following the declaration of a ceasefire. The violence is predominantly within each general ethnic community, rather than between ethnic opponents. In South Africa 'the struggle years had turned black townships into breakaway armed camps ruled by a rough sort of popular justice. These institutions identified and punished police collaborators, thieves and anyone perceived as an enemy of the community' (Scheper- Hughes 1997).

The issue is authority. Factional violence within the Palestinian community continued after the Palestinian Authority assumed responsibility for policing in 1995. In Northern Ireland too, punishment beatings against 'anti-social elements' continued throughout the peace process as both Loyalists and Republicans carried out what they regarded as their policing function. People were expelled from the community and severely beaten for 'anti-social behaviour'.

Violence in the Community

The fragmentation of paramilitary organizations is not the only violent accompaniment to peace processes. Two other forms of violence may also seriously undermine them – the revival of direct confrontations between ethnic rivals, and a rise in the conventional crime rate.

When a ceasefire is declared, the discipline of the military campaign diminishes, but the underlying hatred remains, taking the form of riots and undisciplined confrontations with rivals or the police. The militants who enter negotiations are not divorced from the instincts and antagonisms of their communities, and may feel the need to support them. During the early months of negotiation in South Africa, sectional violence was partly orchestrated between the ANC and the IFP, but spilled over into tit-for-tat killings and more general violence. The emergence of the 'street guerrilla', mostly teenagers, in the Basque Country arose partly from ETA's weakening authority, but was also partly a reaction to the popularity of the peace movement. In Northern Ireland the declaration of the ceasefires and the ending of direct violence between organized paramilitaries and the security forces were marked by a return to more direct violence between Catholics and Protestants, especially during the annual marching seasons.

A rise in conventional crime may appear to present a less obvious threat. There is often an inverse relationship between political violence and conventional criminal activities during periods of civil unrest. Far from leading to a rise in conventional crime, political violence may actually reduce the crime rate. Conventional crime rates were low in the Basque Country and South Africa, for example, while political violence was at its height. During the years of Northern Ireland's 'troubles' the numbers of burglaries, assaults and thefts were consistently lower than those in England and Wales. The reasons are varied. Policing is dominated by security concerns, and many hostile areas are inadequately patrolled, leading to an under-recording of crime statistics. Paramilitary organizations claim, and often exercise, the right to police the areas under their control. This is often done with extreme violence. They are unfettered by the constraints of the law, and the severity of their sanctions is a deterrent to potential criminals. The level of conventional crime is also likely to rise during a ceasefire. It is facilitated by arms stockpiled during and after the war. In 1996 there was at least one firearm in 20 per cent of South African households and in Angola an AK-47 could be bought for the price of a chicken (Naylor 1997). The criminal aspects of paramilitary campaigns often transmute into crime syndicates, particularly involving drug smuggling and dealing, and the security services, more geared to political than conventional crime during the war years, are often ill-equipped to deal with them.

Expectations of immediate economic and other improvements, raised during the period of negotiations, are often disappointed after the accord is signed. This is what happened in South Africa, where the crime rate increased to such a degree as to seriously undermine post-settlement peace-building. It threatened inward investment, tourism and general confidence. By the mid-1990s the high level of conventional crime had far outpaced political violence as a threat to stability. Between 1993 and 1997 two-thirds of all Johannesburg residents were victims of crime. By 1998 the daily homicide rate was sixty-eight, and still rising, the world's highest murder rate. It was not helped by low conviction rates, dramatically pointed out in the Nedcor study: 'Of every 1000 crimes committed in South Africa, only 450 were reported, 230 were solved and 100 brought to trial. Of those prosecuted, only 77 were convicted, of whom 33 were imprisoned but only eight served sentences of two years or longer. Of the eight imprisoned, only one would be rehabilitated' (Sidiropoulos et al. 1998: 58).

More ominously, the barrier between conventional crime and South Africa's underlying racial tensions became increasingly blurred. Fifteen hundred white farms were attacked between 1994 and 1998, resulting in more than 200 murders, and threatening to create a loop back from post-settlement civil violence to the racial violence familiar from the earlier struggle. A succession of inquiries by the ANC government all stressed a common theme: 'the insistence that the primary motive is criminal, not political, with robbery as the most common objective' (Laurence 2000). Some farmers were not convinced, and the Transvaal Agricultural Union accused politicians, 'even cabinet ministers, of creating a psychological and political climate which encourages the attacks'.[8]

A sharp rise in conventional crime may lead to vigilantism. Some of the worst violence in South Africa was caused by Pagad (People Against Gangsterism and Drugs), who engaged in tit-for-tat killings with criminal gangs as well as in no-warning restaurant bombs. Pagad was responsible for twenty bombings around Cape Town, leading the Minister of Justice to step up protection for judges and prosecutors involved in cases against Pagad, and to consider a ban. Pagad's response was to threaten 'one prosecutor, one bullet', a play on the radical mantra 'one settler, one bullet' used during the anti-apartheid war. In Guatemala vigilantes were responsible for the killing of dozens of suspected criminals in the six months after the accords. By 1998 violent crime was ranked as the most serious problem in both Guatemala and San Salvador, raising concern about a possible correlation between high crime rates and disrespect for new democratic institutions.

Violence as a Catalyst for Peace

On 12 July 1998 three Catholic children from Ballymoney, Northern Ireland – Richard, Mark and Jason Quinn, aged ten, nine and seven – were burned to death during the violence that had accompanied the Orange 'marching season' during the previous three years. In 1998 the marching season, culminating in the confrontational demonstration at Drumcree, had threatened to undermine the recently signed Good Friday Agreement. The reaction to the killings was unprecedented. Support among Orangemen for the increasingly violent protest at Drumcree was severely eroded. Many withdrew and some openly condemned it. The atrocity allowed those Unionists who opposed the Orange activities to tune into the general feelings of outrage. The Drumcree demonstration continued, but the deaths in Ballymoney had knocked the heart out of it.

A month later, on 15 August, a splinter Republican group, the 'Real' IRA, planted a bomb in the country town of Omagh, killing twenty-nine afternoon shoppers. The bomb struck indiscriminately against both communities. It appeared to spurn the popular support for the Good Friday Agreement in the recent referendums in both parts of Ireland. Consequently it allowed Gerry Adams to underline their rejection of violence by condemning a Republican bomb 'without any equivocation whatsoever'. Martin McGuinness of Sinn Fein even went further: 'We see our job to be one of stopping the activities of these people'.[9] The Omagh bomb also provided the opportunity for both governments to harmonize and toughen their anti-terrorist powers with virtually no opposition. This in turn allowed the Unionist leader David Trimble, very uncharacteristically, to compliment the Irish Republic. In effect Omagh licensed a number of actors who had intellectually accepted the need to make concessions to actually do so.

Public reaction to the Omagh bomb caused consternation among spoiler groups. Within four days of the bomb those responsible for planting it, the 'Real' IRA, had declared a ceasefire. Three days later the Irish National Liberation Army, one of the most violent of the Republican groups, followed suit with 'a complete ceasefire'.

The responses to Omagh and Ballymoney were dramatic, but not unique in peace processes. Occasionally, in Northern Ireland and elsewhere, certain atrocities provoke universal condemnation and galvanize popular reaction against the perpetrators. The Basque Country and South Africa have experienced similar episodes. After decades of kidnappings and murders, it took the kidnapping and murder of a young Basque town councillor, Miguel Angel Blanco, in 1997 to bring hundreds of thousands of Basque protesters on to the streets in opposition to ETA's violence. In the midst of the most violent period of the South African process, why was the murder of twnty-eight ANC supporters in Bisho in 1992 not followed by the same violent protests after the massacre of forty-eight people at Boipatong three months earlier? Instead, it became a stimulus for the negotiations.

What is the nature of these atrocities that converts them into catalysts for peace? Why did Ballymoney and Omagh have such a powerful effect in Northern Ireland when so many awful actions from the past did not? War-weariness is part of the explanation. The protagonists may have reached Zartman's 'mutually hurting stalemate'. But war-weariness is not sufficient explanation and may persist for years without stimulating massive public demand for compromise. Nor is the nature or severity of the violence. A calculated injection of heightened violence is more likely to apply tensions to a peace process than to advance it. Even the killing of civilians does not always have the effect it had in Northern Ireland after Omagh. The three critical factors in creating catalysts are quality of leadership, the cohesion of the groups in negotiation and timing.

Leadership of a high quality is critical in steadying nerves and restoring confidence when violence threatens a peace process. In 1993 the assassination of the popular black leader Chris Hani by white extremists at a sensitive point in the negotiations was followed by serious rioting. Nelson Mandela agreed to a request by the white government to speak on state television, and was able to restore momentum to the peace process. It was not the only time that Mandela intervened to assure his followers that they should avoid the use of violence. His success, however, raises the question why other interventions from leaders have tended to be less effective.

The answer lies in the level of cohesion within the negotiation parties. While Mandela's charisma was undeniable, it was less important than his ability to maintain ANC unity and dominance during negotiations. The more united and cohesive are the main negotiating parties, the easier they find it to take an effective lead against violence. If strong voices from their own communities are opposing their approach to negotiations, leaders are often forced to be more equivocal in their condemnation. Contrast the effects of violence during the South African negotiations in 1992 and 1993 with its effects in Israel-Palestine in 2000. The dominance of the ANC within the black community underpinned Mandela's ability to provide positive leadership. Barak and Arafat were unable to provide the same leadership to their two deeply divided communities, because many voices were arguing that compromise meant selling out on critical issues, and that only force could achieve their essential demands.

The other key reason why certain violent events, at certain times, become catalysts for peace lies not in the nature or severity of the violence, but in their timing. What converts outrage to action is condemnation within the context, or at least realistic hope, that agreement is possible, and that further violence could threaten it. In such circumstances it is worth paying attention to those catalytic events when an atrocity not only provokes universal condemnation but also galvanizes popular reaction against the perpetrators. The public demand for a renewal of negotiations after Bisho followed a recent reminder of the alternative presented by the Boipatong massacre and from fear that the peace process might collapse. The Omagh bomb closely followed two referendums and an election supporting the Good Friday Agreement. It would stretch the evidence to suggest that there was a peace process in the Basque Country in 1997, but the kidnapping of Miguel Angel Blanco reflected a measurable feeling among Basques that the time had come for a ceasefire by ETA, and one followed a year later.

So the atrocities enabled public outrage to be harnessed, as opposed to simply vented. It is the harnessing that is important. Outrage without a mechanism to enforce it fades away, as earlier peace movements in all three places, and in Israel, had faded away. A peace process, or the prospect of one, creates a mechanism for connecting anger to the political process.

The effects of catalytic episodes are transitory. The often-mentioned 'window of opportunity' is barely ajar and soon slams shut. In January 1999 the start of formal negotiations between the Colombian government and FARC, the country's largest guerrilla group, prompted anti-violence demonstrations. Around five million people demonstrated in 700 cities and towns across Colombia in October 1999, the latest of several major initiatives by civil society to promote a national debate on questions of war and peace. FARC and Colombia's right-wing paramilitary groups were unimpressed by this display of general discontent, and the negotiations made little progress.

The most important effect of catalytic atrocities is not their ability to end spoiler violence. It is that they enable the middle ground to find its voice at a time when the voice of moderation could make a difference. Months after the Omagh bomb the renewed antagonism between the Ulster Unionists and Sinn Fein over decommissioning underlines the speed at which the voice of moderation is muted.

Implications for Policy

It is important to analyse the distinctions between different forms of post-accord violence, because each form requires a different policy approach. The best safeguards against state violence, for example, are external monitors – international and regional organizations, non-governmental groups and a strong independent media reporting illegal actions to the outside world – a reality recognized by the attempts of some governments to exclude or control their access to scenes of violence. An awareness of the distinction between different forms of violence is even more necessary when dealing with militants, because different types of spoilers require different treatments. Policy should reflect these distinctions. It should aim to support those ex-militants who have entered negotiations, to leave the door open for other militants to enter the process under strict conditions, and to apply the rule of law to isolate and sanction the zealots and mavericks who continue to use violence.

Some degree of violence is unavoidable at every phase of peacemaking, from ceasefire to post-war reconstruction, because all sides fear the cost of continuing the war and the consequences of making peace. The use of violence is primarily a matter of calculation rather than spontaneity. So is the use of peace. Höglund and Zartman (2006) have demonstrated that mutual fear may, under certain circumstances, 'accelerate negotiations and the implementation of a peace agreement'. Whether the calculation between war and peace is positive or negative depends on a conscious cost-benefit analysis by both the state and its militant opponents. The challenge is to provide sanctions and incentives that will push them both towards compromise.

Notes

1. See Darby (2001), where some of the issues discussed in this chapter are explored in greater detail. This book in turn draws on a comparative study of five peace processes in South Africa, Northern Ireland, the Basque Country, Israel-Palestine and Sri Lanka, reported in Darby and MacGinty (2000).
2. For an excellent review of this literature see Miall et al. 1998; see also Gurr 1993; Sollenberg (Published annually).
3. Reported in the *Chicago Tribune* 22 September 2000.
4. Republic of South Africa, *Interpellations, Questions and Replies of the National Assembly* (Cape Town: Government Printer, 18 February 1998), 14.
5. *The Economist* (London), 28 June 1997.
6. Among the studies dealing with the implosion of paramilitary organizations are Wieviorka 1993 and Conversi 1997.
7. Ulster Unionist Party (Belfast), Press release, 1999.
8. The growing controversy about the attacks on white farms is outlined in Patrick Laurence, 'South African White Farmers Feeling Increasingly under Threat of Violence', Reuter's Press Agency, 14 August 2000.
9. *The Observer* (London), 6 August 1998,

References

Conversi, D. 1997. *The Basques, the Catalans and Spain: Alternative Routes to Nationalist Mobilization*. Reno: University of Nevada Press.

Crocker, C.A., F.O. Hampson and P. Aall. 1999. *Herding Cats: Multiparty Mediation in a Complex World*. Washington DC: United States Institute of Peace Press.

Darby, J. 2001. *The Effects of Violence on Peace Processes*. Washington, DC: United States Institute of Peace Press.

Darby, J. and R. MacGinty (eds). 2000. *The Management of Peace Processes*. London: Macmillan.

Gurr, T.R. 1993. *Minorities at Risk: A Global View of Ethnopolitical Conflicts*. Washington DC: United States Institute of Peace Press.

Gutierrez, P.R. and E.A. Torriero. 2000. 'Critics: Drug War Cash may Finance Brutality', *Orlando Sentinel*, 22 September 2000.

Hampson, F. 1996. *Nurturing Peace: Why Peace Settlements Succeed or Fail*. Washington, DC: United States Institute of Peace Press.

Haass, R.N. 1990. *Conflicts Unending: The United States and Regional Disputes*. New Haven: Yale University Press.

Höglund, K. and I.W. Zartman. 2006. 'Violence by the State: Official Spoilers and their Allies', in J. Darby (ed), *Violence and Reconstruction*. Notre Dame Ind.: Notre Dame Press.

Laurence, P. 2000. 'South African White Farmers Feeling Increasingly under Threat of Violence', *Reuter's Press Agency*, 14 August.

Miall, H., O. Ramsbotham and T. Woodhouse. 1998. *Contemporary Conflict Resolution*. London: Macmillan.

Naylor, R.T. 1997. 'The Rise of the Modern Arms Black Market and the Fall of Supply-side Control', in V. Gamba (ed), *Society under Siege – Crime, Violence and Illegal Weapons*. Johannesburg: Institute for Security Studies.

Republic of South Africa. 1998. *Interpellations, Questions and Replies of the National Assembly*. Cape Town: Government Printer, 18 February, 14.

Scheper-Hughes, N. 1997. 'Peace-time Crimes', *Social Identities* 3(3): 471–99.

Sidiropoulos, E., A. Jeffrey, H. Forgey, C. Chipps, T. Corrigan, T. Mophuthing, A. Helman and T. Dimant. 1998. *South Africa Survey 1997/98*. Johannesburg: South African Institute of Race Relations.

Sollenberg, M. (Published annually). *States in Armed Conflict*. Uppsala: Department of Peace and Conflict Research, University of Uppsala Press.

Stedman S.J. 1997. 'Spoiler Problems in Peace Processes', *International Security* 22(2): 5–53.

Wieviorka, M. 1993. *The Making of Terrorism*. Chicago: University of Chicago Press.

Zartman, I.W. 1989. *Ripe for Resolution: Conflict and Intervention in Africa*. New York: Oxford University Press.

Index